DATE DUE

HIGHSMITH 45-220

The CIM Handbook of Selling and Sales Strategy

The Marketing Series is one of the most comprehensive collections of books in marketing and sales available from the UK today.

Published by Butterworth-Heinemann on behalf of The Chartered Institute of Marketing, the series is divided into three distinct groups: *Student* (fulfilling the needs of those taking the Institute's certificate and diploma qualifications); *Professional Development* (for those on formal or self-study vocational training programmes); and *Practitioner* (presented in a more informal, motivating and highly practical manner for the busy marketer).

Formed in 1911, The Chartered Institute of Marketing is now the largest professional marketing management body in Europe with over 60,000 members located worldwide. Its primary objectives are focused on the development of awareness and understanding of marketing throughout UK industry and commerce and in the raising of standards of professionalism in the education, training and practice of this key business discipline.

Books in the series

Below-the-line Promotion
Geoffrey Randall

CIM Handbook of Export Marketing
Chris Noonan

CIM Marketing Dictionary, 5th edition
Norman A. Hart

Creating Powerful Brands
Leslie Chernatony and Malcolm McDonald

Market-led Strategic Change
Nigel Piercy

Marketing Logistics
Martin Christopher

Marketing Planning for Services
Malcolm McDonald and Adrian Payne

Marketing Plans, 3rd edition
Malcolm McDonald

Marketing Research for Managers, 2nd edition
Sunny Crouch and Matthew Housden

Practise of Advertising, 4th edition
Norman A. Hart

Practise of Public Relations, 4th edition
Sam Black

Profitable Product Management
Richard Collier

Retail Marketing Plans
Malcolm McDonald and Christopher Tideman

Relationship Marketing
Martin Christopher, Adrian Payne and David Ballantyne

Relationship Marketing for Competitive Advantage
Adrian Payne, Martin Christopher, Moira Clark and Helen Peck

The Marketing Book, 3rd edition
Michael J. Baker

Trade Marketing Strategies
Geoffrey Randall

The CIM Handbook of Selling and Sales Strategy

Professor David Jobber

Published on behalf of The Chartered Institute of Marketing

BUTTERWORTH
HEINEMANN

Butterworth-Heinemann
Linacre House, Jordan Hill, Oxford OX2 8DP
A division of Reed Educational and Professional Publishing Ltd

ℛ A member of the Reed Elsevier plc group

OXFORD BOSTON JOHANNESBURG
MELBOURNE NEW DELHI SINGAPORE

First published 1997

© David Jobber 1997

British Library Cataloguing in Publication Data
A catalogue record for this book is available from the British Library

ISBN 0 7506 3116 3

Typeset by Avocet Typeset, Brill, Aylesbury, Bucks
Printed and Bound in Great Britain by Scotprint, Musselburgh, Scotland

Contents

List of contributors   vii
Preface   xi

Part One   Fundamentals of Selling   1

1   Understanding buyer behaviour: implications for selling   3
    Dr Richard Elliott, University of Oxford

2   Personal selling skills   18
    Professor David Jobber, University of Bradford Management Centre

3   Commercial negotiations   34
    Richard Graham, Huthwaite Research Group Ltd

Part Two   Managing Customer Relationships   53

4   Relationship management   55
    Professor Colin Egan, Leicester Business School

5   Selling to and managing key accounts   89
    Professor David Shipley, Trinity College, University of Dublin
    Roger Palmer, Cranfield University

6   Trade marketing   104
    Belinda Dewsnap, Loughborough University Business School

7   Telemarketing   126
    Michael Starkey, Leicester Business School

Part Three   Salesforce Management and Strategy   153

8   Developing and motivating a salesforce   155
    Dr Bill Donaldson, University of Strathclyde

9 Assessing sales performance   170
   Dr Antonis Simintiras, The Open University

10 Strategic sales planning   186
    Kevin Wilson, Southampton Institute of Technology

11 Sales organization effectiveness   211
    Professor Nigel F. Piercy, Cardiff Business School
    Professor David W. Cravens, Texas Christian University, USA

12 Using IT in the sales function   230
    Lynn Parkinson, Parkinson Training Ltd

Part Four   Sales Applications   259

13 International selling   261
    Dr Susan Bridgewater, University of Warwick

14 Selling a service   276
    Professor Malcolm McDonald, Cranfield University

15 Business-to-business selling   298
    Julian Gibas, Automotive Business Development
    Daragh O'Reilly, University of Bradford

Index   313

Contributors

Susan Bridgewater is a Lecturer in Marketing at Warwick Business School. Susan joined Warwick in 1991. Prior to this she was a Product Manager with Nairn-Forbo, responsible for sales and marketing of home fashion products in Europe, and New Products Manager in the food service sector for Van den Berghs and Jurgens, Unilever.

David Cravens is the Eunice and James L. West Professor of American Enterprise Studies and Professor of Marketing in the MJ Neeley School of Business at Texas Christian University, Fort Worth. He has published his sales research in the most prestigious journals in the world and is recognized as a major contributor to the development of sales management thinking globally. He has extensive practical experience as an executive in the oil industry. In 1996 he was elected Marketing Educator of the Year by the Academy of Marketing Science.

Belinda Dewsnap is a Lecturer in Marketing at Loughborough University Business School. After graduating, Belinda spent several years in sales, operations and product supply management positions with major blue-chip companies at both strategic and operational levels. Her current research focus is on the working interface between brand marketing and sales.

Bill Donaldson is Senior Lecturer in Marketing and Deputy Head, Department of Marketing at the University of Strathclyde. His previous experience included jobs with British Steel, Spear and Jackson Hand Tools and Hepworth Building Products. Author of *Sales Management: Theory and Practice*, published by Macmillan in 1990, his current research interests are in sales operations, customer service and relationship marketing.

Colin Egan is Professor of Strategic Management at Leicester Business School. He is a faculty member of the Chartered Institute of Marketing where he teaches marketing strategy and develops in-company strategic management programmes. Prior to this 'academic life' he had ten years' practical business experience in a sales and marketing environment. He specializes in management development and has recently developed and run sales and marketing programmes for the following companies: Bass, BP, British Steel, BT, Burmah Castrol, Coral, ECC, IBM, Rolls-Royce Industrial Power Group, GPT, National Westminster Bank, Hitachi Europe, Philips, Reed Elsevier and PowerGen.

Richard Elliott is a Fellow of St Anne's College, Oxford and was the first Lecturer in Marketing to be appointed in the University of Oxford. He worked in brand management with a number of multinationals and was Marketing Director of an industrial goods company. He has taught MBA students at the London Business School, ESSEC (Paris), Lancaster and Warwick Universities. He has acted as a consultant for a wide range of companies including Asda, United Biscuits, Sun Alliance, British Airways, BNFL, Guardian Financial Services, Smurfitt and VSEL.

Julian Gibas is Managing Director of the sales and marketing agency and consultancy, Automotive Business Development. Under his guidance, this company has carried out work for many organizations including a number of international manufacturing companies who operate in Europe, America and the Far East. Prior to starting ABD he worked as a Marketing Advisor to the Irish Trade Board. His experience has also encompassed sales management roles in the vehicle security industry and in the drinks industry, where he worked for a major blue-chip company.

Richard Graham is International Business Manager for Huthwaite Research Group. Over the past few years, he has established partnerships in Poland, Hungary, Israel and Iceland as part of Huthwaite's drive to build a global training network. During the same period he has been responsible for developing the existing network which already covers the whole of Western Europe, South Africa, Korea and Singapore. Over the past fifteen years he has been responsible for selling and implementing international sales training projects with companies such as BOC, PTT Telecom (The Netherlands), Datex Engstrom (Finland and Hewlett Packard).

David Jobber is Professor of Marketing at the University of Bradford Management Centre. He previously lectured at the University of Huddersfield and gained sales and marketing experience with the TI Group. He is author of *Principles and Practice of Marketing* (McGraw-Hill) and co-author of *Selling and Sales Management* (Pitman). He is an experienced sales and marketing trainer with organizations including Allied Domecq, BBC, Kalamazoo, Rhone Poulenc and Rolls Royce.

Malcolm McDonald is Professor of Strategic Marketing at Cranfield School of Management. Prior to this position he was Marketing and Sales Director of Canada Dry and before that a Senior Sales Manager in Allied Breweries. Malcolm's current major research interest is in key account management.

Daragh O'Reilly worked in sales and marketing roles for many years before joining the staff at the University of Bradford Management Centre. He spent several years as a business development executive with IDA Ireland, a leading player in the European manufacturing investment market, dealing with Japanese multinational clients. He has had extensive international research, consultancy and training experience including the UK and Ireland, the USA, the Far East, West Africa, and Costa Rica. He is the co-author, with Julian J. Gibas, of *Building Buyer Relationships* (Pitman, 1995).

Roger Palmer is a Teaching Fellow in Marketing at Cranfield School of Management. His early sales and marketing experience was gained with Shell. He subsequently held senior appointments as Marketing Director of Pauls Agriculture Ltd and then General Manager of the UK Animal Health Division of the American Cyanamid Corporation. His consultancy clients include IBM, Pilkington, Monsanto, DHL and SKE. In the not-for-profit sector, he works with an international charity.

Lynn Parkinson runs a marketing training consultancy (Parkinson Training) for organizations in the UK and continental Europe. Her clients include Laporte, Coca Cola and ICL. She has previously worked in the construction industry, tourism and in direct marketing.

Nigel Piercy is the Sir Julian Hodge Professor in Marketing and Strategy at Cardiff Business School in the University of Wales. He worked in retailing and later in marketing with Amersham International. He is author of the best-selling book *Market-led Strategic Change* (Oxford, Butterworth-Heinemann) and consults with many organizations in Britain, the USA, the Far East and South Africa.

David Shipley is Professor of Marketing at the Business School at Trinity College Dublin. He previously lectured at Bradford and Staffordshire Universities and enjoyed ten years' industrial experience with Royal Doulton and Baker-Perkins. Professor Shipley maintains his business involvement as a trainer and consultant with organizations including The Chartered Institute of Marketing, IBM, Nissan, Philips, Sony, The Royal Mail and W. H. Smith.

Antonis Simintiras is a Reader in Marketing at the Open University Business School. He has had many years of industry experience and worked for several companies in Greece and the USA. He holds visiting professorial appointments at various European Business Schools and acts as a consultant for companies and the Greek Government. Dr Simintiras's current interests in research and consultancy are in the areas of international negotiations and sales management.

Michael Starkey is a Senior Lecturer in Marketing at De Montfort University. He has worked in the international trading in food products in both the UK and Hong Kong and was a sales manager for a Japanese precision engineering company before joining De Montfort University in 1992. He is co-editor of the book *Management of Sales and Customer Relations* published in 1996 (International Thomson Business Press) and co-founding editor of the Journal of Selling and Major Account Management.

Kevin Wilson is a Senior Lecturer in Marketing at the Southampton Institute. Kevin has over twenty years experience in industrial selling, having occupied senior sales management roles within the electrical industry working for both American and European blue-chip companies. Research interests in the field of selling and key account management are balanced by continuing involvement with the day-to-day practicalities of salesforce management through a busy consultancy practice.

Preface

The basic business idea for this book was to produce an accessible yet advanced look at the area of selling, sales management and strategy. This was founded on the realization that Europe lacked a guide to the latest thinking in this field. Given the key role selling plays in corporate success, this was a major omission. Within these pages, I hope that you will find practical ideas and techniques to enhance your performance as a sales practitioner.

As editor my challenge was to find experts in key areas of selling and sales strategy. My objective was to find people who were not only knowledgeable about the principles but also had experience of the practice of sales. My belief was that this blend would add a new dimension to the sales literature, recognizing that the selling job was not simplistic but complex, and that the field deserved a higher standard of treatment than that provided by some 'how to sell and manage' recipe books.

The structure of the books follows a logical progression beginning with the fundamentals of selling, through managing customer relationships (a topic of great concern to many companies these days) to salesforce management and strategy. The final section examines specific sales applications in international selling, selling a service and business-to-business selling. A key feature of the book is the in-depth coverage of contemporary issues such as key account management, telemarketing, trade marketing and information technology applications in sales.

I believe that the *CIM Handbook of Selling and Sales Strategy* will provide you with much food for thought regarding new ways of developing your sales operation and many actionable ideas for improving your sales performance.

Finally, I wish to thank all contributors for the fine professional job they have done. I am delighted with the care they have given to their task and the practical slant they have applied to their chapters.

Professor David Jobber

Part One

Fundamentals
of Selling

1

Understanding buyer behaviour: implications for selling

Dr Richard Elliott, University of Oxford

 This chapter introduces models of buyer behaviour in consumer and organizational markets and draws out the implications for selling. In consumer markets the key concepts of involvement and emotion are the focus of discussion, while in organizational markets the additional issues of power, influence and commitment over time are vitally important. Guidance is given on identifying the appropriate model to apply in a selling situation, and how an understanding of buyer behaviour must lay the foundation for selling and sales strategy.

The traditional approach to understanding buyer behaviour is as a sequence of stages through which the buyer moves, gathering information and evaluating competitive offerings before reaching a decision and acting upon it. This is an idealized model which has its origins as a model of how a rational purchaser *should* make purchase choices and only rarely describes how people actually behave. In this chapter we shall consider consumer behaviour and organizational buying behaviour separately, although there are great similarities between them. As we shall see later, although the sequential stage model is usually thought of as a model of consumer choice, it is in fact a reasonable description of how organizations make purchase decisions.

Models of consumer choice

The classical model of consumer decision making

This shows the consumer moving through a series of psychological states and sequences of action before reaching a choice decision. It is an information-processing model which assumes that the consumer is sufficiently motivated to invest the mental and physical effort required to search out and process information. However, if we examine what consumers actually do through the various stages, we find wide divergence from the classical model.

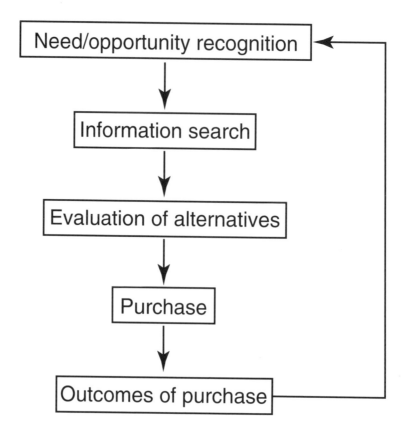

Figure 1.1 *Classical model of consumer choice*

Need/opportunity recognition

Consumers recognize a need or an opportunity for a product when they perceive an important gap between their current state and their ideal or desired state, either because of a change for the worse in their actual state (need recognition), or because their ideal or desired state becomes further away (opportunity recognition). For example, much simple demand is a result of a need recognition because of running out of stock of a product, or of a product failing to deliver satisfaction. Opportunity recognition occurs when life changes prompt a change upwards in expectations, and, as such, opportunity recognition represents much of the growth of consumer product and service markets. However, the level of motivation required to prompt a purchase may be at a much lower level than this

suggests. For example, much consumption is driven by a desire to emulate other people, and this may often be at a subconscious level, thus the emphasis on a process initiated by conscious perception may be overstated. Also low levels of simple curiosity may be sufficient to prompt purchase.

Practical tip

Curiosity is one of the basic human motivations, and its use in selling should always be considered. It can play an important role in opening a sales presentation, as it helps capture the prospect's attention and stimulate his/her interest.

Information search

Having recognized that a product will satisfy a need or an opportunity gap, the consumer will search for information with which to make a decision. Searching for information may involve an internal search of memory and/or an external search of the environment for information. For most consumers of most products an internal search of memory substitutes for external search, and as we shall see, awareness alone may be sufficient to effect choice. Studies of external information search and actual shopping behaviour for consumer durables have found wide differences between individual search behaviour, such that 25% of people visited four or more shops, while 37% bought at the one and only shop they visited; 32% only considered one brand while 16% considered four or more; 52% obtained no independent information, while 11% consulted two sources. Even for the purchase of new cars, more than 30% of people considered only one make of car and visited only one car dealer prior to purchase. The conclusion seems to be that even for expensive goods most consumers only visit one shop, do not gather additional information from advertising and generally process very little information. The extreme of minimal information search may lie with fast-moving consumer goods (FMCGs) where consumers purchasing detergents were found to spend a total of 13 seconds from entering the supermarket aisle, walking to the area where the brand is located and selecting the chosen brand. Over 70% looked at only one package, and only 11% looked at more than two.

Evaluation of alternatives

In order to choose between competing brands the consumer must decide which evaluative criteria will be used and employ some form of decision rule. The evaluative criteria (sometimes called choice criteria) are the product attributes, functional, symbolic and emotional, on which the relative performance of the competing alternatives will be compared. The decision rule is the strategy the consumer uses to deal with the information available and arrive at a choice. However, consumers also use certain tangible attributes as surrogate indicators, or signals, of less tangible attributes. In particular, price and brand name are often used as surrogate indicators of quality. Decision rules can be categorized as either compensatory or non-compensatory. Compensatory rules allow poor performance on one attribute to be offset by good performance on another attribute, while non-compensatory decision rules are simpler strategies in which consumers use one single standard and eliminate those alternatives which do not measure up to it. Rules are developed by experience and stored in memory and can be retrieved when necessary; at other times consumers may construct rules as they go along, using fragments of rules stored in memory to make an on-the-spot choice.

It has become clear in recent years that human information processing limitations greatly effect the way in which consumers make purchase decisions. In conjunction with the dominant perspective of humans as 'cognitive misers' who will always seek to reduce cognitive effort and will be content to merely satisfice rather than maximize their decision outcomes, the study of decision rules has moved towards the study of various simplifying 'rules-of-thumb' used by consumers to shortcut the cognitive process of choice. It has been argued that some of these 'rules-of-thumb' are efficient and accurate, such as the equal weight rule which examines all of the attributes and all of the data but simplifies the process by ignoring the relative importance or probability of each attribute.

However, most 'rules-of-thumb' used by consumers seem to be either inaccurate strategies or to lead to severe and systematic bias when compared with the rational decision-making model of economic theory. Consumers may use simple counts of good or bad features or rely on rules such as 'buy the cheapest brand' or 'buy what my parents buy' or the simplest habit rule 'buy the brand I bought last time'. Perhaps the most ubiquitous is when the consumer retrieves pre-formed evaluations from memory and the one with the highest level of overall liking is chosen. We shall consider this simple use of emotion to drive the choice process later. Consumers also appear to use inferences based on experience of the market place to help them cope with information. For example, it appears that many consumers cannot handle the arithmetic needed to compare prices across different quantities, and instead use a 'market belief' such as that 'if an item is on price promotion then it must be a better buy'. These consumer market beliefs incorporate such brand beliefs as 'own-label brands are just the same as brand leaders sold under a different label at a lower price', and 'all brands are basically the same', and shop beliefs such as 'the more sales assistants there are in a shop, the more expensive are its products', and 'larger shops offer better prices than small shops'.

A class of 'rules-of-thumb' that are more general in their applicability and seem to operate over a wide range of decision areas and to reflect some inherent biases in human judgement are the three judgement rules: representativeness, availability, and framing.

- **Representativeness** refers to the tendency to judge the probability that an object belongs to a category based on how typical it appears to be of that category, ignoring the statistical probability. This is linked to the 'law of small numbers' and the 'gambler's fallacy' in which people seem to not only believe that small samples can accurately represent large populations, but also expect random sequences to look random.
- Of more direct relevance to consumer decisions is the **availability rule** which refers to the tendency for an event to be judged more probable in terms of how easily we can bring it to mind. For example, the performance of products with unusual brand names is more likely to be judged as a failure than the same product performance with less distinctive brand names.

- A further judgemental bias is the **'framing effect'**, in which the way in which product attributes are framed with either a positive or a negative label will affect consumer evaluations. Consumers who were presented with minced beef that was labelled '75% lean' had much more favourable evaluations of the meat than when the beef was labelled '25% fat'. However, this effect was reduced after actually tasting the meat.

Practical tip

Information about consumer benefits should always be positively framed, that is they should always be presented with the competitive advantage first, and with any comparative data ordered to 'frame' the competition in a negative light. The emphasis should be on gains and not on losses. For example, the added cost of an extended warranty should be framed as a substantial saving in the future.

Purchase

Two important aspects of the purchase stage are the extent to which the purchase is actually pre-planned, and the choice of outlet to buy from. There are a range of factors which will intervene between a formed purchase intention and actual purchase. The major factor is time, in that the more time between intention formation and behaviour the more opportunity exits for unexpected factors to change the original intention. However, in many instances a conscious purchase intention is not formulated prior to the purchase act. In supermarket shopping, the displays of products can act as a surrogate shopping list and prompt a type of impulse purchase. This would be more accurately termed a partly-planned purchase as, although no specific intention is formed, a general intention to purchase exists, and it is not a true impulse purchase which involves a sudden strong urge to purchase with diminished concern for the consequences. A large US study of supermarket purchase decisions found that the majority of brand decisions are made in-store, with 83% of snack food choice being decided upon in the shop.

Rather than a choice between brands, for many people and many types of product, shops form the group of brands from which choice is made, and brands may only be chosen once the shop decision has been made. For the increasing number of people for whom shopping is a recreational activity, browsing can lead to many unplanned purchases but is itself a pleasure-giving activity for a significant proportion of the population.

Outcomes of purchase

The essence of post-purchase evaluation is whether the consumer is satisfied or dissatisfied with the product. The major cognitive approach in this area is the expectancy disconfirmation model which points to the importance of prior expectation as determining how we will interpret experience with the product post-purchase. If we have low expectations then poor performance will not cause much dissatisfaction. If, however, we have high expectations then poor performance will result in high levels of dissatisfaction. The opposite is true for satisfaction, in that if we have low expectations and the product performs well then we will be satisfied. However, recent research has emphasized the extra role of emotional aspects in achieving satisfaction versus the purely instrumental aspects of dissatisfaction.

Although dissatisfaction with purchases is common, relatively few consumers actually make complaints. Complaint behaviour seems to be determined largely by individual factors, only 38% of people being likely to take direct action and 14% likely to take no action.

The ability of the consumer to learn from the experience of purchasing and using products is subject to a number of limitations and cognitive biases. In particular, if not highly motivated, consumers may limit learning by relying on previously learned schema, which can often be derived from advertising. In general, it is suggested that consumer learning from experience can be managed, with market leaders having much to gain by impeding learning. The principal method used is to encourage ambiguity by avoiding direct comparisons, and by attempting to control the attribute agenda by suggesting belief structures or schema which consumers can use to interpret consumption experiences. Heinz Tomato Ketchup has set the attribute agenda for sauces by adopting the claim of 'thickness' which can be easily verified and used to judge competing brands. It is left to the consumer to draw the inference that thickness equals flavour.

Consumer involvement

The concept of involvement has been described as pivotal in consumer psychology as it attempts to describe aspects of the relative personal relevance or importance that a product or brand has for an individual. Fundamentally, involvement can be seen as the motivation to search for information and to engage in systematic processing, and it is a motivational state which affects many of the key aspects of consumer behaviour such as decision making, responses to persuasion and processing of advertisements. Although it should properly be understood as a continuum running from very low to very high it is useful to refer to high versus low involvement as a structural aid in locating different individuals' subjective perceptions of the personal relevance of a product, a brand, a purchase decision, or an advertisement.

There are a number of different definitions of involvement and several alternative measurement methods but there is some agreement that involvement is a function of three sources of importance: the consumer, the product and the situation. Individual differences in the characteristics of the consumer include the self-concept, values, personal goals and needs. Product characteristics which will affect the level of involvement include the price, how frequently it is purchased, the symbolic meanings associated with the product and their social visibility, the perceived risk of poor performance or potential for harm, and the length of time one will have to commit to the product once it is purchased. The situational variables include aspects of the purchase situation itself, such as the amount of time available, whether the purchase is made privately or in the presence of others; and more importantly, aspects of the intended use situation such as whether the product is intended as a gift, or will be used in an important social situation. It must always be remembered that involvement is person/product/situation specific, and while we can classify products as high or low involvement for ease of application, no product is low involvement for every person at all times. The key elements of this model of involvement are shown in Figure 1.2.

The classical model of consumer decision making usually only applies to high involvement products and/or when there are important situational factors. In these cases consumers may often seek extensive information prior to purchase. However, a qualification of the simple 'More involvement equals

more information search' hypothesis is only true of functional products, i.e. those which satisfy by their physical performance. Expressive products, i.e. those which help the consumer express their personality or self-concept, are at once both highly involving and are purchased with little information search, as the psychosocial interpretation of these products is less susceptible to explicit information search as it is largely idiosyncratic. This will be addressed when we consider models of emotion-driven choice. But what do we know about how consumers make purchase choices when they are not involved with the product?

Low involvement choice

By combining data from a wide range of studies we can build a picture of the low-involvement consumer. It seems clear that consumers have very little knowledge about the differences between brands and perceive them as all very similar. If they hold any beliefs about an individual brand then they are likely to be very weak, and thus easily changed. Avoidance of mental and physical effort seems to be the key motivation as con-

Figure 1.2 Factors influencing consumer involvement with products

sumers are seeking to be satisfied, not necessarily delighted. Perhaps the major criterion is the that the choice be the one least likely to give them any problems. It has been suggested that for much of the time consumers are paying little or no conscious attention to the information environment, but are relying on past behaviour as a guide.

In most cases awareness of a brand is a key predictor of purchase, in that brands in 'top-of-mind' awareness are the only ones consumers are likely to choose from, unless some situational factor at point-of-sale draws a new brand to their attention. We know that consumers have a very limited number of brands in any category which they can recall from memory, usually 7 plus or minus 2, and in low-involvement categories nearer to 4 plus or minus 1. So building top-of-mind awareness is a crucial task for marketing communications in low-involvement categories.

However, the major route to awareness is through past behaviour. You will recall that one of the factors that predicts that a product will be low-involvement is frequent purchasing, so that once a consumer has purchased a brand several times and found it reasonably satisfactory, they can fall back on habit from then on. On the first purchase occasion, consumers may use trial as a low-risk method of evaluating the brand, before forming any judgements about it. This model of low-involvement choice is shown in Figure 1.3.

So far we have considered the extent to which the consumer engages in mental effort in choosing a brand, that is the extent of information-processing that is carried out.

But many products and services are not thought about coolly and rationally, so what happens when choice is under the control of emotional processes?

Emotion-driven choice

When consumers are highly involved and emotionally aroused then they are ready to suspend disbelief and operate in a state of willing self-illusion as they pursue a promised benefit that they may know to be false but *feel* to be true. The major source of high emotion in consumer behaviour is when a product or service is high in symbolic meaning. This may be because the consumer believes that it may help them construct and maintain their self-concept and sense of identity, and/or because they believe it will help them communicate a desired image to other people. Symbolic meaning is primarily conveyed by non-verbal imagery, and is perceived holistically. That is, it is very hard for people to break down an emotional preference into individual parts. It is also largely directed towards the self, that is we do not evaluate an emotional purchase in the abstract, but in relation to us. In a process of holistic flow, we form a non-rational preference and then seek out information to support our choice in a process of post-hoc rationality. This process is driven by an emotional desire to arrive at a particular decision which we have already made, where biased information search and reasoning processes are used to arrive at those conclusions we want to arrive at. Once events are subjectively perceived to be real, often through

Figure 1.3 *Low involvement choice*

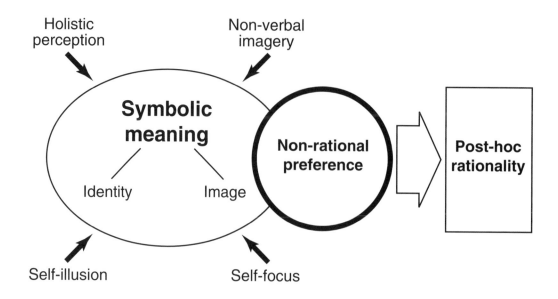

Figure 1.4 *Emotion-driven choice*

imagination and fantasy, then emotional responses overwhelm objective evidence and people search out evidence which supports their non-rational preference and will ignore or 'forget' evidence which might contradict it. This model of emotion-driven choice is shown in Figure 1.4.

Low emotion choice

When consumers are not so involved with the product or service but it is still an area where judgement is largely driven by emotional factors, then studies of the effects of emotion on judgement have shown that even

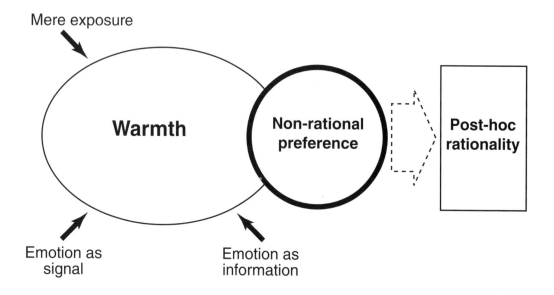

Figure 1.5 *Low emotion choice*

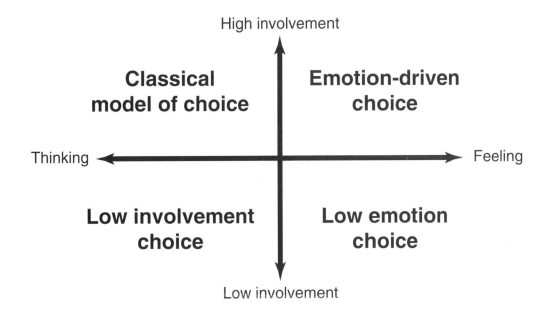

High involvement

Classical model of choice

Emotion-driven choice

Thinking ← → Feeling

Low involvement choice

Low emotion choice

Low involvement

Figure 1.6 *Consumer choice processes*

slightly positive emotional states lead to less thought, less information seeking, less analytic reasoning, less attention to negative cues and less attention to 'realism'. In this state we can consider consumers as seeking a mild sense of warmth, rather than hot emotion, and seeking to choose the brand which they simply feel best about. This feeling of warmth may derive from a number of factors. There is a large amount of experimental evidence that, far from 'familiarity breeding contempt', mere exposure to a brand name over time can result in the development of a non-rational preference. Emotional responses can be used as a signal; in particular a basic emotional signal is that of rejection or dislike. The 'refusal of other tastes' may well be a fundamental process in that we first reject everything we dislike, and that left must be what we like. Also emotional responses can carry information, in that we can consult our feelings for information for a choice decision: 'Well, how do I feel about it?' Because we are not so involved with the choice we may not be motivated to justify our choice with rational arguments, but some people still feel the need to seek out information that justifies

their choice, although this may be a rather more passive operation than that when choice is driven by emotion. This low emotion model of choice is shown in Figure 1.5.

We can thus segment consumer choice behaviour along two dimensions: that of high versus low involvement; and choice that is primarily a rational, thinking process versus choice that is primarily driven by emotional factors. This is illustrated in Figure 1.6.

Models of organizational buying behaviour

The fundamental difference between the buying behaviour of consumers and that of organizations is the number of people involved. When highly involved a consumer will follow a decision process very similar to that followed by organizations, but the people influencing the decision are unlikely to exceed immediate family members and friends, whereas organizational decisions can be influenced by twenty or more individuals each of whom represents another group of people. Identifying the composition of the organizational decision group – the 'buying centre' – is a key task for industrial selling as each member may have different choice criteria, and this is directly related to developing an understanding of the decision process and each member's relative influence, together with the dynamics of inter-organizational relationships. Each of these areas will be discussed in turn.

The composition of the buying centre

The buying centre is a concept rather than a fact, that is its members may never actually meet together, nor should one expect to be able to identify its members by using an organizational chart. It is composed of all those people who have an influence on the buying decision, and will involve different people at different times as the organization moves through the buying process, and will involve more people if it is a new and risky purchase than if it is merely a repetition of a previous purchase. Because the same person may also play a different role in the purchase at different stages, it can be useful to distinguish a limited number of roles in the buying centre, and then seek to identify individuals who perform these roles in a specific organizational purchase situation.

Five roles can be defined in an organizational purchase:

- **Users**: People who will actually use the product or service.
- **Influencers**: All those who influence the decision, even though they may not be directly involved in it, or even be part of the organization. Usually by the supply of information relating to criteria or specifications.
- **Deciders**: The individuals who actually determine the final choice, even though they may not have formal authority.
- **Buyers**: Those with formal authority to place an order and manage its implementation.
- **Gatekeepers**: People who control the flow of information to other members of the buying centre.

The matching of individuals to roles is only the first step in analysing a particular buying centre. It is essential to attempt to understand the distribution of power between members and the specific criteria against which they will evaluate competing offerings. Both of these factors will vary depending upon the nature of the buying process, with the membership of the buying centre changing through the process and sub-decisions being made at various stages.

The organizational buying process

A seven-stage model of the organizational buying process is shown in Figure 1.7 which is very similar to the classical model of consumer choice.

As with the classical model of consumer choice, this is a normative model of what should happen, and in reality the process may not flow in sequential stages but some stages may happen in parallel, and some may not happen at all. The important issue is that at each stage a sub-decision may be taken which will determine the outcomes of successive stages. For example, at the second stage, that of deciding on the characteristics and quantity of the item, the salesperson who is successful in identifying the key individuals and their specific criteria has an opportunity of influencing the sub-decision in such a way that the specified characteristics and/or quantity give them a built-in advantage at stage five, the evaluation of proposals.

Practical tip

A salesperson who succeeds in initiating the buying process, perhaps by demonstrating potential improvements in quality performance, has the opportunity to work with the members of the buying centre through the early stages of the process, thereby building a relationship and influencing the specification of characteristics.

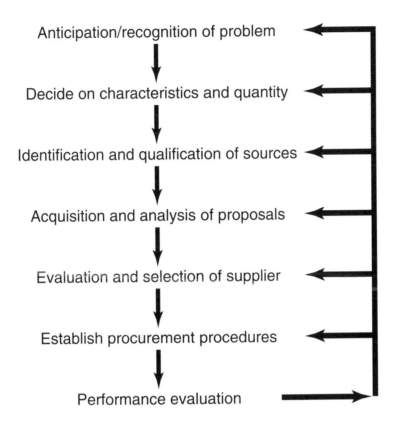

Figure 1.7 *The organizational buying process*

The importance of the last stage should not be under-estimated, as research has shown that it is vital to respond quickly to customer complaints in order to increase the probability of receiving further orders.

Organizational involvement with the purchase decision

Just like consumers, organizations do not put the same amount of effort into all purchases, and we can identify two factors – experience and knowledge – which will determine how much organizational involvement there will be with the purchase decision. The less experience an organization has of purchasing a particular product, and the less relevant knowledge it possesses, the more difficult the purchase decision will become. Three 'buy-classes' have been described in terms of decreasing experience and knowledge which run from a 'straight rebuy' through a 'modified rebuy' to a 'new task'. As the buying situation becomes more difficult it also becomes more important to the organization and so organizational involvement with the purchase decision also increases. This is illustrated in Figure 1.8.

As organizational involvement increases, so the number of people involved in the buying centre increases, and so does their seniority within the organization. A simple guide to the level of management likely to be involved is the total financial cost. In a 'new task' situation where the financial cost is very large and the organization has little or no experience in the area, then it is very likely that board members will be actively involved in

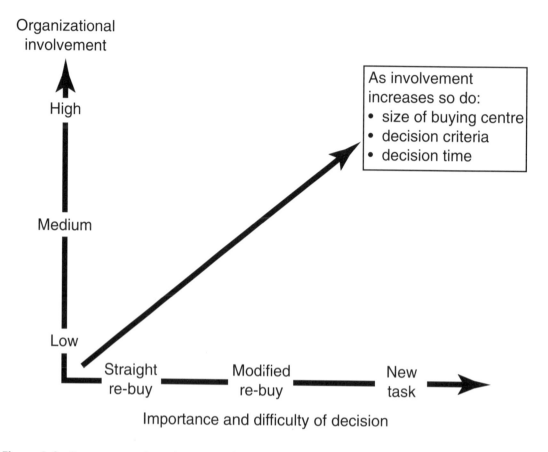

Figure 1.8 *Organizational involvement in the purchase decision*

the decision and the purchasing manager's influence will be relatively small. At the other extreme, in a 'straight rebuy' situation where the financial cost is relatively modest and the experience level is high, then the purchasing manager will be the most senior manager involved, and in a large organization it may not even reach beyond the level of junior management.

Similarly, as organizational involvement increases, so does the complexity of the decision as more purchase criteria are specified by more influencers, and the purchase decision time becomes more extended.

Influences within the buying centre

Because the purchasing department is the easiest one to identify from outside an organization and will be involved in all purchase decisions, it forms the starting point for identifying membership of the buying centre. However, research indicates that for many purchases the key influencers are located in other functional areas, such as production engineering, quality management, or R&D.

The role of the gatekeeper is particularly important, as by controlling the flow of information to other members of the buying centre, the gatekeeper can exert enormous influence on the decision, a degree of influence out of all proportion to the gatekeeper's level of seniority. In many instances, the gatekeeper may be the purchasing manager, who is often attempting to expand his/her influence within the organization. However, the gatekeeper role may be played by another member of the organization and identifying this person may be the key to sales success. Secretaries often act as gatekeepers allowing or denying access to their managers.

Influencers from different functional areas will often lay stress on different choice criteria when evaluating potential suppliers. The purchasing department may emphasize price, engineering may put most value on quality, while production may consider prompt delivery the most important factor. Because these criteria are situation-specific and cannot be generalized across industries, organizations, or buying situations, the key task for the salesperson is to understand the criteria held by members of each buying centre on each occasion.

Relationship marketing versus transaction marketing

Organizations can be categorized on the basis of their attitude towards forming relationships with suppliers and their behaviour over extended periods of time. We can locate most organizations along a continuum of commitment behaviour defined at one end by 'Lost-for-good' customers and at the other by 'Always-a-share' customers. These are illustrated in Figure 1.9.

Lost-for-good customers are committed to a small number of suppliers in whom they have made substantial investment in terms of procedures and thus face very high switching costs in changing suppliers. They perceive that they are exposed to a variety of intangible risks and they are therefore reluctant to change suppliers. However, once they do switch, the account is lost forever (or at least will be very hard to win back). The decision to change suppliers is very infrequent, is considered a serious move and not undertaken lightly.

Always-a-share customers tend to have multiple suppliers, and are much less committed to any single supplier. The organization faces low switching costs and can therefore easily switch suppliers and share out its business between competing suppliers over time. Each purchase is seen as a single transaction and the choice of supplier is taken depending upon the immediate package of benefits being offered in terms of price, delivery, etc. A supplier may lose one piece of business but will still be able to compete effectively for the next piece of business to come along. The decision to switch part or all of its business between suppliers is routine and has few long-term implications.

Both these descriptions are simplifications of extreme positions, and most organizations lie somewhere in from the two ends of the continuum. But if a customer can be identified as tending towards 'Lost-for-good' then relationship marketing is appropriate, whilst if a customer tends towards 'Always-a-share' then transaction marketing is the appropriate approach. The task is to match the marketing

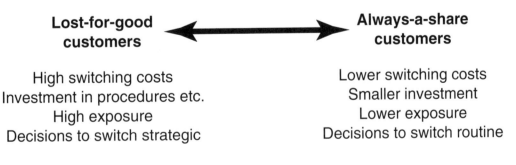

Lost-for-good customers ⟷ **Always-a-share customers**

High switching costs
Investment in procedures etc.
High exposure
Decisions to switch strategic

Lower switching costs
Smaller investment
Lower exposure
Decisions to switch routine

Relationship marketing

Transaction marketing

Figure 1.9 *Relationship versus transaction marketing*

tools to the commitment level of the customer over time.

The salesperson is a key factor in relationship marketing, as the focus is on the individual customer. But the effort also includes the whole marketing activity of the supplier in building commitment and reducing perceptions of exposure. In transaction marketing the focus is on the individual sale, and although a relationship between salesperson and customer should be cultivated it is unlikely to involve the development of sustained commitment.

Practical tip

Identify those customers for whom relationship marketing and the investment it requires is appropriate, and those for whom transactional marketing is more suited.

Implications for selling

The major implication for selling and sales strategy is that the key to success lies in understanding the psychology of the customer and the social influences upon them. By utilizing the models and frameworks described in this chapter, the salesperson can identify the type of decision process likely to be used by the customer and tailor a presentation to suit the specific situation.

In consumer markets the salesperson must decide whether the customer is likely to be highly involved with the purchase, and whether the decision is likely to made largely on a rational or an emotional basis. If they are highly involved in a rational decision then the salesperson must develop a presentation which provides extensive information in support of a number of key benefits. If they are not very involved but it is still a rational decision then the salesperson should offer a smaller number of benefits, and help the customer to develop or apply an appropriate 'rule of thumb' to make the decision easy. For

example, suggest to the customer the 'rule of thumb' that one should 'choose the brand most other people choose'. It is important to balance the raising of expectations in the customer with the likely reality delivered by the product or service as most dissatisfaction is created by a shortfall between the two. Thus care should be taken not to over-sell benefits otherwise this is likely to lead to less customer satisfaction.

If the decision process is primarily emotional in nature, then the salesperson should feel free to over-emphasize symbolic benefits as the customer is unlikely to require 'realism'. For example, a key symbolic benefit is often the extent to which a particular choice of brand will draw admiration from other people and the salesperson should not be restrained in describing the magnitude of this effect as the customer will *want* to believe it. It is vital to help the customer bolster his/her choice by supplying evidence that they can use to justify to themselves and to important others that they made a 'wise' choice. When the customer is not so involved then it may be that sufficient 'warmth' can be generated through the sales interaction itself, in that the inter-personal skills of the salesperson in building a relationship might prove to be the key to success.

In organizational markets it is essential for the salesperson to identify the members of the buying centre, to understand their different choice criteria and to estimate their relative power and influence in the specific purchase. If there is high organizational involvement then the numbers in the buying centre will be greater, and so will the seniority of managers taking part. This suggests that there should be a team-selling approach which attempts to match both seniority and criteria between the selling organization and the customer, with senior managers talking to their opposite numbers and engineers with engineers.

The identification of an organization as tending towards being either 'Lost-for-good' or 'Always-a-share' leads to a requirement to match each type of organization with either a relationship marketing or a transactional marketing approach. Always-a-share customers tend to focus on product features or on the salesperson's ability to provide an immediate service rather than company brand name or corporate image. However, Lost-for-good customers are concerned with the long-term issues of general technological capabilities and the strategic direction of the selling company.

Although Lost-for-good customers demand consistency from suppliers, they do not want static consistency. Instead, they expect suppliers to be consistent in showing concern for the customer but also to be dynamic in their responses to changing market conditions. Thus the salesperson must be constantly alert for changes in their customer's business environment and ensure that they maintain flexibility in what they offer the customer. Although the Lost-for-good customer is highly dependent on the capabilities of their suppliers, they are often not able to accurately assess these capabilities or the staying power of technologies so they look for easily observable signs of competence. This means that the salesperson must be aware that such issues as whether delivery promises are kept and whether documentation was correct, may be used as evidence on the longer-term capabilities of the supplier. So the salesperson must maintain the image of the firm by attending to details and keeping promises as this may have an important influence on the customer's perceptions of their longer-term technological competence. Because the Lost-for-good customer demands heavy commitment and support from the salesperson, the salesforce itself must work with a long-term time horizon and consider the wider concerns of the customer. Building effective long-lasting relationships is a sustained activity and cannot be achieved through short-term efforts, nor by pushing individual products.

Summary

This chapter introduced models of buyer behaviour in consumer and organizational markets and drew out the implications for selling. In consumer markets the key concepts of involvement and emotion were the focus of discussion, while in organizational markets the additional issues of power, influence and commitment over time are vitally important. Guidance was given on identifying the appropriate model to apply in a selling situation, and how an understanding of buyer behaviour can drive the design of appropriate selling strategies in specific environments.

Further reading

Jackson, B.B. (1985) *Winning and Keeping Industrial Customers: The Dynamics of Customer Relationships*. Lexington, MA: Lexington Books.

Parkinson, S. and Baker, M. (1986) *Organizational Buying Behaviour: Purchasing and Marketing Management Implications*. London: Macmillan Press.

Solomon, M. (1992) *Consumer Behavior: Buying, Having, and Being*. Englewood Cliffs, NJ: Prentice-Hall.

2

Personal selling skills

Professor David Jobber, University of Bradford Management Centre

 This chapter explores some of the fundamental skills necessary to conclude a sale. A seven-step procedure is discussed: preparation, the opening, need and problem identification, presentation and demonstration, dealing with objections, closing the sale and the follow-up. Great stress is placed on gaining an understanding of customer needs. Situation, problem, implication and need pay-off questions are examined to provide an in-depth understanding of how a salesperson who is involved in a major sale should probe to understand implicit and explicit needs.

The basic philosophy underlying the approach to personal selling adopted in this chapter is that selling should be an extension of the marketing concept. This implies that, for long-term survival, it is in the best interests of the salesperson and his or her company to identify customer needs and aid customer decision-making by selecting from the product range those products which best fit the customer's requirements.

The sales interview offers an unparalleled opportunity to identify individual customer needs and match behaviour to the specific customer that is encountered.

Research has shown that, far from using high-pressure selling tactics, success is associated with:

1. Asking questions.
2. Providing product information, making comparisons and offering evidence to support claims.
3. Acknowledging the viewpoint of the customer.
4. Agreeing with the customer's perceptions.
5. Supporting the customer.
6. Releasing tension.

All of these findings are in accord with the marketing concept.

In order to develop personal selling skills, it is useful to distinguish seven phases of the selling process (see Figure 2.1). Each will now be discussed.

Preparation

Preparation before a sales visit can reap dividends by enhancing confidence and performance when face-to-face with the customer. Some situations cannot be prepared for: the unexpected question or unusual objection, for example. But many customers face similar situations and certain questions and objections will be raised repeatedly. Preparation can help the salesperson respond to those recurring situations.

Salespeople will benefit from gaining knowledge of their own products, competitors' products, sales presentation planning, setting call objectives and understanding buyer behaviour.

Product knowledge

Product knowledge means understanding both product features and the customer benefits that they confer. Understanding product features alone is not enough to convince customers to buy because they buy products for the benefits that the features provide, not the features in themselves. Salespeople need to ask themselves what are the benefits that a certain feature provides for customers. For example, a computer mouse (product feature) provides a more convenient way of issuing commands (customer benefit) than using the keyboard. The way to turn features into benefits is to view products from the customer's angle. A by-product of this is the realization that some features may provide no customer benefit whatsoever.

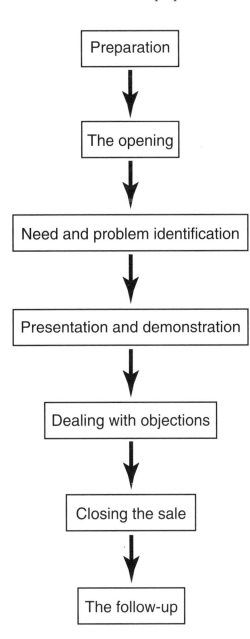

Figure 2.1 *The selling process*

Practical tip

Choose five key products and list their product features. Then identify the customer benefits each of these features provides. When talking to customers, remember to discuss product benefits not just features.

Competitors' products

Knowledge of competitors' products allows their strengths to be offset against their weaknesses. For example, if a buyer claims that a competitor's product has a cost advantage, this may be offset against the superior productivity advantage of the salesperson's product. Similarly, inaccuracies in a buyer's claims can be countered. Finally, competitive knowledge allows the salespeople to stress the differential advantage of their products compared to the competition.

Sales presentation planning

Preparation here builds confidence, raises the chances that important benefits are not forgotten, allows visual aids and demonstrations to be built into the presentation and permits the anticipation of objections and the preparation of convincing counter-arguments. Although preparation is vital there should be room left for flexibility in approach since customers have different needs. The salesperson has to be aware that the features and benefits that should be stressed with one customer have much less emphasis placed on them for another.

Setting call objectives

The key to setting call objectives is to phrase them in terms of what the salesperson wants

the customer to do rather than what the salesperson should do. For example:

- For the customer to define what his or her needs are.
- For the customer to visit a showroom.
- For the customer to try the product, e.g. drive a car.
- For the customer to be convinced of the cost saving of our product compared with the competition.

This is because the success of the sales interview is customer-dependent. The end is to convince the customer; what the salesperson does is simply a means to that end.

Understanding buyer behaviour

Thought should also be given to understanding buyer behaviour. Questions should be asked: Who are the likely key people to talk to? What are their probable choice criteria? Are there any gatekeepers preventing access to some people who need to be circumvented? What are the likely opportunities and threats that may arise in the selling situ-

Checklist 2.1

Remember that successful selling depends on the hard work that is done as part of preparation. This involves:

1. Understanding the features and benefits of the products you are selling.
2. Understanding the features and benefits of competitors' products and how they are better/worse than yours.
3. Planning sales presentations while recognizing a flexible approach may be needed according to what is important to each customer.
4. Setting call objectives in terms of what you want the customer to do.
5. Understanding buyer behaviour in terms of the important issues discussed in Chapter 1.

ation? All of the answers to these questions need to be verified when in the actual selling situation, but prior consideration can help salespeople to be clear in their own minds about the important issues.

The opening

Initial impressions can cloud later perceptions and so it is important to consider the ways in which a favourable initial response can be achieved.

Buyers expect salespeople to be business-like in their personal appearance and behaviour. Untidy hair and a sloppy manner of dress can create a lack of confidence. Further, the salesperson who does not respect the fact that the buyer is likely to be a busy person, with many demands on his or her time, may cause irritation on the part of the buyer.

Salespeople should open with a smile, a handshake and, in situations where they are not well known to the buyer, introduce themselves and the company they represent. Common courtesies should be followed. For example, they should wait for the buyer to indicate that they can sit down or, at least, ask the buyer if they may sit down. Attention to detail, like holding one's briefcase in the left hand so that the right can be used for the handshake, removes the possibility of an awkward moment when a briefcase is clumsily transferred from right to left as the buyer extends his or her hand in greeting.

Opening remarks are important since they set the tone for the rest of the sales interview. Normally they should be business-related since this is the purpose of the visit; they should show the buyer that the salesperson is not about to waste the buyer's time. Where the buyer is well known and where, by his or her own remarks, the buyer indicates a willingness to talk about a more social matter, the salesperson will obviously follow. This can generate close rapport with the buyer, but the salesperson must be aware of the reason for being there, and not be excessively diverted from talking business. Opening remarks might be:

Trade salesperson: Your window display looks attractive. Has it attracted more custom?

Retail salesperson: I can see that you appear to be interested in our stereo equipment. What kind of system had in you mind?

Need and problem identification ■

Most salespeople have a range of products to sell. A car salesperson has many models ranging from small economy cars to super luxury top-of-the-range models. The computer salesperson will have a number of systems to suit the needs and resources of different customers. A bicycle retailer will have models from many different manufacturers to offer customers. A pharmaceutical salesperson will be able to offer doctors a range of drugs to combat various illnesses.

In each case, the seller's first objective will be to discover the problems and needs of the customer. Before a car salesperson can sell a car, he or she needs to understand the customer's circumstances. What size of car is required? Is the customer looking for high fuel economy or performance? Is a boot or a hatchback preferred? What kind of price range is being considered? Having obtained this information the salesperson is in a position to sell the model which best suits the needs of the buyer. A computer salesperson may carry out a survey of customer requirements prior to suggesting an appropriate computer system. A bicycle retailer should ask who the bicycle is for, what type is preferred, e.g. mountain or racing bicycle, and the colour preference, before making sensible suggestions as to which model is most suitable. A pharmaceutical salesperson will discuss with doctors the problems which have arisen with patient treatment; perhaps an ointment has been ineffective or a harmful side-effect has been discovered. This gives the salesperson the opportunity to offer a solution to such problems by means of one of his or her company's products.

When making a major sale, attention to understanding buyer needs is crucial. The Huthwaite Research Group have developed a procedure for identifying two types of needs:

- Implied needs which were expressed by customers as problems, difficulties or dissatisfactions such as 'our existing computing process is too slow' or 'I'm unhappy with the flexibility of our inventory system'. But recognition of a problem or difficulty and the feeling of dissatisfaction does not mean that the customer is ready to buy. For that to happen, the problem/difficulty/dissatisfaction has to be developed into explicit needs.
- Explicit needs which are specific customer expressions of wants, or intentions to act such as 'We need a new computing system' or 'I intend to install a new inventory system'. These are action-orientated needs which trigger purchase.

A key purpose of questioning in the major sale is to discover implied needs and to develop them into explicit needs. Uncovering implied needs alone is insufficient: successful salespeople know how to translate them into explicit needs. A major component of the Huthwaite Research Group's approach is to accomplish this task. They discovered that successful salespeople offered solutions very late in the call after implied needs had been developed into explicit needs. These observations led to the creation of the SPIN® strategy which is outlined in Figure 2.2.

SPIN is an acronym for situation, problem, implication and need pay-off, describing the four types of questioning required to move the customer to the situation where solutions and benefits can be examined. Although it should not be regarded as a rigid formula, the model provides a set of guidelines taking a sales call through the steps of need identification and development until explicit needs are reached.

Situation questions

These are used to identify facts about the customer (e.g. their position, responsibilities and role in the buying decision), their business (e.g. type, sales volume, rate of growth, number of employees) and specific information relevant to the product field (e.g. current products and/or services used, when purchased). These questions establish the background to the customer's existing situation. They are critical to first-time visits but also on repeat calls changes in situations may need to be identified. The problem with situation questions is that they are often boring to the customer who may grow impatient if too many are asked. Successful salespeople do their homework as part of their call preparation so that situation questions can be kept to a minimum.

Problem questions

Instead of dwelling on unnecessary situation questions, successful salespeople spend more time on problem questions. Typical questions are:

'Are you completely happy with your present machine?'
'What are the disadvantages of handling the data manually?'
'Is your equipment entirely reliable?'
'Isn't it difficult to get a service person out quickly to repair your photocopier?'
'Are there any quality problems?'

These are designed to reveal the problems, difficulties and dissatisfactions with the current situations so that the customer's implied needs can be identified. Although important in selling, the Huthwaite Research Group found their use to be more strongly linked to sales success in smaller compared with larger sales. The key in larger sales is not to immediately follow the identification of implied needs with suggested solutions (which often

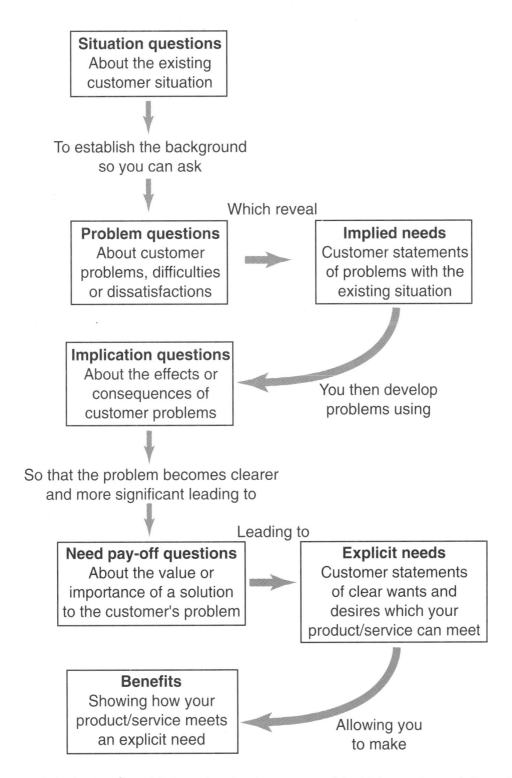

Figure 2.2 *The SPIN® model. Reproduced with permission of the Huthwaite Research Group Ltd, Rotherham, UK. © Huthwaite Research Group. SPIN® is a registered trademark of Huthwaite Research Group*

happens). Rather the salesperson should use implication questions to build up the perceived seriousness of the problem before offering a solution.

Implication questions

Two important differences between smaller and larger sales are the levels of expenditure and personal risk associated with each type of purchase. Making a major sale often involves the purchaser sanctioning large expenditures and accepting a high level of personal risk of a mistake being made. These are the costs of purchase. Customers need to be convinced that the implications of the problems recognized through problem questioning are severe enough to offset the costs of purchase. Some customers can see the implications clearly for themselves, but in many cases the true seriousness of the problem will only be perceived through the salesperson using implication questions.

Implication questions are designed to encourage customers to state the consequences, effects or implications of their problems. They magnify the size of the implied needs (problems, difficulties, dissatisfactions) with the current situation. For example, a problem question may have revealed that a machine is unreliable; an implication question would ask for the consequences of this unreliability, e.g. loss of output, greater personal hassle and aggravation, higher costs because of the need for more overtime payments.

Typical implication questions are:

'What effect does unreliability have on output?'
'Could unreliability lead to increased costs?'
'Does the difficulty of using the computer lead to higher training costs?'
'How does the late delivery of parts affect your customers?'
'What are the implications of your supplier's slow repair service?'

Implication questions are central to success in selling to major accounts because they build up the customer's perception of the seriousness of the problem. Rackham (1987) termed these 'sad questions' because they focused on problems such as increased costs, lower output and slow delivery. The next step is to use need pay-off questions to build up the customer's perception of the value or usefulness of a solution.

Need pay-off questions

Need pay-off questions move the focus of attention from problems, difficulties and dissatisfactions to a more positive solution-centred discussion. For example, problem questions may have revealed that a machine is unreliable; implication questions may have discovered that the implications are higher costs and lower output. Need pay-off questions can now focus on the value of a solution.

Seller: ... so your main problem is machine unreliability leading to higher costs and lower output (need pay-off question). So, from what you've said, you'd be interested in a machine that would be more reliable?

Customer: Yes, we need to sort out this problem.

Seller: (Need pay-off question). If your machine only had a downtime of two hours for maintenance every six months, how would that affect costs?

Customer: It would drastically reduce overtime payments; it might save £50,000 a year.

Seller: (Need pay-off question) And how would output be affected?

Customer: Output might go up 5% producing an extra £100,000 worth of components.

Need pay-off questions were called 'happy' questions by Rackham because they focus on the usefulness or value of solving a problem; they produce responses from customers that are pleasing. Typical need pay-off questions are:

'How would reducing down-time help you?'

'Why would reducing preparation time be important to you?'

'What benefits would you see in a faster machine?'

'Why would you like to see a reduction in inventory levels?'

'Would eliminating the need to train staff save you money?'

Because they focus on the value of solving the problems the customer is facing, they create a positive helpful atmosphere in which to do business. Furthermore, they are asking the customer to tell the salesperson the benefits, not the other way around. They are convincing themselves of the value of solving their problems. Crucially, the process provides the opportunity for the customer (decision-making unit member) to rehearse describing those benefits to other people in the decision-making unit.

By giving customers the chance to explain to the salesperson the usefulness of the solution, it is valuable practice for when they need to give a convincing explanation to other people in their company. This aids the internal selling so often necessary in major account sales.

The combination of implication and need pay-off questions, then, has moved the customer from describing implied needs (e.g. a problem with machine unreliability or difficulty with using a computer) to developing explicit needs ('I need a more reliable machine' or 'I would like a computer that is easier to use'). The dual effect of building up the seriousness of the problem (through implication questions) and recognition of the value of the solution (through need pay-off questions) is to convince the customer of the need to find a solution through a purchase.

Usually need pay-off questions will follow problem and implication questions as suggested in the SPIN® acronym. Indeed the Huthwaite Research Group found that top salespeople built up the perception of problems before asking need pay-off questions. But there are exceptions to this sequence depending on the sales situation.

For example, if the customer volunteers an explicit need (e.g. we must buy a more reliable machine) early in the call, then it would be sensible to go to need pay-off questions immediately to build up perceived value of a new machine. There are also circumstances when need pay-off questions should not be used. If, for example, a customer suggests an explicit need, for example, 'I need a photocopier that can copy colour slides' a need pay-off question like 'Why do you need copies of colour slides?' would be appropriate if the salesperson was able to supply a copier that met this need since it would encourage the customer to consider and build up the importance of that need. However, if the salesperson could not meet that need, asking a need pay-off question would be the worst thing to do for the very same reason.

Practical tip

Identify and practise using situation, problem, implication and need pay-off questions that are relevant to the products you are selling. The result will be a greater awareness of the value of your products in customers' eyes.

Presentation and demonstration ▬

The presentation and demonstration provides the opportunity for the salesperson to convince customers that the salesperson can supply the solution to their problem. It should focus on customer benefits rather than product features. These can be linked by using the following phrases:

'Which means that…'
'Which results in…'
'Which enables you to…'

For example, a machine salesperson might say that the machine possesses proven technology (product feature) which means that the reliability of the machine (customer benefit) can be depended upon. Evidence should then be supplied to support this sales argument. Perhaps scientific tests have proved the reliability of the machine (these should be shown to the customer), satisfied customers' testimonials could be produced or a visit to a satisfied customer could be arranged.

Practical tip

Using the features and benefits identified in the first practical tip exercise of this chapter, practise linking them by using the terms 'which means that', 'which results in' and 'which enables you to'.

The salesperson should continue asking questions during the presentation to ensure that the customer has understood what the salesperson has said and to check that what the salesperson has mentioned really is of importance to the customer. This can be achieved by asking 'Is that the kind of thing you are looking for?'

Many sales situations involve risk to the buyer. No matter what benefits the salesperson discusses, the buyer may be reluctant to change from the present supplier or change the present model because to do so may give rise to unforeseen problems – delivery may be unpredictable or the new model may be unreliable. Assurances from the salesperson are, of themselves, unlikely to be totally convincing – after all, they would say that, wouldn't they! Risk is the hidden reason behind many failures to sell. The salesperson accurately identifies customer needs and relates product benefits to those needs; the buyer does not offer much resistance, but somehow does not buy. A likely reason is that the buyer plays safe, sticking to the present supplier or model in order to lessen the risk of aggravation should problems occur.

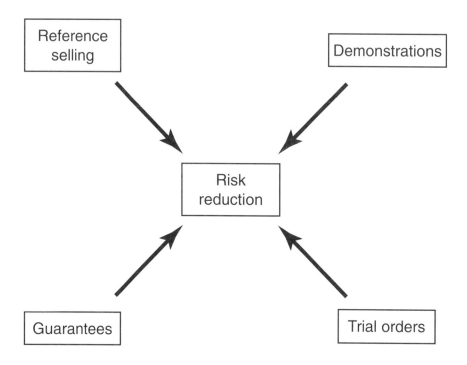

Figure 2.3 *Reducing risk for customers*

How, then, can a salesperson reduce risk? There are four major ways (see Figure 2.3):

- reference selling
- demonstrations
- guarantees
- trial orders.

Reference selling

Reference selling involves the use of satisfied customers in order to convince the buyer of the effectiveness of the salesperson's product. During the preparation stage, a list of satisfied customers, arranged by product type, should be drawn up. Letters from satisfied customers should also be kept and used in the sales presentation in order to build confidence. This technique can be highly effective in selling, moving a buyer from being merely interested in the product to being convinced that it is the solution to his or her problem.

Demonstrations

Chinese proverb: 'Tell me and I'll forget; show me and I may remember; involve me and I'll understand.'

Demonstrations also reduce risk because they prove the benefits of the product. A major producer of sales training films organizes regional demonstrations of a selection of them in order to prove their quality to training managers. Industrial goods manufacturers will arrange demonstrations to show their products' capabilities in use. Car salespeople will allow customers to test drive cars.

For all but the most simple of products it is advisable to divide the demonstration into two stages. The first stage involves a brief description of the features and benefits of the product and an explanation of how it works. The second stage entails the actual demonstration itself. This should be conducted by the salesperson. The reason behind this two-stage approach is that it is often very difficult for the viewers of the demonstration to understand the principles of how a product works while at the same time watching it work. This is because the viewers are receiving competing stimuli. The salesperson's voice may be competing for the buyers' attention with the flashing lights and noise of the equipment.

Once the equipment works, the buyers can be encouraged to use it themselves under the salesperson's supervision. If the correct equipment, to suit the buyers' needs, has been chosen for demonstration, and it performs reliably, the demonstration can move the buyers very much closer to purchase.

Guarantees

Guarantees of product reliability, after-sales service, and delivery supported by penalty clauses can build confidence towards the salesperson's claims and lessen the costs to the buyer should something go wrong. Their establishment is a matter for company policy rather than the salesperson's discretion but, where offered, the salesperson should not underestimate their importance in the sales presentation.

Trial orders

The final strategy for risk reduction is for salespeople to encourage trial orders, even though they may be uneconomic in company terms and in terms of salespeople's time in the short term, when faced with a straight re-buy. Buyers who habitually purchase supplies from one supplier may recognize that change involves unwarranted risk. It may be that the only way for a new supplier to break through this impasse is to secure a small order which, in effect, permits the demonstration of the company's capability to provide consistently high-quality products promptly. The confidence, thus built, may lead to a higher percentage of the customer's business in the longer term.

Dealing with objection

If the questioning sequence described earlier (SPIN®) is effectively used, fewer objections can be expected since the value of the product has been built up. This is called objection prevention. Nevertheless, in many calls some objections may arise and how the salesperson handles them can be crucial for success. Objections should not always be viewed with dismay by salespeople. Many objections are simply expressions of interest by the buyer. What the buyer is asking for is further information because he or she is interested in what the salesperson is saying. The problem is that the buyer is not, as yet, convinced. Objections highlight the issues which are important to the buyer. For example, Ford, when training salespeople, make the point that a customer's objection is a signpost to what is really on their mind.

An example will illustrate these points. Suppose an industrial salesperson working for an adhesives manufacturer is faced with the following objection: 'Why should I buy your new adhesive gun when my present method of applying adhesive – direct from the tube – is perfectly satisfactory?' This type of objection is clearly an expression of a desire for additional information. The salesperson's task is to provide it in a manner which does not antagonize the buyer and yet is convincing. It is a fact of human personality that the argument which is supported by the greater weight of evidence does not always win the day; people do not like to be proved wrong. The very act of changing a supplier may be resisted because it may imply criticism of a past decision on the part of the buyer. For a salesperson to disregard the emotional aspects of dealing with objections is to court disaster. The situation to be avoided is where the buyer digs in his or her heels on principle, because of the attitude of the salesperson.

So, the effective approach for dealing with objections involves two areas: the preparation of convincing answers, and the development of a range of techniques for answering objections in a manner which permits the acceptance of these answers without loss of face on the part of the buyer. The first area has been covered in Chapter 1. A number of techniques will now be reviewed to illustrate how the second objective may be accomplished. These are shown in Figure 2.4.

Listen and do not interrupt

Experienced salespeople know that the impression given to buyers by the salesperson who interrupts the buyer in midstream is that the salesperson believes that:

- the objection is obviously wrong
- it is trivial
- it is not worth the salesperson's time to let the buyer finish.

Interruption denies the buyer the kind of respect he/she is entitled to receive and may lead to a misunderstanding of the real substance behind the objection.

The correct approach is to listen carefully, attentively and respectfully. The buyer will appreciate the fact that the salesperson is taking the problem seriously and the salesperson will gain through having a clear and full understanding of what the problem really is.

Agree and counter

This approach maintains the respect the salesperson shows to the buyer. The salesperson first agrees that what the buyer is saying is sensible and reasonable, before then putting forward an alternative point of view. It therefore takes the edge off the objection and creates a climate of agreement rather than conflict. For example:

Buyer: The problem with your tractor is that it costs more than your competition.

Salesperson: Yes, the initial cost of the tractor is a little higher than competitors' models, but I should like to show you how, over the life-time of the machine, ours works out to be far more economical.

This example shows why the method is sometimes called the 'yes but...' technique. The 'yes' precedes the agree statement, while the 'but' prefaces the counter-argument. There is no necessity to use these words, however. In fact, in some sales situations the buyer may be so used to having salespeople use them that the technique loses some of its

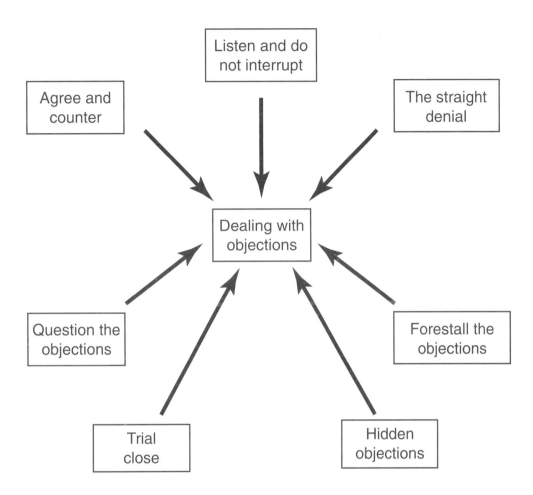

Figure 2.4 *Dealing with objections*

effectiveness. Fortunately there are other approaches which are less blatant. For example:

1. 'I can appreciate your concern that the machine is more expensive than the competition. However, I should like to show you....'
2. 'Customer XYZ made the same comment a year ago. I can assure you that he is highly delighted with his decision to purchase because the cost savings over the life-time of the machine more than offset the initial cost difference.'
3. 'That's absolutely right! The initial cost is a

little higher. That's why I want to show you....'

The use of the reference selling technique can be combined with the agree and counter method to provide a powerful counter to an objection. For example, salespeople of media space in newspapers which are given away free to the public often encounter the following objection:

Buyer (e.g. car dealer): Your newspaper is given away free. Most of the people who receive it throw it away without even reading it.

Salesperson: I can understand your concern that a newspaper which is free may not be read. However, a great many people do read it to find out what second-hand cars are on the market. Mr Smith of Smith Motors has been advertising with us for two years and he is delighted with the results.

The straight denial

This method has to be handled with a great deal of care since the danger is that it will result in exactly the kind of antagonism which the salesperson is wishing to avoid. However, it can be used when the buyer is clearly seeking factual information. For example:

Buyer: I expect that this upholstery will be difficult to clean.

Salesperson: No, Mr. Buyer, absolutely not. This material is made from a newly developed synthetic fibre which resists stains and allows marks to be removed simply by using soap, water and a clean cloth.

Question the objection

Sometimes an objection is raised which is so general as to be difficult to counter. For example, a customer might say he or she does not like the appearance of the product, or that the product is not good quality. In this situation, the salesperson should question the nature of the objection in order to clarify the specific problem at hand. Sometimes this results in a major objection being reduced to one which can easily be dealt with.

Buyer: I'm sorry but I don't like the look of that car.

Salesperson: Could you tell me exactly what it is that you don't like the look of?

Buyer: I don't like the pattern on the seats.

Salesperson: Well in fact this model can be supplied in a number of different upholstery designs. Shall we have a look at the catalogue to see if there is a pattern to your liking?

Another benefit of questioning objections is that, in trying to explain the exact nature of objections, buyers may themselves realize these are really quite trivial.

Forestall the objection

With this method, the salesperson not only anticipates an objection and plans its counter, but actually raises the objection as part of his or her sales presentation.

There are two advantages of doing this. First, the timing of the objection is controlled by the salesperson. Consequently, it can be planned so that it is raised at the most appropriate time for it to be dealt with effectively. Second, since it is raised by the salesperson, the buyer is not placed in a position where, having raised a problem, he or she feels that it must be defended.

The danger with using this method, however, is that the salesperson may highlight a problem the buyer had not thought of. It is most often used where a salesperson is faced with the same objection being raised time after time. Perhaps buyers are continually raising the problem that the salesperson is working for one of the smallest companies in the industry. The salesperson may pre-empt the objection in the following manner: 'My company is smaller than most in the industry which means that we respond quicker to our customers' needs and try that bit harder to make sure our customers are happy.'

Turn the objection into a trial close

A *trial close* is where a salesperson attempts to conclude the sale without prejudicing the chances of continuing the selling process with the buyer should he or she refuse to commit himself/herself.

The ability of a salesperson to turn the objection into a trial close is dependent upon perfect timing and considerable judgement. Usually it will be attempted after the selling process is well under way, and the salesperson judges that only one objection remains. Under these conditions, he or she might say the following: 'If I can satisfy you that the fuel consumption of this car is no greater than that of the Vauxhall Cavalier, would you buy it?'

When dealing with objections, the salesperson should remember that heated arguments are unlikely to win sales – buyers buy from their friends, not their enemies.

Hidden objections

Not all prospects state their objections. They may prefer to say nothing because to raise an objection may cause offence or may prolong the sales interaction. Such people may believe that staying on friendly terms with the salesperson and at the end of the interview stating that they will think over the proposal is the best tactic in a no-buy situation. The correct salesperson response to hidden objections is to ask questions in an attempt to uncover the nature of the objections. If a salesperson believes that a buyer is unwilling to reveal his or her true objections, he or she should ask such questions as:

- 'Is there anything so far which you are unsure about?'
- 'Is there anything on your mind?'
- 'What would it take to convince you?'

Uncovering hidden objections is crucial to successful selling because to convince someone it is necessary to know what he or she needs to be convinced of. However, with uncommunicative buyers this may be difficult. As a last resort the salesperson may need to 'second guess' the reluctant buyer and suggest an issue which they believe is causing the problem and ask a question such as: 'I don't think you're totally convinced about the better performance of our product, are you?'

Closing the sale

The skills and techniques discussed so far are not, in themselves, sufficient for consistent sales success. A final ingredient may be necessary to complete the mix – the ability to

> **Practical tip**
>
> Think of the possible objections that customers might raise when selling the latest product introduced by your company. For each objection work out how you will respond. This might mean doing your homework to provide convincing evidence to support your case.

close the sale. It should be noted, however, that the use of closing techniques is not always appropriate (e.g. too early in the decision-making process or when talking to a specifier). In such circumstances an action agreement (described later) should be used. The following discussion assumes that closing is the correct course of action.

Some salespeople believe that an effective presentation should lead the buyer to ask for the product without the seller needing to close the sale himself/herself. This sometimes happens, but more usually it will be necessary for the salesperson to take the initiative. This is because, no matter how well the salesperson identifies buyer needs, matches product benefits to them and overcomes objections, there is likely to be some doubt still present in the mind of the buyer. This doubt may manifest itself in the wish to delay the decision. Would it not be better to think things over? Would it not be sensible to see what a competitor has to offer?

The plain truth, however, is that if the buyer does put off buying until another day it is as likely that he or she will buy from the competition. While the seller is there, the seller is at an advantage over the competition; thus part of the salesperson's job is to try to close the sale.

Why, then, are some salespeople reluctant to close a sale? The problem lies in the fact that most people fear rejection. Closing the sale asks the buyer to say yes or no. Sometimes it will be no and the salesperson will have been rejected. Avoiding closing the sale does not result in more sales, but rejection is less blatant. The most important point to grasp, then, is not to be afraid to close. Accept the fact that some buyers will inevitably respond negatively, but be confident that more will buy than if no close had been used.

A major consideration is timing. A general rule is to attempt to close the sale when the buyer displays heightened interest or a clear intention to purchase the product. Salespeople should therefore look out for such **buying signals** and respond accordingly.

There are statements by customers that indicate an interest in buying. For example: 'That looks fine', 'I like that one', 'When could the product be delivered?', 'I think that product matches my requirements'. They all indicate a very positive intention to buy without actually asking for the order. They therefore provide an excellent opportunity for the salesperson to ask the customer to make a commitment to buy.

A time will come during the sales interview when the salesperson has discussed all the product benefits and answered all the customer's questions. It is, clearly, decision time; the buyer is enthusiastic but is hesitating. There are a number of closing techniques which the salesperson can use.

Simply ask for the order

The simplest technique involves asking directly for the order:

- 'Would you like to buy it?'
- 'Do you want it?'

The key to using this technique is to keep silent after you have asked for the order. The salesperson has asked a closed question implying a yes or no answer. To break the silence effectively lets the buyer off the hook. The buyer will forget the first question and reply to the salesperson's later comment.

Summarize and then ask for the order

This technique allows the salesperson to remind the buyer of the main points in the sales argument in a manner which implies that the moment for decision has come and that buying is the natural extension of the proceedings. 'Well, Mr Smith, we have agreed that the Vectra model meets your requirements of low noise, high productivity and driver comfort at a cost which you can afford. May I go ahead and place an order for this model?'

The concession close

This involves keeping one concession in reserve to use as the final push towards agreement: 'If you are willing to place an order now, I'm willing to offer an extra 2½ per cent discount'.

The alternative close

This closing technique assumes that the buyer is willing to purchase but moves the decision to whether the colour should be red or blue, the delivery should be Tuesday or Friday, the payment in cash or credit, etc. In such circumstances the salesperson suggests two alternatives, the agreement to either thus closing the sale.

- 'Would you like the red one or the blue one?'
- 'Would you like it delivered on Tuesday or Friday?'

This technique has been used by salespeople for many years and consequently should be used with care, especially with professional buyers who are likely to have experienced its use many times and know exactly what the salesperson is doing.

The objection close

This closing technique has been mentioned briefly earlier in this chapter. It involves the use of an objection as a stimulus to buy. If the salesperson is convinced that the objection is the major stumbling block to the sale, he/she can gain commitment from the buyer by saying 'If I can convince you that this model is the most economical in its class, will you buy it?' A positive response from the buyer and reference to an objective statistical comparison by the seller effectively seals the sale.

Action agreement

In some situations it is inappropriate to attempt to close the sale. For many industrial goods the sales cycle is long and a salesperson who attempts to close the sale at early meetings may cause annoyance. In selling pharmaceutical products, for example, salespeople do not try to close a sale but instead attempt to achieve 'action agreement' whereby either the salesperson or the doctor agrees to do something before their next meeting. This technique has the effect of helping the doctor–salesperson relationship to develop and continue.

Practical tip

Identify in your selling job situations where it is sensible to use closing techniques and where to do so would be inappropriate. Would using the action agreement technique be suitable? If so, think of the types of action agreement you could use.

Follow-up

This final stage in the sales process is necessary to ensure that the customer is satisfied with the purchase and that no problems with such factors as delivery, installation, product use and training have arisen. Salespeople may put off the follow-up call because it does not result in an immediate order. However, for most companies repeat business is the hallmark of success and the follow-up call can play a major role by showing that the salesperson really cares about the customer

rather than only being interested in making sales.

The follow-up call can also be used to provide reassurance that the purchase was the right one. As we have already seen, many customers suffer from cognitive dissonance, that is, being anxious that they have made the right choice.

Summary

This chapter has explored a number of key issues relating to personal selling skills. A major task for salespeople is to recognize that customers have different wants and expectations and these need to be understood in order to sell successfully. This means that salespeople need to develop their questioning skills and their abilities to build the perceived value of their products in the customers' minds. They must understand how to translate product features into customer benefits, know how to handle the psychological aspects of objections and recognize when it is appropriate to close the sale. Attempting to close at unsuitable times will cause customer annoyance and disrupt the harmony of relationships.

References and further reading

Burnett, K. (1992) *Strategic Customer Alliances*. London: Financial Times/Pitman.

Futrell, C. (1995) *Fundamentals of Selling*. Homewood: Irwin.

Jobber, D. and Lancaster, G. (1997) *Selling and Sales Management*. London: Pitman.

Rackham, N. (1987) *Making Major Sales*. Aldershot: Gower. (This reports the findings of the Huthwaite Research Group.)

3

Commercial negotiations ————————————

Richard Graham, Huthwaite Research Group Ltd

 Negotiation is one of the most mission-critical commercial skills. Effective negotiation can make a significant contribution to marginal profitability and at the same time play a major role in building the commercial partnerships which are widely acclaimed as the foundation for long term success.

Yet negotiation remains one of the least understood business processes. Very few of those whose job requires them to negotiate frequently could explain a coherent model of the planning methods and skills they use. Even self-styled experts, who claim to give training in best practice, often preach a win–win philosophy but actually teach little more than a series of win–lose dirty tricks.

In this chapter we will attempt to dispel some of the myths about commercial negotiation and present a model for effective negotiation based on rational analysis and research. Specifically, we will

- define negotiation and its functions, as opposed to selling
- explore the outcome options and mindsets available to commercial negotiators
- review the preparation and planning methods that effective negotiators are observed to use
- present research which sheds light on the face-to-face behaviours used by skilled negotiators in persuading, bargaining and managing the power balance.

Negotiation – a definition ——————

Negotiation is one of the least understood, and most abused, words in our language. Consider the following:

- Estate agents like to refer to themselves as negotiators yet, particularly in domestic house sales, what do they ever do except discount the price of the property?
- One of the world's largest management consulting firms bought a selling skills training course for its consultants. To avoid offending their sensitive egos (and so that they would actually attend) the course was re-titled Negotiating Profitable Engagements, even though it contained not one word of advice about negotiating.

- An IT company is bidding for a major mainframe installation against three aggressive competitors. At a meeting with the client the account manager says, 'This is an important deal for us, so I think it's time to negotiate. Since training is so important to you we'll increase the on-site training from four weeks to eight weeks at no extra cost.'
- During a recent Middle East hostage crisis the government was castigated by the mother of one of the hostages. 'They're not doing anything,' she said. 'I'm not saying they should make concessions, but at least they could negotiate.'

So what is negotiation? The estate agents' Dutch auction, where the price starts high and is discounted until someone is prepared to buy? Is it just a euphemism, a more respectable word for selling? Was the IT account manager negotiating when he gave away free training, or, being in a competitive bid, was he differentiating his offering by matching it more closely to his client's buying criteria? Finally, as the distraught mother suggested, is negotiation something you can do without making concessions?

Of course, negotiation is none of these things, but the examples illustrate how loosely and thoughtlessly the word is used. Not surprisingly, a short dictionary definition brings us much closer to the truth. Negotiation is 'conference and bargaining for mutual agreement'. Simple though this is, it does allow us to deduce that for negotiation to take place two preconditions must be satisfied.

Both parties must have some level of commitment to do a deal

If one side, usually the buying company, is not committed to some extent (they realize they have a need, have evaluated their options and recognize that you have a superior capability to meet their needs), why would they want to confer or bargain? The management consultants cited above were not being trained to negotiate, they were

being trained to sell: to develop a need and demonstrate that their services could meet it.

Negotiation occurs only after both sides have recognized a need to do business. Thus, negotiation and selling are two different skills with two different functions. Selling employs skills which create a desire to do business. Negotiation employs skills which optimize the terms under which the business will be done.

Perhaps the most conclusive evidence of the essential difference between selling and negotiation lies in the behaviour of the participants. In selling the behaviours of seller and buyer are totally different: persuader and persuadee. In negotiation, as we shall see later, both parties use the same set of skills or behaviours, because both have the same commitment to reach a workable agreement.

Both parties must have the authority and the will to vary the terms of the agreement

Bargaining, a key word in our dictionary definition, implies trading something you have for something the other party has which is important to you. So both sides must make concessions on some issues to gain advantage on others.

In the examples we quoted the estate agents and the account manager are both making concessions without seeking matching concessions from the other side. Nor were the other sides in both cases sufficiently committed to the deal to consider concessions, so negotiation was not taking place, merely product differentiation. The hysterical plea by the hostage's mother is simply self-contradictory. You cannot negotiate if you do not intend to make concessions.

Outcomes and mindsets

Before we begin the detailed preparation and planning for a negotiation, it will be useful to explore, at a macro level, the various types of outcome and associated mindsets which are available to the commercial negotiator, for our choice of outcome and mindset will be the main factor influencing our tactical decisions at the micro level.

Practical tips

- Try to minimize specific, unilateral concessions in the early stages of the sale. Concentrate on maximizing the other party's commitment to the deal by demonstrating that, in overall terms, you have the best fit with their buying criteria.
- Check the mandate and authority levels of the other side before you start negotiating. Set expectations of mutual concessions by discussing likely trades in terms of general principles. These tactics should forestall the later use of a common 'dirty trick': accepting your concessions, but claiming that any concessions they have made need to be cleared with, and will not necessarily be approved by, some higher authority.

There are, logically, four possible outcomes:

- **Lose–lose**: Neither party is happy with the outcome and each believes that the other has, unfairly, got the better part of the deal. Alternatively, one side has accepted such disadvantageous terms that, in the cold light of day, they wish they had not done the deal at all. In either case, one or both parties is likely to sabotage the implementation. No-one ever plans for a lose–lose result. These outcomes happen precisely due to lack of foresight in planning.
- **Lose–win**: This outcome occurs when the first party, perceiving itself to be in a very weak position, nevertheless decides to get the business at all costs. After a series of kamikaze unilateral concessions they secure a deal which is, in fact, a Pyrrhic

victory: they have achieved their goal, winning the business, but will they ever recover from their success?
- **Win–lose**: In this situation the first party has exploited its position of power, usually due to monopoly, purchasing power or restricted supply, without any consideration for the needs of the second party. The winner may achieve short term benefit, but the long term implications are aggrieved suppliers seeking revenge or exploited customers looking for an alternative supplier.
- **Win–win**: Both parties view the negotiated agreement as being mutually beneficial and are committed to co-operating to achieve a successful implementation. Words like synergistic and symbiotic are often used to describe such idealized outcomes. Leaving the fantasy world of management theory, however, we must ask how the concept of a win–win outcome translates into the real world.

Having understood the theoretical outcomes, let us now look at the associated mindsets and consider the dangers, opportunities and realities.

- **Lose–lose**: As we have said, it is very difficult to imagine anyone planning a lose–lose outcome, but it is important for negotiators to constantly ask themselves whether anything they are doing or planning to do is likely to cause the negotiation to deteriorate into a lose–lose scenario.
- **Lose–win**: If the negotiation is a one-time event there is no point in considering adoption of a lose–win mindset. If, conversely, the negotiation is intended to be part of an on-going commercial relationship there must be some point below which the terms are so undesirable that to perpetuate them in the long term would be commercial suicide. If that walk away point is identified, the mindset is no longer lose–win, but has begun to have win–win characteristics as defined below. If the walk away point is not identified, the

lose–win mindset runs every risk of degenerating into the lose–lose outcome we have already described. Thus the common but simplistic management mandate to 'get the business at all costs' is not only unhelpful but actually threatening to the establishment of viable long term commercial relationships.

- **Win–lose**: In the case of a one-time negotiation win–lose is a practicable mindset if the party adopting it can rationalize the ethical issues created by the unbridled exploitation of a position of power. As with lose–win, however, the on-going relationship is a different case. If the win–lose mindset is maintained beyond the point where the deal is viable for the other party, the probability is that the actual outcome will, sooner or later, be lose–lose. But if the powerful party considers the needs of the other party and the level at which they will lose commitment to implement the deal their mindset is no longer purely win–lose, but has, again, taken a step in the direction of being win–win. To equate this 'how far can we push them' mindset with win–win may shock the more idealistic reader, hence the need to define very carefully what effective commercial negotiators mean by a win–win mindset.
- **Win–win**: This is a term which has been overused to the point of meaninglessness. Any business proposition, no matter how shady, can be sanitized, so the belief goes, by labelling it win–win. But what does win–win really mean in the real world of commercial negotiation?

Some theorists advocate what we might term the ethical approach. The purpose, they say, of negotiation is to reach an agreement which the world will recognize as wise, just and fair. This may be entirely appropriate if one is trying to resolve conflict in the Balkans, but it might be considered a little naive if you are supplying baked beans to a major supermarket chain. It also, of course, ignores the problem that concepts of justice and fairness have confounded the great philosophers for three millenia, so it seems unlikely that they will finally be defined by we humble commercial negotiators.

Effective negotiators were observed to have a much more practical win–win mindset:

> The best result for us which will still allow the other side to believe that they achieved a reasonable agreement under the circumstances.

Note the feel good factor and the pragmatism:

- We want the other side to feel good about the agreement so that they will co-operate in its implementation.
- The feel good factor relates to the circumstances – if the other party perceives us as being more powerful they will be happy with less, which means we can take more and still have a win–win outcome.

Thus, as we said earlier, a negotiator may start with a lose–win mindset, but if they give thought to the limits below which they do not wish to do a deal they are starting to think win–win. And the win–lose negotiator is also becoming win–win if he fears that the other party may sabotage the deal if pushed beyond a certain point.

Practical tip

A pragmatic win–win mindset is the only practical approach to commercial negotiation. Any other mindset runs too great a risk of resulting in a lose–lose outcome.

Pragmatic win–win is not naive or philanthropic. It is a mindset which underpins systematic planning to give the best deal for you which has a high probability of successful implementation.

Having defined negotiation and what we mean by a win–win mindset, we are left with two key questions:

- How do we define and plan for a win–win outcome in any specific situation?
- How do we interact with the other party to achieve it?

The rest of this chapter is devoted to answering these questions.

Research method

In the introduction to this chapter we stated that we would be presenting some of the key findings from a research project which investigated the preparation and planning methods and face-to-face skills used by successful commercial negotiators. It is therefore appropriate at this stage to explain briefly how the research was conducted.

Since the purpose was to establish what skilled, effective negotiators did differently from their average counterparts it was necessary, first, to identify a 'skilled' sample group. Candidates were required to have:

- a demonstrable track record of successful negotiation,
- recognition of their skill and effectiveness by both sides, and
- a record of very low implementation failure.

The researchers eventually found 49 negotiators who satisfied these criteria and observed them preparing and executing 103 negotiations.

The other parties with whom the skilled group were negotiating provided a convenient random sample, which was referred to as the 'average' group – largely experienced negotiators, but with random abilities which ranged from weak to fairly skilled. Thus, in reporting the findings, we shall make frequent reference to the differences in practice between 'skilled' and 'average' negotiators.

During the preparation and planning phase the researchers were mainly concerned to observe:

- the analysis methods and processes used by the two groups
- the content of their discussions and the amount of time devoted to different issues.

Research into face-to-face skills used a totally different research tool, known as behaviour analysis, or BA for short. BA is a method for observing, categorizing and quantifying objectively what people do in interactive situations, like negotiations – particularly what they say to each other.

Researchers observed the face-to-face negotiations and sub-divided the interactions, or discussions, into behaviour categories such as proposing, seeking information, giving information, summarizing and disagreeing. The goal of such research is to identify those categories of behaviour which skilled negotiators use significantly *more* or significantly *less* than their average counterparts.

It is reasonable to surmise that if we can then train ourselves or others to emulate the behaviour pattern of skilled negotiators our face-to-face negotiating skills will be more effective.

Enough, then, of the research sample and methodology. Let's see what skilled negotiators are actually doing.

Preparation and planning

One of the researchers' early expectations was that the skilled group would devote more time to preparation and planning than the average group. This was false; in fact both groups allowed about the same amount of time. The key differentiator was how the time was spent.

Skilled negotiators made a clear distinction between:

- **Preparation** – *what* we want to achieve in the negotiation and *what* constraints there are on us achieving it, especially *what* the other party wants; and

- **Planning** – *how* we are going to use the positions we analysed in the preparation phase to achieve our goals, including *how* we are going to persuade the other side to accept our positions, *how* we will manage the power balance and create appropriate trades.

The average group used virtually all the available time for preparation, whereas the skilled group allowed approximately equal time for preparation and planning. As a result, we shall see, they had a much more flexible, creative approach when they came face-to-face with the other side across the negotiating table.

Practical tips

- Allocate adequate time for preparation and planning of your negotiations. Unless you are already using models similar to those described in this chapter you are probably not currently allowing enough time. Increase it.
- Set a timed agenda, allowing approximately equal time for preparation and planning. Stick to it – or you will not give enough time to planning.

Preparation

For the sake of simplicity and structure we can consider preparation, as practised by the skilled negotiators, as a sequence of five stages.

1 Set objectives

This may sound like an obvious starting point, but we must be careful to understand what the skilled negotiator means by a statement of objectives.

If you ask the man in the street, the average negotiator, what are their objectives for a negotiation, they will probably just itemize their targets for each of the negotiable issues: £5.00 per tonne, 150 tonnes per month, a 24 month agreement, etc.

To the skilled negotiator, however, the statement of objectives is a broad summary of the outcome they desire in the negotiation and how it will integrate with and serve their long term interests, e.g. We are seeking a short term agreement at a competitive price which will allow us to penetrate the account and increase price and profitability in the medium term.

Compare that objective, appropriate for a new, well-differentiated competitor attacking a new account, with the objective which might be set by the incumbent supplier trying to defend the account, e.g. We are seeking a long term agreement at a substantial volume to create a barrier to competitive entry.

What is the purpose of these general or strategic objective statements? Quite simply, to create a context and a focus for the rest of the preparation and planning process; to ensure that all decisions about detail serve the company's long term goals. Without such a focus there is a danger that the positions taken on specific issues may be inconsistent, or, indeed, that the preparation is overtaken by some irrational spirit of machismo which sets unrealistically ambitious targets on all issues, even those which are unimportant and which should be used as bargaining chips for concession.

Finally, the skilled negotiator tries to anticipate what the other side's objective might be. This principle of putting oneself in 'their shoes' recurs frequently throughout the preparation phase. At this stage the skilled operator is trying to anticipate how much congruence or conflict there might be between the two sides' objectives and, therefore, how tough the negotiation is likely to be. If they anticipate a great discrepancy they may consider modifying their own objective to reduce the incongruence.

This attempt to estimate and reconcile the other side's objective is the first example we have seen of the pragmatic win–win approach we discussed earlier. The skilled negotiators are trying to set themselves an objective which will still allow them to give the other side enough of what they want to satisfy them that they did a reasonable deal under the circumstances.

Practical tip

To make sure that your objective for this negotiation serves your long term interests, practise making your objective statement in two distinct clauses: We want X, so that in the medium/long term Y.

Keep your objective to statements of principle. Do not introduce hard figures which will later inhibit your more detailed preparation.

---

2 Fallback position

Another potential source of confusion. In common parlance 'fallback' is used to mean the worst deal you will accept in the negotiation. This is not how skilled negotiators use the word. They mean something very different:

> The best alternative course of action you have if this negotiation fails completely.

Using this definition, why is your fallback position so important? Because it governs your position on many elements within the negotiation:

- your perception of your own power
- the other party's perception of your power
- the best case you will try for on specific issues
- the worst case you will accept on specific issues
- therefore, what the limits of a win–win outcome are likely to be 'under the circumstances'.

Fallback needs to be as specific as possible. Buyers' fallback is very often to source the same or a similar product from an alternative supplier. But what about sellers? Unless there is an excess demand situation it is not really credible for them to say that their fallback is to sell the product to another buyer. If, as most frequently happens, there is an excess of supply, why not sell the product to both buyers?

Very often, for most sellers, the key issue is how they can best invest their time. If this negotiation is becoming unprofitable, at what point would it be better to invest their time selling to and negotiating with an alternative buyer? So for many sellers, their fallback position is only as strong as their prospect list. Their fallback is: if and/or when this negotiation fails, I will invest my time more profitably selling to prospects A and B.

Thus sellers, in particular, must not only be specific about their fallback, but must be confident that the fallback has a very high probability of achievement, i.e. that they can actually do a deal with prospect A or B. Your fallback will be put to the test if you are driven to your planned walk-away point in this negotiation. If you do not have complete confidence in it, you are likely to lose your nerve and make an unplanned concession when you should have walked away.

Practical tip

Buyers usually believe they have a stronger fallback position than sellers because they have the option of buying from an alternative supplier.

To weaken the buyer's position, ensure that you have differentiated your product as much as possible, in terms of both tangible and intangible benefits, before you negotiate. The buyer's fallback is greatly weakened if he believes he cannot source exactly the same product elsewhere.

3 Prioritize the negotiable issues

Having looked at the big, strategic issues of objectives and fallback, the skilled negotiator now moves on to the finer detail of the negotiating positions (unfortunately this is where the average negotiator often starts his or her preparation).

The first question is what are you going to bargain about? In other words, what are the negotiable issues? Some of the most obvious are:

● Price
● Contract length
● Delivery
● Promotion
● Volume
● Payment terms
● Warranties
● Exclusivity.

There will obviously be others which are specific to a particular industry or a particular negotiation.

The golden rule for negotiable issues is the more the merrier. Particularly in tough negotiations (with conflicting objectives) the probability of achieving a win–win outcome is greatly increased if you are negotiating about ten different variables rather than just two, like price and volume.

On this subject, try to discourage your company from having too many negotiable issues set in concrete in the small print of a standard contract. Do you or your company really want to walk away from a profitable, multi-million pound deal because the customer wants to pay in 30 days and the small print in your contract insists on 21 days? If you enforce the small print, that could happen. If you are not going to enforce the small print, why have it? Give yourself more tradables from the outset.

While most negotiators considered what the negotiable issues might be, the skilled negotiator group performed an extra, but important, stage of analysis: they prioritized the issues from their point of view and then estimated the priorities of the other side (Table 3.1). High (H) indicates an issue which is important to you (or to them) and on which you will make concessions only with great reluctance. Low (L) indicates an issue which is rated as unimportant and on which you would probably move more readily.

The purpose of this exercise is to highlight those areas where trading will be most difficult and concessions most hard won, and those issues where there is most scope for leverage and mutually beneficial trades. Consider the two scenarios below.

Table 3.1 *Preparation*

Negotiable issues	Priorities		Limits			Their target	Cost of concessions
	Us	Them	Best	Target	Worst		
Volume	M	H	8k	10k	12k	15k	Over 12k – cannot meet Halfords' demand
Contract length	H	M	2 yr	9 mth	6 mth	6 mth	They can get comp. prodcut at 6 mths
Price	L	M	10%	5%	0	–5%	1% = £315/k/mth
Payment terms	M	L	14 dys	14 dys	30 dys	30 dys	0.19%/7 days

Scenario 1

Negotiable issue	Us	Them
Price	H	H
Volume	H	H
Contract length	M	M
Delivery	L	L

What sort of negotiation is this likely to be? Of course it will be tough – assuming both parties have conflicting objectives. Neither side can offer the other a concession with leverage, i.e. a concession which is worth more to them than it costs us. Deadlock is a real risk.

Scenario 2

Negotiable issue	Us	Them
Price	M	M
Volume	H	L
Contract length	H	L
Delivery	L	H

What about this example? Obviously it will be a much easier negotiation. We can even speculate pretty accurately about the likely outcome: we will get concessions on volume and contract length in return for a concession on delivery. Price will probably be settled slightly in favour of them, because they have already made two concessions to our one.

Prioritizing the negotiable issues, therefore, allows us both to predict points of potential conflict or deadlock and to identify areas of movement for both sides. The question now is how much movement there will be.

4 Set trading limits

In this stage we see yet another major difference in the practices of skilled and average negotiators. As the sample preparation sheet

in Table 3.1 shows, the skilled negotiators set a range of limits: best, target, worst. Average negotiators, by contrast set only a single target point for each issue.

The single target point may seem reasonable planning practice – we are constantly told to set targets, or objectives – until we consider the implications:

- A single target point gives you no help in deciding where your opening position must be: above your target, but how high?
- You cannot make a concession and go below your target without feeling that you have 'failed', so you may reject a perfectly acceptable deal only marginally below your plan.
- If you do decide to drop below your target you now, effectively, have no plan, so where do you stop? An unprofitable or impracticable deal (lose–lose) is now a real possibility.

Skilled negotiators set a trading range to avoid all these negative consequences of a single target:

- **Best** – means the best deal for us on this issue which still allows the other side the perception of a win–win outcome.
- **Worst** – means the worst case we will accept on this tradeable under any circumstances; usually the point at which our fallback position would be more attractive than continuing with this negotiation.

- **Target** – is not a mathematical mean between best and worst, but a realistic aspiration of what we feel we should achieve if our best is impossible. It is not, however, a strait-jacket.

The final column in this section of the sample preparation sheet (Table 3.1) is headed 'Their target', which is self-explanatory. Trying to estimate their best–worst range is probably over-ambitious, but a shrewd guess at 'Their target' could be informative:

- If 'Their target' is comfortably within our best–worst range we can plan our concession strategy accordingly and anticipate a relatively easy agreement.
- If, conversely, 'Their target' is below our worst we must be aware of the danger of deadlock, especially if this negotiable issue has a H–H priority. We must review our worst position and look for other concessions we could make to persuade them to accept a deal on this issue below their target.

Having now set best–worst limits, we know how much we are prepared to move or bargain, so we can progress to the final stage of preparation: calculating how much each movement is worth to us.

5 Calculate cost of concessions

The purpose of calculating in advance the cost of concessions is to facilitate the bargaining process and increase the negotiator's sense of control. It avoids stressful and time-consuming calculator punching or repeated 'time outs' to discuss tactical issues each time a new offer is made or a new concession demanded.

There are essentially two types of cost associated with concessions: those which can be calculated arithmetically, and risks and opportunities which occur when a certain degree of concession is reached.

Arithmetic costs are illustrated by the issues of price and payment terms in Table 3.1. In this case the seller is renegotiating a

contract for the supply of a motor accessory to a chain of DIY stores. He would like to increase the price, which is a low priority to him, but believes the buyer will be looking for a discount of 5%. A discount of 1% is worth 31.5p per unit, but the contract will be for the monthly supply of many thousands of units so, for ease of calculation, the seller has expressed that cost of concession as £315 per thousand units per month. A 1% discount on a contract for 8000 units over 12 months therefore has a value of £30,240, a figure which focuses the mind rather more effectively than 1%!

Calculating the cost of concession on payment terms is even easier. This company values money at 10% per annum, thus the cost of receiving payment seven days later is $10 \div 52$ or 0.19% (leaving aside cash flow considerations). On this point, it is often surprising to note how often negotiators will readily give an additional 1% discount rather than an extra 14 days for payment, a concession which costs less than half as much.

Risk and opportunity costs are illustrated by the volume and contract length issues in Table 3.1. The selling company has a very limited supply of product, which is currently outstripped by demand. They know the DIY store in this negotiation wants more than the 10k per month they are currently getting, but the sellers know that if they agree to a contract for more than 12k per month it will leave them insufficient stock to satisfy the demands of Halfords, another major and arguably more important customer. On the issue of contract length, the sellers know that a competitor is going to enter the market in six months. Any contract in excess of six months with a major retailer like the DIY chain will therefore both secure the market a little longer for our seller and create an additional entry barrier for the competitor.

Planning

We said earlier that in the planning phase the skilled negotiators considered how they were going to use all the information produced in the preparation phase. In broad terms there were two major questions: first, what tactics would they adopt for bargaining or trading, yielding concessions and controlling the power balance, and, second, what face-to-face behaviours or skills would they use to implement the tactics.

So as we examine the planning of these very effective negotiators we will also develop an understanding of the face-to-face skills they use to give them an edge over their more average adversaries.

As we start this section of the chapter it is important to reinforce one point: some of the methods and skills we will be looking at have been attacked as manipulation. So, indeed, they are. Any persuasion, for example, is manipulative by definition. The point about skilled win–win negotiators, however, is that they use their manipulative skills only within the constraints of the win–win, best–worst limits they have defined in their preparation. It is, in that sense, benign manipulation to ensure a win–win outcome, rather than allowing the lack of skill on the other side to engineer a lose–lose one.

Planning – general principles

Whether they were considering persuasion, bargaining or power, there were certain recurring themes that characterized the planning of the skilled negotiator group.

- **Common ground** – 38% of comments in planning were about areas of anticipated agreement or common ground, compared with only 11% for the average group. The purpose seemed to be to maintain a positive climate by stressing common interests rather than points of conflict.
- **The long term view** – again, there were twice as many comments (8.5% versus 4%) by the skilled group about long term issues. Partly, this may be due to the discipline imposed by the statement of objectives, which emphasized that the outcome of the negotiation must serve the company's long term interests.
- **Non-sequential planning** – the average group tended to plan in sequence: 'We'll handle price first, then volume, and then the minor items like delivery and payment terms.' This has the obvious drawback that if the other side has also formulated a sequential, but different, plan, the first big conflict in the negotiation will be not about terms, but about the agenda. Skilled people were seen to consider each negotiable issue in isolation and have a plan for all the possible linkages with the other tradable issues. As evidence, they discussed five options per issue, compared with only two for the average group.

Planning – behavioural skills

In Table 3.2 we present the complete behaviour profiles of skilled and average negotiators resulting from the behaviour analysis of more than 100 negotiations. Some of these behaviours, or skills, are used in certain clusters to achieve desired results in persuading, bargaining and managing power, but it is worth looking briefly at the overall behaviour plan of the skilled negotiator. Although superficially complex, it can, without sacrificing too much subtlety, be reduced to a list of dos and don'ts:

Skilled negotiators do:

- Ask lots of questions – more than twice as many as average. Questions seek information, reasons, feelings and proposals. They give control, they give thinking time and they are an alternative to outright disagreement.
- Maintain clarity by testing understanding and summarizing – more than twice as much as average. Testing understanding can also be useful for creating movement. How would you react to the question, 'Let me get this straight, are you saying you came to this negotiation with a mandate to move by only 1%?'
- Give feelings. Contrary to popular opinion, skilled negotiators are not poker-faced. They express their feelings almost twice as often as the average negotiator, both to create trust and as an alternative to giving hard facts.

- Label behaviour – massively more than average, except for labelling disagreement. We all know the focusing effect of phrases like 'Can I ask you a question', 'Let me just make an important point', or 'May I summarize'.

Skilled negotiators don't:

- Counter propose. This is the instant turn-off. If you are not prepared to give due consideration to the other side's proposal, why should they listen to yours?
- Label disagreement. The best way to ensure your argument does not get a fair hearing is to announce in advance to the other party that you are going to contradict their argument.
- Use irritators. Do you find it persuasive if someone says to you 'Listen, young man, I think you're going to find this a very fair and generous offer'? Of course not. Your reaction is 'I'll be the judge of your offer, and don't patronize me.'
- Dilute their arguments. Our language – the weight of argument, the decision hangs in the balance, the scales of justice – suggests that, in argument, more is better. The problem is that as you advance more and more arguments they tend to become progressively weaker. The other side will not attack your first argument, they will destroy your sixth. Successive weak arguments dilute the power of the first strong ones. Skilled people would rather repeat one strong argument, and introduce a second reason only if the first argument is successfully undermined.

If you practise nothing else from this chapter, integrate those four dos and four don'ts into your negotiating behaviour and you will significantly improve your effectiveness.

Planning – persuasion

We must be clear at this point what we are persuading about. We are not persuading the buyers that they need the product. That must have been done before the negotiation begins, or one of our key criteria – both parties must have some level of commitment to do a deal – has not been met.

In negotiation we are usually persuading the other side that our position is right and theirs is wrong or untenable. How do we do this? The answer lies mainly in the skilled negotiators' heavy use of questions.

Logic, it seems, is not persuasive. Boxing is a good analogy or model for the common idea of persuasion: the two sides stand toe to toe and trade arguments, like blows, until the one with the heavier arguments wins.

The effective negotiator does not do this. As we can see from the behaviour profile (Table 3.2) they give a lot less information, or arguments. It seems that they have a different model of persuasion which is more like judo: first to create instability, or doubt, in the minds of the other side, and then, when they are unbalanced, to create movement by pulling the other side toward them. They do this principally with planned questions:

- To create doubt – seeking other and testing understanding:
  'Exactly what is your position?'
- Seeking reasons (to cause argument dilution):
  'Why do you believe that?'
  'Is that your only reason?'
- Seeking feelings:
  'Are you confident about that?'
  'Aren't you concerned about ...?'
- To create movement – seeking proposals:
  'Can you suggest a better solution?'
- Building:
  'That's a good proposal, but we could also ...'
- Proposing terms:
  'Since you now seem to be saying that the market is under-supplied, could I suggest a 10% price increase?'

To summarize, as practised by the experts, persuasion in negotiation is mainly based on planned sequences of questions. You only need one, at most two, strong and credible arguments to support your own position.

Table 3.2 Comparison of average and skilled behaviour profiles in negotiation. (Percentage figures indicate usage of that behaviour as a percentage of all the negotiator's behaviour)

Behaviour	Definition	Average profile	Skilled profile	Comments
Proposing terms	A behaviour which puts forward new terms or actions for consideration by the other party	More	Less	Skilled negotiators tend to trade (conditional proposal) at every opportunity. Only use proposing terms when in a position of power
Conditional proposal	A behaviour which puts forward new terms which are subject to stated conditions or concessions	Less	More	
Counter proposal	A proposal of any type which follows a proposal given by the other party without first demonstrating consideration of their proposal	3.1/hr	1.7/hr	Skilled profile tries to minimize Tends to damage the climate
Procedural proposal	A behaviour which puts forward a new suggestion or course of action regarding the process of negotiation	Less	More	Skilled people use this technique to control negotiation flow and to imply they are in the chair, i.e. powerful
Building	A proposal which extends or develops a proposal made by the other party in a mutually beneficial way	Less	More	Used in persuasion to make other side's proposals mutually beneficial
Supporting	A behaviour stating a conscious or direct declaration of agreement or support for another person, his/her opinions or proposals			Skilled negotiators sometimes 'low react' (supporting and disagreeing less than 10% of all behaviour) to apply pressure and gain information
Disagreeing	A behaviour which states direct disagreement or raised obstacles or objections to another person's proposals or opinions			
Defend/attack	A behaviour which attacks another person either directly or by defensiveness	More	Less	Destroys the climate. Average profile six times higher. Skilled minimize to 1% of all behaviour
Open	A behaviour which admits error or guilt in a non-defensive way	Less	More	Used by skilled people to defuse escalating arguments caused by own error

Behaviour	Description			Comment
Testing understanding	A behaviour which seeks to understand whether or not a previous contribution has been understood	4.1 %	9.4%	Used to maintain clarity – key reason for low implementation failure of skilled people
Summarizing	A behaviour which summarizes or otherwise re-states in a compact form the content of previous discussions or events	4.9%	7.0%	Maintains clarity, but is also a chairing behaviour, like procedural proposing
Seeking proposals	A behaviour which invites ideas or proposals from the other party	less	More	Skilled profiles for all types of seeking is 21.3% compared with an average profile of only 9.6%
Seeking reasons	A behaviour which invites from the other party reasons or justifications for proposals or arguments	less	More	Skilled negotiators ask more of all types of questions, but especially seeking reasons and proposals as part of their persuasion technique
Seeking feelings	A behaviour which invites feelings or reactions from the other party to proposals, events or statements	less	More	
Seeking other	A behaviour which seeks from the other party information other than proposals, reasons or feelings	less	More	
Giving feelings	A behaviour which expresses feelings and emotions rather than facts and figures	7.8%	12.1%	Skilled profile substitutes feelings, which are not useful to the other party, for information which might be giving feelings is also thought to create trust
Giving information	A behaviour which states information, reasons or opinion rather than feelings or emotions	28.9%	17.3%	
Irritators	A behaviour which irritates the other party through self-praise/or condescension	10.3/hr	2.3/hr	Skilled people minimize because they are not persuasive, but damage the climate
Labelling other	A behaviour which announces the behaviour about to be used	1.2%	6.4%	Used to slow negotiation and focus on key points
Labelling disagreeing	A behaviour which announces that the behaviour about to be used is disagreeing	1.5%	0.4%	Avoided by the skilled. Causes other party to switch off, not listen to argument
Argument dilution	The use of an increasing number of arguments to support a proposal or position	3.1/issue	1.8/issue	Skilled try to use only one strong argument per issue

Behaviour analysis exercise

Actually observed by a researcher: a negotiator was having difficulty convincing the other side that his position was valid. After a pause for thought, he introduced his next argument:

'Look, I've been fairly honest with you so far.'

Is this an irritator? What does it mean? We have no idea!

Planning – bargaining

The basis of successful bargaining is leverage, a word that was used in the preparation phase when we were prioritizing the negotiable issues. Leverage occurs when there is a mismatch in priorities: us H, them L; or us L, them H.

In general, we want to make concessions on issues which are low to us and high to them, in return for concessions from the other side on issues which are high to us and low to them. We call these non-zero-sum trades: both sides get more value than they have given (in a zero-sum trade the sides exchange concessions of equivalent value).

The first step in planning, therefore, is to identify all the priority mismatches and look for appropriate trades and linkages. Remember that skilled negotiators consider five options per issue. If there are high–high priority potential deadlocks we should also think at this stage about bundling two or three low–high mismatch concessions to bargain against an issue which is important to both of us ('I'll give you this and this and this if you'll give me the thing I want most.')

Having planned the possible trades we must then start the bargaining by making general principle conditional proposals: 'If you could move on contract terms, we might be able to do something on price.' As the negoti-

ation progresses and the linkages become more firm, so the conditional proposals will be more specific: 'If you could make the terms 24 months, we could offer 7½% discount.'

Within this general planning and trading framework there are several specific pieces of advice drawn from the tactics of skilled negotiators:

- Plan a high, but credible opening – it must be above your best, but not so high that you have to make a ridiculous concession to get back within your best–worst range.
- Don't open on a contentious, high–high issue – establish the principle of trading using medium priority issues.
- Don't settle minor issues early, tempting though it may be – you may need them as tradeables later.

Having looked at leverage, linkages and how you are going to open the negotiation, the final stage of planning for bargaining is your concession strategy. Consider what message you would send with this series of concessions:

2% - 5% - 9% - 14%

It says 'Keep pushing, there's a lot more to come.' How about:

3% - 6% - 9% - 12% - 15%

'Wait ten minutes and we should give you another 3%.' Compare that with:

4% - 7% - 9% - 10% - 10.5%

We call these diminishing return concessions because they send the message that each extra unit of persuasive effort the other side applies will yield an ever-smaller return. In effect this strategy asks the question, do you want to argue for another hour for a quarter of a percent.

To summarize this strategy, then:

- identify a realistic settlement point (between best and target)

- plan a high but credible opening
- plot a series of decreasing steps
- stick to it!

Practical tip

Think twice before introducing your manager, or some other superior from your company, into the negotiation. Think what message you are sending to the buyer.

As one very experienced buyer said, 'As soon as the salesman brings his manager to see me I know there is more discount available, because only the manager is authorized to give it.'

By all means agree with your manager a change to your negotiating mandate, but don't signal to the buyer 'we've lowered our worst case' by taking your manager to the negotiation meeting.

Planning – power

Power is often talked about, but seldom defined. In negotiation, we have chosen to define power as anything which confers a bargaining advantage. If this sounds rather nebulous, it is because, in negotiation at least, power is nebulous. In fact, the first important thing to understand is that power is in the head.

How do we know this? Thanks to a very simple experiment which you can try yourself. Find two sides who have completed their preparation and planning and are about to start a face-to-face negotiation. Ask each side, confidentially, to estimate its share of the power balance: 60:40, 70:30, etc. Almost invariably you will find that there is more than 100% power available: both sides frequently claim more than 50% of the power. This cannot be reality, because in reality there is only 100% power available. So if both sides are claiming 60% it means that, through the

process of preparation and planning, either one or both sides have convinced themselves that they have more power than is actually the case.

What does this tell us? Simply that to manage power we must manage the other side's perception. Certain things cannot be altered: the basic facts of the situation, the size and status of the company you are selling to – whatever you say, IBM remains IBM and Exxon remains Exxon. But you can manage perceptions of the detail of this particular negotiation and perceptions of you, your authority and your skill.

There is a simple, but wonderfully effective tool which will help you plan to manage the other party's perception of the power balance. It is called a strengths and weaknesses analysis or STREAK, for short. See Figure 3.1.

Use of the STREAK analysis involves only two steps:

- brainstorm all of your strengths and weakness, their definite strengths and weaknesses, and other possible strengths and weaknesses they may have, but of which you cannot be certain;
- prepare appropriate tactics and behaviours to make optimum use of your analysis during the face-to-face negotiation, as shown in Figure 3.1.

Finally, on the subject of power, there is one more strategy you can try. We have already suggested that skilled negotiating behaviour, in itself, should command respect, and respect confers power. But there is one other cluster of behaviours which is particularly associated with power: chairing behaviour.

The chairperson of any meeting is automatically acknowledged by the participants to have control, and therefore power. If, therefore, you adopt the behaviour of a chairperson, subtly and without being too obvious, you can become the de facto chairperson of the negotiation and be accorded the control and power that go with the job.

Chairing behaviours have already been mentioned in the Comments column of Table

	Strengths	**Weaknesses**
Ours	EMPHASIZE Re-state frequently Use only strong reasons	HIDE Do not mention Prepare arguments to rationalize
Theirs	MINIMIZE Avoid mentioning Prepare counter-arguments Question validity Refer to your fallback	EXPOSE Prepare questions Seek evidence of weakness Seek feelings
Their possible	MINIMIZE As their strengths	EXPOSE As their weaknesses

Figure 3.1 *STREAK analysis*

3.2, but we will summarize them here for clarity. As you would expect, they are behaviours which contribute control and clarity, but not content, to the meeting:

- Seeking – especially information
- Testing understanding
- Summarizing
- Procedural proposals.

Power, then is about perceptions: analyse and play to your strengths, minimize their strengths and expose their weaknesses, and use the authority of chairing behaviour to manage the process.

Summary

If you need to create a long term business relationship with the other party, the 'pragmatic win–win', as we have defined it in this chapter, is the only viable approach. Any other approach will, sooner or later, degenerate into a lose–lose.

Set an overall objective for the current negotiation which serves the long term interests of your company. The discipline of the 'we want X, so that Y' format will help focus your thoughts.

Identify your strongest fallback position. In selling, your fallback is frequently only as strong as your prospect list.

Brainstorm as many negotiable issues as possible. Prioritize them for your company and the other party to highlight mismatches of priorities which offer potential for leveraged trades.

Set best/target/worst limits for each negotiable issue. Best is the most you can get while maintaining a win–win. Worst is governed by the strength of your fallback. Target is an optimistic aspiration.

Calculate the cost of concession for each tradeable. Simplify arithmetic formulae for speed of calculation during the negotiation. Consider other non-arithmetic risks and opportunities.

In general, when planning, think about the long term and how areas of common ground can be used to maintain the climate of the negotiation. Avoid sequential planning. Take each negotiable issue on its own and consider as many options as possible for linkages and trades.

Have an overall plan to emulate the behaviour profile of the skilled negotiator. This will involve increasing questions, testing understanding and summarizing, giving feelings and behaviour labelling, reducing labelling disagreement, counter proposals, irritators and argument dilution.

Plan for persuasion with questions which will destabilize the other side by creating doubt about their position. Then create movement by seeking proposals or proposing terms. Use only one, strong argument to support your position.

Plan for bargaining by looking for leveraged, non-zero-sum trades. Use conditional proposing as much as possible. Devise and use a diminishing return concession strategy. Plan for power by making a STREAK analysis and devising tactics and behaviours to emphasize your strengths and expose their weaknesses. Give yourself authority by using chairing behaviour.

Above all, whatever strategies, tactics or skills you use – keep it win–win.

Part Two

Managing
Customer
Relationships

4

Relationship management ————————————

Professor Colin Egan, Leicester Business School

 In this chapter an emerging approach to marketing known as relationship management is examined. Key points covered include:

- Marketing the old way: the transaction mindset.
- Marketing in the modern world: the relationship era.
- An examination of trends in industrial buyer behaviour.
- How 'networks' of relationships underpin marketing activity in turbulent business environments.
- Why firms need to think about *supply chain links* when developing sales and marketing strategies.
- The principles and practice of 'partnership'.
- Why *internal* marketing is *essential* for external relationship marketing success.
- The important role of market segmentation in the relationship management approach to marketing.

Introduction ▬▬▬▬

Marketing is a huge discipline which has grown dramatically over the last thirty years or so. Like many subjects before it, this extraordinary expansion of knowledge and understanding has led to a core set of generic principles and a vast array of specialist areas of interest. This chapter deals with one of the topics which has grown rapidly in prominence over recent years, i.e. the approach to marketing described as relationship management. Before we explore the exciting possibil-ities of the relationship approach to marketing practice, however, it makes sense to reflect on the more traditional ways of doing business.

Marketing as transactions ▬▬▬

The term 'marketing' derives from 'market', a noun which describes a venue where buyers and sellers meet and are involved in transactions, typically, in the modern world, an exchange of goods for cash. Imagining a fruit and vegetable market such as Covent Garden gives a good impression of the transaction scene: there are many sellers displaying their wares and many buyers wandering around the stalls evaluating the quality of the produce. Price will be a major consideration and buyers will be strongly inclined to frequently switch to suppliers who have the best 'deal' on any given day. In this scenario the power in the relationship rests firmly with the buyers since they have an abundance of choice and a high propensity to exercise it.

Consider now a different scenario. Passengers arriving in Hong Kong, London, Frankfurt, Kuala Lumpur, Taipei, Milan, Brussels or, indeed, most international airports, have no choice of taxi supplier whatsoever – they simply stand in line and await their turn. The odds on the randomly allocated taxi driver ever encountering the traveller again are extraordinarily low. In this case the exchange – cash for journey – is a pure transaction. The driver knows that he is unlikely ever to see this customer again and he is therefore in a strong position to extract a 'rip-off' price. This simple fact explains why virtually every international airport taxi system is highly regulated by the authorities so that the transaction is conducted in a fair manner.

The two transaction scenarios outlined above are extremes, each describing a situation where neither party to the exchange is dependent upon the other for ongoing satisfaction or business success. In the first scenario, the buyer is all powerful and can pick and choose at leisure. In the second scenario the supplier is in control, albeit regulated. The reward for the taxi driver's patience in the long queue for a customer is a lucrative fare. He can be courteous or grumpy, depending upon his mood. Put simply, his business survival does not depend upon repeat purchase.

For a variety of reasons which are examined in this chapter the transaction mentality associated with the above two scenarios is inappropriate for modern business practice. In most market sectors customers are demonstrating a desire for consistency and continu-

ity, in many cases, paradoxically, because they have too much choice! Suppliers, meanwhile, can considerably enhance their profitability if they can secure long term customer loyalty. It is a well known adage in marketing that it costs six to nine times more to win a new customer than it does to retain an existing one. A famous Harvard Business Review study, for example, demonstrated that increasing customer retention by 5% could enhance profitability by 100%. With these facts in mind, a customer should be viewed as an asset and not, as many firms appear to treat them, as a liability! The strategic challenge for companies is to identify ways and means of 'locking-in' their customer base, but to achieve this in a fashion which is not felt to be oppressive. As we will see, an emphasis on building relationships in an atmosphere of partnership is a powerful way of meeting this challenge, an approach which increases customer dependency while at the same time significantly raising their satisfaction with the overall 'package' they receive. This brief introduction to the 'way things were' signals tremendous prospects for companies who are astute enough to shape the future, i.e. to grasp the opportunities presented by what has been described as a paradigm shift to an era of relationship marketing. While this trend in marketing thought extends to consumer goods manufacturers (e.g. Procter & Gamble) and service providers (e.g. Tesco) the main focus in this chapter is the business-to-business sector. As we will see, fundamental changes in the nature of industrial supply chains are forcing relationship marketing on to the agendas of many board room meetings.

Marketing as relationships

The increasing complexity of the industrial purchasing process and unprecedented changes in organizational markets are combining to radically alter the nature of exchange relationships in industrial supply chains. Key changes include the growing professionalism and sophistication of the purchasing management function, the internationalization of firms and markets and the impact of developments in information processing and communications systems on the way in which business is undertaken. As supplying firms constantly seek business opportunities and new ways to service new markets, procurement professionals are increasingly demanding more from the purchasing process. For different reasons, but in an inexorable trend, both suppliers and buyers are seeking longer term relationships with each other.

Professor Martin Christopher and his colleagues (1991) have conducted extensive research into these trends and the impact which they have had on marketing practice. They have demonstrated that a key task in the contemporary business environment is to secure long term relationships of mutual advantage through building strong bonds between suppliers and customers. To meet this challenge companies should create internal co-ordination between customer service, marketing and quality control. Furthermore, to successfully enact the principles of what is described as relationship marketing the superordinate goal of the business should be customer retention and every employee should have a close involvement in the marketing process. Despite the obvious importance of these lofty ideals, it is clear from research evidence that far too many firms tend to concentrate their efforts on attracting new prospects rather than placing the emphasis on securing repeat business. Davidow (1986) has convincingly demonstrated the positive relationship between *customer retention* and profitability but he expresses his frustration at the neglect of many companies to recognize this simple fact:

It has always been incredible to me how insensitive companies can be to their customers. Most of them don't seem to understand that their future business depends on having the same customer come back again and again.

The main reason this happens is because they are still locked into the transaction mentality described in the introduction to this chapter and they have yet to embrace the relationship mindset alluded to above. The transaction approach is a way of doing business which focuses on short term issues and is based on the principles of a zero-sum game, i.e. a win–lose scenario. In stark contrast, the underlying principle of relationship marketing is based on a positive sum outlook, i.e. it has a sharp focus on creating win–win scenarios. With this in mind three statements can be made:

1. Changes in the business *environment* should be forcing companies to fundamentally alter the way in which they conduct business. In a context of radical change, adaptation and survival of the fittest is the order of the day.
2. Firms need to develop a *strategy* for dealing with turbulence in the business environment. They must proactively shape the future, not wait for forces beyond their control to drive them to commercial disaster.
3. The first two propositions are easier said than done! Firms must reshape their organizational structures and functional processes if they are to have any chance of *implementing* relationship marketing principles and procedures.

The marketing challenge which emanates from these three statements can be represented as a triangle of environment, strategy and organization, with equilibrium being achieved when there is 'fit' amongst each of the three components. Figure 4.1 illustrates this strategic marketing triangle.

A common feature of all frameworks which claim to explain superior business performance is the proposition that it is the interaction between the elements of the model rather than their consideration in isolation which fundamentally explains competitive success. In this sense, the whole is greater than the sum of its parts. Given this, firms must ensure that the bonds between environment, strategy and organization remain

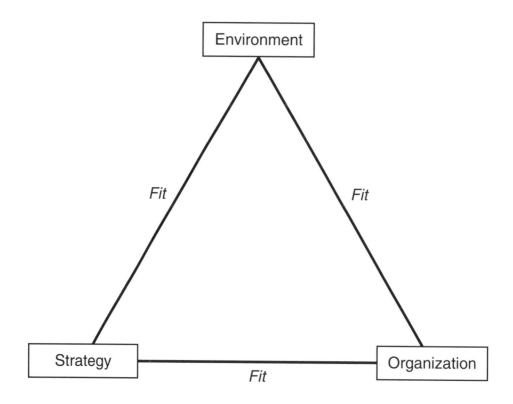

Figure 4.1 *Strategic marketing triangle*

intact, i.e. they must create and maintain a strong degree of 'fit' along each axis of the triangle in Figure 4.1.

The starting point to ensuring this 'fit' is to understand trends in the firm's *macro environment*, typically defined as social, legal, economic, political and technological (SLEPT) factors. Some of these trends will have an immediate impact (for example, a deep recession) while others will have longer term implications (for example, an emerging technology). Some trends will pose major threats, others will provide potential business opportunities. Checklist 4.1 provides a simple framework for you to evaluate key macro environmental trends in your company's business sector. It requires you to assess the implications of these trends and to note the required response your company should make.

Responsiveness to environmental trends and the ability to be flexible are essential for long term organizational survival. Example One discusses the downfall of the Swiss watch industry and illustrates how even the most successful companies, or in this case an entire industry, can rapidly collapse when failing to *understand* the implications of environmental change.

On a more positive note, Example Two examines how changes in the macro environment can present opportunities for growth, in this case, the growing awareness of green issues and the important influence of lobbying groups on governments and firms. Such market *opportunities* are often described as 'strategic windows'.

In the next section the key factors which are changing the nature of competition in many industrial markets are profiled – a set

Checklist 4.1
Macro environmental analysis

The following exercise requires you to identify key trends in the *macro environment* your business operates in. Examples of key factors to address are given (social, legal, economic, political, technological). The 'etc...' category is for those factors which are particularly relevant to your industrial sector. Consider the impact of these trends for your company and note the required response. When assessing the impact of the environmental trends consider three time frames: (i) now; (ii) 1–3 years; (iii) 3–5 years. This will allow you to prioritize key actions for immediate attention and to prepare for those factors which present a longer term threat or opportunity.

Macro environment trend	Impact on your company	Required response
Social		
Legal		
Economic		
Political		
Technological		
etc...		
etc...		

**Example One
The Swiss watch industry**

One of the most remarkable examples of what can happen when there is a failure to recognize environmental threats is that of the Swiss watch industry. Swiss watch companies arrogantly underestimated emerging Japanese rivals and were dismissive of the notion of changing customer needs. The industry collapsed, seriously damaging the Swiss economy. A remarkable recovery was made, with industry consolidation and product innovation (including the 'Swatch' phenomenon) restoring Swiss fortunes. The man responsible for the turnaround, Nicolas Hayek, is determined to ensure that the industry does not repeat past blunders. Speaking to shareholders in the company's annual general meeting he gave the following warning:

The seeds of failure lie in success itself. We must be energetic and tireless, and every day fight against the beginnings of arrogance towards our customers. We must also be energetic and tireless against any tendency to become presumptuous, to rest on our laurels or fall back into old habits. This would be deadly for the enterprise.

In making this observation Hayek is warning against complacency, a poison which permeates many successful companies and often triggers their demise. The key problem is that firms, however successful they may be at a certain point in time, tend to be very poor at understanding important changes in their business environment. Quartz technology was actually invented in Switzerland but it was Japanese companies who exploited the potential of this key market opportunity.

of issues which can collectively be described as constituting the firm's *micro environment*. The implications these factors have for firms intending to adopt a relationship marketing philosophy are then identified. Supplying firms really must understand what is happening among their customer base and a crucial starting point for this information gathering process is to identify and be responsive to key marketplace trends. The next section explores the major trends in industrial purchasing behaviour.

Trends in buying firms' purchasing management

A combination of highly efficient competitors (many of whom are global) and emerging technologies have raised the role of purchasing to a strategic one in many organizations. Firms now use a range of techniques to improve the efficiency of purchasing while at the same time raising its effectiveness. The following list gives an indication of key trends in industrial purchasing management:

**Example Two
Green steel**

British Steel, like most major steel producers, has experienced declining demand over recent years, particularly in important sectors such as the automotive industry which has struggled in the prolonged recession of the early 1990s. There is an opportunity, however, to increase the amount of steel used in each car produced. Car manufacturers are under tremendous pressure from environmental groups to make vehicles wholly recyclable, a goal which is difficult to achieve with composite materials and plastics. Steel, meanwhile, is a very 'green' material in that it is perfect for recycling time and time again. The technological challenge for British Steel is to make their products lighter without compromising the other important characteristics of steel, for example, its strength and finish.

- The consolidation of purchasing, transportation and inventory control functions into a single materials management function;
- The centralization of procurement at headquarters for geographically separated manufacturing units;
- A growing demand for 'total quality' zero-defects supply and manufacturing;
- The widespread adoption of just-in-time (JIT) inventory management systems;
- A growth in the use of sophisticated and computerized techniques such as materials requirements planning (MRP);
- A strong emphasis on the total cost of ownership, where the pre-, during and after-sales costs are considered rather than the more tangible 'ticket price';
- An ever greater use of electronic data interchange (EDI) where routine transactions are automatically handled by computers;
- Widespread functional disaggregation, i.e. in the classic 'make or buy' decision many firms are choosing to focus on core competencies and contract out those business functions which are performed better by specialist firms;

- A much greater degree of marketing awareness amongst procurement professionals;
- A supply chain focus, whereby there is a recognition by firms that the complete supply chain should be considered as the unit of competition, not its individual members;
- Many firms are opting for systems contracting, where the buying firm delegates certain project management tasks to a prime contractor who then subcontracts the work appropriately and monitors and controls progress of the main task. This leads to a 'first' and 'second tier' supply base, a corollary of which is a sharp reduction in the number of primary suppliers;
- There is a dramatic growth of strategic supply chain alliances, a trend known generically as partnership sourcing.

Checklist 4.1 lists a number of factors which are associated with the general trends identified above. The aim is to identify the extent to which your company's key customers are adopting a strategic approach to purchasing, i.e. it assesses their 'purchasing philosophy'.

Checklist 4.2
Strategic purchasing philosophy

The following list of statements relate to the major characteristics of strategic purchasing. Identify a number of key accounts and record the extent to which you agree with each statement. Add the numbers and determine the average score. A low average indicates that the customer has a commitment to strategic purchasing. The questions can also be presented to key customers for them to complete. It is a useful exercise to evaluate the gap between your perception of their purchasing philosophy and the customer's own assessment.

	Strongly agree		Neither agree nor disagree			Strongly disagree	
Benchmarking is used to meet superior performance targets	1	2	3	4	5	6	7
Benchmarking is used to improve purchasing activity	1	2	3	4	5	6	7
There is a clearly defined purchasing mission statement	1	2	3	4	5	6	7
The purchasing mission is translated into objectives and plans	1	2	3	4	5	6	7
Purchasing is regarded as a strategic multifunctional process	1	2	3	4	5	6	7
The key goal is to optimize the supplier base	1	2	3	4	5	6	7
Suppliers are regarded as partners	1	2	3	4	5	6	7
Supplier selection and development are regarded as key strategic activities	1	2	3	4	5	6	7
There is a formal review process to drive continuous improvement	1	2	3	4	5	6	7
Education, training and professional development are seen as essential elements of the purchasing function	1	2	3	4	5	6	7
Purchasing and suppliers actively participate in new product development (NPD) processes from a very early stage to optimize time to market, total cost and quality	1	2	3	4	5	6	7
Purchasing assumes a proactive role in NPD	1	2	3	4	5	6	7
Integrated logistics systems (e.g. just-in-time, kanban) have been implemented	1	2	3	4	5	6	7
Repeat purchasing is supported by an effective, reliable logistics planning system	1	2	3	4	5	6	7
There is a comprehensive supplier measurement/rating system covering quality and logistics performance	1	2	3	4	5	6	7
Regular feedback of performance ratings is provided to the supplier	1	2	3	4	5	6	7
Support for supplier improvement (e.g. training, consultation, etc.) is provided	1	2	3	4	5	6	7
Electronic data interchange (EDI) is used for the transfer of operational information with the supplier	1	2	3	4	5	6	7
Purchasing is organizationally responsible for supplier quality	1	2	3	4	5	6	7
There is an emphasis on continuous improvement of the supply base quality, cost and performance	1	2	3	4	5	6	7
The supply chain target is zero defects	1	2	3	4	5	6	7

Checklist 4.3
Operational purchasing policy

The following list of statements relate to the major objectives which firms pursue when determining their operational purchasing policy. Identify a number of key accounts and record the extent to which you feel each goal is an important factor in determining supply policy. Add the numbers and determine the average score. A low average indicates that the customer has sophisticated operational purchasing procedures. The questions can also be presented to key customers for them to complete. It is a useful exercise to evaluate the gap between *your perception* of their purchasing policy and the *customer's own assessment*.

	Very important					Not at all important
To obtain better service from suppliers	1 2 3 4 5 6 7
To improve delivery reliability	1 2 3 4 5 6 7
To reduce transportation cost	1 2 3 4 5 6 7
To improve after-sales service support	1 2 3 4 5 6 7
To improve quality of technical advice	1 2 3 4 5 6 7
To achieve greater security of supply	1 2 3 4 5 6 7
To achieve as low a price as possible	1 2 3 4 5 6 7
To improve product quality	1 2 3 4 5 6 7
To establish co-ordinated forecasting systems and methodologies	1 2 3 4 5 6 7
To improve dialogue with suppliers	1 2 3 4 5 6 7
To have a greater choice of products	1 2 3 4 5 6 7
To encourage supplier involvement in new product development	1 2 3 4 5 6 7
To reduce overall purchasing administration costs	1 2 3 4 5 6 7
To be able to control suppliers better and/or make better use of information	1 2 3 4 5 6 7
To continuously reduce lead times and increase supplier flexibility	1 2 3 4 5 6 7
To sustain mutually profitable business allowing all supply chain members to invest and grow	1 2 3 4 5 6 7
To continuously improve product quality and functionality to satisfy end user requirements	1 2 3 4 5 6 7

Checklist 4.2 deals with the *strategic* dimensions of purchasing policy. It is also important to understand the *operational* aspects of purchasing, particularly those goals which underpin the overall policy on procurement.

Checklist 4.3 tests the importance of a variety of goals in underpinning your customer's operational purchasing policy.

A corollary of the above identified trends in industrial purchasing is that members of industrial supply chains now find themselves in a relationship of mutual dependency, a situation which is forcing them into developing much tighter bonds between each other. Partnership sourcing must be matched by relationship management, i.e. marketing should be undertaken within a framework of long term relationships as opposed to the ad hoc basis of business associated with the transaction mentality. Two key benefits accrue to all companies in a supply chain who operate within a relationship configuration:

1. There is a dramatic reduction in the uncertainty surrounding business operations.
2. Transaction costs are considerably reduced.

In the past these benefits would typically be achieved by vertical or lateral integration, i.e. by firms at different levels within the supply chain merging their operations. The complexity of the contemporary business environment, however, tends to preclude this option. As we have seen, the general trend is towards *disaggregation* as firms focus on their specialist core competencies. Example Three provides a good illustration of this trend.

The outcome of disaggregation and the other trends outlined above is a form of 'soft' integration, an arrangement whereby firms remain independent but work closely with their supply chain 'partners'. A general term to describe arrangements of this type is *networks*. The impact of network solutions on maintaining equilibrium in the strategic marketing triangle is demonstrated in Figure 4.2.

Example Three
Core competencies

Marks & Spencer is one of the world's most profitable retailers. It is noted for the quality of its customer service and the human resource policies which are the foundations of this reputation. A major determinant of its profitability, however, is the strong bonds it builds with its suppliers and the array of outsourcing arrangements it manages. For example, M&S uses external logistics firms to manage the complex and highly specialized daily task of keeping its hundreds of stores fully stocked with a vast array of fresh foods. As a consequence of this approach it does not have to tie up huge amounts of capital in distribution assets (e.g. trucks, warehouses, etc.). M&S also use a specialist distribution and warehousing firm to manage all the things they do not sell, for example, mannequins, cash registers, stationery, uniforms, etc. This frees up store space thus giving more opportunity to sell more products! M&S also has very tight relationships with its major suppliers and works closely with them in quality control and new product development. Being a supplier to M&S is not an easy task! Despite this, companies who can meet their stringent quality control requirements will be 'world-class' in terms of competitiveness.

The supplier policy taken by M&S allows them to focus on and invest in their unique core competencies. It also makes their organization very flexible and responsive to opportunities and threats from the general business environment.

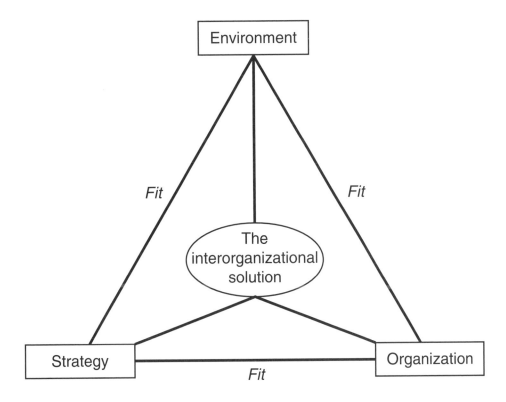

Figure 4.2 *Network solutions and the strategic marketing triangle*

Network solutions: collaboration for competitive edge

Networks have come to play a major role in the conduct of business, particularly those where international competition is intense. Many definitional problems are associated with the term networks but, in their broadest sense, they describe *inter-* rather than *intra-*organizational solutions to coping with the dynamics and complexity of the business environment. Networks provide an intermediate solution to the problems caused by this environmental turbulence. They can offset the uncertainties associated with market-based transactions and they avoid the complexities of integration. They are not without their problems and there are strong criticisms of their existence. Many economists, for

example, would argue that collaboration rather than competition will stifle innovation and allow companies to become inefficient, the customer being the ultimate victim of cartel-like business practices. Organizational theorists will point to the difficult task of managing *within* organizations, let alone *between* them. Despite this, there is growing evidence that network solutions provide extraordinary competitive advantages, whether this be through the giant Japanese *Kieretsu* and Korean *Chaebol* networks or amongst the exporting networks of Scandinavian producers.

Many writers have argued that the network form of organizational behaviour is especially pertinent to markets which are characterized by sophisticated and rapidly changing technology and those which are exposed to continuous shifts in international trade and competition. In this context traditional organizational structures have failed to cope and the network has emerged as a superior form of organizational design. Here we encounter the notion that organizational advantage is a superior and more sustainable source of competitive edge than technological- or product-based competencies. In the case of networks, however, the challenge is to understand how successful inter-organizational relationships can be sustained and to evaluate the factors which deliver strong and sustainable performance over time. Relationship marketing is the key to success but, as we have seen, firms have typically been very poor at putting its principles into practice. In the following sections we examine why this is the case. A recognition that the relationship approach must be managed strategically is followed by a detailed evaluation of the types of interactions which take place in buyer–seller relationships.

Process solutions: relationship management

As a discipline, marketing is very good at describing the things which firms should do strategically to achieve competitive success. It tends to be less successful at dealing with the trickier task of implementing marketing programmes. Having said this, a number of marketing academics have made significant contributions to the understanding of the factors involved in the transition from the traditional product orientation of companies to the 'resource' orientation which underpins the relationship approach. Three mainstream schools of thought have emerged:

1. The Nordic school of relationship marketing;
2. The collective writings of the Industrial Marketing and Purchasing group;
3. An integrative approach centred upon research undertaken at Cranfield University.

These streams of thought are increasingly converging and, taken together, their emphasis on matching internal marketing programmes with external marketing strategies provides a common agenda. All three schools recognize the importance of internal processes for partnership success and each approach acknowledges the sensitive impact of the 'atmosphere' which surrounds the relationship between two or more parties. A common thread is the importance of networks and the emphasis on *internal* re-organization to secure successful *external* relationship management. Figure 4.3 builds upon the strategic marketing triangle. It incorporates the impact of networks and, in its final format, draws attention to the critical importance of designing appropriate internal processes to ensure that external relationships are effectively managed. The notion of 'balanced solutions' is proposed as an umbrella term to describe the comprehensive nature of the approach.

In the following sections each mainstream approach to relationship management identified above is examined in more depth.

A Scandinavian perspective on relationship management

The Nordic perspective on relationship marketing is concisely summarized by Professor Christian Grönroos (1996). Firstly, he identifies three *strategic* elements of the relationship approach:

1. Companies must strive towards a *service* business orientation;
2. Companies must break down functional boundaries and adopt a *process* management perspective;
3. Companies should *actively* seek involvement in partnerships and networks.

Taken together these three strategic elements constitute a paradigm shift in business orientation and serve to underline that companies must strive to develop a relationship philoso-

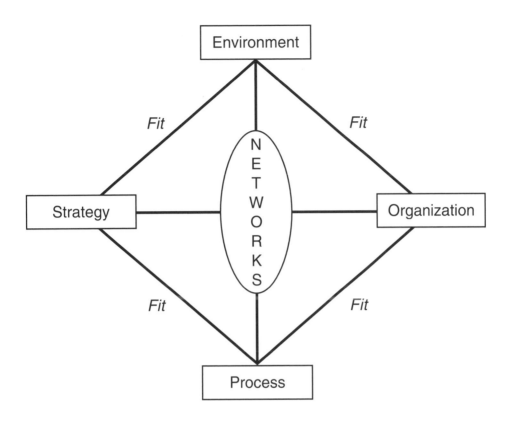

Figure 4.3 *Internal processes for the management of external relationships*

phy. Grönroos also gives an indication of the three *tactical* elements which underpin the relationship approach:

1. Companies should seek direct contact with customers and other *stakeholders*, for example, suppliers, suppliers of suppliers, customers of customers, etc.;
2. Companies should adopt the principles of database marketing, employing information technology to accurately determine the needs and preferences of *segments* of their customer base;
3. Companies should develop a customer-oriented service delivery system.

The Nordic relationship marketing philosophy is based upon the premise of integrated customer care, an interactive management and marketing approach which is built upon

the following resource base:

1. Personnel
2. Technology
3. Knowledge
4. Time.

The importance of time is central to all perspectives on network solutions, the argument being that unless a long term perspective is adopted, relationship management will tend to flounder before it can be successfully implemented. The focus which the Nordic school bestows upon people is also critical, particularly the emphasis on the importance of *internal marketing*. Put simply, this states that if a strategy cannot be sold internally it is highly unlikely to succeed in the external environment. The emphasis on networks, relationships and interactions provides the bedrock of the relationship marketing approach, a guiding principal being that a company can leverage a whole set of resources which are external to it, thus reducing the need for it to expand its own resource base. In the next section the IMP studies are examined and a comprehensive model which embraces much of the discussion relating to relationship management is discussed.

Insights from the Industrial Marketing and Purchasing group ■

Relationship management has been described as a phenomenon which underpins a 'new age' of industrial marketing. The emphasis is on *relational* exchange and the overall goal is customer retention. From an operational point of view the key challenge is to understand the dynamics of the buyer–seller interface and to manage them accordingly. Amongst the most influential researchers in this area are the Industrial Marketing and Purchasing group (IMP) who have developed a model which integrates important concepts such as risk reduction, power, dependence, interpersonal behaviour,

distribution channel behaviour and industrial buying behaviour. The model has four main groups of variables, i.e. those factors which both surround and are part of buyer–seller interactions:

1. Variables which describe the elements arising in the *process* of interaction;
2. Variables which characterize the participants involved in this process, i.e., organizations and individuals;
3. Variables which describe the environment in which the interaction takes place;
4. Variables which serve to portray the atmosphere which both affects and is affected by the interaction processes.

The full range of variables identified by the IMP group is shown in Table 4.1.

The IMP studies examine *why* relationships between organizations develop and they extend this analysis to a broader based discussion of *how* such relationships emerge. The former issues relate to the network principles discussed above while the latter explain the processes by which networks actually come into existence. The IMP group profiles how networks are developed over

Table 4.1 *A profile of the IMP model variables*

Elements in the process	Participants	Environment	Atmosphere
● products and service ● information ● finance ● social values	**Organization** ● technology ● structures ● experience ● resources ● strategy **Individuals** ● aims ● experiences ● resources	● market structure ● dynamism ● internationalization of the market ● social system and cultures	● power/dependence ● co-operation ● closeness (or distance)

Source: Hakansson (ed.) (1982) *International Marketing and Purchasing of Industrial Goods.* Chichester: John Wiley

time and also identifies the organizational challenges which managing these relationships presents. IMP group member Professor David Ford (1980) has modelled the development of buyer–seller relationships as a five stage process:

1. *Pre-relationship stage* – where a company is evaluating potential suppliers.
2. *Early stage* – involving the negotiation of sample delivery and a heavy investment of management time.
3. *Development stage* – where contracts are signed and deliveries commence.
4. *Long term stage* – where purchase has become regular, uncertainty is vastly reduced and commitment is enhanced.
5. *Final stage* – a characteristic of long established markets whereby supply chain relationships become institutionalized.

Underpinning the IMP research is the concept of *distance*, i.e. a recognition of a link between the elements being exchanged and the atmosphere surrounding the interaction processes. The closer the distance, the more enduring the relationship. It has been demonstrated, for example, that in the process of supplier evaluation, buyers' assessments are based as much, if not more, on relationship skills than technical and commercial skills. Five categories of 'distance' have been identified:

1. *Social distance* – the extent to which both the individuals and the organizations in a relationship are unfamiliar with each other's way of working.
2. *Cultural distance* – the extent to which the norms and values of the two companies differ because of their separate national characteristics.
3. *Technological distance* – the differences between the two companies' product and process technologies.
4. *Time distance* – the time which must elapse between establishing contact or placing an order and the actual transfer of the product or service involved.

5. *Geographical distance* – the physical distance between the two companies' locations.

Different buying situations mean that the characteristics of distance and the importance of each component will vary considerably. Despite this, Ford (1980) has demonstrated that reduction in distance and the associated increase in perceived commitment on the part of the buyer is a significant discriminator in the supplier assessment, selection and evaluation process. This finding is typical of those found in the general IMP literature and much of the related research which can be broadly categorized as the interaction approach to industrial buying. The next section explores the practical relationship management issues which arise from the conceptual and empirical work of the IMP group.

Working the interaction: developing supply chain linkages

Over the last decade firms have faced increasing pressures to continuously improve productivity. Throughout this period the principal focus has been on the re-alignment of production factors, particularly regarding the more effective use of technology. In this search for higher productivity the emphasis has been essentially internal, with little effort being placed on the possibilities of cost reduction through enhancing supply chain linkages, especially through reconfiguration of physical distribution processes. The important point to note here is that while relationships are paramount they cannot replace the service operations which underpin successful supply chain management. It is beyond the scope of this chapter to elaborate fully on the operational aspect of the logistics dimension of relationship management. Suffice to say, in establishing a physical distribution system which is both effective and efficient, the following factors are amongst the most important considerations:

- evaluation of the customer service standards to be achieved;
- selection of appropriate transportation modes;
- determination of the optimal number and location of warehousing facilities;
- the design of order processing and information systems;
- determination of production scheduling;
- establishing inventory management and control procedures.

Many researchers would add that the implementation of an effective 'total distribution solution' in a strategic sense requires infusion of the 'logistics concept' throughout the organization. Essentially, this notion embraces both materials management and relationship management and is made up of the following elements:

- customer service;
- logistics and distribution strategy;
- just-in-time management;

Checklist 4.4
Identifying sources of differentiation

For each element in the following list rate your company's effectiveness in differentiating itself from a 'best-in-class' rival. Add the individual scores and find the average. A low average suggests a very strong competitive position. This exercise will also allow you to prioritize actions to deal with areas of identified weakness.

	Very effective in differentiating					Not at all effective in differentiating
Your ability to understand correctly the requirements of your customers	1	2	3	4	5	6	7
The skills of your employees who are in close contact with your customers	1	2	3	4	5	6	7
The creative input and innovation of your company in meeting customers' needs	1	2	3	4	5	6	7
The quality of your customer base	1	2	3	4	5	6	7
Your ability to communicate with the customer	1	2	3	4	5	6	7
Your ability to meet accurately the stated requirements of your customers	1	2	3	4	5	6	7
The method by which your product is delivered to the customer (e.g. JIT)	1	2	3	4	5	6	7
The image you portray to the customer	1	2	3	4	5	6	7
The ability to meet the requirements of the customer on time	1	2	3	4	5	6	7
Your reputation in the marketplace	1	2	3	4	5	6	7
The back-up service you provide to your customers	1	2	3	4	5	6	7
The way customer enquiries are handled	1	2	3	4	5	6	7
The way customer complaints are handled	1	2	3	4	5	6	7
The systems set up to deal with customer service	1	2	3	4	5	6	7

Checklist 4.4 *(Continued)*

	Very effective in differentiating						Not at all effective in differentiating
The amount of customization of your products offered to the customer	1	2	3	4	5	6	7
The internal communication procedures of your company	1	2	3	4	5	6	7
The relationship of your company with other firms (e.g. suppliers, media) necessary for delivery of your product	1	2	3	4	5	6	7
Your ability to attract new clients	1	2	3	4	5	6	7
Your promotional activities	1	2	3	4	5	6	7
Efficient administration of orders and invoices	1	2	3	4	5	6	7
Senior managers available to customers if required	1	2	3	4	5	6	7
Proactive sales representative available to address and understand your customers' problems	1	2	3	4	5	6	7
Expertise in addressing individual technical problems	1	2	3	4	5	6	7
Price/cost competitiveness	1	2	3	4	5	6	7
Quality of products	1	2	3	4	5	6	7
Range of products	1	2	3	4	5	6	7
Rate of innovation (new products)	1	2	3	4	5	6	7
Ability to handle emergency situations	1	2	3	4	5	6	7
Support and information of health and safety and environmental issues	1	2	3	4	5	6	7
Delivery service (on time, flexible and well handled)	1	2	3	4	5	6	7
Keeping your customers informed of changes and problems	1	2	3	4	5	6	7
Able to provide additional services, e.g. maintenance, pre- and post-sale advice and support	1	2	3	4	5	6	7
Overall corporate reputation and trustworthiness	1	2	3	4	5	6	7
Past performance	1	2	3	4	5	6	7

- supply chain management;
- information technology in logistics and distribution;
- people.

In recent years there has been a growing awareness amongst buyers and sellers of the importance of physical distribution, particularly the substantial potential for cost reduction and profit improvement which is inherent in this business process. The trade-off has always been that indiscriminate cuts in physical distribution investment tend to compromise customer value. Integrated distribution systems incur costs such as transportation, warehousing and inventory management as well as the hidden costs arising from lost sales, cancelled orders and dis-

satisfied customers. The cost structure of physical distribution and logistics is complex, particularly, as mentioned above, when one considers the interdependence of costs and customer service and the inevitable trade-offs this generates. Typically, an inverse relationship exists whereby the provision of enhanced customer service incurs higher costs while, conversely, cutting logistics costs tends to compromise service levels. These aspects of customer service include:

- those activities which are involved in accepting, processing and delivering customer orders and which follow up on deviations from agreed schedules;
- those activities which are targeted at ensuring reliability and timeliness in the

delivery of goods in line with customers' expectations;

- the range of business activities which, taken together, combine to deliver and invoice the company's products in a way which delivers customer satisfaction while at the same time meeting the company's own objectives;
- activities underpinning total order entry, including all communications with customers, all shipping, all freight, all invoicing and total control of product repair and general complaints handling;
- business processes which secure accurate delivery of products, timely issuing of invoices, accurate follow-up where required and efficient response to routine inquiries.

Delivery of effective customer service provides value in terms of timeliness and convenience and, from a relationship management perspective, this must embrace processes which take into account pre-transaction, mid-transaction and post-transaction considerations which surround the exchange process with the customer. Quality customer service provision fundamentally involves the identification of how additional value can be added to the core product or service being offered. More generally, relationship marketing sees customer service in a broader supply chain/marketing channel context, i.e. as embracing the company's customers, its downstream relationships with the end-consumer and also its upstream relationships with suppliers and, ultimately, its suppliers' suppliers.

The ability to successfully implement relationship marketing strategies based on the operational provision of superior customer service – i.e., a generic strategy of differentiation – requires a clear understanding of the company's competitive advantage. Fundamentally, this requires two broad categories of knowledge. Firstly, the company must understand its own ability to differentiate its market offering with reference to well understood customer needs. Secondly, when pursuing strategies of differentiation it is

essential to have detailed competitor information. Checklist 4.4 lists a range of factors which have been identified as sources of differentiation and requires you to evaluate how effective your company is at achieving them.

It is not enough to understand customer value – rivals may know that too! Nor is it possible to claim to be 'different' if you have not identified a high quality rival to benchmark upon. For these reasons, a strong competitor awareness is essential. Checklist 4.5 gives a detailed list of items associated with competitor awareness and requires you to evaluate how well your company performs on these criteria.

This section on the operational and practical issues associated with relationship marketing has been necessarily brief but it needed to be included for completeness. Another reason for its consideration here is that many supply chain professionals (e.g. logistics managers, stock controllers, salespeople, buyers, etc.) remain extremely cynical about the possibilities of the relationship approach. Stock and work-in-progress is tangible: it can be monitored, measured and controlled, as can delivery times and quality levels. In stark contrast, relationship concepts are extremely intangible. Like many 'soft' aspects of management, they often require fundamental attitudinal and behavioural changes before they are generally accepted within organizations. Partly in recognition of this problem, a group of researchers based at Cranfield University has developed a framework which embraces *stakeholder principles* but which also makes relatively abstract concepts accessible to practising managers. The next section profiles their contribution.

An integrated perspective on relationship management: the Cranfield six markets model

A third approach to relationship marketing has been developed by a group of researchers at Cranfield University. A central thrust of this group's work has been to integrate the major dimensions of relationship management within a framework which they describe as the 'six markets model'. This draws heavily on 'stakeholder' principles and recognizes the complexity of industrial markets. The six categories of market are as follows (Millman, 1993):

1. *Customer markets*. This category is what is traditionally understood as a 'market' in the mainstream marketing literature. From a relationship marketing perspective the focus should be on building partnerships and the appropriate sales approach is via key account management. In a later section the important principles of segmentation which underpin key account management are discussed in more detail and the characteristics of buyer–seller partnerships are fully evaluated. The principles and practice of key account management are explored in Chapter 5.

2. *Internal markets*. In recent years there has been a growing interest in the concept of internal marketing, an approach which aims to transcend functional boundaries so that everyone in an organization has an awareness of their role in the marketing process. Internal marketing programmes are essential for transforming attitudes and beliefs within organizations and should form a central plank of any relationship management strategy. Internal marketing is discussed more fully in a later section.

3. *Supplier markets*. The move towards a much more strategic role for purchasing is forcing companies to recognize that the supply chain is the unit of competition. New technologies (such as electronic data interchange) and inventory management systems (such as JIT) require a much more co-ordinated and cohesive approach to the management of buyer–seller relationships.

4. *Recruitment markets*. The basic premise here is that employee retention should be central to an organization's strategic direction and that employees should be seen as assets, particularly, but not exclusively, those staff who interact with cus-

tomers. The notion of 'moments of truth', whereby a customer's perception of a company is formed by multiple interactions with its employees, was an early attempt to draw attention to the need for excellent service quality amongst contact personnel. The emphasis here was upon careful selection, motivation and training of employees. Similarly, the highly successful 'Investors in People' initiative has brought many companies into an awareness of the power of *strategic* human resource management.

5. *Influence markets*. This is a recognition that opinion formers (e.g. journalists, analysts, academics) and reference groups (e.g. trade associations, regulators, lobbyists) can have a tremendous impact on general perceptions of a company. Word of mouth communications are very powerful and companies must try and shape these third party influences to create favourable impressions. For many companies public relations is taking on a much more strategic role, particularly as public scrutiny of business practice intensifies.

6. *Referral markets*. This category acknowledges the role of experts and professionals in shaping the decisions of purchasing organizations. For example, steel companies who would like to see the construction industry use a greater percentage of steel must persuade architects and structural engineers of the functional and aesthetic attributes of, say, tubes and pipes. More generally, the role of endorsement is critical and strong relationships with such 'influencers' can lead to enhanced credibility for the supplying firm and deliver much greater proximity to the specifications process. An important concept in the theory of relationship marketing is the notion of a 'loyalty ladder'. This describes how companies progress from seeking prospects towards developing a focus on customer retention, the ultimate goal being not only to have a loyal customer but also to create a scenario where the customer is a strong advocate of the company.

Checklist 4.5
Competitor awareness

The following list of statements all relate to the knowledge a company has or needs about its key competitors. Indicate the degree to which you agree or disagree with each proposition. A low average suggests a high degree of sophistication in competitor intelligence gathering and, other things being equal, a strong competitive position. The exercise can also be used to prioritize key actions to deal with the identified weaknesses in competitor awareness.

	Strongly agree			Neither agree nor disagree			Strongly disagree
We know the strengths and weaknesses of our main competitor	1	2	3	4	5	6	7
Our firm routinely monitors the activities of our main competitors	1	2	3	4	5	6	7
We subscribe to trade and industry publications in order to find weaknesses that we can take advantage of	1	2	3	4	5	6	7
Our firm devotes a lot of effort to figuring out the strategy of our competition	1	2	3	4	5	6	7
We know the pricing policies of our competition very well	1	2	3	4	5	6	7
We know which major customer segments our competitors are trying to serve	1	2	3	4	5	6	7
We know who our main competitors are	1	2	3	4	5	6	7
We have survived the recession better than most of our competitors	1	2	3	4	5	6	7
In this industry there really is not that much difference among the top few firms in technology development and the functional quality of products	1	2	3	4	5	6	7
We're geared up to respond quickly to competitors' actions	1	2	3	4	5	6	7
We tend to be the trend setter in this industry	1	2	3	4	5	6	7
We have a person or group responsible for monitoring the actions of our competitors	1	2	3	4	5	6	7
It costs us less to provide our service than it does our largest competitor	1	2	3	4	5	6	7
We make better use of technology than our competitors	1	2	3	4	5	6	7
We are actively developing a strategy to deal with international competition	1	2	3	4	5	6	7
We find ourselves frequently adjusting the nature of the product and service support we provide to respond to our competitors	1	2	3	4	5	6	7
Because of the competition we have little control over the prices that we charge	1	2	3	4	5	6	7

Checklist 4.5 *(Continued)*

	Strongly agree		Neither agree nor disagree		Strongly disagree	
We provide a substantially different product than most of our competitors	1	2	3	4	5	6	7
We react quickly to competitive moves	1	2	3	4	5	6	7
We are probably more profitable than our largest competitor	1	2	3	4	5	6	7
We monitor the competition so that they won't catch us by surprise	1	2	3	4	5	6	7
It's impossible to predict who the dominant firm in our industry will be in five years	1	2	3	4	5	6	7
Start-up costs are high to enter this industry	1	2	3	4	5	6	7
Our analysis of the competition is more informal than formal	1	2	3	4	5	6	7
In our industry we have to worry about indirect competition every bit as much as direct competition	1	2	3	4	5	6	7
Our top managers frequently meet to discuss the strategies of our competitors	1	2	3	4	5	6	7
I believe that if you focus on satisfying the needs of customers then you don't have to worry about the competition	1	2	3	4	5	6	7
We are more prepared to take advantage of the end of recession than most of our competitors	1	2	3	4	5	6	7
We tend to react to industry trends	1	2	3	4	5	6	7
Our competitors are not very strong	1	2	3	4	5	6	7
Understanding our competitors is an integral part of our firm's planning	1	2	3	4	5	6	7

The Cranfield research has made a valuable contribution to our understanding of how relationship marketing works in practice. Few deny the powerful nature of the relationship marketing concept. It is only by understanding its core processes in more detail that we can hope to make it a sustainable and stable approach to business practice. In concluding the section on the six markets model we will present what the Cranfield group identify as 'an agenda for research', i.e. those areas which, upon investigation, will reveal more knowledge about this important topic. It is clear that the majority of these areas can and should be addressed by practising managers. After all, academics merely record and interpret what practitioners do in the first place! The following summary indicates the broad scope of required activity (after Millman, 1993):

- Characterizing types of relationships and the frequency/quality of interaction in specific industry contexts;
- Developing external market scanning systems and internal information systems to support relationship marketing;
- Examining the nature of continuity and discontinuity of client/contractor relationships in project-based industries;
- In-depth studies of multi-level, multi-functional relationships in key account management and how these might best be integrated into existing/new organization structures;
- Exploring barriers to migration from transactional to relationship marketing;
- Developing accounting techniques for evaluating customer profitability;
- Understanding networking relationships driven by electronic data interchange;

A recognition that a company has a number of stakeholders, each of which has differing needs, is a fundamental starting point for the relationship management approach to marketing. The following checklists simply require you to profile the needs of different stakeholders alongside a statement of your needs of them. Five stakeholders are mentioned. In the final list the question mark relates to any company- or industry-specific stakeholders, for example, the regulator in the privatized utility sectors.

For each stakeholder identify the needs which they have of your company. Evaluate the current situation, i.e. note how well you presently meet these needs. Profile the desired situation and, finally, list the actions which are essential to achieve this optimal scenario.

Stakeholder: Customers

Customers' needs of us	Current situation	Desired situation	Action points

Our needs of them	Current situation	Desired situation	Action points

Stakeholder: Distribution intermediaries

Channels' needs of us	Current situation	Desired situation	Action points

Our needs of them	Current situation	Desired situation	Action points

Checklist 4.6 *(Continued)*

Stakeholder: Suppliers

Suppliers' needs of us	Current situation	Desired situation	Action points

Our needs of them	Current situation	Desired situation	Action points

Stakeholder: Employees

Employees' needs of us	Current situation	Desired situation	Action points

Our needs of them	Current situation	Desired situation	Action points

Stakeholder: Investors

Investors' needs of us	Current situation	Desired situation	Action points

Our needs of them	Current situation	Desired situation	Action points

Checklist 4.6 *(Continued)*

Stakeholder: ?

? needs of us	Current situation	Desired situation	Action points

Our needs of them	Current situation	Desired situation	Action points

- Assessing the potential for applying "internal marketing" techniques to improve core processes such as product innovation, marketing planning and customer service.

The latter point is central to all studies of relationship marketing. In understanding the factors driving the provision of superior customer satisfaction many insights can be drawn from the services management literature, amongst the most important being the notion of internal marketing. The concept is operationalized as an approach to business which, as previously mentioned, recognizes that firms which wish to become market-led must first demonstrate the importance of so doing to all employees.

Having said this, research undertaken on internal marketing by Payne and Walters (1990) suggests that formal internal marketing rarely exists. Some of their findings include:

- internal marketing is generally not a discrete activity – it is implicit in quality initiatives, customer service programmes and broader business strategies;
- where it exists, internal marketing comprises formal structured activities

accompanied by a range of less formal ad hoc initiatives;
- communication is critical to internal marketing success;
- internal marketing performs a critical role in competitive differentiation;
- internal marketing performs an important role in reducing inter-functional conflict;
- internal marketing is evolutionary, involving the slow erosion of inter-functional barriers.

Internal marketing underpins *shared values*, a concept which features very strongly in the marketing and strategic management literature. An important role of internal marketing is to ensure that all employees, but especially those who have regular contact with customers, believe in the company's products and that they are motivated to promote a favourable image of the company. Achieving this level of customer satisfaction, in turn, requires considerable effort and it must be led and underpinned by top management commitment. In this sense, effective internal marketing requires the creation of a 'service culture' throughout the organization.

This statement underlines the importance of cross-functional integration in the traditional marketing philosophy sense of 'everybody does marketing'. A growing body of evidence is demonstrating that such an approach is amongst the most effective and sustainable sources of competitive advantage. A recurrent theme of this chapter has been that the lofty ideal of 'customer first' often breaks down on the failure of organizations to reconfigure their processes to achieve this apparently simple goal. Despite this, many companies are genuinely striving to seek organizational advantage based on a sharper market focus.

In the next section we briefly consider a common thread which permeates the three perspectives on relationship management discussed thus far: the importance of multiple groups of relationships in industrial marketing activity.

Stakeholders and multiple relationships

Relationship management is making a tremendous impact on a number of broad fronts. Much has been heard of the 'stakeholder' principle recently, a concept which has long been part of the vocabulary of management. Checklist 4.6 provides a practical tool to analyse a firm's relationship with its various stakeholders.

Central to the stakeholder concept is the notion of multiple relationships and there is a strong ethical underpinning to its practical foundations. Applying this perspective to relationship marketing, Takala and Uusitalo (1996) argue that, for such an approach to be successful, there are two essential conditions:

1. A relationship is a mutually rewarding connection between the provider and a customer, i.e. both parties derive benefit from the contact;
2. Parties have a commitment to the relationship over time.

As we have mentioned elsewhere in this chapter, the importance of commitment is central to a long term partnership approach but in practice it is very difficult to measure, i.e. it is a 'soft' aspect of management, intangible yet of critical importance. Takala and Uusitalo (1996) have gone some way to make the notion of commitment more tangible, identifying three key components:

1. Stability;
2. Sacrifice;
3. Loyalty.

Stability is a central issue since it balances the conflicting interests of different stakeholders. They go on to argue that a stable relationship pre-supposes trust and that, fundamentally, it is only mutual trust which can be the cornerstone of successful relationship marketing activities. There is much debate about the characteristics of trust in social science theory but, where consensus exists, it tends to relate to the intangibility of the concept. Having said this, research demonstrates that trust is used by managers as a proxy for a broad range of issues associated with strong and long relationships. In this sense, the feeling of trust is essential to establishing an atmosphere of mutual co-operation. Figure 4.4 presents a summary of the key dimensions of trust.

What many of the dimensions of trust indicate is that achieving a feeling of trust is fundamentally a function of time. In this sense, a manager will describe a relationship of trust with reference to *cumulative* positive experiences. The emphasis on 'cumulative' indicates that trust is a long term issue and that it must be built up over time. Similarly, a key factor which will allow trust to emerge is the 'atmosphere' within which the relationship develops. A positive atmosphere is essential for a trusting relationship, i.e. a climate created by a joint philosophy of co-operation. A negative atmosphere, meanwhile, is typical where conflictual relationships are the norm. It is essential that effort is put into building an atmosphere of co-operation, a process which is elaborated upon below in the section on partnership. It is equally important to predict and contain conflict. Checklist 4.7 lists a number of

Figure 4.4 *Key dimensions of trust*

factors which have been identified as potential sources of conflict and requires that you assess the risk of these arising in your own supply chain relationships.

The notion of trust can be applied to a broad range of marketing concepts. For example, *brand loyalty* is underpinned by cumulative satisfactions, a trust relationship which can pass through many generations. In the brand example, however, the relationship is with an inanimate object which manufacturers have managed to standardize. Interpersonal relationships, meanwhile, have the added dimension of variability, i.e. they are marred by the inconsistencies associated with human behaviour! This explains why trust relationships must be *managed*, a process which also recognizes that any relationship where people or organizations rely on each other has a dependency dimension.

The generally accepted solution involves a recognition of this dependency and a positive outlook on dealing with it for mutual advantage, i.e. an adoption of a philosophy of partnership. In the next section we consider the partnership philosophy in more detail.

Developing a philosophy of partnership

The partnership approach does not refer to a legal agreement but rather describes a supportive relationship between supply chain members which is built around a recognition of each party's mutual roles. There are three basic phases of the partnership approach to supply chain management:

Checklist 4.7
Identifying conflict sources

The following items have been identified as major sources of conflict between supply chain members. Rate whether or not each factor is a major cause of conflict in your company's relationship with *specified* supply chain members. It is not appropriate to take an overall average in this exercise. Rather, prioritize actions on those factors where a low score is given. It is essential to identify conflict sources in order to contain their negative impact.

	Very important cause				Not an important cause	
Infrequent communication	1 2 3	4	5 6 7
No discounts offered	1 2 3	4	5 6 7
Probation period required	1 2 3	4	5 6 7
Length of credit period offered	1 2 3	4	5 6 7
Delivery service	1 2 3	4	5 6 7
Requirement to carry too many products	1 2 3	4	5 6 7
Length of supply agreement (too short)	1 2 3	4	5 6 7
Poor managerial capability of supplier	1 2 3	4	5 6 7
Pressure on supplier to carry excess stock	1 2 3	4	5 6 7
Suppliers' technical support inadequate	1 2 3	4	5 6 7
Your product range not competitive	1 2 3	4	5 6 7
Conflicting objectives of 'partners'	1 2 3	4	5 6 7
Terms and conditions of agreement	1 2 3	4	5 6 7
Documentation	1 2 3	4	5 6 7
Usefulness of sales visits	1 2 3	4	5 6 7
Volume rebates	1 2 3	4	5 6 7
Competititors' prices	1 2 3	4	5 6 7
Communication of price policy	1 2 3	4	5 6 7
Certification analysis	1 2 3	4	5 6 7
Stability of personnel	1 2 3	4	5 6 7
Not understanding customer needs	1 2 3	4	5 6 7

1. An explicit statement of policies should be made by suppliers in areas such as product availability, technical support, pricing, etc. Given this, supply chain member roles can be determined in terms of the marketing tasks to be performed and the compensations to be received.

2. Jointly assess all existing supply chain members with reference to their capabilities for fulfilling their supply chain roles. Help each other overcome identified weaknesses by developing appropriate and sharply focused support programmes in these areas of need.

3. Each supply chain partner must continually assess the appropriateness of the poli-

cies guiding the relationship, particularly in the face of a rapidly changing environment.

It has been demonstrated repeatedly in this chapter that a *supply chain* is the unit of competition, not individual firms within it. Crucially, the actions of one member (whether positive or negative) will impinge on the other members. Clearly then, the goal should be to foster a relationship whereby *individual* activities deliver *mutual* gain and this fundamental fact is the essence of partnership. The benefits suggested to accrue from a partnership approach to supply chain management are as follows (Shipley, 1984):

- it facilitates effective two-way communication;
- it enables integrated planning;
- it allows for co-ordinated operations;
- it fosters mutual assistance when required;
- it creates the best environment for avoiding or minimizing potential conflicts that can arise from myriad sources.

Given the importance of the partnership approach to supply chain management and the obvious benefits it is capable of delivering, it should not be too surprising that extensive research has been undertaken regarding how strong relationships are developed and maintained. In an extensive series of publications Professor David Shipley has developed a comprehensive insight into the characteristics and challenges of a partnership approach to supply chain management. Collective practical recommendations for manufacturers based on this research output are summarized below:

1. Begin by prioritizing partnership as the supply chain philosophy.
2. Set clearly determined and jointly developed marketing objectives for the relationship.
3. Clearly communicate the marketing strategy to all network members. Partners should work towards mutually acceptable financial objectives and devise indi-

vidual formal marketing plans for each party.
4. Supply chain policies and arrangements should be based on a comprehensive understanding of the market and analysis of key trade-offs.
5. Agree division of tasks and clarify the roles and responsibilities of each partner.
6. Ensure financial rewards are equitable to fully compensate partners for performing the marketing functions they undertake.
7. Understand the partner's views, needs and profit-making formula. Assess the needs of supply chain members and understand *their* competition. Provide support which will give them competitive edge. Appeal to the partner's self-interest to achieve joint goals.
8. Evaluate the balance of power in the relationship, monitor changes and pursue realistic options.
9. Recognize that conflict is always likely to emerge and develop contingency plans to deal with it. Make sure that communication channels are kept open and use formal and informal meetings for airing views. Constantly strive for better working relationships. Appoint an independent ombudsman for resolving conflicts.
10. Train boundary personnel to work effectively with partners and maintain communications in a manner which they understand. Make sure that partners can recognize potential trouble-spots in the relationship, e.g. the return of goods, complaints handling, flexibility, etc.
11. Deliver flexible, innovative performance which will allow the partners to maintain a competitive edge.
12. Deliver good logistical performance. Strive together to provide better end-customer service.
13. Periodically audit relationships to ensure that they remain viable and provide robust pathways to the target markets. As markets develop over time, customer buy phases and selection criteria should be monitored to ensure that appropriate service levels are being offered.

14. Treat the supply chain as a strategic asset. Signal commitment to partners and seek ways to utilize the complete supply chain to provide a competitive edge.
15. Re-prioritize partnership.

Positive supply chain management should provide a balance of effort between administering effectively and efficiently the existing ongoing business relationships and all the while considering the strategic options available from enhancing system performance. As mentioned above, for this to be successfully implemented it is essential to create an atmosphere of co-operation. Checklist 4.8 lists a number of identified items which work to create a co-operative climate and requires you to indicate how

---

Checklist 4.8
Identifying sources of co-operation

The following items have been identified as major sources of co-operation between supply chain members. Rate whether or not each factor is a major source of co-operation in your company's relationship with *specified* supply chain members. Once again, it is not appropriate to take an overall average in this exercise. Rather, prioritize actions on those *relevant* factors where a *high* score is given. It is essential to create a co-operative climate for a relationship management approach to be successfully implemented.

	Very important source				Not an important source	
Supplier is independent	1 2 3 4 5 6 7					
Competition is controlled	1 2 3 4 5 6 7					
Process accreditation	1 2 3 4 5 6 7					
Training offered	1 2 3 4 5 6 7					
Marketing support given	1 2 3 4 5 6 7					
Financial support given	1 2 3 4 5 6 7					
Management advice given	1 2 3 4 5 6 7					
Shared objectives	1 2 3 4 5 6 7					
Length of supply agreement (extended)	1 2 3 4 5 6 7					
Suppliers' investment in compatible systems	1 2 3 4 5 6 7					
Suppliers' general marketing	1 2 3 4 5 6 7					
Business partners relationship	1 2 3 4 5 6 7					
Effective two-way communication	1 2 3 4 5 6 7					
Broad range of products offered	1 2 3 4 5 6 7					
Fair pricing policy	1 2 3 4 5 6 7					
Good personal contact	1 2 3 4 5 6 7					
Equitable relationship	1 2 3 4 5 6 7					
Customer understands our needs	1 2 3 4 5 6 7					
Customer understands our problems	1 2 3 4 5 6 7					

well your company performs in achieving these factors.

The points made in this section integrate and summarize many of the fundamental behavioural aspects of relationship management which have been made throughout this chapter. In concluding the chapter, however, we need to revert to basic economics. Relationship marketing is expensive! It demands tremendous resources for successful implementation, both economic and emotional. It is wholly inappropriate to have a blanket policy for the relationship approach and the effort expended in implementing it should be rewarded by extracting value from *selected* supply chain partners. The marketing process which can achieve this is segmentation, a principle which works to extract the maximum value for both supplier and buyer, but only if mutual advantage is delivered to both parties.

Segmentation for profitable relationship management

A basic tenet of marketing is that companies should not seek any customer at any price, i.e. they should focus their efforts on *profitable* customers. The best way to achieve this is to employ the principles of market segmentation and to develop tailored marketing programmes accordingly. From a relationship management perspective, there are two key segmentation variables: (i) usage rate; (ii) loyalty. We will consider each in turn.

Usage rate

The importance of this criterion for a relationship management approach should be immediately apparent. It simply does not make sense to invest time and resource in customers who are unlikely to demand significant quantities of product. A useful approach when segmenting on this customer characteristic is to consider three categories of usage rate:

1. Heavy users;
2. Medium users;
3. Light users.

This generic classification allows us to recognize that different industrial sectors will have different orders of magnitude for each category. For example, industrial fasteners will be measured in terms of thousands of pieces whereas machine tools will be measured in tens. This approach to segmenting an industrial market is also powerful in that it moves beyond the classic distinction of small versus large purchasing organizations. For example, a relatively small firm could be a large user of a certain type of industrial gas. It also gives us insights into how to *service* a market. Heavy users clearly warrant a relationship management approach, particularly if they are potentially very loyal to one supplier. Example Four demonstrates how even producers of such a basic commodity as electricity can creatively segment a market. In contrast to heavy users, light users are probably best served through the use of industrial intermediaries such as distributors or dealers.

The usage rate segmentation base also gives us strategic insights into how a company can grow its business in mature markets. If a company recognizes a potential to displace an alternative technology its strategic approach is to encourage light and medium users to switch to its product. Example Five provides a good illustration of this point.

Loyalty profiles

An equally strong segmentation base is to establish the degree of loyalty amongst customers. Once again, a threefold classification provides insight and guidance:

1. Solus;
2. Major;
3. Minor.

Solus users are those companies who are 100% loyal, and who have a policy of work-

Example Four
Powerful segmentation

National Power have successfully segmented the market for electricity based on a combination of customer benefits and usage rates. Firstly, heavy users are identified, in this case those customers who spend in excess of £250,000 per year. Secondly, the nature of the customer's business is used to assess the benefits they require from long term electricity contracts. Hospitals, for example, have completely different demand patterns than those of a continuous manufacturing process facility. An airport is different again. By understanding this and customizing their offering, National Power are able to raise customer satisfaction and customer loyalty amongst highly profitable heavy users.

Example Five
Increase usage!

British Steel would like to see far more steel used in construction. Steel tubes are aesthetically pleasing, structurally strong, they can serve as conduits for wiring and plumbing, and compared to alternative materials they are relatively inexpensive. Despite this, they are under-used in the construction industry. The challenge for British Steel in this case is to build strong relationships with architects and structural engineers to encourage them to specify greater usage of steel. A stunning success story is Stansted Airport, a steel tube construction which has won major architectural awards, these plaudits commending both its low cost and striking design.

ing on a sole supplier basis. The marketing challenge with these customers is to 'ring fence' this loyalty and, in order to protect this status, a relationship management approach is central to the process. Major users will have more than one supplier although they will be predominantly loyal to one firm. This is a very common scenario since purchasers do fear the dependence associated with the sole supplier approach. The marketing challenge is again to secure loyalty and reduce switching to a minimum. Minor users fall

Table 4.2 *Segmentation matrix for relationship marketing*

| Usage rate | Loyalty profile | | |
	Solus	Major	Minor
Heavy	• VIP status • Multi-level contacts • Ring-fence accounts • Pursue joint product development opportunities • Entertain • Innovate, innovate, innovate!	• Relationship marketing • Sacrifice short term proift for long term growth • Multi-level contacts essential • Entertain • Educate	• Convert • Maintain market presence and build technological edge • Continuously review • Employ high-level managers to engage in courtship
Medium	• Relationship marketing • Defend and ring-fence • Multi-level contact • Find substitutes and complements	• Strive harder • Find substitutes and complements • Undertake joint workshops	• Keep watching brief • Innovate for sustainable advantage • Convert/ignore
Light	• Careful resource managemnt • Consider telesales/database marketing	• Telesales • Encourage distributors to support your brands	• Ignore

into one of two categories: (i) fickles, i.e. those purchasers who are always chasing deals and will readily switch suppliers for each transaction; (ii) a rival's loyals, i.e. those purchasers who are solus or major customers of a competitor. Fickles should be avoided at all costs since they are highly unlikely to be convertible to profitable accounts. Careful consideration should be given as to whether or not a rival's loyal customers should be targeted, particularly if the available evidence suggests that they are highly satisfied. The fundamental principle of segmentation is to allocate resources to market clusters which will deliver the most profitable returns. Chasing a

lost cause makes little sense, especially if the higher potential segments have not yet been ring fenced. Table 4.2 combines the two segmentation bases we are considering and makes suggestions as to appropriate ways of servicing the market.

The important thing to understand about any such models is that each case should be given specific attention. Chapter 5 on key account management gives further insights into how you can develop profiles for individual customer targets – the main point is that the focus of any relationship management approach to industrial marketing should seek to identify *profitable* market segments.

Summary

In this chapter we have discussed the core principles of what has emerged as one of the most exciting developments in marketing for many years. Relationship management has definitely become a major talking point in the marketing world and many firms are striving to adopt its ideals. Despite this, boundless frustration surrounds the concept of relationship management as companies find it so difficult to put the principles into practice. Figure 4.5 gives a profile of the multiple dimensions of relationship management and serves to indicate the comprehensiveness of the subject.

Two key themes emerge from this chapter:

1. As an approach to strategic selling, the benefits of a relationship management approach are indisputable;
2. The fine principles of the relationship management approach are extraordinarily difficult to apply in practice.

In the discussion presented in this chapter we have examined the potential and pitfalls of the relationship management philosophy in some depth. On balance, we can safely say that strategic selling is closely intertwined with the relationship marketing approach. As the trends identified in earlier sections accelerate, it is essential that industrial marketing organizations get closer to their customers. Industrial purchasers are using fewer suppliers and offering the chosen few longer contracts based on a partnership philosophy. Those companies who fail to recognize this fundamental marketing fact of life will flounder in the modern competitive world.

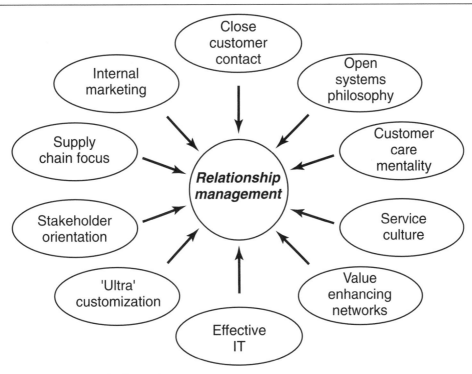

Figure 4.5 Dimensions of relationship management

References

Christopher, M., Payne, A. and Ballantyne, D. (1991) *Relationship Marketing*. Oxford: Butterworth–Heinemann.

Davidow, W.H. (1986) *Marketing High Technology*. New York: The Free Press.

Ford, D. (1980) The Development of Buyer–Seller Relationships in Industrial Markets, *European Journal of Marketing*, **23**, 1, 52–60.

Grönroos, C. (1996) Relationship marketing: strategic and tactical implications, *Management Decision*, **34**, 3, 5–14.

Hakansson, H. (ed.) (1982) *International Marketing and Purchasing of Industrial Goods*. Chichester: John Wiley.

Millman, T. (1993) The Emerging Concept of Relationship Marketing, *Proceedings of the 9th IMP Conference*, University of Bath.

Payne, A. and Walters, D. (1990) *Internal Marketing: Myth or Magic?* Working paper. Cranfield School of Management.

Shipley, D.D. (1984) Selection and Motivation of Distribution Intermediaries, *Industrial Marketing Management*, 13, November, 249–56.

Takala, T. and Uusitalo, O. (1996) An Alternative View of Relationship Marketing: a Framework for Ethical Analysis, *European Journal of Marketing*, **30**, 2, 45–60.

5

Selling to and managing key accounts ___

Professor David Shipley, Trinity College, University of Dublin
Roger Palmer, Cranfield University

 The objective of this chapter is to extend insight of key account management and to position it as an effective strategic response to market adversity which enables suppliers to increase market share, profits and customer loyalty through building sustained relationships of mutual gain with strategically important customers. The key account relationship approach is depicted as superior to a transaction orientation to selling although it is acknowledged that the former approach is not always desirable or feasible. Emphasis is placed on the need to establish and maintain strong, enduring professional relationships between all the relevant functions of both the supplier's and customer's company. Attention is also given to the responsibilities of the key account manager and the skills and empowerment required to perform this role effectively. A description is provided of the key account management process for shifting a buyer–seller dyad from the pre-relationship stage to a fully synergistic relationship.

Key account management is a crucially important management function for numerous companies. This is particularly the case for suppliers whose immediate customers are in industrial or commercial sectors such as manufacturing, assembly, retailing, banking, government and public services. Relative to consumers, customers in these types of markets tend to exhibit:

- Large size, but fewer companies
- Technical complexity
- Fierce competitive behaviour
- Professional management
- Sophisticated purchasing personnel
- Stringent buying requirements
- Buying power
- Strong demands on suppliers.

Key account management evolved as a means to enable suppliers to prosper when confronted by these kinds of difficult customers, conditions and fierce competitors. However the key account management approach as practised by its most successful exponents is not merely a sales and marketing activity of the company. Rather, it involves multiple functions of the business united by the common objective to build and sustain tight long term relationships with strategically important customers. Thus, effective key account management is central to the implementation of effective relationship marketing addressed in Chapter 4. It is also fundamental to the success of many companies and requires harmony, extensive communication and unrelenting co-operation among the functions of the firm to deliver irresistible and sustained differential advantage to its key customers. Customers often need dialogue with specialists in, for example, the development, technical, logistics, finance and service functions of the supplier's organization. Hence, these personnel are important members of a key account management team and success requires that they are available to support the sales and marketing specialists as required.

Practical tip

To increase your probabilities of success in a key account management programme, ensure an appropriate mix of cross-functional specialists is deployed to the key account team. Further, train them to converse meaningfully with and in the technical language of specialist managers in the customer's organization when called upon to do so.

Historically, particular customers were defined as key accounts if they purchased large quantities of a supplier's output or provided a large proportion of profits. Many firms continue to apply this unsophisticated definition. Typically they perform an 80/20 or Pareto analysis to define large accounts. Some firms are unable to conduct even this apparently straightforward exercise however, due to inadequacies in their internal marketing information systems.

More importantly, specifying customers as key accounts solely on the criterion of large size can be myopic. What is required is a broader set of criteria based on the strategic or long term importance of specific customers to the supplier. Large customer size can be a valid criterion of key account status in this context. However other strategically valid criteria include:

- Accounts that have strong long term growth prospects by building market shares in their existing markets.
- Customers with growth potential from being major players in small but expanding markets.
- Accounts that will permit a supplier to test new products in their production processes or will even form formal new product development alliances.
- Customers that are early adopters of new products and therefore encourage others to adopt likewise.
- Customers that are highly prestigious accounts which can be used as reference sites for potential buyers.
- Accounts that are currently served by competitors that the supplier has decided to attack.

Another historical error concerning key account management also remains in common practice. This is to treat it as the responsibility of a super salesperson. The training and development of many key account managers still centres on practical skills such as negotiation, the 'six steps of selling' and perhaps insight into the workings of the customer's purchase decision making unit (DMU). However key account management involves far more than a discontinuous series of unconnected negotiations or sales episodes with DMU participants. Rather it centres on regular and/or continuing discussions and exchanges with the DMU members at both formal and social levels. Hence key account management is an ongoing process concerned with building and maintaining tight relationships between, on the one hand, the supplier company and its account team and, on the other, the customer company and its DMU. The prime objective of this is to manage the relationship to provide superior value and satisfaction to the customer and increased market share, revenue and assurance of buyer loyalty to the supplier.

Conditions for effective key account management

Adoption of a key account approach is not always appropriate or feasible. Three relevant factors require consideration:

- Is this approach acceptable to the customer?
- Is the sales and marketing approach of the supplier suitable?
- Does the supplier have or can it obtain personnel with the necessary skills and capabilities?

Suitability to the customer

Despite a supplier's best intentions, if it is supplying say paper clips and bin liners to the BBC it is unlikely that the supplier would ever be perceived as a strategic supplier. Conversely in 1995 demand for colour PC monitors was buoyant but world production capacity for colour monitor tubes was 30% below demand. Hence manufacturers of monitors such as Toshiba and Gold Star perceived producers of monitor tubes such as Phillips as critically important strategic suppliers with which they urgently required partnership status.

In this context customers can be visualized as occupying a position along the transactions–relationships orientation continuum shown in Figure 5.1. Wholly transaction orientated customers perceive no benefits for themselves in forming relationships with suppliers. They want to buy as a series of one-off transactions. Alternatively, customers at the opposite end of the continuum encourage supplier relationships to obtain the advantages associated with them.

For example, the head of a large electrical retailing firm recently stated in an interview that he was transaction orientated and actively discouraged a relationship approach. What was of primary importance to him in the highly competitive retailing business was the buying price. A branded goods supplier to this organization noted that it was not even allowed to place their point of sales promotional literature into the store to assist with marketing to consumers.

In stark contrast, one of Britain's major brewers opened a bottling plant on a site that shares an adjoining wall with a bottle manufacturer. This formal relationship enabled the brewer to gain the major benefits of guaranteed just-in-time delivery, close quality control, zero stocking costs and free inbound logistics. Similarly the bottle manufacturer enjoys a locked in customer and zero outbound logistics costs.

Customer buying orientations have important implications for suppliers. In addition to avoiding relationships with suppliers, transaction orientated buyers retain dual or multiple sourcing and play vendors off against each other to gain buying advantages. Alternatively customers toward the relationship focused end of the continuum are more loyal to their preferred suppliers, tend to be less price sensitive and provide other advantages. However while such a buyer is likely to overlook an occasional mistake by a supplier, once the trust and harmony of a relationship is broken, regaining the customer's patronage may be extremely difficult. The implications for the supplier of differences in buyer behavioural styles are clear. It is critical to identify the

Transactions ———— Relationships
orientation   orientation

Figure 5.1 *The customer buying orientations continuum*

buyer's orientation and to allocate resources so as to manage the selling approach accordingly.

Practical tip

Research the customer's buying orientations and allocate resources to manage the selling/marketing approach to fit it. Once a profitable relationship is established with a key account do all that is necessary to sustain it. Never break the customer's trust of there may be no way back.

Indications of a customer's buying attitude can be obtained from various considerations:

- *How strategic are your products to your customer's business?* Does your company supply paper clips and envelopes or computer mainframes or bespoke components to a robotic just-in-time production line?
- *What is the customer's generic attitude to suppliers?* Where are they positioned along the continuum in Figure 5.1? What are the influences on them from the end user or consumer?
- *Does the customer face high switching costs?* Is it risky and costly for the buyer to change suppliers and do your firm's offerings provide superior benefits? If not the customer may be able to play-off your firm against rivals.
- *Does your firm offer a bundle of products and services?* Products are easy to copy but sustainable superiority can often be

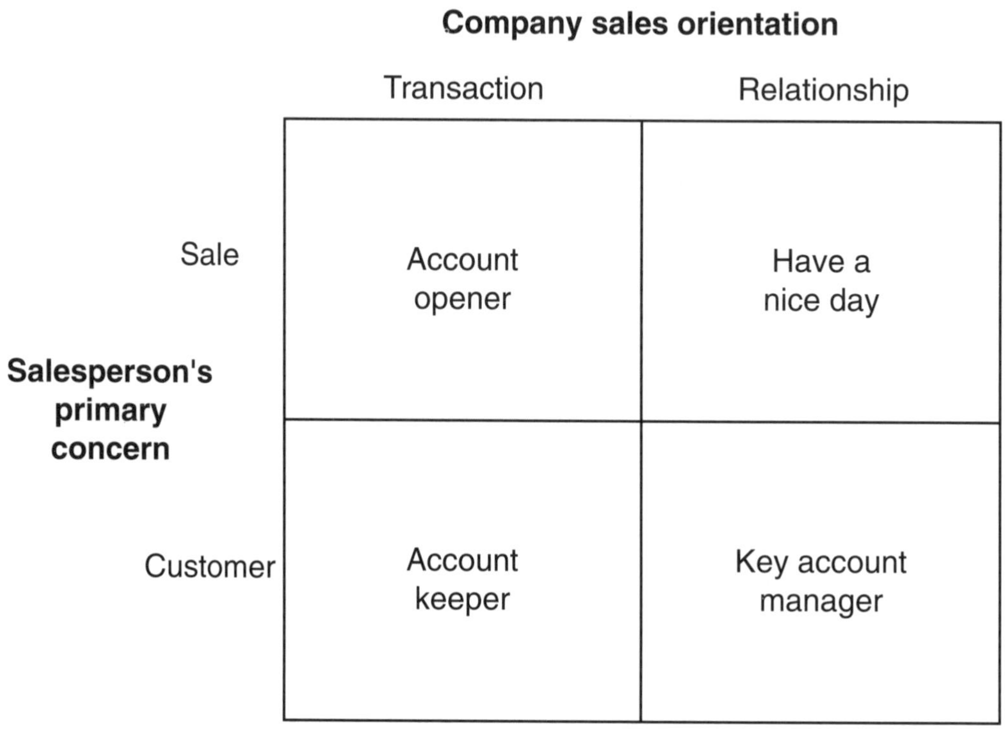

Company sales orientation

	Transaction	Relationship
Sale	Account opener	Have a nice day
Customer	Account keeper	Key account manager

Salesperson's primary concern

Figure 5.2 *Supplier sales and marketing approaches*

Example One

A supplier of industrial cleaning materials was serving catering and hotel chains populated by well trained and enthusiastic buyers. The supplier realized that its products were little different from those of its rivals. Their response was to redefine their product range and introduce a range of cleaning systems tailored to the context in which the products would be used. For example their hotel products were supplied in bulk containers from which the cleaning staff could fill hand-held spray applicators. All the dispensing and application equipment was designed for ease of use and made from durable, high quality materials. The products were carefully designed to meet the precise needs of the cleaning staff. For example there were air fresheners for hotel rooms used by smokers.

In addition the supplier provided staff training on room cleaning and product use. This was very popular in an industry where training is scant. They also innovated in the area of pricing by offering to charge either on a per unit of product basis or on a per room basis. Occupancy is a critical profit factor in the hotel trade and the opportunity to treat room servicing as a variable cost was very attractive.

Finally the supplier guaranteed reliable delivery to avoid stock outs and the whole relationship was managed by a key account manager whose primary concern was the satisfaction of the customer.

achieved by augmenting them with distinctive services tailored to the customer's needs. Outstanding service is difficult to imitate as rivals usually need to adapt their organizations, which takes time and resources. Examples of service differentiation include small batch production, ultra reliable delivery, highly effective after sales service, market research updates, staff training, integrated ordering and payment systems, problem solving facilities and a keep in touch service.

Suitability of the supplier's sales approach

A range of generic sales/marketing approaches exist for suppliers to select from.

These are summarized in Figure 5.2 which shows the sales and marketing approach on the horizontal axis and the salesperson's primary concern on the vertical axis. The transaction orientation (preference for a series of one-off sales) versus the relationship orientation (preference for a long term arrangement of mutual gain) was discussed above in the context of the customer. The concern of the salesperson is typically positioned along a continuum running from concern for gaining the sale to concern for managing the well-being of the customer. The salesperson's style will be influenced by the firm's orientation. For example, the latter will reflect the culture and the ethos of the company and the methods and criteria for salesforce leadership, evaluation, motivation and rewards. The four generic approaches illustrated in Figure 5.2 are now discussed.

Account opener approach

This option is common among firms that sell a product once or very seldomly to each of many different customers. For example, a double glazing sales representative and his/her company relies on a continuous supply of cold calls which can be rapidly qualified, in the classic 'six steps of selling' approach, and hopefully converted into sales. Such a high transaction focus by the company and concern for the sale by the representative renders a key account management approach unnecessary and inappropriate.

Have a nice day approach

Here the company is seeking to build repeat sales via relationships but fails to ensure its salespeople demonstrate sufficient genuine customer care. For example, it is a common occurrence when checking out of a hotel to be wished 'have a nice day' or 'have a safe trip' by an often patently bored and distracted receptionist. This is meant to indicate concern for the relationship with their guest. However, the observant guest will also often notice that the receptionist's body language is screaming 'thank goodness they've gone, now we can get down to the important work or have a cup of coffee'. This signifies that the real concern is to conclude the transaction. Firms with these kinds of problems clearly need to address their staff (salesforce) problems and perhaps restructure their organizations before they can hope to implement an effective key account management programme.

Account keeper approach

This approach characterizes situations in which the salesperson perceives value in building ongoing business through customer relationships but where his/her company does not recognize the benefits of this and consequently fails to provide sufficient support.

The salesperson utilizes personal talents, handles complaints well and is generally helpful so as to build personal relationships with customer personnel. However, concerned about individual transactions and the costs and/or profitability thereof, the company offers too little cross-functional back-up to allow the salesperson to create a company-to-company relationship which is prerequisite to an effective key account management process.

Key account manager approach

Here the salesperson attaches great importance to both providing ongoing high level customer satisfaction and to achieving the objectives of the company. Moreover, since the company is orientated to prosper in a situation of mutual gain with its customers, it provides the cross-functional support and adequate resources needed for the key account manager to succeed.

Amplification of this approach is provided below. However, it should also be noted that relationship marketing is never easy in a tough and changing business world as Example Two illustrates.

Skills of the key account manager

Changes in the personnel fulfilling the role of the account manager is one of the main reasons why firms lose key accounts. For example, one highly competent and popular manager in the hand tools business has been poached by several successive employers to obtain the accounts that follow him when he moves. The role of the manager is thus vital and involves several major responsibilities including:

- managing customer satisfaction
- co-ordinating the offering
- facilitating the relationship between customer and supplier
- promoting the customer's interest within the supplier's organization.

The manager takes a lead role in the selling

Example Two

The Ford Motor Company recently announced that it would be reducing the number of its suppliers. Hence, a high priority of these suppliers would be to remain on the list. At the same time Ford announced that it would be working with suppliers to hold current price levels for the next five years. Adoption of a key account management programme and retaining Ford's business in these difficult circumstances for suppliers is unlikely to remove the problems, but at least it may enable them to continue – which is perhaps preferable to being delisted!

process. However, a critical responsibility is to establish and maintain a harmonious and mutually beneficial relationship between his company and the customer. Traditionally, buyer–seller relationships were managed as illustrated in Figure 5.3 (left) with inter-firm contact occurring almost exclusively between the supplier's sales manager and the cus-tomer's purchasing manager and each attempting to out-negotiate the other. Effective exponents of the modern key account management approach, however, manage the dyad relationship with multi-functional levels of interaction involving the various relevant functions of both organiza-tions as shown in Figure 5.3 (right).

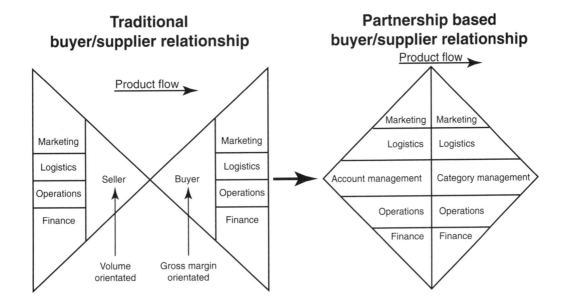

Figure 5.3 Buyer–supplier relationships

To make this happen, the manager must ensure that functional specialists within his or her own firm are motivated and able to interact with their counterparts in the customer organization. This requires that the manager has a diverse set of high level skills and with the nature of the internal responsibilities it has major implications concerning relative job status, reporting relationships, remuneration and career development.

As a baseline the manager needs to have a high level of commercial skills, technical competence in the products of the firm and deep knowledge of customer needs, competitors and the industry. A substantial difficulty for many account managers is that often their multi-functional colleagues do not recognize the need for them to interact with customer personnel. They perceive sales and marketing as being none of their business and resist being involved in them. Hence, the account manager requires internal credibility and the authority to drive multi-functional involvement with customers. Similarly, managing the interface between the two organizations calls for considerable interpersonal and communicatio skills. Without this extensive range of skills, it is unlikely that any company can operate a key account management system effectively.

Practical tip

Select, train and support qualified people for the key account manager role. Ensure they possess finely-tuned commercial skills, products, customer and market knowledge, interpersonal skills and communication talents. Empower them to drive cross-functional participation in customer interaction and reward them appropriately for the difficult and demanding duties they perform.

The key account management process

When a key account management (KAM) approach is considered appropriate and feasible it is necessary to assess the actual process involved. Not all buyer–seller relationships are at a stage where systems are fully integrated, staff contributing positively at all levels and highly skilled managers in place. The dyad relationship needs to be built over time. A process through which this can be achieved is illustrated in the relational development model in Table 5.1. This indicates that various stages of a relationship can be identified and that each has characteristic features. Actively managing this process enables selected accounts to be managed from a simple transactional relationship through to a synergistic one.

The pre-KAM stage

Here the two firms are at the very start of a relationship and each will be assessing the opportunities according to their own criteria. Since a key account is by definition of strategic importance to the seller's business, it is at this stage that the supplier is scrutinizing the potential payoff from forming a relationship. Similarly, the buyer will be evaluating the supplier's offering and comparing its value to that being offered by competitors. It is important at this stage that both firms recognize that the benefits of forming a strategic relationship outweigh those of a transactional approach to trade. Personal relationships are also founded at this stage and these are critical for future progress and success.

Early KAM

At this stage the supplier has gained some of the customer's business although it is likely that the latter will still be multiple-sourcing. However, the account manager can now

Table 5.1 *Stages in buyer/seller relationships*

Pre-KAM	Early KAM	Mid-KAM	Partnership KAM	Synergistic KAM	Uncoupling KAM
Product need established	Transactions commence	Selling company now one of a few 'preferred suppliers'	Selling company is now in partnership with buying company	'Quasi-integration' – selling company and buying company together deliver value to the end customer	Relationship disintegrates or product fails to keep up with the market
Buying company scrutinize price and other terms	Key account manager/key contact relationship strengthens	Operational staff get to know their opposite numbers	Contacts at all levels	Focus teams at all interfaces between supplier and customer	
Key account manager's focus is to establish relationship	Key account manager working to increase volume of business	Key account manager working to establish distinctive advantage	Key account manager looks for opportunities for process integration	Key account manager is co-ordinating large matrix team	

start to exert more influence by pointing out the benefits to the buyer of a single point of contact. He/she must though be seen to have the internal status and authority to pursue the customer's interests internally. It is also important to be providing a seamless delivery of product and service. Also at this stage volume begins to grow and the customer will be closely monitoring the supplier's performance so that problems need to be avoided and rapidly corrected. The producer should also be searching for ways to customize the offering or to otherwise establish irresistible differential advantage. The account manager will be striving to establish credibility with the customer, to deepen personal relationships with the customer's staff and encouraging functional specialists within his/her own firm to do the same.

Mid-KAM

By now the supplier is one of a very few preferred sources for the product. Trust has been established, especially with the account manager, and there are a range of contacts on each side communicating regularly. The relationship may even extend to social functions which help to deepen contacts across the two organizations.

While there is an assumption of continuing business, the buyer may still be sharing equally good relations with other suppliers. Hence, the manager and the company will be striving to 'go the extra mile' to win clear preference to progress to the next stage.

Partnership KAM

The relationship has now matured and the supplier is a trusted key external strategic resource to the buyer. This will be evident in various ways. For example, joint product development, sharing of sensitive information, mutual training of the other firm's personnel and joint market research programmes.

The relationship will be mutually acknowledged as a long term one, supported by agreement on prices for example. There is typically co-operation on long term projects and special arrangements to cater for unique circumstances such as product shortages and new product introductions. Often there is a close integration of systems to remove mundane paperwork. Other routine aspects of the relationship, previously the subject of internal scrutiny, will be allowed to run themselves in the knowledge that they are being well managed.

Overall, there is a positive spirit in the relationship and mutual commitment to it. An important task of the account manager is to

reinforce the prevailing high levels of trust to freeze out potential rivals.

Synergistic KAM

There is now a highly involved relationship between the two firms and breaking it is likely to be both difficult and traumatic. There is extensive joint working from the two boardrooms downward. Planning systems are closely integrated and staff from the two organizations work so closely together that boundaries are often not discernible. Joint teams are deciding mutual objectives and priorities in delivering distinctive value to the customer's customers. Unnecessary costs are being driven out of the system and product and process improvements are sought mutually. However, the supplier must ensure that its contribution to the end product is clearly understood by end cus-

Example Three

A producer of fresh produce had been a supplier for many years to a processing company which in turn supplied some of the big high street retailers. Quality, consistency and assurance of supply were important factors in the relationship. The Food Safety Act increased the requirements for traceability and demonstrable commitment to hygiene and high standards in all aspects of the process.

The buyer and supplier responded to this by reviewing together all aspects of their business. This resulted in a long term pricing agreement which removed the uncertainties of the notorious cyclicality associated with some foodstuffs; profitability was shared rather than competed for in frequent pricing discussions. In addition, a computerized batch tracing system was installed which spanned both the supplier's and buyer's system and provided the evidence and security required by retailers. Also an EDI (electronic data interchange) system was installed which removed much unnecessary paperwork. Payment terms were agreed and then automatically handled by the system. Invoicing was also automated with routine checking of invoices against suppliers' dispatch notes. The accounting system was then left to run itself, resulting in a substantial reduction in paperwork and administration.

tomers or risk the brand equity that is rightfully attributable to itself inadvertently passing to the buyer.

Uncoupling KAM

It is always possible for a strategic relationship to deteriorate and end. Price conflicts are often blamed although at root the cause is usually a breakdown in personal relationships. One of the most common problems is that the key account manager leaves the supplier, retires or dies. Changes in staff more generally can also result in attitudinal or personal incompatibilities. Then behavioural changes are sometimes seen as breaches of trust which can lead to rapid erosion of the relationship which may be very difficult to recover from.

Changes in the market place and business environment can also lead to a breakdown of relationships. For example, the customer may lose its strategic value to the supplier as a result of financial problems, image lapses or loss of market share. Similarly, the customer may decide to terminate the relationship if through complacency the supplier began to consistently fail to meet delivery, quality or service requirements.

Motives for key account management

This section outlines some of the obstacles to and benefits of developing key account relationships from the perspectives of both suppliers and buyers.

Example Four

As part of the industry rationalization which was taking place at the time, one large engineering group acquired another. Each was supplied with lubricants by a different supplier and each supplier had a long standing relationship with their buyer.

The merged companies went through a rigorous process of rationalization and product range alignment. Each lubricant supplier maintained their contacts within the evolving new organization. Eventually issues of structure rose to the top of the agenda and functions were merged and redefined. The new structure was dominated by staff from the acquiring company. Whilst they entered into a process of supplier evaluation, the supplier to the acquiring company was informally assured that they were the preferred supplier to the new organization, providing that price and other factors were satisfactory.

Their competitor recognized that their contacts had been removed in the restructuring and sought to retain the account by offering an exceptionally attractive price.

The net result was that the preferred supplier retained the business but at a much reduced price. Their competitor offered increasingly attractive prices and this encouraged the buying team to adopt a transactional approach to the new circumstances in which they found themselves, and used this as a one-off opportunity to exercise their increased buying power.

The competing supplier had different objectives from the company that retained the business and this in turn influenced the buyer to focus on price.

Practical tip

Select your key account targets and then work enthusiastically through the key account management process to establish a synergistic relationship for the account security and other benefits it can provide. Guard against becoming a less attractive partner for the customer but remain alert to market or other changes which decrease the customer's strategic attractiveness to your firm. Be willing to withdraw from the relationship when its attractiveness diminishes irreparably below your tolerance level.

From the seller's perspective _____

One of the main obstacles encountered by sellers attempting to establish key account relationships is the buyer's short term focus on price. Sellers are often frustrated by buyers' refusal or inability to consider the longer term and wider dimensions of a potential relationship. Without some degree of appreciation and commitment by the buyer, how-ever, the seller's endeavours may come to nothing.

The seller's major motives to found key account relationships centre on improving market share, increasing profitability and strengthening customer loyalty and so assurance of the business. These benefits arise in several ways:

Customer retention

Sustaining an ongoing relationship is far less costly than winning new accounts since it avoids all the costs of identifying, pitching to and converting unfamiliar customers. Further, tight integration between the buyer and the seller strengthen security from competitor attack and particularly from short term price rivalry.

Increased account penetration

As a trusted supplier of proven reliability there is strong potential to supply additional products on a range-sell basis. Alternatively, there may be opportunities to sell into other parts of the customer's organization such as another division or an overseas branch. The key account managers will be alert to opportunities such as these and can drive the

---

Example Five

A major supplier of chemical acts as an intermediary to a manufacturer of pharmaceutical products. Discussions with the buying director revealed that a major end user was located near the intermediate supplier's factory. This suggested the opportunity to backload delivery vehicles with raw materials and in addition rationalizing to full pallet and lorry loads as part of the agreement. This, together with improvements and demand forecasting, eased production scheduling. The real savings which arose led to a collection discount for the purchaser and efficiency savings for the supplier.

process by asking for introductions and recommendations and by making suitable products available.

Improved value

This can be achieved either by reducing costs and sharing the benefits or by delivering higher perceived benefits at the same cost to the buyer. There is likely to be a learning curve effect as the organizations and their staff gain experience and then actively cooperate to improve value (see Example Five).

Increased competitive capability

The key account supplier enjoys competitive benefits aside from those arising out of continuous efforts to drive customer costs down and benefits up. The 'inside track' position it occupies provides the suppliers with access to new opportunities within the account not available to outsider-competitors. Also, a satisfied customer can act as a reference to other potential accounts, particularly when the customer is the market leader. For example, many suppliers prize their relationships with Marks and Spencer for this reason.

From the buyer's perspective

Buyers committed to the process of key account management with suppliers understand that it takes time to adapt and change. In seeking to develop a new understanding with suppliers buyers have found that, despite their patience, sellers are slow to adapt. The early indicators already discussed, primary contact staff and administrative systems, are seen as bellwethers of future success of this new strategic direction. At this stage buyers are likely to decide with whom they can work in the future. Particular factors which are likely to indicate a shift to a relationship approach are all underlaid with profit improvement in mind. They include:

Outsourcing

The buyer deliberately selects areas which are strategic to the business as a basis for future partnership arrangements. Those areas not regarded as strategic can then continue to be handled in house or outsourced. If the buyer believes that they have no distinctive competence in such areas as building maintenance, catering, etc., these can be quickly and easily outsourced and typically this is done. There has also been a strong move to the outsourcing of computer services. Critical considerations here are the cost and complexity of the resource and the tendency of these two characteristics to rise alarmingly. However, the argument for outsourcing is not always straightforward as many businesses, particularly in the service sector, rely on their systems as a source of competitive advantage. Outsourcing in these circumstances may indicate lack of clear strategic planning.

Downsizing

This is a common contemporary approach to achieving major cost reductions, usually by reducing the scale of fixed capacity. When this is combined with outsourcing from a strategic supplier it enables the same volumes to be produced as previously but with lower average costs (see Example Six).

Economies of scale

Many producers are striving to achieve greater economies of scale by, for example, holding larger or highly specialized factories or by pursuing global strategies. This has raised new difficulties for their suppliers to meet highly specialized requirements and the number of suppliers that can reach higher levels of performance is constrained, perhaps even declining in some industries. Hence, when customers find reliable suppliers it is strongly in their interests to enter into key account relationships with them.

Realizing the benefits of KAM

If key account management is to be successful as a strategy then there are a number of critical features to bear in mind.

Example Six

A major European airline used to monitor a fleet of aeroplanes that was sufficient to meet high level summer demand. A problem was that such aeroplane capacity was left grounded during off-peak periods, particularly during the winter months. Hence, the airline carried very high average fixed costs, that were not giving a constant return. The solution was to downsize the fleet to meet high level winter demand and then lease sufficient aeroplanes to meet summer demand from a South American airline. The happy outcome of this strategic relationship is that the South American line generates revenue in its winter from aeroplanes that would otherwise be grounded and the European airline enjoys much lower average costs.

- **Process** – KAM is a process involving not just the sales team but all those with appropriate and relevant skills and knowledge to contribute to the satisfaction of the customer and increasing the value delivered.
- **Output** – The output of the process is an enhanced relationship with the customer giving higher satisfaction and better value to the buyer and higher levels of customer loyalty to the supplier. Ultimately the supplier increases their competitive advantage relative to other potential suppliers and increases the quality of their market share.
- **Staff** – The key account manager is the driver of the process, responsible for co-ordinating input to the customer and managing colleagues internally to deliver what is required of them. In addition the key account manager will have the primary responsibility for sales, and will almost certainly be responsible for revenue and perhaps profitability. A high level of skills and capabilities are required. Obviously a high level of sales skills and the ability to operate at a senior level is needed, but so also is good technical knowledge to give

credibility and act as the genuine first point of reference. Additionally good interpersonal skills are needed not least to manage across the supplier's functions and co-ordinate and at times cajole colleagues and their contribution.
- **Responsibility and reward** – The key account manager requires a daunting list of attributes. Such staff are difficult to find and develop and almost certainly attractive to competitors. Their remuneration, status, reporting relationship and authority all pose challenges to the organization. This is particularly so where the change is dramatic rather than gradual, and people are required to take higher levels of responsibility and work more independently in a business staffed with fewer, better people. The reality is that a high proportion of key accounts are lost due to changes in staff and the disruption of relationships, both on the buyer and seller side.
- **Product quality** – No matter how good and comprehensive the level of service given to the buyer, fundamental problems with the quality of the product cannot be compensated for. High levels of reliability

and quality are an essential precursor for the success of key account management.

- **Company culture** – Key account management means that high levels of responsibility are devolved within the organization and that managers have authority to act as they judge appropriate in the light of circumstances. The organization must not only be prepared to allow this to happen but must act to encourage and support managers through the process.

Summary

Conventional selling philosophy emphasizes the confrontational nature of the buyer/seller relationship. There are driving forces which suggest that a mutually beneficial approach can work and should be adopted, based on partnership and enduring relations rather than a series of discrete sales. Recent research has shown the steps involved in the process as the relationship develops and the critical factors at each stage.

Buyers are having to adapt their businesses in response to the competitive environment. Working with fewer, better suppliers brings benefits to the business and releases management time and resource to focus to customer facing issues. Equally such a policy limits the number of potential suppliers to the business. Suppliers see themselves being squeezed by increasingly short term pricing pressures and recognize that adding value by improving service rather than reducing price is a better alternative.

Key account management is a process which provides a route map as to how increasingly more productive relationships can be achieved. Fundamental to this is the role of the key account manager. Such people require a comprehensive list of professional, technical and interpersonal skills and have a high level of responsibility. In return they need training to maintain and compensate for skill gaps, appropriate and probably high levels of reward as well as status and authority in the organization.

Such combinations of skills are rare enough and it is unlikely that those possessing them are going to undervalue themselves in the marketplace. This begs the difficult question of managing career expectations against the requirement to maintain continuity of contact. Changes in personnel are one of the major reason for account decoupling.

The underlying motivation is improved profitability as well as security of business and quality of market share. Key account management represents a stepwise and important change in the way that buyers and sellers respond to each other.

References

Jackson, B. (1985) Build Customer Relationships That Last, *Harvard Business Review*, **63**, Nov–Dec, pp. 120–28.

McDonald, M.H.B, Millman, A.F. and Rogers, E. (1996) *Key Account Management: Learning form Suppliers and Customer Perspectives.* Cranfield School of Management.

Miller, R.B., Heiman, S.E. and Tuleja, T. (1988) *Strategic Selling: Secrets of the Complex Sale.* Kogan Page.

Payne, A.F.T. (ed.) (1995) *Advances in Relationship Marketing.* Kogan Page.

6

Trade marketing ———————————————————

Belinda Dewsnap, Loughborough University Business School

 The objective of this chapter is to show how trade marketing can help companies achieve both customer and brand objectives.

Whilst it is written from the angle of the manufacturer supplying branded goods to the retail trade, its content should be of interest to anyone keen to know more about new ways to manage trading relationships.

The questions we shall explore are: What is trade marketing? Why is it needed? What is the trade marketing process? How should the infrastructure for trade marketing be built?

What is trade marketing? ▬▬▬▬

Trade marketing is essentially the application of fundamental marketing principles to the trade customer. It involves understanding and satisfying trade customer needs.

In practical terms trade marketing translates into the need to focus on:

1. Building and maintaining strong brands.
2. Delivering superior levels of customer service to the retailer.

Whilst we shall see how manufacturers are setting up trade marketing – variously called customer marketing, category management, trade planning, as well as trade marketing – our focus will be about trade marketing as *a way of doing business*, rather than as a function or department. Thus heavy attention is paid to what needs to be done in the trade marketing approach, and it is not until the final section on infrastructure that the we address the issue of assigning tasks to roles and departments.

Why do we need trade marketing?

...if the retailer won't put the product on the shelf, then it doesn't matter how well designed the box is. (Bidlake, 1990)

Previously, mass marketing to the consumer and the resulting consumer demand was sufficient leverage to gain stocking by retailers. The trading environment has now changed on a range of fronts which means that this approach is no longer appropriate: it is now vital to *market to* the intermediary customer as well to the consumer. The factors driving companies to adopt a trade marketing approach are interrelated and can be grouped under the three headings shown in Figure 6.1.

Trade

The sum of the trade-related factors driving trade marketing is *trade strength* and intense *inter-retailer competition*. It is strength gained both on the basis of trade concentration, where responsibility for retail buying is in the hands of a decreasing number of retailers, and on the basis of an ever-increasing sophistication in retail management practices. At a time when manufacturers had the information and marketing edge with respect to the consumer, retailers were very receptive to advice on which products to stock. This is no longer the case. Major retailers now have information and have become proficient marketers. This shift of power away from manufacturers is most marked in the UK grocery trade. Competition between major retailers drives the need for differentiation of their entire retail offering – their image, their service, their merchandising and their marketing.

Let us further explore the sources of trade strength and the differentiation strategies they have available to them.

Knowledge is power

Scanning technology (EPOS) delivers to retailers immense amounts of information on the consumer, and on the impact of all merchandising and marketing variables. In addition, as manufacturers' ability to mass-deliver brand messages to consumers decreases, so more and more product decisions will be made in store. Not only does the retailer have the *information* to target consumers but also the vehicle to execute the marketing.

Direct product profitability (DPP) systems mean that retailers know better than ever before the profitability of each individual stock item, and this is information which is key to their product stocking decisions.

Space planning systems in conjunction with EPOS and DPP have given retailers the ability to achieve optimal allocation of valuable shelf space.

Finally, technology is also allowing retailers to focus on managing whole product categories, rather than individual products, and is even allowing them to pre-test the effects of product-mix, pricing and promotion before implementing any changes.

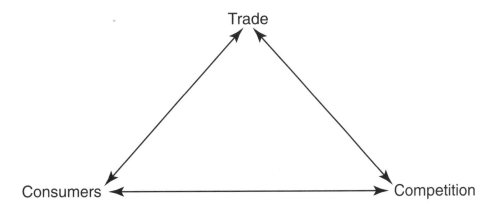

Figure 6.1 TCC triangle

Increased professionalism

Retail management is altogether more sophisticated. The calibre of staff has improved greatly – some are even imports from manufacturing companies. Furthermore retail managers receive training in all areas of business to enable them to become all-round business managers. Not only does the 'trade', then, now have more understanding of everything consumer-related, it also has a better understanding of how to deal with manufacturers.

Competition and the need to differentiate

In the face of intense competition retailers have to adopt a differentiation strategy. Retail businesses are now effectively huge branded businesses. Differentiation is based on store image, product assortment, the way products are merchandised and promoted, and the service which is given. Importantly for manufacturers to observe, own label products are a part of this retailer differentiation strategy. Inter-retailer competition also drives the need to optimize operational efficiencies throughout the entire supply chain.

Consumers

Consumers are more sophisticated. They view themselves very much as individuals and not part of a mass market. As a result markets are undergoing more segmentation. This presents additional challenges for consumer marketing by manufacturers and increases their need for consumer information.

Consumers are less influenced by mass advertising and less brand loyal. They are also more value-conscious. All of these factors explain the increase in 'repertoire buying' and share of own label.

Media effectiveness overall is reduced. Fragmentation of audiences across an increasing array of media makes it difficult to reach a mass audience. And as the productivity of each advertising pound declines, so the manufacturer focuses more resources on communicating *in store* by way of trade and consumer promotions. This in itself may be behind the trend for consumers to be more price- and deal-conscious.

In terms of lifestyles and shopping habits the reduction in consumer shopping trips made constitutes a significant decrease for both manufacturers and retailers in the number of opportunities they have to influence consumers.

Competition

As product ranges expand and diversify so the pressure on shelf space becomes more intense. This naturally intensifies the competition between suppliers to deliver the products and customer service which retailers want.

All of the above factors combine to make the traditional way of using the trade customer – as nothing more than the manufacturer's distribution arm – obsolete. Manufacturers must now market *to* retailers in order to gain shelf space, and more often than not, alongside own label products.

This puts increased emphasis on co-ordinating brand and customer strategies. Criticism by retailers of the lack of communication between brand marketing and account handlers is common. There is equal criticism of each other internally; of brand marketing for their ivory-tower lack of knowledge of commercial realities, and of account handlers for their over-attendance to the trade at the expense of the brand. This further explains the re-organization of the approach to sales and marketing and the emergence of 'trade marketing'.

The trade marketing process

To re-state our opening definition, trade marketing is a process of understanding and satisfying trade customer needs. For the brand manufacturer, however, it is not possible to separate brand and trade, which is why we underline the need for a strategy focused on brand and customer service. Trade-focused and brand-focused managers work together to achieve brand and customer goals.

Let us now look at the brand component of the trade marketing approach.

Building and maintaining brand equity

The challenge overall for manufacturers is to develop the effective merchandising and promotion of products at the level of individual retailers while at the same time building brand equity on a national level.

What we shall examine here is the importance of brands to both retailers and manufacturers and how, notwithstanding substantial threats from declining brand loyalty and the increase in the share of own label, the case in favour of building brands is still very strong.

The longevity of really big brands – Kelloggs, Gillette, Mars, Colgate, Heinz – together with their strength in global markets indicates that strong brands really are wanted by consumers. More importantly for the trade marketing approach, retailers want successful brands because brands with high market share deliver them more profit.

The following facts presented by Doyle (1989) reveal why manufacturers should still focus on building successful brands:

- Products with a market share of 40% generate three times the return on investment than those with a market share of only 10%.
- The number one UK grocery brand generates over six times the return on sales than the number two brand, while the number three and four brands are totally unprofitable.

Financial returns are also, Doyle reports, the reward for manufacturers who invest in achieving perceived brand quality:

- Brands with high perceived quality earned double the return on investment and return on sales of low quality brands.

His advice in terms of overall strategy for delivering growth and profitability is one based on brand differentiation rather than cost and price. In theory the best strategy is low cost and high differentiation but it is beneficial to trade some cost savings in order to achieve very strong differentiation.

As a plan of action this translates into a need for substantial investment in innovation, quality, service and the development and maintenance of brand imagery.

With respect to innovation manufacturers have the headstart over retailers, and continual investment in innovation will ensure they maintain the competitive advantage.

As evidenced by the increased share of own label, consumers have become less willing to pay a premium for brands in cases where brand imagery is either less important or less well-established. This underlines the need for investment in brand values, particularly for brands with established personalities. Manufacturer marketing spend patterns over recent years, however, do not reflect this way of thinking. Their meeting of retailer demands for increases in trade promotion leads to cuts in consumer advertising which give rise to concerns about the long term effects on brand equity. Whereas advertising builds long term profitability through image differentiation, it is felt that promotion, by its focus on price and discounts, only serves to weaken brand values. Yet in an era where the stakes for individual accountability in business are ever higher, it is far easier to justify the increased spend in promotion where the effects are more easily measurable (e.g. by EPOS) than those of advertising. So the tactic to reduce advertising is understandable but is not in line with our key trade marketing thrust to build and maintain strong brands. Advertising is essential if manufacturers are to be able to communicate their brand's unique benefits and to position their brand's values to appeal to target customers.

Addressing the brand/trade balance with respect to deployment of marketing resources is a key concern for manufacturers. To protect brand image and deliver customer service requires a partnership approach between customer-facing and brand personnel, and the ideal process involves the simultaneous development of brand and customer plans and the continuous flow of consumer and customer information between the two. These operational facets are central to trade marketing success.

To understand how brands fit a retailer's strategy and objectives, the manufacturer must understand their wider needs as a customer.

Understanding and responding to customer needs

The fundamental question for a manufacturer ... is changing from 'How do I drive my own profits? to 'How do I drive my retailers' profits?'
(Weisz, 1994)

Co-operation and close working relationships with retailers are essential for trade marketing. A total understanding of the retailer's business will enable the manufacturer to help the retailer achieve its objectives, to capitalize on its opportunities and to provide support for the challenges it faces. Furthermore, empathy demonstrated in this way by a supplier drives an even stronger bond of co-operation between the two.

The three essential elements to be addressed are:

1. Understanding the retailer's business.
2. Knowing the people to influence.
3. Being clear about how the retailer rates the manufacturer's performance.

Understanding the retailer's business

Delivering against retailer needs requires gaining an objective and detailed understanding of:

- The company's strategies and objectives.
- How the business works across all functions?
- Its strengths, weaknesses, opportunities, threats.
- Its use of technology and information.
- Category management practices.

Much of the intelligence a company gains on its customer will be from the salesforce and from any other parts of the company which have a regular dialogue with the customer. Published reports such as the 'Account Management Series' from the Institute of Grocery Distribution (IGD) represent an important and objective source of information on major retail customers and are useful to retailers and manufacturers alike.

Areas covered by a typical report would be:

- Market share data.
- Grocery industry challenges and the company's response.
- Strategy – what differentiates the company from its competitors?
- Financial analysis.
- Store operations – geographical locations, new store openings, closures.
- The buying function – department structure, performance criteria, category management, range development and NPD, merchandising, systems.
- Marketing – customer profiles, pricing and promotion strategies, customer services.
- Distribution – policies, systems, depot locations.

The company's strategies and objectives

The key facets of a retailer's strategy and its long term objectives will determine the framework for the relationships with its suppliers. For the purpose of trade marketing it is useful to view a retailer's strategy from the perspectives of its overall market positioning, its merchandising and its policy with respect to own label products.

Market positioning in retail will be based on factors which it is felt clearly distinguish the retailer from competing retail operations. Positioning could be based on the products sold: for instance a retailer may enjoy a reputation for breadth of range, for speciality products, for own label, and so on. Equally its reputation could be based on low price, on store layout, the helpfulness of its staff or indeed on any other elements of its service to customers.

> ### Practical tip
>
> Important questions for consideration are, what is the retailer trying to achieve with its product range and merchandising: is it endeavouring to present a value-for-money image or trying to move 'up market'? Which products or product categories are to be the image builders, the traffic builders, the profit builders?

Knowing the trade customer's positioning strategy will enable a manufacturer to understand where *its* products could, or do, fit the retailer's strategy and objectives. Its usefulness would extend from providing an input to new product development plans, to developing tailored promotions, right down to the sales presentation itself in terms of influencing the kind of products offered and the selling arguments developed.

Merchandising strategy is built on positioning strategy and encompasses issues of what products to stock, how to display them and how to promote them. Knowing this strategy enables a better targeting of a manufacturer's entire marketing mix. Deriving from merchandising strategy will be actual merchandising policies which will set out, for example, how often shelves are to be refilled. Shelf refill policy itself has implications for packaging size and configuration and therefore directly impacts the manufacturer. Furthermore merchandising policies constitute a critical input to space planning systems. The manufacturer which takes the time and trouble to fully understand its customer's merchandising ethos and operations will be in a position once again to meet the retailer's needs for the right product in the right packaging and supported with the right promotion.

In the grocery sector *own label* became important in the 1980s when supermarkets were competing mainly on price. Own labels were used as part of this strategy. In most cases they were a slightly inferior version of the leading brand, sold at a lower price and with packaging to reflect this positioning. Now own label competes as an equal with manufacturers' brands, and many have to be viewed as brands in their own right.

A knowledge of the retailer's strategy with respect to own label would allow a positioning of manufacturers' brands within this context. In a fiercely competitive retail environment the benefits of own label to retailers can be:

1. a means of *differentiating* themselves from competition – a tool to build store image and store loyalty;
2. a source of higher margins;
3. a way of offering price promotion to attract and keep customers.

Over and above being aware of own label strategy and the potential competitor status of own label, the manufacturer needs to decide whether or not manufacturing own label for a particular retailer is to be a part of delivering what that customer wants. Manufacturers such as Kelloggs whose policy is strongly against manufacturing own label continue to gain shelf space for their strong brands. So how should a manufacturer decide its approach?

This will not only depend on the manufacturer's corporate mission and strategy, but will also be driven by more commercial and practical realities. The checklist could look something like the one shown in Checklist 6.1.

How the business works across all functions

It is important that anyone who manages a trading relationship with retailers has a working knowledge of the different retail functions; how the retail operation works and its key measures of performance. This extends to making sure that the inter-company relationships extend beyond the interface of buyers and sellers. The wider role of the account handler is to bring together from both sides experts in other functions, for example, logistics, systems and finance, who will work together to jointly explore opportu-

**Checklist 6.1
To manufacturer own label or not?**

- Are our brands strong enough to hold up against the brand leaders and own label? It is now widely accepted that brands below second position in the category will be delisted.
- Do we have a profit and sales gap which cannot be filled with new brands, and do we have the ability anyway to develop viable new brands?
- Do we have excess production capacity above industry norms?
- Do we have the skills to make own label and to do so profitably?

nities and address challenges across the whole supply chain.

Strengths, weaknesses, opportunities, threats

Published data as discussed earlier, together with information gained from personal contact, will provide a sound database from which to produce a SWOT on each retailer customer.

Gaining an awareness of the major threats facing the retailer will, if it were needed, help to explain many of the demands placed on the manufacturer by the retailer. For leading edge suppliers this knowledge also delivers scope for proactively offering support and sharing resources.

Let us examine the most major threats faced by retailers.

- **Competition** between retailers has been identified as the factor driving attempts at differentiation of the entire retail offering. Competition derives from existing retailers, from new forms of retailing (for example warehouse clubs) and from new entrants from abroad (for example discount operations such as Netto and Aldi). Where possible the manufacturer's marketing mix should be tailored to support the retailer in all of its differentiation efforts.

  The tailoring of promotions, from the

type of promotional packaging used, to promotional pricing, to devising promotions complementary with retailer own brands, is just one opportunity to meet retailer needs. Merchandising policies represent another important source of differentiation for the retailer, and for the manufacturer they provide the opportunity to proactively share technology and space planning expertise. Manufacturing own label presents a clear opportunity for a manufacturer to contribute to differentiation attempts. Service will undoubtedly form a part of the focus for competitive advantage, and again the manufacturer has a key role to play. Keeping products in stock whilst at the same time minimizing inventories demands that the manufacturer becomes proficient in supply chain management, and seeks to capitalize on any opportunity which exists to improve supply chain performance with a retailer.

- **Financial market** pressure for consistently high price/earnings ratios leads to an ongoing search for sales growth, profitability and return on capital employed (ROCE). This places enormous emphasis on retail buyers and category managers to achieve optimal product assortments, space allocation and promotion, and to squeeze additional margin out of their suppliers. Possible manufacturer responses to the merchandising challenge have been examined already. The margin issue could first be addressed by ensuring that all supply chain costs are minimized. Beyond that the only thing manufacturers can do is to ensure that their negotiators are armed with as much information as possible about the profitability of their products, both from their perspective and from that of their customers.

- **The final threat** we shall address is that of the *changing habits and expectations of consumers*. Fewer shopping trips made by the consumer, and their higher expectations of product quality and total service, bring issues like merchandising and product availability into sharp focus. As seen already, the manufacturer's scope for response includes an opportunity to tailor the entire marketing mix, to share resources and expertise, and to assist the retailer in all areas of supply chain management.

Use of technology and information

Retailer sophistication and much of their current bargaining power is derived from technology, applications and information. The manufacturer needs to be fully conversant with the technology employed and to understand how it can fit with retailers' technology strategy and opportunities. In addition the manufacturer needs to be sensitive to the impact of its own actions on retailer technology. All opportunities to proactively assist the retailer should be sought because sharing information and technology resources is cost-effective for both sides.

Electronic point of sale (EPOS)

The main benefit of EPOS and retail scanner systems is the amount of timely and accurate information they deliver. Advances in technology have significantly aided the scope for data analysis. In addition to the original scanner-related data on sales rate, stock levels, stock turn, price and margin, retailers now have information about the demographics, socio-economic and lifestyle characteristics of consumers. They can in addition assess the impact of a whole host of variables – price, promotions, advertising, position in store, shelf position, number of facings, and so on. This information drives their choice of product mix, allocation of shelf space and promotional tactics.

EPOS has certainly changed the relationship between buyer and seller. Before the availability of scanner data the trading relationship depended on information provided by manufacturers from retail audits, information which was at least several weeks old. More detailed, accurate and timely data from scanner systems gives the retailer significant bargaining power. Not surprisingly therefore, information finds its way onto the negotiating agenda. Manufacturers do buy EPOS data from their customers but they can also trade the information and capabilities they have in exchange for it. Market knowledge is still the manufacturer's forte and this national market picture is of great use to the retailer. Additionally, armed with the retailer's EPOS data, the manufacturer could deliver well-targeted trade marketing programmes beneficial to both sides. In true trade marketing spirit, co-operation is the overall preferred approach.

Space management systems

Maximizing the sales and profitability of selling space is critical. Space management systems which try to systematize the merchandiser's decision making processes are used widely by retailers and manufacturers alike. In many cases manufacturers have not only bought packages but have set up departments which specialize in space management. Opportunity exists for their proactive use by manufacturers, particularly in situations where the retailer is short of resources. More importantly manufacturers can put themselves forward as product category specialists. In the soft drinks sector Coca Cola Schweppes Beverages act as category specialist. A key function of the trade marketing role at CCSB is to advise the retail trade on the allocation of space to the soft drinks category in totality.

Direct product profitability (DPP)

The output from DPP systems can affect retailer decisions on product stocking, store position, pricing and even trading terms demanded. It is vital therefore that the manufacturer understands DPP and the extent and manner in which individual retailers use it.

DPP replaces gross margin as a much more accurate measure of a product's contribution to total company overhead and profit. It takes account of the fact that products differ with respect to the amount of resource they use; that is, the amount of transport costs, warehouse and back-of-store space, staff handling time, share of shelf space, even head office costs. As a minimum the manufacturer needs to be aware of how the retailer is using DPP and have sufficient expertise to argue the results of the retailer's analysis. For example a product with a low DPP may still be essential to a retailer's success if it generates in-store customer flow, and if deleting it would lead to a loss of customers.

It can be used by manufacturers and retailers to examine the costs in their individual ends of the distribution chain, and by both to estimate the costs and profits in the other's field for use in negotiation. In some instances manufacturers have taken the lead in introducing DPP and in so doing have capitalized on the potential gains for both sides. Proctor & Gamble (USA) claims it may modify its packaging, its trading terms and other variables on the basis of DPP analysis. Proactive use of DPP by manufacturers works better with actual cost data from the retailer; without this only standard retail industry data can be used. And to continue a theme already begun, manufacturer–retailer co-operation here in the sharing of data is the preferred strategy in order to maximize gains for both parties.

Category management

Technology is also the enabler for category management – a subject to be explored in more detail below. Scanning technology delivers information at a level of detail which allows customized merchandising strategies (tailored product assortments, space allocations, pricing, promotions) to be devised for categories/types of store. Furthermore, sophisticated computer modelling programs allow such marketing programmes to be pre-tested before they are implemented.

Retailers will respond to those manufacturers who establish themselves as experts in the category. Manufacturers can step in to save the retailer's time, to analyse and to identify significant consumer and category trends. The appointed 'category captain' is looked to for category insight and strategic recommendations. This of course presumes the adoption by the manufacturer of the relevant technology and applications, but the gains to the proactive manufacturer are substantial. Manufacturers may have extensive information on brand performance but would welcome any additional information on consumer behaviour and competitor activity which the retailers can share with them as category expert. The manufacturer would then be in a position to more adeptly target merchandising and promotional efforts.

Electronic data interchange (EDI)

The direct linking of manufacturer and retail computer systems is driving wider co-operation between buyer and seller and creating gains in costs and efficiency too. EDI is used in the whole ordering–delivery–invoicing cycle to achieve a reduction in transaction costs, to assist in speeding-up supply, and to minimize stock levels. Based on inventory control models, for example, EDI provides the means for automatic re-ordering.

Category management practices

Category management represents the most recent development by retailers and manufacturers in the marketing and selling of their products. Category management helps manufacturers deal with the two biggest challenges they now face:

- To better understand consumers
- To build mutually beneficial relationships with retailers.

and for this reason we include it under the heading of trade marketing.

The move on the part of manufacturers to create a category management focus and to develop category expertise is based on a need to fit with the latest retail buying processes where the focus increasingly is on categories, not individual products or brands. (A category is defined as a grouping of products all satisfying the same broad consumer need. Examples would be soup, detergents, dog food, toothpaste, yoghurts, and cooking sauces.)

For the retailer, category management involves managing product categories as individual business units, charged with satisfying consumer needs whilst optimizing sales and profit of the category overall. Central to this approach is the use of sophisticated computer programs used in the development of category merchandising and marketing programmes, customized to meet the needs of identified consumer profiles.

Category management offers retailers a new way to improve profitability by a focus on the optimization of selling and marketing practices:

- product selection
- pricing
- promotion
- planograms
- merchandising.

As competition in the retail sector becomes increasingly more aggressive, so the focus on improving the profitability of categories becomes more of an imperative. Forging strategic alliances with manufacturers – nominating them as category specialists – is the most cost effective way to achieve this. The benefit to manufacturers of such an alliance, aside from the chance to build a stronger trading partnership, is the opportunity to influence how categories are driven forward. An example of this is Proctor & Gamble's launch of its stumpy 'Fairy' washing-up liquid bottle. As category specialists, P&G were able to persuade retailers that the mould made much more effective use of shelf space. All other manufacturers in the category were, as a result, forced to move to a similar size – with the obvious adverse effects for their planning and operations.

Realistically retailers can only manage one specialist per category. As a consequence they will respond to those manufacturers who establish themselves as experts. Not surprisingly most category specialists are also market leaders, for example Coca Cola Schweppes Beverages as category specialist for the soft drinks category overall. Occupying this position would mean that retailers would look to them for strategic category insight and recommendations; for example, CCSB would provide demand forecasts for the total category, and advice on category space allocation. Smaller manufacturers do, however, have an opportunity to be category specialist. Competing against multinationals Mars and Unilever, Homepride (Richards, 1995) were able to employ category management to its advantage. In 1994 they invested heavily in category management and now advise customers on the future direction of the cooking sauces category.

In order to gain category leader status, a manufacturer must demonstrate that they have the vision, the resources (i.e. people, time and technology) and the board level commitment to help drive categories, rather than just their brands.

The impact on account handlers

It is imperative that account handlers gain an understanding of category management practices, and that when dealing with a customer which operates on category principles they tailor their account plans and sales presentations accordingly.

Practical tip

Category management and key account planning:
    Produce a detailed strategy by retail account for product mix, pricing, promotion, and shelf-space within a category.

The impact on brand management

Many manufacturers have re-organized their brand management structures along category lines. Under this new system brand managers report to a category manager who is responsible for the total category. The major difference between this orientation and former brand and product-line structures is chiefly one of mindset. This mental shift involves moving away from brand-driven decisions to decisions which are based on maximizing sales and profit from the category overall. Their broad category view would entail, for example, making decisions on the manufacturing

of own label – a decision based on whether it makes sense from the point of view of maximizing total category business.

Team approach

A move to category management is sometimes accompanied by the development of a team approach to selling and the creation of category-focused multi-functional teams. This delivers category focus combined with specialist support for account handlers and retailers from other functions to improve operational efficiency and customer service.

Know the people to influence

Building long term mutual relationships is at the heart of trade marketing and as relationships are all about people, so knowing as much as possible about the people involved in any trading relationship is crucial. For the manufacturer this means the account handler being aware of all the people who need to be included in the trading relationship. What are their goals, their motivations, their performance measures and the problems they

---

Checklist 6.2
The category-focused sales presentation

Overviews:
- Category
- Our brands
- Brand/retailer consumer purchasing patterns/profiles

Recommendations:
- Product mix
- Pricing
- Promotion
- Space planning

Notes:
Relate to retailer's target customer and retailer's financial objectives. Explain how proposed strategies will help retailer attract more customers to its stores and improve category volumes and profits.

Use outputs of computer modelling to show how pricing and promotion strategy for manufacturer's brand will affect brand itself and performance of category overall.

face? How have their roles changed in the past few years?

The people to influence may or may not be the company's decision makers, so it is important to know who makes decisions and who controls information. What is the decision making process? How do member roles relate by decision type – that is, for a new-buy, re-buy, modified re-buy (e.g. range extension)? It also helps if the customer's corporate culture is understood. Does a bureaucratic or an empowering culture prevail? This will help in understanding and tuning into the decision making process.

Be clear about how the retailer rates the manufacturer's performance

The application of marketing principles should lead the manufacturer to ask, not only, 'What does the customer want from us?' but also 'What does the customer think of us?' Answers could be achieved by the manufacturer undertaking a survey to assess levels of customer satisfaction on a range of service-related topics. Alternatively the task could be delegated to a market research firm specializing in trade research. Either way the aim is to obtain objective information on how trade customers rate supplier performance. This could then be fed into a plan to improve the effectiveness of the company's trade marketing efforts.

Building the infrastructure for trade marketing ▬▬▬▬▬▬

In this section we shall examine the infrastructure requirements of marketing to a powerful retail trade in terms of:

- roles and organization structure
- people and skills
- technology and information.

Roles and organization structure ——

Up until this point we have been less concerned about who does what in the trade

---

Checklist 6.3
Trade satisfaction audit

What is the level of trade satisfaction in terms of:

- volume/profit?
- DPP?
- delivery?
- shelf-life?
- product/packaging?
- promotions?
- product movement?
- sales/display aids?
- space utilization?
- new product development?
- quality of personnel?
- trading relationship (flexibility/responsiveness)?

marketing approach or how organizations are structured, and more concerned to emphasize the core principles of trade marketing as a way of doing business. However as the purpose of this section is to look at how to put in place the infrastructure for trade marketing, it is necessary to consider possible ways of organizing.

Because the term trade marketing is applied in so many different ways and with an equally varied array of titles (trade marketing manager, customer marketing manager, trade planning manager, category manager) it is important to find some common ground which is shared by those currently practising trade marketing. From those companies observed, this common ground equates to the key drivers behind adopting trade marketing; that is to say, the list of new challenges and new tasks which marketing to the trade throws up. Central to this list are:

1. The need for improved communication and co-ordination
2. New trade marketing related tasks
3. Category management

In each of the organization structures which follow, all of which are examples of current practice by FMCG manufacturers, one or a combination of the above three factors is apparent. Before taking a look at example organization structures let us further explore these factors.

Improved communication and co-ordination

One of the common criticisms levied by retailers is the apparent lack of internal communication in their supplying companies. Ensuring that any marketing programmes satisfy both customer and brand objectives forces a closer co-operation between marketing and sales. At a time when it was appropriate for all resources to be focused on the achievement of brand objectives, sales planning departments would provide this marketing–sales integration. The key thrust of sales planning was tactical and was to ensure the implementation of marketing plans. Any

tailoring of plans for trade customers took place when the generic brand plans had already been signed-off. The trade marketing approach, however, demands the fusion of sector/account perspectives with brand/consumer perspectives at all stages of planning. Further, this need to combine perspectives extends across all planning horizons: long term strategic to short term tactical. Constant capturing of the customer angle, and building it into marketing plans, demands massive improvements in communication and co-ordination. Another factor driving the need for enhanced marketing–sales co-ordination is the dramatic increase in workload and job complexity for account managers brought on by the increasing demand by retailers for tailored promotion programmes.

New trade marketing related tasks

In addition to the list of responsibilities traditionally held by sales and marketing, today's relationship with retailers provides a list of new jobs which are either not done now, or are in need of more focused attention. It is useful to group these under four headings:

● tailored promotions
● computer models
● information
● order to invoice cycle.

Tailored promotions

We have already highlighted the increasing need to tailor promotional programmes to the individual retail customer, and the increased time account handlers would need to spend on this area without support. In order to allow account handlers to refocus their efforts on developing the face-to-face relationship with customers, many companies have allocated the responsibility for planning and developing trade-orientated promotions to a new trade marketing team. Trade marketing would work closely with brand marketing and key accounts to develop promotions which satisfy the objectives of both. In many instances trade marketing maintain budget responsibility for all sales promotions, leaving brand marketing free to focus on consumers and brand equity.

Computer models

This category refers to any computer system or package which the retailer/manufacturer *could* use to deliver solutions for better management of the business. Included here would be space planning models, DPP (direct product profitability), promotional evaluation software, and category management models. The use of the word 'could' is intentional, because whether the retailer is currently using technology solutions or not, the manufacturer should aim to know as much as possible about their operations and benefits: first, so that it can understand where the retailer is coming from with the use of technology, and second, so that it can take a proactive step in delivering a solution to the retailer. This extends to the manufacturer buying appropriate packages and developing expertise in their use.

The department or centre of expertise charged with the knowledge and application in this area could liaise directly with retailers or act as the support arm to account handlers – producing the actual computer-based output for use in their sales presentations to retailers, and providing training to account teams on the models and their application.

Information

Management of information for trade marketing involves responsibility for the strategy and management of a database on customers, consumers and competitors to the point of ensuring accessibility/availability of information for use in presentations to the trade. In some instances this will involve trade marketing supporting account handlers by collecting, analysing and presenting data for their use in accounts. Where more sophisticated systems exist the focus is on an integrated database of information accessible to all who need it, and so far as the account handler is concerned, ideally made available on his/her own personal computer.

Order to invoice cycle

Falling under this heading would be any of those projects/tasks linked to improving the operational efficiency of the order to invoicing cycle. This could include steps to implement EDI links to automate routine re-ordering and to minimize the time and cost of paperwork flows in all stages from order to delivery to invoice.

It is assumed here that any wider supply chain initiatives, that is, major projects designed to optimize product availability, to minimize product inventory and to improve product handling, would be managed either by a dedicated logistics department or by the relevant persons in the product supply department.

Category management

Many major grocery retailers have implemented category management structures and practices. A corresponding category management focus in manufacturer organizations provides the base for understanding and meeting their retailer customer needs. (See page 121 for a detailed explanation of category management.)

Examples of organization structures

The organization charts shown in Figures 6.2 to 6.8 are based on current practice in the UK and are an attempt to illustrate how companies in the re-design of their marketing–sales structures have responded to the demands of trade marketing in today's marketplace.

There are no prescriptions for organization structure: each will be contingent on the size, needs, capabilities and culture of the company concerned. In addition we can expect sales/marketing structures to be dynamic and varied as companies learn more – and at different rates – about the intricacies of trade marketing. Some believe that trade marketing units which have been set up are merely

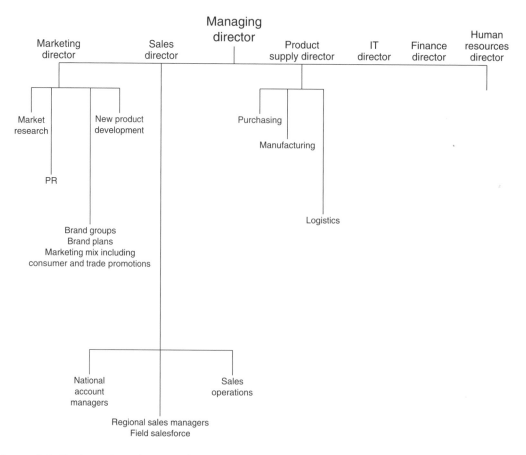

Figure 6.2 *Traditional marketing–sales organization structure*

a vehicle for manufacturers to learn the wider role of managing relationships with trade customers, and that, on this basis, the units may well outlive their usefulness and disappear.

Figure 6.2 shows a traditional marketing–sales structure with no trade marketing department. Sales operations would ensure implementation of brand plans by sales teams. In all probability the responsibility for above-the-line and below-the-line promotional budgets would rest with marketing.

Figure 6.3 shows a revision of the traditional organization to include a trade marketing department. This trade marketing department provides an interface between marketing and sales to co-ordinate brand and customer plans and undertakes the new tasks of trade marketing. Trade marketing here reports to the sales director, and would typi-

cally hold responsibility for below-the-line promotional budgets.

Figure 6.4 depicts an organization similar to that shown in Figure 6.3, the key difference being in reporting: here trade marketing reports to the marketing director. Equal application of resources to both trade and consumer needs would be critical here to ensure achievement of both brand and customer objectives.

The importance of the trade dimension is underlined in Figure 6.5 by the inclusion of a director for trade marketing. This would guarantee the required level of authority for trade marketing decisions.

In Figure 6.6 the roles of brand development manager and customer development manager replace those of brand manager and sales manager. The key thrust here is to provide a clear division between purely brand-

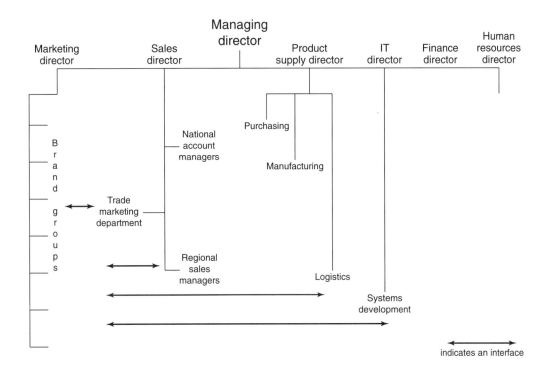

Figure 6.3 *Traditional structure with addition of a trade marketing department*

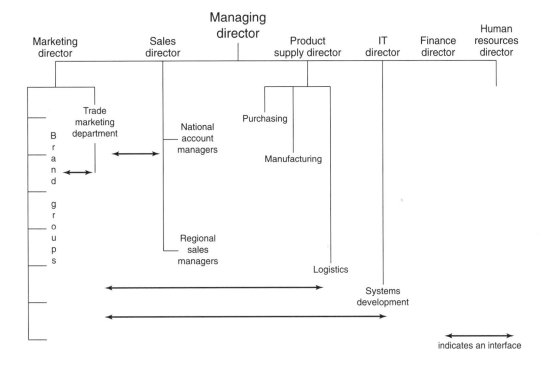

Figure 6.4 *Trade marketing department reporting to marketing*

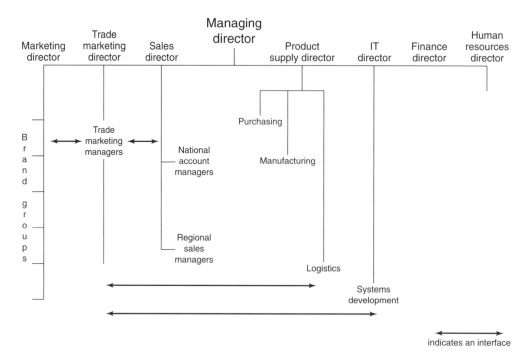

Figure 6.5 *Inclusion of trade marketing director*

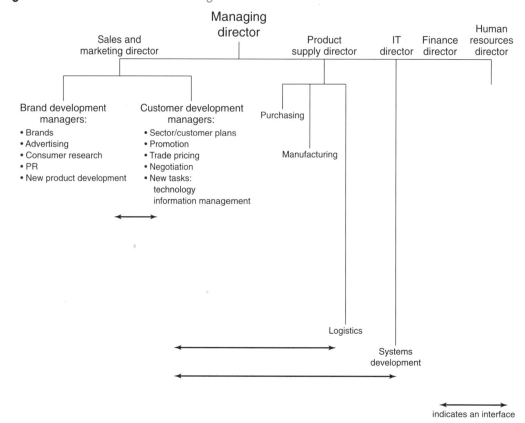

Figure 6.6 *Separation of brand-focused and customer-focused tasks*

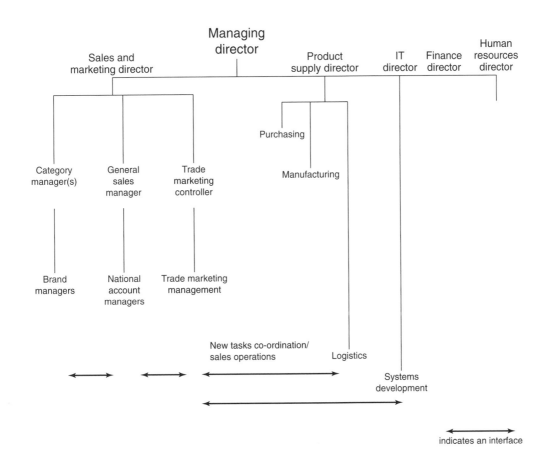

Figure 6.7 *Category management replaces brand focus*

focused activities on the one hand and customer-focused on the other. Thus the customer development manager takes over the
former brand marketing responsibility of
promotion. Overall the aim is to improve service to retail customers and allow a dedicated
focus by the brand team on brand strategy
and innovation. Better co-ordination between
marketing, sales and operations is achieved
by cross-functional teamwork.

Brand management receives category
focus by the creation of the category management role (Figure 6.7). Brand managers now
report to a category manager role which has
broad category focus. The number of category managers will depend on the number of
categories the individual brands/products
fall into, as well as on more practical opera-

tional considerations. Trade marketing co-
exists here to undertake all of the new sys-
tems/information-related tasks.

Figure 6.8 depicts a category management
structure which operates a cross-functional
business team in each category. A category
controller manages this category-focused
team and has responsibility for the profit of
the category. Trade marketing in this instance
undertakes all of the new systems/informa-
tion-related tasks.

People and skills

The issue here is not merely one of how to
staff trade marketing and category management, but also one of the implications for

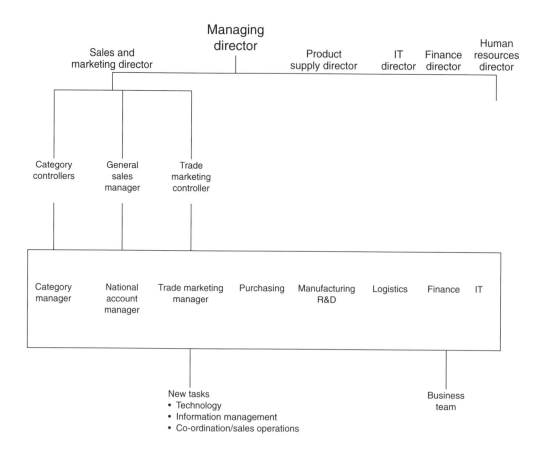

Figure 6.8 *Category management with business team*

existing roles in the business, particularly for sales managers dealing with their high-calibre and well-trained retail contacts.

This presents the manufacturer with three important tasks:

1. List the skills and aptitudes required of each job role
2. Vis-à-vis the output of task 1 above, audit the calibre and skills of the people findings to establish skills gaps
3. Produce a plan for training and recruitment.

Let us now review the skills requirements of new and existing sales/marketing roles and the consequent impacts on training and recruitment.

Account management

As servicing retailers becomes more and more the job of everyone in the corporation, so the account manager finds himself/herself in the role of integrator internally, making sure that the appropriate specialists from the manufacturer side are working with their opposite number on the retailer side. As an integrator and as the person whose key task is managing face-to-face relationships with highly-trained retail buyers/category managers, the account manager needs be to familiar with all business functions. In short they need to be all-round business managers, and in order to develop category expertise they need marketing skills to analyse and use consumer data. The addition of profit responsibility to the account manager's list of accountabilities, and the associated addition of customer profitability models, adds to an ever-increasing list of computer skills required to perform the role.

All of this adds up to a need to recruit and train high-calibre individuals, and for those already in post, the task of training them to handle the challenges of a broader account role and a more professional retail trade.

Trade marketing and category management

To influence without authority has traditionally been the preserve of the brand manager. The trade marketing position is now very often working in the same context, with one key difference, the need to produce results which satisfy the twin goals of customer and consumer. Not only does this role demand well-developed persuasion skills but also a knowledge of product *and* trade in order to achieve credibility.

This *combination* of skills and experience presents a serious staffing challenge. Even existing personnel with experience of either brand management or sales management would be very sceptical about moving to a role which allowed them no direct authority.

One solution could be to make the role a development position; one which all ambitious brand and sales people need to spend time in at some stage. On the other hand in situations where profit responsibility for a whole category/cross-functional business team is assigned to the category manager no problems of accountability and authority exist. The opportunity to manage a business unit like this makes this position very attractive to managers in all functions. Furthermore, it opens up the opportunity for a customer-focused role to managers of any function, and in the context of today's flatter organizations provides a way of maintaining the best talent in the business.

Brand marketing

Customer service and building strong brands, as we have said many times, are the two objectives for the manufacturer of branded consumer goods. The brand marketing department is accountable for brands. Yet increases in trade spending, at the expense of media advertising, the streamlining of marketing staffs and the emergence of new trade marketing teams have done little lately for the morale of the brand manager. And the move to deliver consumer information directly to account handlers without intervention for analysis and collation by brand teams can only add to the angst.

This is not good news. Any problems can, however, be minimized by ensuring utter clarity of accountability of all roles and of baton changes between roles. And on the positive side, brand marketing managers now have the benefit of singular focus on the brand and innovation.

Training requirements

Any training to achieve trade marketing focus needs to satisfy two main aims:

1. to develop new skills (category expertise, technical training on new systems and applications), and
2. to develop an appreciation of the interdependent nature of all roles and an awareness of their contributions and constraints.

Technology and information

In the earlier section on understanding and meeting customer needs we have looked at the importance of fitting in with retailers' use of technology. The advantages offered by technology:

- the ability to process massive amounts of

data into information for decision making;
- the facility to automate processes and therefore improve operational efficiencies.

are equally valid to both retailer and manufacturer, which explains why we advocate investment in technology by manufacturers in line with retailer strategies.

Practical tips: Training development

1. Hold joint training sessions between sales and marketing managers.
2. Formalize career paths to include significant periods of time spent in both customer-focused and consumer-focused functions.
3. Use trade marketing or sales managers to train brand marketing on how retailers use category management, DPP and space planning systems.
4. Use brand marketing managers to train trade marketing and sales on how to analyse and interpret consumer data.
5. Aim to develop general business managers throughout the organization.

Although investment in information technology solutions will vary widely on the basis of resources available, there is a step before any investment is made which is not related to size of budget. This is the need to devise an information strategy: the thinking and planning which goes into working out what information sales and marketing need to support their tasks of managing customer relations and developing brand programmes, and beyond that how this information will be brought together.

Information should relate to customers, consumers and competitors, and will be from internal and external sources.

Internal
- Customer profitability (by major customer, by sector, by brand)
- Product profitability
- Budgets and reports
- Demand forecasting
- Product information
- Shipments information
- Customer contact reports
- Database of retail outlets.

External
- Market information (market size, structure, brand shares)
- Consumer information (including brand information)
- Information on customers
- Competitor intelligence
- Customer satisfaction survey (what the customer says about you as supplier).

Information provision is vital to trade marketing success. However as technology delivers the means of processing masses of data the result could simply be a deluge of reports. Wading through increased amounts of information is time-consuming, and steals from available customer contact time. Heading the priority list in all cases, then, is the need where possible to replace paper systems, and to capitalize on all opportunities to integrate fragmented data. The aim should be output – analyses and exception reports – which support decision making.

Access to information is also key. As advancements are made in technology and applications, so both hardware and software are moving into the hands of those managing the customer interface. Based on the ability to integrate information managers are being given a 'workbench' or 'toolbox'. This is a database of integrated information accessible on their own laptop computers. Much of the internal and external information listed previously is, using appropriate software, integrated to deliver information which is targeted to decisions. This same toolbox can use software, such as Lotus Notes which, by allowing information to be shared, supports teamworking. An example of this could be the sharing electronically of the outcomes of a customer meeting. This would obviate the need to photocopy a contact report to all team members; instead the salient points of the meeting would be accessible to all via their individual laptop computers.

Technology and information increase the scope for adding value to the customer relationship and as such are crucial components of the infrastructure for trade marketing.

Summary

- Significant changes in today's trading environment:
  - the shift in power to retailers
  - changes in consumer expectations and buyer behaviour
  - increased competition between manufacturers
    have combined to force manufacturers to re-appraise their selling and marketing practices and organizations.
- Trade marketing as a way of doing business is essentially the application of basic marketing principles to the trade customer.
- Trade marketing as a function or department appears under a variety of different titles
  - customer marketing, trade marketing planning, category management, as well trade marketing – and as an ethos, a way of doing business, affects all sales and marketing roles.
- Trade marketing is a process which is based on understanding and responding to the needs of intermediary customers.
- For the manufacturer of branded goods this involves an equal focus on brands and customer service.
- Very often this requires a fundamental rethink of processes, job roles and organization structures; an audit of the available people skills to deliver trade marketing objectives; and an increased focus on new technology and information provision.

References and further reading ■

Bidlake, S. (1990) Sales War. *Direct Response (UK)*, March.

Davies, G. (1993) *Trade Marketing Strategy*. Paul Chapman Publishing.

Doyle, P. (1989) Building Successful Brands: The Strategic Options. *Journal of Marketing Management*, **5**, No. 1, 77–95.

Kotler, P., Armstrong, G., Saunders, J. and Wong, V. (1996) *Principles of Marketing*. Englewood Cliffs, NJ: Prentice Hall.

Nielsen (1992) *Category Management*.

Randall, G. (1994) *Trade Marketing Strategies*. Oxford: Butterworth-Heinemann.

Richards, A. (1995) Supermarket Superpowers. *Marketing*, August 10.

Weisz, P. (1994) P&G, Lever: Forget Brand, Grab Shelf. *Brand Week*, **35**, Pt 3.

7

Telemarketing ———————————————

Michael Starkey, Leicester Business School

 In this chapter we will examine the fast growing subject of telemarketing. We begin by examining a number of different definitions of telemarketing and looking at its history and growth. Telemarketing can be used for lead generation, telesales, database building and customer service.

A main focus of the chapter is 'selling over the telephone'. The types of selling skills and selling behaviours that successful sales people use are examined. We also look at ways to improve the chances of success in telesales. Guidance is provided for those organizations considering using telemarketing in choosing whether to set up an in-house operation or whether to buy-in.

Finally, we consider the importance of ethics in telemarketing and delivering service quality.

What is telemarketing? ▬▬▬

Telemarketing means different things to different people. The Direct Marketing Association, in a booklet called *What is Telemarketing?* states, 'More and more companies are using the telephone as a means of hearing from or contacting people who are, or who may become, their customers. This is called telemarketing'. Telemarketing just like many other disciplines has its own jargon. For instance, when telephone calls are made by a firm to a customer or potential customer this is referred to as 'outbound telemarketing'. Similarly when calls are received by an organization, perhaps in direct response to newspaper or television advertisements with a Freefone number, this is referred to as

'inbound telemarketing'. The people who talk to customers on the telephone in call centres or telesales operations are often referred to as agents, operators or customer service advisors.

Michael Stevens in his book *Telemarketing in Action* provides a broad definition of telemarketing: 'Telemarketing is the planned and controlled use of telephone communication to build profitable long term relationships with members of influential audiences who impact on an organization's success.' This definition can be split into five key elements:

- **Planned** – Calls are both planned in terms of objectives and structure.
- **Controlled** – Call outcomes and costs can be kept under review.

- **Communication** – A two-way communication process takes place.
- **Profitable long term relationships** – Just as in any sales situation, the intention must be to turn suspects into prospects and turn prospects into long term customers. It is now recognized that it is much more profitable to retain customers rather than to keep looking for new ones.
- **Influential audiences** – The telephone can be used to build a relationship with all key stakeholders that affect a business.

Telemarketing is not just a fancy word for telesales. There is an important difference. Michael Stevens, in his earlier book *The Handbook of Telemarketing*, explains that traditional telesales operations are often badly planned and controlled. Furthermore, telemarketing involves far more than just selling. Yet research conducted by the Henley Centre in 1994 revealed that 50% of those questioned thought that telemarketing was selling by phone and 17% thought it was cold selling. Other activities include lead generation, lead tracking, database building, appointment making, providing information, handling enquiries, order taking, market research and customer service. Some of these will be examined in more depth later in this chapter.

The development of telemarketing

The history and growth of telemarketing

The use of the telephone for selling started in the USA in the 1950s and early 1960s as a cost effective method for selling newspaper advertising space. The Henley Centre's Teleculture 2000 report describes how the late Murray Roman, the 'father of modern telemarketing', set up the first outbound telemarketing operation, whilst working for the Ford Motor Company in the USA in the 1960s.

Roman wanted to identify and qualify prospects who were contemplating buying a new car within the next three to six months. He employed a team of telephone operators

throughout the country, who worked from home, thus benefiting from local telephone call rates. Qualified prospects, who were considering buying a new car, were offered a test drive at the local Ford dealership. The leads were handed on to dealers, who then followed up. Initial tests proved so successful that in total 22 million calls were made and this still holds the record for the biggest single outbound campaign in the history of telemarketing. The first telesales operation in the UK was set up by Thomson Regional Newspapers in Sheffield in the mid-1960s.

In the UK the 0800 (Freefone) and 0345 (Locall; local call rates) market is growing at a phenomenal rate (see Figure 7.1). The Teleculture 2000 report estimates that per capita usage will rise from 10 calls per year in 1993 and peak at about 60 calls by the year 2010. In the USA the annual per capita usage was 70 calls in 1993 and this is expected to peak at about 90 calls in the year 2005. Although the UK market has lagged behind the American market, the Teleculture 2000 report states that the UK market has grown at a much faster rate. BT estimate that in 1996 the total volume of telemarketing calls across their network to be about 20 million calls per week. The Henley Centre's latest report (on the use of the telephone), *Teleculture Futures*, states that the use of Freefone and special numbers will continue to grow with emphasis on customer service and will extend 'throughout the business community from large to small organizations and across sectors that are now more resistant to the teleculture'.

Based on research with 500 companies with over 100 employees, The Henley Centre estimate that there are 800,000 people employed in what they term the telebusiness industry and that the total spend is £10.4 billion.

Telemarketing today

Telemarketing in some form is used in many organizations, from banking to builders' merchants. Whilst the most prominent users may be financial services and insurance compa-

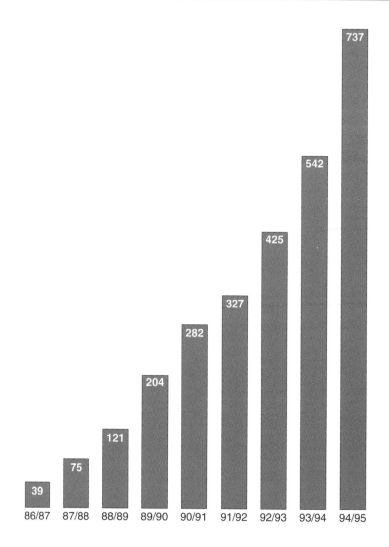

Figure 7.1 *The growth in Freefone (0800) and Lo-call (0345) (millions). Source: BT*

nies others include charities, government (careers service), motor manufacturers, accountants, utilities, food distributors, estate agents, builders, electrical wholesalers, car rental companies, newspapers, metal stock holders and mail order catalogue companies. In fact, any organization that communicates with its customers by telephone, although it may not realize the significance of it, is in fact using some form of telemarketing. This creates both an opportunity and a threat.

● An opportunity because more and more consumers are prepared to do business over the telephone.

● A threat as The Henley Centre's Teleculture 2000 report states that 68% of people would prefer not to deal with an organization again if *a single call* is badly handled.

Research published in 1990 by Arthur Anderson on 'what business customers want most in customer service' showed that in 1970 business people ranked contact with an outside sales person as most important. However, by 1990 this had slipped to ninth place and the most important was then considered to be contact with a capable inside sales person.

The Henley Centre's Teleculture Futures report provides a very clear warning to those that have ignored the message from Teleculture 2000. The report concludes by saying:

> If businesses continue to ignore the clear demands from their customers for the use of the telephone and fail to put customer care interaction and response at the heart of the organization, using today's technologies, then there is no guarantee they will survive into the 21st century. And if a British business fails to respond to today's challenge as a proxy for preparing for tomorrow's, the prospects for UK plc in the global race for 'wired' domination may not be good, despite the benign consumer environment here, and our established skills in the areas of creativity, content creation and excellence in communication.

Telemarketing and direct response TV (DRTV)

Along with telemarketing, direct response TV is also growing at a phenomenal rate. Research conducted by BT and Channel 4 showed that DRTV has grown by 46% between 1993 and 1995 with 19% of all TV advertisements now carrying a telephone number as a response mechanism. Figure 7.2 shows why DRTV is growing so fast. This seems to confirm the Teleculture 2000 view regarding the increasing willingness of customers to buy using the telephone.

Daewoo, the Korean automobile manufacturer, wanted to break into the UK market without using the established dealer network. The following case study shows how they did this using DRTV and telemarketing.

Applications for telemarketing

The discussion on the definitions of telemarketing reported that the number and scope of applications is much wider than might at first be imagined. Telemarketing can be used as a replacement for the traditional field sales force particularly for low value items or low value accounts; to provide some support activities for the traditional field salesforce so that they can maximize their selling time in front of the customer; or as part of the

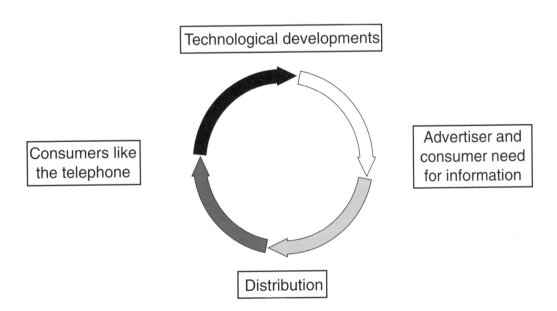

Figure 7.2 *Why DRTV is growing so fast: four key factors. Source and copyright: BT/Channel 4.*

Example One
Daewoo: the launch of a new company

Daewoo have, in the space of a year, literally leapt from obscurity to their enviable position as a household name.

Daewoo have embraced the notion of an outstanding customer driven service. Information drawn from a survey of 200,000 UK car buyers showed consumer dissatisfaction with the traditional dealer approach, so from the beginning Daewoo introduced a new concept in car sales and aftercare, cutting out the middleman, and, in doing so, both lowering and standardizing costs.

Their package consists of three types of outlets: motor shows, car centres and support centres. A vital element was needed to link customers to the concept and to define the product and its associated benefits – something that united all Daewoo outlets in the consumer consciousness and allowed exceptional ease of access to the customer.

The ideal answer was to offer a Freefone number. Merit Direct undertook to represent Daewoo in time for the April 1995 launch, confirming that the concept of linking the customer to the network via the phone is accepted as a central part of the Daewoo philosophy.

The Freefone number was incorporated into all Daewoo literature and advertising (principally DRTV) and forms a strategic part of the company's sales information package. Daewoo hoped that by providing an outstanding purchase package they might pull in responses of around 3360 in the month following the launch.

The response they actually received was staggering: 43,137 enquiries within the first month. By August 1995 (a total of four months from the launch) the Freefone number had attracted 190,269 calls on a previously unknown product.

Daewoo achieved a remarkable 3.32% of total UK sales in July 1995, after just three months on the market. This approach has been an unqualified success for Daewoo and is proof positive of the acceptability and accessibility of the Freefone number. The campaign has achieved response figures way in excess of the projected volume (a factor of 14 times greater than expected), taking Daewoo from being an unknown to ninth place in the manufacturer's league table in just five months.

The telephone and the effective call handling were vital components in the overall success of the campaign.

Source: Merit Direct Limited

response mechanism in direct response marketing. Sales managers need to keep a careful watch on expenditure and consider whether telemarketing might be appropriate for their organization. This includes both selling and other activities involved in the sales cycle. Typically the cost of a sales call may vary between £150 and £500, therefore it is important that time in front of the customer is both productive and cost effective. There are four main applications for telemarketing. These are lead generation, telesales, database building and customer care.

Lead generation

It is now commonly accepted that it is more profitable to retain existing customers than to keep churning them over and continually looking for new ones. Even organizations that excel at retaining their customers will still lose some and have to replace them. Lead sources can be obtained from a number of origins such as replies to direct response advertisements, lapsed customers, contact names on the company database and purchased lists. The telephone can be used to approach, screen and qualify potential customers, and once enquiries are generated to keep track of the customers.

In some instances it may be better for the salesforce to work on converting qualified sales leads into orders rather than specifically spending a lot of time searching for potential new sales leads. Many of the major automobile manufacturers use telemarketing as a response mechanism for TV or newspaper advertisements in order to generate sales leads. These are then passed on to the dealers to follow up.

For companies employing a field salesforce, both inbound and outbound telephone calls can be used to make appointments for sales representatives. Relieving sales representatives from making their own appointments means that more time can be spent face to face with the customer. Inbound calls generated from a direct response television (DRTV) advertisements can be routed to agents with a computer based diary management system to make an appointment at a convenient time for the potential customer. The objective for the agent is to sell the appointment and not the product or service.

Enquiries and orders may originate from a number of sources such as mail shots, newspaper or TV advertisements or even billboards. Predicting the number of likely callers is essential to ensure that agents are productive and calls are answered promptly.

One of the key messages from the 1995 Channel 4/BT joint research into UK DRTV was the need for more companies using DRTV to ensure effective planning and the integration of call handling into the process from the outset. During the study only 63% of calls in response to DRTV advertisements were answered, meaning that 37% were lost, primarily due to insufficient call handling resources at the time the advertisement was transmitted. The removal of eight 'rogue' campaigns reduces the failure rate to 23%. Among the horror stories was one company which answered 1200 calls during a campaign and lost 54,000! It had hooked up its number to an answering machine.

If a telemarketing bureau is being used, it is essential that they are fully briefed about the timing of all advertisements. It is not unknown for a client to forget to tell the bureau that an advertisement has been booked or for one to be booked at the last minute because a special deal has been obtained.

Response rates to DRTV are rising as UK television viewers become more ready to use the telephone to respond to DRTV advertisements. The Channel 4/BT study found that a good response rate had increased nearly five fold from 380 calls per million viewers in 1993 to 1800 calls per million viewers in 1995. Eighty per cent of calls come in within 15 minutes of the transmission time of an advertisement.

Telesales

Telesales – the traditional use of the telephone in telemarketing

Whilst initially telesales may have, in some instances, gained a bad reputation, this is no longer generally the case. Telesales is now a way of life that is often preferred by both customer and supplier alike. Since the 1960s telesales has continued to be the main means for selling classified advertising space in newspapers using both inbound and outbound calls. The impact of information technology has enabled newspapers to build up a data-base of customers.

Sales people at the Hong Kong Refrig-erating Company act as both traditional sales representatives and telesales people.

Replacing the field salesforce

Some organizations are finding they can no longer justify the cost of keeping a field sales-force on the road. Simon Jersey is one com-pany which decided to replace their entire field salesforce with telemarketing agents. At the 1995 Telemarketing awards, they won the top award in the 'best use of telemarketing for selling' category.

Telephone account management

Some organizations, such as Royal Mail, are switching over part of their operation to tele-phone account management as a more effec-tive way of handling small and medium size customers. Telephone account management (TAM) was set up with the aim of building relationships with existing and potential cus-tomers, generating new business and provid-ing customer service. Key accounts are still handled by the salesforce and the 300,000 minor accounts worth less than £40,000 per annum are now handled by telephone account executives. Whereas a field salesper-son might make around 3.4 calls a day, a tele-phone account executive can make about 18 calls a day.

Although it may be easy to justify using telemarketing for low value accounts there is an increasing application of the use of tele-marketing in handling key accounts in a sup-port function between the regular calls by key account executives or key account managers.

Example Two
The Hong Kong Refrigerating Company

The Hong Kong Refrigerating Company is a food trading company that imports meat, vegetables and dairy products from the major food exporting countries for sale to hotels, restaurants, wholesalers, retailers and street traders throughout Hong Kong. From 1976 turnover has increased from about £5 million to an estimated £90 million for the year ending 1996. Food trading in Hong Kong is a dynamic fast moving business with prices frequently fluctuating on both international and the domestic markets.

Because of transit time by ship, market conditions and lead time required by the exporters, products may be bought forward by the company from 3 to 9 months prior to arrival in Hong Kong. Some sales are contracted with customers on a back to back basis for delivery several months ahead and others are done on a daily basis from stock held in the company's cold store. The principal method for selling is by telephone. In the morning the sales people contact customers with the latest offers and in the afternoon they are out visiting and collecting payments. The telephone is a highly effective method for conducting and negotiating business deals with customers.

**Example Three
Simon Jersey**

Simon Jersey is a leading supplier of uniforms to the business community, especially the hotel and catering industries. The family-owned company has its headquarters and manufacturing base at Accrington in Lancashire with offices in London and Strasbourg and distributors in 22 countries.

The company faced a classic business dilemma – how to maintain high levels of service and customer satisfaction, while cutting overheads and increasing profits – all within a short time frame. The company decided to transform the way it communicated with its market and at the same time reduce one of its heaviest areas of expenditure, the field salesforce. The solution was to replace the field salesforce with a fully integrated telemarketing system handling both inbound and outbound calls staffed by 50 telemarketing agents.

Now, whenever Simon Jersey makes or takes a call, customer account histories are available to agents at the touch of a button, allowing every customer to be treated more personally, and for their details to be accessed or altered while they are on the telephone. Agents are able to satisfy virtually any of their needs there and then, from order enquiries, catalogue requests and invoice or account details to information on stock availability, entering orders and arranging 24 hour delivery. The system can also access new lists of potential customers and assimilate them into its database – while weeding out duplicates and non-contactable numbers.

Chris Houghton, head of information management at Simon Jersey, said 'We can be more scientific about buying databases now, cross referencing data so we give agents a better quality lead and we get a better response as a result. We achieved well over 33,000 conversions in 1995, that's in addition to our existing customer base. Telemarketing has allowed us to grow in a way that was not going to happen otherwise.' Over the last three years Simon Jersey's turnover has increased by 250% from £8 million to £20 million.

Database building

The database is becoming an essential element in sales and marketing strategies. Both acquiring data and maintaining the accuracy of data stored on the database costs money. The telephone is now being widely used both to acquire data and maintain the database. A consumer database with 100,000 names might, according to the Hewson Consulting Group, cost between £20,000 and £40,000 annually to contact customers and prospects in order to validate the details. Yet the database must be accurate if it is to be of value. Merit Direct estimate that, in a 12 month period, up to 30% of records will become out of date. Information on customers such as contact names must be validated at least every 6 months. A much higher response rate will be obtained by using the telephone than by using direct mail alone.

The NWS Bank won an award at the 1995 Royal Mail/Direct Marketing Association Awards. The bank supplies car finance through some 200 dealerships. Contact is maintained with customers by both direct mail and telemarketing. By talking to customers at least four times a year, NWS promises to alert dealers immediately of customers' intentions to change their vehicles or where car service is required. This 'dealer alert' programme is database driven, operated by 40 programming and analytical staff. It has resulted in the amount of business received from dealers increasing by 55%.

Customer care

Customer carelines

Carelines, whilst relatively new in the UK, have been in existence in the USA for several years. Tom Peters in the BBC TV training video, the 'Tom Peters Experience', refers to how the inclusion by one company of the home telephone numbers of all the senior executives on the back of business cards resulted in a huge increase in the use of the Freefone number on the front of the card because customers felt that the company cared about the quality of its products and took customer service issues seriously. Care lines are defined in the Careline Report published in 1995 by the L&R Group as 'Telephone numbers printed on-pack which the consumer can ring for advice or information about the product, often free of charge'.

The L&R Group carried out a three part study to determine the penetration of carelines in FMCG products in the USA, UK, France, Germany, Australia and New Zealand.

- **The shopping test**: In all the countries ten products from ten categories were selected to see if they carried carelines. In the USA 81% of the products contained carelines as opposed 22% (up from 8% from a study published two years earlier) in the UK.
- **The careline responsiveness test**: The careline numbers displayed on the packs were then tested by consumers for speed of response, product knowledge, quality of

service and range of information. The study also established whether the manufacturers obtained information from consumers and if this was used for database building.

In the UK the average response time was 2.7 seconds, but it varied between 1 second and 20 seconds. This was much better than all other countries tested except the USA, where the average response time was 1.4 seconds (range 1 second to 10 seconds). Evidence was found that some firms were having difficulty in striking the right balance between using carelines primarily for customer care or for marketing purposes. Careline operations in the USA and the UK came out best for product knowledge and the quality of call handling.

- **The consumer survey**: The L&R Group also wanted to find out about consumer awareness of and attitudes towards carelines in the UK. Fifty-eight per cent of the UK consumers surveyed said they expected careline numbers to be free of charge. No over-the-counter pharmaceutical products carried a careline number in the UK (90% did in the USA), yet 52% of consumers would welcome the provision of such a service. If there was a choice between one product with a careline and one without, 32% of consumers said they would favour the product with a careline.

Crisis management

Management needs to think carefully about both what and how they will communicate with their customers if there is an unexpected disaster. Unless the situation is handled properly, long term harm may be caused to the company's image. Several years ago sales of Perrier Water fell dramatically after the product became contaminated with benzene and even several months later sales were only at 60% of the pre-scare level. Sometimes crises can affect a whole industry.

In 1996 sales of beef throughout Europe collapsed after it was announced in the House of Commons that there might be a link between a new strain of CJD and BSE. In the UK sales fell by one third, but soon recovered to 80–85% of their former level. Consumer reaction to such a statement was inevitable. However, if the Ministry of Agriculture and the Department of Health had co-operated to formulate a clearly co-ordinated 'communications strategy' then consumer confidence might have been restored very much more quickly. Effective crisis management could have involved placing advertisements in the national newspapers and using DRTV with a dedicated 0800 number to call for information.

An automated answering service could have been set up very quickly, which would have been capable of handling large volumes of traffic 24 hours per day. A clear pre-recorded message giving factual information could have been made by a senior health official. There could have been other options, i.e. to receive further details by mail or ask more detailed questions from an expert. If the number of calls was higher than had been predicted then the overload could have been diverted to other call centres. An operation of this nature would have been well within the scope of the larger telemarketing bureaux.

The BSE crisis presents the case for planning for the unforeseen crisis. If your organization faces an unexpected disaster will you be able to cope? The next day your switchboard may be jammed solid with worried customers and there may possibly be thousands more who just cannot get through.

Selling over the telephone

Telemarketing people need to have the right knowledge, skills and attitude just as ordinary field sales representatives do. A morning training course followed by starting work in the afternoon is just not good enough. Yet far too many organizations fail to pay adequate attention to making sure employees are equipped for the job. Inadequate training means that people are more likely to under perform and the image they portray is likely to reflect badly on the company. To customers, sales people are the company. Companies need to consider carefully the consequences of providing insufficient training or cutting training budgets. As previously mentioned, research by The Henley Centre has shown that customers would prefer not to do business again with a company after a call has been badly handled.

Selling over the telephone does not just involve servicing low value accounts or selling low value products. Some sales made over the telephone are both high value and may take some time to negotiate over a number of calls. Some of the skills and methods used in high value sales are equally applicable to telephone selling in business to business sales. The main focus in this section is on business to business selling.

Planning the call

Planning calls is essential. The purpose of a plan is to provide a framework that will enable the agent to stay in control of the call. It does this by providing a framework for both:
- Structure – what to talk about
- Process – how to go about talking to clients.

Preparing the call

Making outbound calls to customers or prospective customers requires careful planning and accurate targeting of the key decision makers (see Checklist 7.1).

There are two types of framework that can be used, namely scripts and prompts. Both have their advantages and disadvantages. Scripts may be best for inexperienced sales agents, when dealing with basic standard products or taking payment details. A bureau that is handling calls for several clients would almost certainly use scripts. Scripts can sound very 'wooden'. Prompts provide greater flexibility and may be more suited to more complex products, more experienced sales people and an in house telesales operation.

Checklist 7.1
Preparing for the call

1. Consider the client you want to talk to
Have there been any recent changes in the company, i.e. acquisitions, mergers, changes in management structure, that can justify your reason for the call? Try and identify the best person to speak to before the call. This may involve making an initial call a few days beforehand.

2. Decide what to say
Have an attractive statement for both the person you want to speak to and the gatekeeper, who may be preventing you from reaching that person.

3. Consider the call objectives
These will vary depending on the purpose, i.e. whether it is to sell, or to obtain information for later use. It is useful to have both.

- a main objective, i.e. persuade them to buy, and
- a fallback objective, i.e. agree to an appointment for a sales representative to call, or that you may call them back in two weeks time.

Scripts

A simple (abbreviated) dummy script for processing an enquiry might read as shown on page 137.

Prompts

Two types of prompts will be examined that can be used for selling a product or service together with a range of associated options. In the following example the product is an ink jet printer with associated options.

Product planner

The product planner helps telesales agents think though the associated options and the reasons why a customer might be interested in them. One potential danger of the product planner is that an inexperienced agent may be tempted just to read though the planner as though it were a list. A few careful and focused questions about the problem or need that the product is likely to meet should ensure a more willing listener. A more detailed discussion of questions to ask is given later in this section under the heading 'Selling behaviours'. Only a few options are shown in the planner given in Table 7.1.

Using a bubblegram

If the sales agent is clear why customers might be interested in a product and the options that go with it then it might be helpful to use a bubblegram. The advantage is that a bubblegram is not sequenced and is intended to give a map of how issues might be linked together in a customer's mind. Once the customer has expressed interest in a product the agent can start to develop the sale from where the customer is most interested.

In Figure 7.3 the product itself is the central

1. Good morning/afternoon/evening.
   Thank you for calling 'CLIENT NAME'.

2. Is there any specific service or product which you would like to receive information on:
   Product 1
   Product 2
   Product 3
   Product 4
   Product 5
   General information

   Thank you

3. May I start by taking your name and address details and full post code please?

4. And a contact telephone number?

   ....(day time)   ....(evening)

   Thank you

5. May I ask if you are already a customer of ours?

   Yes   [ ]
   No   [ ]

6. Can I ask where you saw or heard our number advertised?

   Television   [ ]   (Go to 8)
   Radio   [ ]   (Go to 8)
   Press   [ ]   (Go to 7)
   Other – please specify

7. Which newspaper/magazine did you see the number in?

8. To help us target our advertising and information in the future, would you mind telling me which of the following age brackets you fall into?

   Under 25   [ ]
   25–34   [ ]
   35–44   [ ]
   45–54   [ ]
   55–64   [ ]
   65+   [ ]
   Do not wish to give age [ ]

9. Thank you for your call. A full information pack is now on its way to you.

Source: Merit Direct Limited

bubble, in this case a portable printer. Then customer facts such as travel and business use that might make it relevant to pursue the various options are located in other bubbles. Questions to develop customer needs or difficulties that might be resolved by the various options can be noted. A question such as, 'While I check availability on our computer system, could you tell me what you're planning to use it for?' will help to guide where to proceed and which other options might be useful.

Cross selling and upselling

Using the bubblegram as a prompt makes cross selling much easier and more natural than reading through a list of options. However, before cross selling, agents could consider whether upselling is appropriate or in the client's interest. Upselling consists of either selling a higher value product or a larger quantity. For example, a few questions will ascertain whether in fact a heavier duty model might be more appropriate. Aggressive selling techniques that ignore customer needs will frustrate customer retention, lead to a high 'churning' of customers and make customer acquisition the main focus. Neither

upselling nor cross selling should be used to boost company revenue or agents' commission at the expense of the customers' interest and needs. Customers who have been the victims of overzealous sales techniques are less likely to buy again.

Seller behaviours

In Chapter 2 the SPIN®[1] questioning model was introduced. This was the outcome from probably the largest research study on effective selling behaviours. Neil Rackham and his colleagues at Huthwaite Research Group analysed 35,000 sales transactions over a 12 year period. Using behaviour analysis they found that in major sales:

- Using closing techniques loses you the business with the increasing size of the sale.
- Classic questioning methods such as asking open and closed questions don't help.

---

[1] The acronym SPIN® is a registered trademark. European trademarks for SPIN® are held by Huthwaite Group Limited. North American and certain other trademarks for SPIN® are held by Huthwaite, Inc.

Table 7.1 *Product planner for ink jet printer. Source: © Huthwaite Research Group Limited*

Product	Basic facts that indicate if options are worth exploring with a customer:
Ink jet Printer	Travel, heavy business usage, presentations
Options	**Problems or needs that would make an option valuable to a customer**
Option 1: Sheet feeder	Quality important so registration critical Time valuable – not waste time feeding in single sheets Desk space important – minimize printer space
Option 2: Carrying case	Concerned about damage if in and out of offices, trains and cars Want one case for PC, printer, cables, documents
Option 3: Ink cartridges/refill kits	Can't estimate usage – don't want to run out

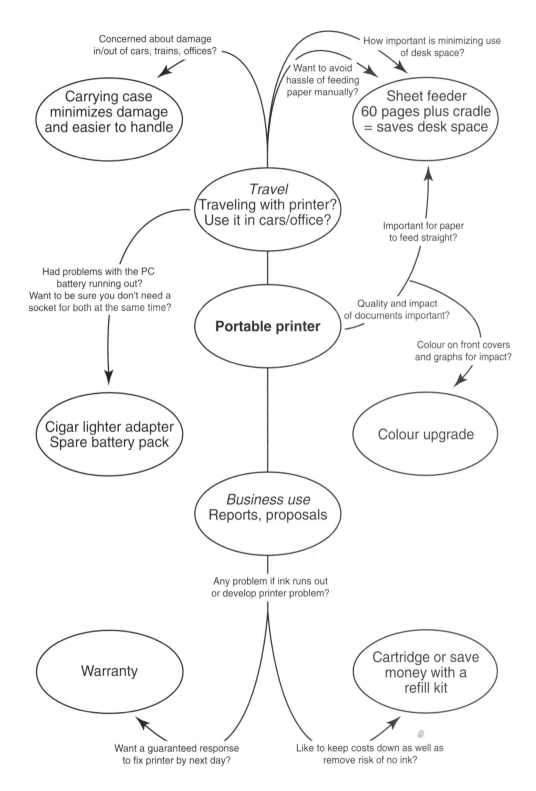

Concerned about damage
in/out of cars, trains, offices?

How important is minimizing use
of desk space?

Want to avoid
hassle of feeding
paper manually?

Carrying case
minimizes damage
and easier to handle

Sheet feeder
60 pages plus cradle
= saves desk space

Travel
Traveling with printer?
Use it in cars/office?

Important for paper
to feed straight?

Had problems with the PC
battery running out?
Want to be sure you don't need a
socket for both at the same time?

Portable printer

Quality and impact
of documents important?

Colour on front covers
and graphs for impact?

Cigar lighter adapter
Spare battery pack

Colour upgrade

Business use
Reports, proposals

Any problem if ink runs out
or develop printer problem?

Warranty

Cartridge or save
money with a
refill kit

Want a guaranteed response
to fix printer by next day?

Like to keep costs down as well as
remove risk of no ink?

Figure 7.3 *Bubblegram for portable printer and options. Source: © Huthwaite Research Group Limited*

- Objection handling techniques are of little help in sales effectiveness, because successful sellers concentrate on objection prevention.

The study found that there are four interrelated questions that successful salespeople ask. These are known as SPIN® and are described in the book *Making Major Sales* by Neil Rackham. They are:

- **Situation questions**: Facts and details about the customer's background.
- **Problem questions**: Difficulties, problems that the customer is experiencing that can be resolved by the seller's products or services.

- **Implication questions**: Develop the customer's perception of the seriousness of the problem.
- **Need pay-off questions**: Explore the benefits or value of resolving the problem.

In some complex and high value sales conducted over the telephone and where the telephone is used in account management then the SPIN® model may be appropriate. This would be particularly so in industrial selling, selling banking and other financial services, because the model helps to reveal a customer's *explicit needs* (not just implied needs). Once salespeople have elicited strong explicit needs, they can demonstrate how the benefits of their product or service will be of

Table 7.2 *Seller behaviours. Source: © Huthwaite Reserach Group Limited*

Name and definition	Examples	Usefulness
Situation questions Ask for facts about the customer's situation	*Are you likely to be advertising on a regular basis? So what sort of holiday are you considering?*	Help to establish whether it's worth trying to sell additional products or service and what the appropriate option is
Need questions Ask about the customer's need, wants and aspirations for things you can provide	*What facilities would you need for the evening? How useful would it be if …? Would it help if …?*	Identify exactly what the customer wants and why. Also help the customer consider needs previously touched upon
Benefits Explain how your products or services will meet the customer's specific needs	*You've said you want good sound quality which the noise reduction facility on this machine will certainly provide.*	The most powerful way of describing your product
Advantages Explain how your products or services can help in general	*The plasma screen on the F100 means you can read it in any lighting conditions. By taking an extra advert you can save 10% on the overall cost.*	Early in the call to get the customer's interest
Features Statements of fact, opinion or descriptions of products or services	*Because the paper path inside this printer bends three times, it won't take card. The 'Easirest' chair has an adjustable backrest.*	For giving facts which the customer needs to understand in order to use the product or service appropriately

real value. In many telesales situations the time permitted per call is just a few minutes and does not allow the model to be properly used. In this case the following adaptation of the model developed by Linda Marsh at Huthwaite may be more appropriate. In this instance two types of questions that the telesales agent will get most value from are *situation questions* and *need questions*.

It is also most important to get the balance right between each of the behaviours. For instance poorly trained salespeople will do a 'feature dump' on customers, whereas what they should be doing is asking plenty of need questions and then following up these with benefits that meet the customer's explicit needs. Many books talk about the value of providing benefits, but look at it from the seller's point of view rather than the customer's. Consequently sellers may describe the advantages their products or services may provide, rather than real benefits which meet the customer's needs (readers who want to find out why this is so should read Chapter 7 in *Making Major Sales* by Neil Rackham).

Table 7.3 summarizes the attention effective and ineffective sellers will pay to each of the selling behaviours.

It is also important for telesales agents to understand customer behaviours. For instance, it is all too easy to make assumptions based on factual statements made by customers. Using needs based questions will help to identify what the customer wants. Table 7.4 summarizes customer behaviours.

How clients decide – using decision guidelines

Although a customer may have identified a need for a product there may inevitably be a selection process to eliminate competing products. The influences that determine guidelines may come from a number of sources such as research, past experience, word of mouth, published information (magazines, reports, etc.), and the client's existing circumstances – they might, for instance, be short of cash. Work carried out by Huthwaite Research Group found that successful sellers understand the 'decision guidelines' their customers use to make the final purchase decision. They do this by:

- finding out what existing guidelines a customer has, and
- assessing the relative importance of the guidelines.

They can use the needs-related questions to check the importance of each need. If there is uncertainty about the relative priority, a question such as 'So which is the most important, the final amount or the flexibility of the payments?' may be asked. A final question to check no guidelines have been overlooked might be 'Is there anything else that will affect your decision?' or 'Are there any other criteria you will be using to decide which ink jet printer to buy?'

Table 7.3 *Differences between effective and ineffective sellers. Source: © Huthwaite Research Group Limited*

	Effective sellers	**Ineffective sellers**
Situation questions	Are focused	Too many and irrelevant
Need questions	Most emphasis	Not enough
Benefits	More	None
Advantages	Targeted and specific	Lots!
Features	Focused, needed for explanation	Lots!

Table 7.4 *Customer behaviours. Source: © Huthwaite Research Group Limited*

Name and definition	Examples	Usefulness
Facts Statements by the customer about the basic situation	*There will be four of us going* *I'll be using the printer for proposals*	To position your response and questions appropriately and provide a focus to allow you to explore needs
Needs Clear statements by the customer of wants desires and intentions which can be met by the seller's products or services	*I want to go somewhere which is sunny but not baking hot in July* *Quality is absolutley critical* *If you could offer me a discount for bulk purchase I'd be interested*	Help to ensure the original request is met appropriately, and help the client appreciate the value of additional products or services

When not to influence guidelines

Customers may be deeply committed to some guidelines, because they have put a lot of preparatory work into them, or they may relate closely to the policy or the culture of the organization. In this case no attempt should be made to influence them.

Influencing guidelines you can meet

Guidelines that can be met can be reinforced using need based questions to stress their importance.

Influencing guidelines you cannot meet

There are three possibilities to consider for guidelines that cannot be met.

- **Reducing the importance of those you cannot influence by 'trading off'.** Use SPIN® to explore the guideline that can be met and neglect the other one.
- **Introducing new guidelines.** Sellers can sometimes use their superior expertise to raise issues the customer has not thought of. SPIN® can then be used to get the customer to consider the new issues and their importance.
- **Modifying the guidelines.** This is particularly useful for guidelines based on cost. Instead of thinking of purchase price

alone, the customer should be encouraged to consider other associated costs.

Assessing call success

How can a successful call be defined? Neil Rackham in his classic book *Making Major Sales* states that in simple small sales there are two possible outcomes, i.e. 'order' or 'no sale'. In the more complicated higher value sales there are two other possible outcomes – a 'continuation' or an 'advance'. Understanding the difference is important in order to analyse call success. A continuation is where the customer has agreed to receive a telephone call in the future, so the relationship will continue, but with no specific topic, date, or action that will *move the sale forward*. An advance can be defined as a future action that moves the sale forward towards a decision. Huthwaite Research Group have found that many salespeople and their managers tend to be over-optimistic about call outcomes feeling they have made advances when they are only continuations. Closer attention to which customer actions or commitments will progress the sale can help improve both forecasting and planning the next steps in the sale.

Here are some statements made by potential customers at the end of a sales call. Place in the box after each statement either O (order), A (advance), C (continuation) or NS (no sale) depending what you think is the outcome of the call.

1. 'Can I give you my credit card details so you can arrange cover immediately?' ☐
2. 'I wouldn't take any of your lousy products if you were giving them away.' ☐
3. 'I am deeply impressed by what you have to offer and I also like the way you presented it.' ☐
4. 'Call me next month and we can continue the discussion when I have got the updated figure.' ☐
5. 'I can't make a decision on my own, but I'll arrange for your rep to meet the office manager next week.' ☐
6. 'We'll think about it and we'll probably call you sometime in the next few months.' ☐

Answers
1. Sale. If the customer is prepared to give their credit card details there can be no doubt.
2. No sale.
3. Continuation. Although it is nice to hear complementary remarks, there is no clear evidence of the sale progressing.
4. Agreement to another call just continues the sale, there is no advance towards a purchase decision. However, it would have been an advance if the client had said, '...in the meantime I'll present your proposal to the financial director and try to arrange a conference call'.
5. Advance. This is action (a meeting with the office manager) and the action moves the sale forward.
6. Continuation. The door is not closed, but this could be the typical brush-off to get rid of the caller without actually saying no. Just saying 'I'll think about it' is not strong enough action to move the sale forward.

Improving call success

It has been shown above that calls can be classified into the four possible outcomes:

order, advance, continuation or no sale, the first two being successful outcomes and the last two unsuccessful outcomes. The 'general outcomes matrix' shown in Table 7.5 can help in understanding the way a telephone call is handled and suggest ways it may be improved so as to increase the chance of either an 'advance' or an 'order'.

> ### Practical tip
>
> 1. Get your agents to write down statements made by the clients at the end of the call and categorize them into order, advance, continuation or no sale.
> 2. For each call consider what steps were made towards advancing the sale.
> 3. Next time calls are made ensure precise objectives are set that will lead towards advancing the sales rather than merely to continuations.

Telemarketing operation – in-house, buy in or both?

Some companies that have large telemarketing operations also use telemarketing bureaux for handling additional call volume generated by specific campaigns. According to Simon Roncoroni of the L&R Group, 99% of the total volume of all telemarketing business in the UK is carried out in-house by companies, with only 1% of the volume being done by telemarketing bureaux.

In 1992 research in the USA also showed that the majority of all telemarketing calls were handled in-house. However, there may be some movement towards the greater use of telemarketing bureaux as they may be able to provide a similar or better level of service than can be obtained in-house. An in-house operation might be considered appropriate if there is already sufficient management expertise and personnel with telemarketing skills. However, using a bureau would require a

Table 7.5 *General outcomes matrix for various types of telephone call. Source:* © *Huthwaite Research Group Limited*

Type of call	Excellent	Good	Standard	Below standard or unsuccessful
Information request	Taking an order for the items information was requested about	An 'advance' towards an order for the items	Gives the required information courteously	Gives the required information but is not courteous
Order request	Order plus another order from cross/up sale	Order plus an advance to a cross/up sale	Takes order as specified	Fails to take the order
Incorrect order For example, out of date codes, old and out of stock items	Sells more expensive item the client could use as a substitute	Sells alternative items where the price is the same or cheaper	Seller sorts out the right item codes and checks status	Refers client directly to another department
Problem solving	Solves problem by selling additional products or service (where this will help the client)	Cause and importance of the problem is identified. Client is confident the seller will take action and that the problem will be solved	Problem is discussed in depth and client is told who to talk to and what to do	Refers client directly to another department
Outbound or other proactive call	Placing the order over the phone then and there	The client: – Agrees to talk to someone in his or her organization and present the seller's suggestion positively – Agrees to come to a demo or be visited by salesperson – Agrees to next phone call and to have made a decision by then	The client: – Agrees to receive a quote – Agrees to think about it – Agrees to next call but does not make any other commitment	The client says not and does not want further contact on this subject Or It is not known if there is a need

Table 7.6 *Basic charges*

Costs	Inbound	Outbound
Set-up costs*	£4500–£7500	£750–£1250
Running costs	80p–£1.20/call plus telephone, i.e. 0800 call costs.	£28–£35 per operator hour (includes all call costs for UK campaign)
	Monthly management fee – approximately 10% of total costs	

* This can vary according to the amount and depth of any product training required.
Source: The L&R Group Ltd

smaller initial investment, allow a faster start-up, and provide volume capacity with 24 hour operation 365 days a year.

The four development options

There are four basic options that can be considered for developing telemarketing as part of the marketing mix:

Set up an in-house operation to handle inbound and outbound calls

This requires a substantial capital investment in telecommunications equipment, computer hardware and software and recruitment and selection of telemarketing agents and an in-depth training programme. Any training programme of less than two weeks is likely to be of little value unless the agents already have the right skills and all that is required is product and company knowledge.

Buy in all activities from a third party bureau

Unless the call volume is large and regular, without peaks and troughs, then using a third party bureau may be cheaper than in-house. Factors affecting call level and frequency include the nature and frequency of advertising campaigns; the more varied and irregular these are, the more likely a bureau is to be cost effective. When comparing costs it is important to consider in-house overheads as well as call costs to the total costs of using a bureau.

Bureau costs usually include the basic charges listed in Table 7.6.

Choosing the right telemarketing bureau

Once a decision has been made to use a telemarketing bureau then it is essential to choose the right one. The Checklist 7.2 provides some guidelines to help this process.

Use a bureau to test the service and once the service has been identified as profitable then move it in-house

This option might be best when considering moving say low value or medium size accounts from the traditional field salesforce to a telemarketing operation. Trials could be conducted in one region and then if this proves successful the programme could be rolled out nationwide.

Use a bureau to test before moving in-house, but still retain the bureau for specific tasks

A bureau may be used:

- when you don't have the experience in a specific application;
- when there are employment constraints, i.e. overflow and out of hours work in order to balance call loads;
- for short term projects;
- for pilot projects.

Checklist 7.2
Choosing the right telemarketing bureau

1. Consider at least three bureaux.
2. Seek specialist advice from consultants to help make the right decision.
3. Check whether the bureau has worked on your type of application, industry sector and media before.
4. Ask for testimonials from clients who have run similar projects.
5. Visit the bureau and see how they handle calls.
6. Ask for examples of the type of reports you will want.
7. Talk to the agents who will be working on your campaign.
8. What is the capability of the technology? Do they have automatic call distributors (ACD), adequate number of lines to cope for busy periods, and capability to update the database?
9. Ask what training is provided for agents.
10. Always provide a full brief. Don't give the bureau any late surprises.
11. Ask for a price in a standard format so that you can easily compare all bureaux prices.
12. Are the management professional and responsive to your requirements?

Source: BT

Selecting the right telephone numbers for incoming calls

For inbound telemarketing there are a number of different types of telephone lines that can be used such as Freefone (BT 0800), Lo-call (BT 0345) and national call rates (BT 0990). Other network operators provide a similar service. Selecting the wrong tariff option can be an expensive mistake according to a report called 'The Numbers Game: The L&R Group guide to selecting telephone numbers for marketing and business'. The report estimates that a 'company receiving 50,000 calls per month on a Freefone may overpay by as much as £12,000 per annum if they select the wrong tariff option, receive bills that vary by as much as 26% per annum depending on network provider, and waste £5,000 per annum by placing an average of 15% of calls on hold for an average of 32 seconds'.

Table 7.7 shows BT's Freefone, Lo-call and national call rate telephone numbers, together with the benefits for both the company and the caller.

Delivering service quality

Delivering service quality requires giving careful attention to every aspect of how the customer is handled. Customers' expectations are continually rising as they are requiring higher and higher standards. We know from The Henley Centre report, Teleculture 2000, that if a single telephone call is mishandled customers would prefer not to buy from the company again. There is much talk about customer satisfaction. Of

Table 7.7 *What's in a number? Source: BT (prices correct as of June 1996)*

	How much do callers pay?	What does it cost you?	What does it say to the caller?	What does it mean for your business?	What's it for	Who uses it?
Freefone 0800	Nothing	12p per minute (daytime) 9p per minute (night-time)	It's a free call – we want your business	You'll get a huge response to your campaign	Lead generation, order taking, carelines DRTV	First Direct, Freemans, Rank Xerox, Boots, Apple
International Freefone 0800	Usually nothing but some countries apply local rate charges	Per minute charge varies from country to country	We are offering you easy access to quality UK products	You can gain a presence in markets abroad quickly and for minimal cost	Global customer support, widen catchment, test new markets	Thomas Cook, Shell, American Express
Lo-call 0345	Local rate	9p per minute (daytime) 6p per minute (night-time)	It's worth a quick local call to get what you need	You're as accessible as a local firm	Inbound order taking, advice and information lines	First Direct, Next, Porche Cars (GB) Ltd, local authorities
National call 0900	National long distance	Nothing	This company is easy to reach and has a strong national presence	You can rationalize your service on a single easy to remember number	Advice and information lines, brochure request, DRTV	Walt Disney, Center Parcs, Eurotunnel, Hoover

course customer satisfaction is important and every effort must be made to ensure that customers are fully satisfied with the product or service being provided. For many companies the primary aim must be customer satisfaction, because they may not yet be fully meeting the customer's aspirations. However, world class companies are going way beyond customer satisfaction as they realize that customer satisfaction alone is not sufficient and that even satisfied customers may defect to the competition. World class companies appreciate that to retain customers they need to delight them. It is beyond the scope of this chapter to explain the concept of delighting customers and a full discussion can be found in the book *Management of Sales and Customer Relations* by Bob Hartley and Michael Starkey.

Whilst the L&R Careline report showed the response in the UK to be quick (average 2.7 seconds), for many industrial organizations such a rapid response may be impractical. Avery Berkel believes in responding quickly to customers. The poster in Figure 7.4 shows that the company considers answering the telephone promptly to be an important part of its total customer service – if it takes five rings to answer the telephone then that can be considered poor customer service.

If a decision is made to use a bureau for running the telemarketing operations, then it is imperative that a service level agreement is drawn up by the bureau. If DRTV is used, it is essential that the bureau is fully briefed about the media campaign and given a detailed schedule of all advertisements on television or radio. It is important that the right number of agents is on duty because 80% of telephone calls come in within 15 minutes of the transmission of a TV advertisement. Companies might find it useful to consult the DMA Broadcast Guidelines produced by the Direct Marketing Association (UK) Ltd. For example, inbound response handling will need to cover issues such as:

- The number of rings within which calls should be answered.
- Acceptable average call length.
- Acceptable rate of failed calls (a failed call is defined as one where the caller does not leave sufficient information necessary to complete the follow-up).
- Deadlines by which fulfilment must take place relative to when the call was received, dependent on campaign criteria.
- The reporting system: what information the client will receive, in what form, and when.

Consideration needs to be given as to how calls will be handled that are not related to the campaign. Arrangements will need to be made so that these calls are:

- Handled either by the bureau there and then.
- Referred to an external careline or customer service number.
- Diverted direct to the client so that they can answer the query themselves.
- Or brief details are taken so that the

enquirer can be called back later either by the bureau or the client.

If a bureau is used for an outbound telemarketing campaign then targets will need to be specified regarding the decision maker contact rate and the conversion rate per operator per hour.

Ethics in telemarketing

In the past telemarketing has had a poor image, however, the industry has taken a number of steps to put this right. For instance, the Telephone Preference Service was established in early 1995 to help companies make sure that they do not make telephone calls to those people who do not want to be called without prior agreement. The Direct Marketing Association has also produced a 'code of practice' booklet which covers telemarketing. Unless the industry is able to regulate itself then it is inevitable that legislation will be introduced in order to bring about changes.

By mid-1996 a total of 77,000 consumers had registered with the Telephone Preference Service. It is important that consumers who do not want to receive unsolicited telephone calls register and that all commercial organizations engaged in telemarketing support the service. If unsolicited telephone calls are seen to be increasing and causing an unwarranted invasion of privacy then legislation is inevitable. The Telephone Preference Service scheme covers calls made to consumers at home. It also only applies to those calls from companies with whom the consumer has no ongoing or contractual relationship. At the end of 1995 the European Parliament voted against the recommendation of the European Commission and rejected proposals for the banning of cold calling using the telephone. However, if, in the future, outbound telephone calls were found to be becoming more intrusive then the threat of legislation would reappear. Meanwhile, the European Commission is preparing a directive on the processing of personal data and the protection of privacy in the telecommunica-

Figure 7.4 *Answer promptly. Source: Avery Berkel*

tions sector. This will regulate the information that may be stored on the use of telecommunications systems by subscribers and the use of personal data for marketing.

The code of practice booklet produced by the Direct Marketing Association provides clear guidelines on ethical and professional conduct for members on using the telephone for marketing, sales or customer service purposes. The recommendations include the following:

● The name of the organization on whose behalf a sales, marketing or service call is made or received shall be voluntarily and promptly disclosed.

● The purpose of the call shall be clearly stated early in the conversation.

● Telephone marketers shall not evade the truth or deliberately mislead.

● Sales, marketing or service calls shall not be executed in the guise of research or a survey.

● Calls should normally be made between the hours of 8 am and 9 pm.

● Telephone marketers shall avoid the use of high pressure tactics which could be construed as harassment.

Summary

Telemarketing will continue to grow for many years to come. The increasing costs of keeping salespeople on the road means that more and more companies are turning to telemarketing in order to replace or supplement the field salesforce. Telemarketing is also playing an increasing role in generating sales leads, database building and improving customer service.

With more and more sales being conducted using the telephone it is essential that telesales people have the right skills and are able to ask questions that focus on customers' needs. This is essential both for gaining and retaining customers. Poorly trained salespeople are likely to lose a company business, as customers are no longer prepared to be badly treated. Telesales agents need to understand how to move the sale forward and distinguish between successful and unsuccessful call outcomes.

There are four basic options that can be considered for developing telemarketing:

1. Set up an in-house operation to handle inbound and outbound calls.
2. Buy in all activities from a third party bureau.
3. Use a bureau to test the service and once the service has been identified as profitable then move it in-house.
4. Use a bureau to test before moving in-house, but still retain the bureau for specific tasks.

Delivering service quality requires giving careful attention to every aspect of how the customer is handled. Customers' expectations are continually rising as they are requiring higher and higher standards of service. Companies engaged in telemarketing need to incorporate 'best practice' in their relationship with customers and potential customers.

Acknowledgements

Grateful acknowledgement is made to Mike Gibson-Sharpe, Market Development Manager, BT Telemarketing Services for provision of materials and commenting on drafts of this chapter, Linda Marsh of Huthwaite Research Group for provision of telesales training material, Richard Wood of The Henley Centre for provision of materials and many others who have provided materials or assistance.

Useful contact telephone numbers

BT *Telemarketing Services*
Freefone 0800 660099

Direct Marketing Association
0171 321252500

The Henley Centre
0171 3539961

Huthwaite Research Group Ltd
01709 710081

Institute of Direct Marketing
0181 9775705

L&R Group
0171 7354000

Merit Direct
01789 299622

References and further reading

Direct Marketing Association (1993) *Code of Practice*.

The Direct Marketing Association (UK) Ltd (1996) *DMA Broadcast Guidelines*.

Hartley, R.A. and Starkey, M.W. (1996) *Management of Sales and Customer Relations*. International Thomson Business Press.

Leiderman, R. (1995) *The Telephone Handbook*. McGraw-Hill.

Rackham, N. (1987) *Achieving Major Sales*. Gower.

Stevens, M. (1995) *Telemarketing in Action*. Maidenhead: McGraw-Hill.

Stevens, M. (1991) *The Handbook of Telemarketing*. Kogan Page.

The L&R Group (1995) *Careline Report*.

The L&R Group (1995) *The Numbers Game: The L&R Group Guide to selecting telephone number for marketing and business*.

The Henley Centre (1994) *Teleculture 2000*.

The Henley Centre (1996) *Teleculture Futures*.

Part Three

Salesforce Management and Strategy

8

Developing and motivating a salesforce —

Dr Bill Donaldson, University of Strathclyde

 In this chapter we consider a prime task of management, i.e. getting the best from salespeople. To achieve this requires an understanding of the differences between managing and doing activities, clarification of sales tasks and management of the motivational mix. We consider training, leadership, remuneration, management controls and feedback mechanisms to be important. These are the issues discussed in this chapter.

Introduction

At any one time individual ability and superior technique may make the difference as to whether a sale is won or lost, but the key factor in sales performance over time is motivation. The problem is how to develop and motivate a field salesforce who operate on their own, away from head office, in a hostile environment, geographically distant, at a relatively high cost, to do their job well in the way management wants it to be done. Motivation can be defined as the amount of effort a salesperson expends on each of the activities or tasks associated with their job. Salespeople respond to stimulus and sales managers can influence this process.

While many sales managers rather fancy themselves as leaders and team builders, and hence as good motivators, the truth is that the motivation of salespeople is neither easy nor straightforward. Part of the complexity of

this problem is the multiplicative nature of the variables which impact on performance. These variables include individual skills, sales aptitude, accurate perceptions of the salesperson's role and other components of motivation. The problem is compounded by the individuality of the selling job where the nature of the task, the individual's selling approach and the prospect's reaction to sales stimuli all vary. Industry specific contexts, the type of selling, the characteristics of individuals, all hamper the search for definitive solutions and create unique problems. To prescribe a solution requires management to consider a number of factors and influences which can then be adapted to particular circumstances.

Managing versus doing

Many sales managers achieve their position on the basis of their performance as sales

Practical tip

Analyse your own activities over two or three typical days in any one month. Try to identify how your time is spent and on what kind of tasks. There is no right or wrong balance but if most of your time is doing as opposed to managing then you are not doing the job you are employed to do.

people but there are important differences between managing and doing. Good salespeople do not necessarily make good sales managers although they may do so. Many organizations, and their customers, expect sales managers to deal with larger accounts, to keep in contact with senior level customer staff and to negotiate for important orders. Further, managers often spend a good deal of their time dealing with enquiries on the tele-

phone, handling customer problems and in liaison internally on supply hiccups or service problems. While these activities are important they are doing tasks and should be distinguished from managing tasks such as organizing, planning and controlling sales effort including training subordinates, supervising, leading and motivating your sales team.

Clarifying the sales task

Fundamental to effective management is to specify exactly the job to be done. This requires a job specification, a job description and measurable indicators of performance. Before these elements are considered it is worthwhile considering the unique problems of the selling job:

● Salespeople have inadequate or incomplete information about their job,

**Checklist 8.1
Managing or doing?**

1. Progressing important customers' delivery queries with production.
2. Calling on an important account with one of your salespeople.
3. Setting out sales targets by specific account.
4. Giving a talk to your local association or club.
5. Booking a hotel for a regional sales meeting.
6. Solving a problem with a customer which one of your sales team has brought to your attention.
7. Talking to staff about a new sales idea you have.
8. Reporting on sales progress to senior management.
9. Deciding on your budget for sales operations.
10. Changing allocation of accounts between salespeople.

Of these ten activities the first five are not managing tasks, the second five are. Analyse your own time; make a list of the activities or tasks in which you are involved and assess whether your are really managing.

especially concerning the needs and preferences of customers and customer organizations.

- Salespeople mostly work alone and independently without direct supervision. Although considered by many to be an advantage this independence creates other problems of role clarity.
- Salespeople operate in an inter-organizational boundary position which creates role conflicts.
- The sales job is demanding in terms of the degree of innovation and creativity required. There is no one right approach in all circumstances.
- The job requires adaptability and sensitivity by salespeople to the needs of customers yet is frequently met by different degrees of antagonism, hostility and sometimes aggression.
- Sales decisions may have to be made quickly requiring decisiveness and mental alertness.
- Individual sales performance evaluation lacks direct observation of inputs; only outcomes are assessed.
- Evaluation is often inferred and subjective, i.e. people biased.
- Salespeople often have little control over the conditions in which they operate.

As a result of these peculiarities managers fail to measure the complete job, instead relying on inadequate definition of the necessary inputs to achieve the desired outputs. That is, the use of sales, call rates or other easily assessed measures are preferred to the more difficult quality dimensions of the job. The quality measures are often the most important if the task is to hold customers and develop the business these customers do with our firm.

Further, most sales managers place an over-reliance on subjective factors. Seemingly contrary to the previous point, many managers seem to evaluate salespeople on selected personality traits or qualities. These characteristics are seldom proven measures of quality in sales performance. More likely, they are factors managers consider made

them successful when they were selling. Evaluation will be a greater motivator if used in a positive, rather than a negative way. The unique nature of the selling job should force managers to consider the effect their communication content and style has on their subordinates.

Practical tip

Next time you are sending a memo or circular to salespeople reminding them about cost cutting on telephone expenses, why not emphasize the positive by suggesting e-mail, fax and telephone be used in that order, which reflects their relative costs.

A job description is important for a salesperson but in preparing such a document the sales manager must define in general terms what the organization really expects salespeople to do. Is it to win new business, new customers, provide technical advice, obtain product specifications, service existing customers, or all of these? (See Checklist 8.2.)

Basic theory of motivation

Most people will be familiar with some of the basic theories of motivation such as Maslow's hierarchy of needs, Herzberg's motivation-hygiene theory, Vroom's expectancy theory and Adam's equity theory. These theories have a strong conceptual basis and prove useful generalizations but none can claim to be universal as applied to the sales job. Vroom's theory (adapted by Churchill and Ford, 1977) is perhaps the most appropriate to the selling job. Basically this theory suggests that a salesperson's performance is a multiplicative function of the level of motivation (effort × performance × reward), sales aptitude and perceptions of how the role should be performed. These variables are influenced by various antecedent conditions such as the personal characteristics of the

Checklist 8.2
Selling tasks

- Demonstration/presentation
- Negotiation on quality, price and delivery
- Explanation of company policy
- Market information on competitors
- Market information on conditions and trends
- Stock availability and customer stock levels and stocking policies
- Dealer support
- New outlets and new business
- Display and merchandising
- Customer relations
- Credit policies and account management
- Complaint handling
- Looking after company property.

Management must decide which of the above each salesperson is expected to do on a routine or exceptional basis. Warning! If you expect salespeople to do all of these tasks all of the time don't ask for 10/12 calls per day.

salesperson, company characteristics, environmental factors and particularly competition. In addition, it can be postulated that the salesperson's performance can be affected by the type and amount of reward received. Salespeople will only put in the effort if they feel (expectancy) the effort will result in performance being achieved and that the rewards for increased performance are of value to them. Expectancies are the salesperson's perception of the link between effort on various activities and the level of performance which results.

For example, salespeople will increase their hours worked and their call rate if they perceive the increased effort will achieve the desired performance and that the improved performance produces the desired reward (increased pay, recognition, self-esteem). This expectancy will be a function of the accuracy and magnitude of their perceptions of

reward. If these are accurate the result will be as expected. The sales manager has to identify important influencing variables such as age, experience, education, competition and so on and assess how these affect salespeople. For example, an individual's expectancy in terms of both accuracy and magnitude (importance) is likely to be positively related to their experience, their ability to assess their environment accurately and their skill in predicting customer and competitor actions and reactions. Their assessment of what they can do about it and what they are prepared to do reflects another dimension in their motivation.

Finally, they will only be motivated if they feel the rewards are attractive to them. Different people are influenced in different ways according to their stage in their career, their gender and the level of existing rewards, so this is neither a simple nor an easy task. Financial rewards, recognition of achievement and career advancement are the strongest but don't apply to all salespeople in the same way.

Practical tip

Categorize your salesforce, in groups or on an individual basis. Just as a lot can be learned from segmenting a market so a salesforce will have groups, some of whose needs are similar to others, yet different from other groups. For example, young people are more likely to value career opportunities and training while older salespeople put more emphasis on remuneration and recognition of achievements.

Practical application of motivation theory

To apply expectancy theory in practice, the job of the sales manager is to realize that there is a combination of motivational factors which influence performance. For example, the salesperson is influenced not only by the amount of reward but by the desirability of receiving increased rewards through extra efforts which influence performance. An important and related factor is the level of job satisfaction the salesperson experiences. Job dissatisfaction means lower sales and less enthusiasm for the job, affecting drive and hours worked. Staff turnover will be higher as good salespeople leave to join more stretching companies. Dissatisfaction will lead to 'bad press' for the company with customers and colleagues. The more dissatisfied the salesperson is with current pay and conditions, the higher the premium that will be attached to an increase in those rewards.

However, increased job satisfaction does not necessarily result in improved job performance. There are many salespeople who are relatively satisfied with their job and thus are not hungry enough to perform to their full potential. The sales manager must avoid or overcome such staleness and complacency in their salesforce. The salesperson must also be accurate in their assessment of their own capability to achieve increased performance. Salespeople are influenced by the clarity of their task, their need to achieve, their satisfaction with the remuneration and the quality of management. Managers can have a significant influence on salespeople's perceptions of these influences.

To provide some help for sales managers, we would suggest solutions must be sought within the relevant context of the sales job. Service calling and development selling, organizational and individual customers, industrial, consumer or service selling can be so varied as to require separate, perhaps unique, analysis. In the complex trading situations now encountered, the use of sales volume or value is itself incomplete if not inadequate. Further, the mix of hard and soft data, both quantitative and subjective, causes real assessment problems. The search goes on but we can recommend some positive actions.

Job specification

With the provisos outlined above, sales managers can do a number of things. First, recruit the right sort of people. That is, those with a need to achieve, whose personal and personality characteristics, aptitude and skills best meet the requirements of the job. This requires a job specification. Sales managers need to concentrate on improving these attributes through training and relating them to the buyers and needs of the market. The right people, experience, skill and role clarity do matter but only when matched to the prospect. This confirms what successful salespeople and sales managers already know but few seem able to achieve in practice.

A job specification should set out the requirements for the appropriate type of person to fill the job. It should be a combination of qualities based on management experience and any available evidence of what is required to do the job. As much objective rea-

Profile of our more successful salespeople:

1. Age 25–30.
2. Average/above average in height and weight and physically fit.
3. Definite career aspirations, mobile and willing to re-locate.
4. Graduate but not necessarily outstanding academically.
5. Has a range of other activities and interests but not too many.
6. Determined to pursue a career in sales.
7. Good interpersonal skills.
8. Some sales experience but not necessarily in this industry.

Outline of requirements for a salesperson:

● Education: College graduate. Average performance with some distinguished achievements.
● Range of activities and more practical orientation.
● Personality: Seeks challenge and enthusiastic. Combination of innovative approach and creativity, at least in some areas. Evidence of both individual achievement and team playing.
● Experience: Some sales experience. Evidence of commitment, not too many different jobs, with some outside interests.
● Physical: Age 25–40, average in height and weight, physically fit, energetic, good appearance.
● Maturity: Stable, reliable evidence of perseverance.
● Motivation: Has career aspirations, willing to re-locate, financially motivated and competitive.
● Other: Clean driving licence, interest in business and current affairs.

soning should be applied as possible but inevitably the outcome is highly subjective. It should cover such characteristics as age, experience, technical knowledge and selling skills thought to be required to do the job. Remember, the more highly trained and experienced the recruit, the more expensive and scarce they are likely to be. Further, those involved in missionary or detail selling require different skills and qualities from those involved in more routine service selling, hence the need for a job specification.

The job description

The second area of importance is in the job itself. If a salesperson doesn't find the job challenging or interesting there will be a motivation problem. Compared with many jobs this problem will be less for salespeople than, for example, an assembly-line worker. Sales managers should be careful that excessive routines, job simplification or too strict a discipline do not de-motivate. Part of the attraction to the job is the freedom of action

Activity Days	1	2	3	4	5	6	7	8	9	10	Total	Average	% of total
Preparatory:													
Customer knowledge													
Proposal preparation													
Target planning													
Productive:													
Contact making													
Presentation													
Unproductive:													
Travel													
Waiting													
Routine admin.													
Complaint handling													
Attending meetings													
Personal:													
Lunch and breaks													
Other													
Call management:													
Account servicing													
Evaluation of results													
Maintaining records													
TOTALS													

Figure 8.1 *Sales tasks*

which is permitted. This autonomy combines with variety of tasks and their perceived importance. For this reason a job description is vital.

As suggested, it is incumbent upon the sales manager to specify the tasks expected to be performed by the salesperson on both a routine and exceptional basis. This can be formulated into a job description which is a written statement of the tasks to be performed and their relative importance (Figure 8.1). A good job description will be a clear written statement which has the agreement of experienced salespeople themselves as well as management. It should be as specific as possible in terms of tasks and performance evaluation yet it should not be too long.

Measures of performance

The third area in which motivational theory can be applied is in clear and unambiguous measures of performance. As shown above these are part of the job description but they require special consideration.

Practical tip

Before writing up a job description conduct an analysis of one or two salespeople and assess how they currently spend their time. The Checklist 8.4 can be used for this purpose.

**Checklist 8.4
Example of a job description**

Job title:
Sales representative.

Job function:
To achieve sales objectives in line with the company's marketing and sales plans. This will be done by developing and maintaining existing accounts and by winning new business and new accounts. Important to our business is good relationships with customers through help, advice, training and high levels of customer care.

Job duties and responsibilities:
- Accomplish product sales targets by securing existing business and developing new business at minimum cost.
- By direct selling, maintain and enhance customer contact thus increasing the business our customers do.
- Generate and exploit sales opportunities within your area.
- Use company information to keep abreast of market and competitive conditions and contribute to this information by timely reporting of relevant market information.
- Maintain adequate customer records and up-date information on customers.
- Provide high level service support for customers through technical, market and promotional information. Ensure price changes are implemented to the company's and customer's satisfaction.
- Provide adequate and timely reports as directed by the regional manager.
- Follow company rules and procedures and take appropriate care of company equipment.

Performance measurement:
- Sales against target
- Profitability of the territory
- Individual profitability of named customers
- Expense control
- Customer records
- Number of customers
- Periodic customer satisfaction index.

The job description must relate to the situation characteristics of the selling job. It should be more specific than the generalized approach taken here.

**Checklist 8.5
Measures of performance**

Quantitative
- Sales by volume or value
- Sales by product
- Expense to sales ratio
- Gross margin on sales
- Market share
- Sales versus area potential
- Calls made
- Call frequency
- Order to call ratio
- Average order size
- New orders to repeat orders
- Return on investment.

Qualitative
- Ability to do the selling job
- Service to existing accounts
- Search out new customers
- Keep stocks at appropriate level
- Keep customers informed
- Assist customers to sell product
- Technical advice and assistance
- Training customer staff
- Solving customers' problems
- Collecting and reporting information
- Customer service
- Company reputation.

Practical tip

Before deciding the most appropriate performance measures, involve salespeople themselves to find out what they feel best encapsulates the essence of the job they are expected to do. If they participate in the process they are more likely to accept the measures.

Managing the motivational mix ▬

The importance and complexity of motivation and its effect on performance has led to the idea of the motivational mix which represents the combination of factors to be considered including training, leadership skills, remuneration and incentives, management controls and feedback mechanisms. These factors, which managers can influence and control, will affect an individual's motivation to work and, ultimately, their job performance.

In addition to recruiting the most appropriate people for the job based on the job specification every sales manager must try and improve their subordinates' individual effectiveness by appropriate training. Much training is wasted because it covers areas which the person already knows about. For this reason, it is important to separate induction training for new recruits from that suggested for existing staff. Again, planning is important so the first stage, prior to training, is to conduct some audit of training requirements. Checklist 8.6 can be used for such a purpose.

This is stage one in the process, determining needs; stage two is designing the programme; stage three is conducting the training; and the final stage is evaluating the results. The vice president of the US pharmaceutical giant Merck, with a sales force of 3000, on receiving an award as the sales company of the year in 1993 declared that 'training is the key'. To reinforce this a 1993 study

**Checklist 8.6
Training audit**

Name:
Area:

Factor	Good (knows this, needs no training)	Above average (knows this, tries to do it)	Below average (knows this, does not do it)	Poor (does not know this, does not do it)	Training recommen-dations
Knowledge: product market customers					
Skills: probing questioning demonstration closing					
Abilities: time management territory management planning reporting records care of car and equipment					

suggested that it is not the amount of money spent on training that counts but how the money is spent. Higher performers do not outspend lower performers, but they allocate the funds in different ways. High performers have longer induction training – three to nine months – whereas lower performers spend less than three months with new recruits. High performers do less classroom and role playing but more on-the-job training. Training also has an important role in estab-lishing the values and beliefs that an organi-zation represents – that is, in establishing cor-porate culture within the salesforce.

Leadership

As referred to earlier, the ability to get the best from subordinates is a valued character-istic and is referred to as leadership quality. However, leadership is best explained in the context in which it is exercised and sales managers should assess their leadership style and its appropriateness to the people and circumstances in which it is applied.

In today's organizations where rationalizing, downsizing and restructuring are being implemented, sales managers must enable their people to adapt and be flexible. Such movers and shakers have been called transformational leaders; they can get their salespeople to perform beyond typical expectations. However, in most situations, sales managers who have not proved themselves as having previously been a successful salesperson will find it hard, if not impossible, to be convincing in this role. Qualities thought to be important in sales managers vary and often extend to a variety of characteristics usually ending with an ability to walk on water and other super-human powers.

Perhaps more revealing are studies which reflect how salespeople feel about their boss. The major complaints usually focus on the following:

- Managers do not spend enough time with their salespeople.
- They do not listen to salespeople's concerns.
- They do not take these concerns seriously, and
- They do not follow up.

Again the problem is that many sales managers have not been trained in management or prepared for the new skills and tasks that they are now asked to perform.

Remuneration

Closely allied to motivation and arguably the most influential factor in the motivational mix is remuneration, which can be both basic financial rewards and special incentives. This explains why financial incentives are a popular and effective means used to motivate sales personnel. Sales managers can remunerate salespeople using salary, commission bonus

Checklist 8.7
Management style

Use the following grid and asses where your position is most likely to be. For example, if you normally consult a subordinate before taking any action you are likely to be consultative. If you contact your team, you are probably democratic. If you are confident and self-opinionated (not always a bad thing), you are autocratic. Remember that there is no one right way and the appropriate style will vary depending on the age, experience, education and personality of the person being led as much as on the characteristics of the leader.

AUTOCRATIC		DEMOCRATIC
	CONSULTATIVE	
PATERNALISTIC		LAISSEZ-FAIRE

or a combination of these. Most sales managers, based on their experience, seem to feel that a balance of types of remuneration is most appropriate

A recent study, conducted by the author, found that most UK companies offer combination remuneration comprising salary and commission or salary and some form of bonus, especially performance related pay. This research also found that a number of salespeople consider job security of higher value than the level of remuneration. Other studies into the effects of pay on the motivation of salespeople have found, for example, that older salespeople with larger families valued financial rewards more whereas younger better educated sales staff who had no family valued the so-called higher order rewards such as recognition, liking and respect and sense of accomplishment. The variety of payment plans in operation, even within similar industry and sales situations, suggests that management do not fully understand the effect of payment on their employees' motivation. If a company's main objectives are on relationship building and long term customers, a higher salary and lower incentive component would be recommended. The difficulty with such rules is that within any one salesforce there is no one remuneration package that suits everyone and we have to settle for one that best meets the needs of most of our salesforce.

Management systems and controls

Setting targets and quotas for salespeople has a direct effect on their motivation. Targets not only direct sales effort and provide evidence for performance evaluation but they can also act as an incentive and motivation. It is not only the target and system of control that is important but the way the target is determined, communicated and applied. For this reason, I have argued elsewhere that a system of management by objectives which is based on participation and involvement of salespeople themselves, is an appropriate option (Donaldson, 1990).

Accuracy and feedback

A problem already identified is that sales tasks and sales effort often can have an indirect rather than a direct effect on sales performance. Missionary selling, such as pharmaceuticals, is particularly prone to this difficulty. For others, organizational complexity or dual effort with intermediaries may confuse the sales process and its effect on performance. Nevertheless, accurate and timely feedback for salespeople has a positive effect on job performance and job satisfaction.

At one level evaluation of salespeople is easy – they either make target or they don't! The problem with the link between sales effort and sales response is that it is neither simple nor direct. Most companies do conduct some form of evaluation but few do this in a formal way which evaluates the cause as well as outcomes. Part of the problem with evaluation is that to do it properly, far from being easy, is time-consuming, costly and downright difficult. At the individual salesperson level, evaluation is necessary to identify above and below average performers, to identify possible candidates for promotion or dismissal, and to identify areas of weakness in salespeople in carrying out their tasks in meeting sales objectives. For management, evaluation is necessary to assess the efficacy of sales management practices such as territory deployment, recruitment, training, remuneration and so on. Again, our starting point is an audit of current performance.

Finally, evaluation is necessary to modify the sales tasks in line with customer and company needs so that sales plans, and assessment of these plans, is against the most appropriate criteria for improved sales performance. A good salesforce evaluation programme should be realistic and fair. It should be positive, contribute to motivation and improve job performance. It should be objective, involve salespeople themselves and be economic in cost and time to administer. These aims inevitably conflict. Accountants,

Checklist 8.8
Performance evaluation

	Low	1	2	3	4	5	6	7	8	9	High
1. Product mix											
2. Customer mix											
3. Work organization											
4. Workload											
5. Product knowledge											
6. Customer knowledge											
7. Competitor knowledge											
8. Relationships											
9. Customer service											
10. Sales techniques											

Approach: taking each area in turn indicate the optimum expected performance, recognizing that a 9 would represent the top 5% or 10% of the salesforce. For an individual salesperson indicate their actual performance on each dimension with a cross. Where there are gaps, indicating weak areas of performance, these should be evaluated and corrective action taken.

operational researchers, behaviourists, management scientists, economists and many other disciplines have tried to find better and more accurate measures of sales performance with varying degrees of success. It appears that evaluating salespeople is still something of an art struggling to be a science.

Overview of salesforce motivation

The individual may respond, positively or negatively, to the different factors which management can deploy to motivate the salesforce. The quest for understanding the components of motivation and its impact on performance should lead to at least some tentative formula for improving salesforce motivation. This is outlined below but before

doing this, we highlight the problems created by a lack of motivation. One problem is that sales will be lower. Enthusiasm, drive and hours worked will be less if individuals are not fully motivated. These directly affect sales performance. A related problem is that sales staff turnover will be higher, especially amongst better performing salespeople more able (and motivated) to find work elsewhere. A lack of motivation not only results in less hours being worked but often higher expense claims, more give-aways to customers, higher mileage, etc. Lower motivation often coincides with indiscipline or 'bad mouthing' to other colleagues or customers. As in most occupations, the importance of minor complaints becomes magnified, diverting management time to peripheral issues. Things to avoid which may exacerbate the problem include poor working conditions, poor reporting procedures, unfairness in rewards, lack of promotion opportunity, lack of individual involvement and participation, no incentives, a disproportionate number of older salespeople and poor communication between subordinates, supervisors and top management.

A more positive approach is to take actions which will increase motivation. Such actions involve the elements in the motivational mix previously described. Among the most vital are likely to be:

- **Motivated people**: Salespeople who have drive and a need for achievement will have higher sales performance. Motivation can be expressed as a function of a salesperson's economic needs, social needs and self-actualizing needs.
- **Participation**: There is a greater commitment and involvement when salespeople take an active part in decision-making. The use of management by objectives or similar schemes can have a positive effect on salesforce motivation.
- **Being part of the company**: As for participation, so involvement is increased by salespeople who are committed to their company, their colleagues and supervisors. This belief extends to the products being sold (task importance) and that sales effort will make a contribution to the company's prosperity and the prosperity of other employees.
- **Morale**: Motivation is affected by morale. Morale is itself a difficult thing to define but is a mix or sum of a person's feelings towards their job, pay, other employees, conditions of work, competitors and other factors. Good morale by itself is not sufficient to motivate but poor morale can be a de-motivating factor.
- **Discipline**: Views on the correct amount and type of discipline vary but it is a factor. Too strict a discipline can turn people off, but no or weak discipline leads to a situation of anarchy. A fair code of things not allowed (e.g. dishonesty), of areas requiring

improvement (e.g. late reports, poor appearance) and areas of freedom (e.g. call patterns) should be established. Generally negative factors are weak motivations.

- **Monetary rewards**: As noted, the type and level of reward has different effects on different people but remuneration is likely to be one of the most influential factors in performance outcomes.
- **Good management**: Although management practices are a difficult concept to measure with the necessary degree of precision to make conclusions on sales motivation and performance; it should be recognized that they do have a combined impact. Factors such as goal setting, evaluation, control, coaching, understanding and know-how, contribute to individual salespeople's motivation.
- **Status enhancement**: Acknowledgement of a job well done, a more prestigious title, a management training course, an above average pay increase are not only important in themselves but as recognition of effort and a stimulus to greater effort.
- **Positive communication**: People are less motivated if they have negative views about the job, the company, their performance. If these views are accurate the cause of dissatisfaction must be corrected via product, price, distribution policies or organizational and managerial changes. If the views are inaccurate then management must improve their communication message. This can be done by measuring existing levels of satisfaction, by a complaint procedure, suggestion box, formal survey, exit interviews (leavers) or by keeping close to employees. Whatever the technique or approach, good two-way communication is vital for effective management of the salesforce.
- **Individual recognition**: Salespeople exist in an environment of relative isolation. It follows they will be sensitive to the distance between themselves and control of the operation. They require not only rewards for work done but frequent and

positive acknowledgement of their performance.

- **Ability to handle rejection**: In doing the job salespeople will inevitably get many rejections, re-buffs and lost sales. To overcome these negatives, especially in newer recruits, management must train salespeople to handle and expect rejection. These problems relate to an individual's role perceptions and, in particular, role conflict and ambiguity.
- **Group involvement**: Since salespeople operate on their own, fostering team spirit, camaraderie and group involvement are part of the management task.
- **Be available and understanding**: As with any employee individuality is important. At any one time salespeople may face personal problems such as health, finance, marital difficulties and so on. These can only be treated on an individual basis.

Summary

The formula for the management of motivation is first, give status rewards. Second, pay particular attention to role problems and handling rejection especially for new recruits. Third, arrange frequent communication individually and through regional or team meetings. Fourth, provide coaching and training for sales staff including special assignments for older, more experienced staff. Finally, stay close to subordinates, be available and understanding.

References

Donaldson, B. (1990) *Sales Management: Theory and Practice*. Basingstoke: Macmillan.

Walker, O.C., Churchill, G.A. and Ford, N.M. (1977) Motivation and performance in industrial selling: present knowledge and needed research. *Journal of Marketing Research*, May, 156–68.

9

Assessing sales performance

Dr Antonis Simintiras, The Open University

 It takes no profound understanding to realize that sales performance determines the viability, if not the very existence, of any entreprenurial activity. It is not necessary to embrace the 'nirvana approach' and believe that no matter how good sales performance is, it is nowhere near being perfect. However, it is important that questions concerning factors contributing to any deviation from the 'perfect norm' of performance are addressed by any contemporary organization. We will devote most of our attention in this chapter to such questions. Therefore, the purpose of this chapter is three-fold. First, we discuss the nature and role of forecasts, sales quotas and selling budgets. Second, we describe methods for evaluating the efficiency of the sales organization. Finally, individual salesperson performance, and methods for its appraisal, are discussed in the context of meeting or deviating from the 'perfect norm'. The use of these evaluations to take corrective action is also outlined.

To achieve sales objectives, sales managers must effectively control the sales effort. The process of controlling consists of the following three steps:

1. Establishing performance standards.
2. Evaluating actual performance by comparing it with established standards.
3. Taking corrective action to reduce the difference between 1 and 2.

The first step in the process is a decision about what needs to be accomplished. This should result in the specification of expected levels of performance. The second step determines whether actual performance measures up to performance standards. When a negative discrepancy between actual and expected performance occurs, corrective action must be taken, which is the third step in the controlling process.

The focus of the next section is on establishing performance standards with the use of sales forecasts, quotas and budgets.

Sales performance in context: the role of sales forecasts, quotas and budgets

Sales forecasts

In recent years there has been a marked improvement in the way companies plan and implement their sales effort. For example, in many organizations sales forecasts form the basis for setting sales quotas and allocating resources, and sales performance is carefully monitored and evaluated. Since performance evaluation begins with predictions or forecasts of company and industry sales, such forecasts are indispensable for decision making in sales management.

A *sales forecast* refers to the expected level of company sales for a level of company effort that is likely to be made in a given market for a specific time period. A *market forecast* is the expected level of industry sales for a level of industry effort that is likely to be made in a given market for a specific time. Thus, various levels of company effort will lead to different levels of sales. Theoretically, actual sales achieved could equal any desired

level of sales the company or industry wants to achieve – simply increase the effort! This, of course, cannot hold true since there is an upper limit of sales which can always be reached. The terms used to describe these upper limits are sales potential and market potential. More specifically, *sales potential* is the 'upper limit' of company sales as a company's effort goes to infinity in a given market for a specific time period, whereas *market potential* is the 'upper limit' of industry sales as an industry's effort approaches infinity in a given market for a specific time period (see Figure 9.1).

Knowledge of market and sales potential allows a sales manager to make accurate market and sales forecasts and plan the allocation of the available resources in a more effective and efficient manner. For example, if one geographic region has four times the market potential, it should tend to receive four times as much sales effort. The sales forecast is a prediction of the level of company sales in the future (usually a year). These are used to determine sales quotas for sales territories, districts, regions, zones or entire markets.

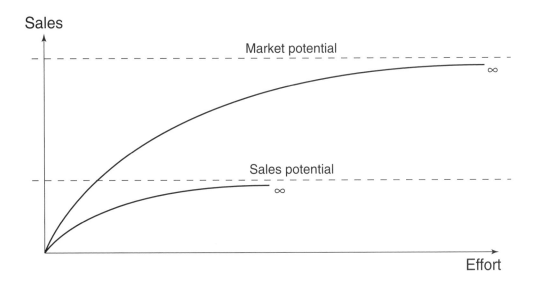

Figure 9.1 *Sales and market potential*

Establishing sales quotas

A *sales quota* is a sales performance objective assigned to a salesperson, branch office, distributor or dealer. Unless accurate sales forecasts are used for establishing sales quotas, the outcome of the evaluation of sales performance will be questionable.

It is rare for a company to achieve sales that are equal to sales potential. Numerous factors (e.g. salesperson experience, competitor activities, customer accessibility) constrain the firm's ability to reach that sales potential. Accordingly, it is very unusual for a company to equate its sales forecast to its sales potential. Rather, sales forecasts are always set at lower levels than the sales potential. This provides the flexibility to set the sales quota above or below the level of the sales forecast. For example, sales quotas may be set at higher levels than the sales forecasts in an attempt to stimulate high performance and ensure that salespeople are continuously 'hungry' for a sale. Alternatively, by setting sales quotas equal to or lower than the sales forecasts, the salespeople are provided with the psychological incentive of being able to achieve or outperform their sales quotas. It can be seen that sales forecasts should provide the basis for establishing sales quotas, and that the accuracy of these forecasts depends heavily upon the accuracy of the estimated levels of sales potential.

The purpose and types of sales quotas

The main purpose of sales quotas is to help managers with planning and evaluating salespeople's performance. More specifically, sales quotas are used, amongst other things, in order to:

- provide a sales objective for the salesforce;
- direct and control salespeople's activities;
- plan and control sales expenses;
- assess the productivity level of the sales effort; and
- improve the effectiveness of compensation plans and rewards.

The most common types of sales quotas used by sales managers are those that are based on:

- sales volume;
- expenses/costs;
- profitability;
- activities; and/or
- any combination of the above.

The use of a particular type or combination of sales quotas depends upon many organizational and environmental factors (i.e. nature of product, structure of market, competition, etc.). Clearly, there are several advantages and disadvantages associated with each type, and these are illustrated in Table 9.1.

Gaining salespeople's acceptance for the sales quotas is extremely important. If salespeople do not agree on the sales forecast which forms the basis for establishing sales quotas, this may result in low levels of motivation and high levels of dissatisfaction and turnover. One way to overcome such problems is by using the bottom-up instead of the top-down forecasting approach. According to bottom-up approach, sales forecasts are initially made at the account level by salespeople, and subsequently sales managers combine the account forecasts into territory, zone, region and eventually company forecast. The top-down approach suggests that company forecasts are first developed by individuals at the business unit level; sales managers then break down these company forecasts into region, zone, territory and account forecasts.

Selling budgets

All resources which are allocated for the personal selling function represent the total selling budget. The basic objective of a sales budget is to identify and determine the lowest expenditure level that is needed to accomplish the sales quotas. It is important to note at this stage that sales managers must resist the temptation to try and reduce or cut down the expenditures to the lowest possible level in order to achieve short term profitability

Table 9.1 *Types of Sales Quotas and their advantages and disadvantages*

Types of sales quotas	Advantages	Disadvantages
Sales volume	• Easy to calculate and administer • Simple to understand	• Emphasis is only on sales volume but not on profits • Leads to imbalances in selling activity (e.g., stress volume sales at the expense of non-selling activities)
Expenses/cost	• Makes salespeople aware of their expenses and profitability of their effort	• Minimizes expenses instead of boosting sales of profitable products and may become the primary aim of salespeople
Profitability	• Places emphasis on profits rather than volume • Indicates that high volume salespeople may not be the most profitable • Reveals the most profitable products and customers	• Complex in their calculation • Difficult to understand • Salespeople have no control over profit quotas unless the quota is on salesperson contribution to profit (i.e. salesperson's gross margin less direct expenses)
Activities	• Can stimulate a fully balanced sales job	• Difficult to determine whether an activity has been performed • Problems in assessing how well the activity has been performed
Combination	• Provides salespeople with the flexibility to assign more value to some elements than others	• Complex to administer • Difficult to understand • Emphasis still on one element despite the use of more than one

gains, because these are likely to be offset by long term losses. For example, cutting down the duration of a sales training programme may reduce the level of the training expenditure, thus providing a short term profit improvement, but may result in lower productivity levels in the long-run due to under-trained sales personnel.

Although often complicated and difficult, determining expenditure levels is an extremely important task. The reason is that a firm's long term profitability is dependent upon sales managers' ability to allocate sales expenditures in a productive way. The key to effective allocation of sales expenditures is to develop a list of major activities and a list of associated categories of controllable sales expenses (i.e. selling expenses, administrative expenses, credit and collection expenses). By allocating sales expenditures into various identifiable categories, sales managers can have detailed information concerning activity-related expenses and the level of expenditure in relation to each activity.

There is an obvious relationship between sales forecasts, sales quotas and selling budgets. For example, when budgets and quotas are set, they become evaluation devices which provide sales management with standards against which performance can be measured. Failure to reach sales quotas and operate within the pre-specified budgetary constraints raises questions concerning the realistic nature of both. Forecasting, on the other hand, goes hand-in-hand with budgeting because the purpose of expenditures is to generate revenue and revenues can only be generated if expenditures do occur. Having established the relationship between forecasts, sales quotas and selling budgets, the next section will focus on the various types of analyses for the evaluating both the organization and the individual salesperson.

Practical tip

There is a growing number of reasonably priced, user friendly, computer packages which can assist the sales manger in performing the forecasting task. An extended list of such packages/programs is provided by D. Jobber and G. Lancaster (1997) *Selling and Sales Management*, Pitman Publishing, UK.

Evaluating an organization's sales performance

While many of the methods and techniques discussed in this section can be used to evaluate individual salesperson performance, the main focus is on evaluating the total sales effort (i.e. to determine the effectiveness of the entire sales organization). It should always be remembered that the evaluation of an organization's sales performance must be undertaken within the framework provided by the sales forecasts, sales quotas and sales budgets. That is, only after performance standards have been established will perfor-

mance assessment mean anything.

The task of evaluating sales organization performance can now be broken down further.

1. Compare the performance standards (i.e. sales quotas, selling budgets) with actual sales performance. Is there a negative discrepancy between what was planned and what has been achieved? What is the magnitude of the difference?
2. Undertake detailed analyses in order to identify the causes of the differences observed.
3. Determine a course of action for improving on unsatisfactory conditions and capitalizing on favourable ones.

At first glance, these tasks may look simple. In fact performance assessment is a complicated and difficult process; it is, however, vitally important.

Sales organization effectiveness refers to the achievement of the entire range of sales and sales-related objectives and goals. It therefore requires the use of multiple measures in order to determine how well the sales organization has performed. Due primarily to the broad focus of the evaluation and the involvement of multiple performance measures, the effectiveness of a sales organization can only be determined by using a comprehensive and multi-stage approach.

The most extensive form of assessment is the *sales management audit* which is a thorough evaluation of all aspects of a sales organization. A sales management audit is a comprehensive, systematic, diagnostic and prescriptive evaluation tool used to assess the effectiveness of the sales management process. It offers guidelines for improvement and prescriptions for required changes. The sales management audit, as the most comprehensive form of evaluation, provides assessments in several areas:

- evaluation of the internal and external sales organization environment (e.g. marketing mix, socio-demographic, competitive forces);

- evaluation of the entire range of sales management functions (e.g. territory design, training and motivating salespeople);
- sales organizations planning system (e.g. objectives and overall strategic plan); and
- sales management evaluation (e.g. adequacy of sales personnel).

Sales management audit is only a part of a broader evaluation programme which is called the *marketing audit*. The sales *management audit* must be carried out by a knowledgeable and independent third party who is both objective and critical.

Analysis of performance results

Given the time, cost and difficulty involved in a sales management audit, it is not uncommon for sales organizations to evaluate some specific functional areas only. For example, a company may wish to evaluate the effectiveness of the sales effort in a particular region without necessarily conducting an assessment of the entire organization. In this case, limiting the assessment to the specific region only may prove adequate in terms of identifying problems and determining their causes.

There are four different types of analysis for evaluating the effectiveness of a sales organization. These are:

- sales analysis;
- cost analysis;
- profitability analysis; and
- productivity analysis.

Each of these is explained and discussed in the following sections. It is important to mention at this stage that more than one type of analysis can (and often should) be used in conjunction when conducting a comprehensive evaluation of organizational sales performance.

Sales analysis

Since the basic purpose of a sales organization is to generate revenue, a comprehensive analysis of its sales is, perhaps, the most important element when evaluating its effectiveness. Sales analyses can be conducted either at the level of the entire sales organization or for an individual salesperson. In this section, we concentrate on assessing the effectiveness of the entire organization.

The term *sale* can be used when an order is placed or received, when the products are delivered or when payment for an order has been received. Determining the exact meaning is important for establishing a consistent approach in calculating and interpreting the results. Also, sales can be measured either in terms of units sold or in revenue. Unless both measures are incorporated, the conclusions of a performance evaluation can be misleading. Consider, for example, the following scenario which highlights the danger of ignoring this issue. On the one hand, price increases of a product due to high inflation rates may reflect positively on revenue sales even when sales in terms of units remain at the same level. On the other hand, unit sales may remain the same but the revenue generated may be lower if salespeople are prone to giving out large discounts to their customers. Therefore, it is advisable for managers to use both revenue and unit sales in their sales analysis.

Sales analysis is the process of gathering information on sales, classifying this information (e.g. type of product, type of customer, type of market, geographical area) and comparing it with forecasts, sales quotas, sales data from previous periods and competitors' performance. Analysis based on sales data can reveal areas of strength and weakness at the organizational level as well as opportunities and threats in the marketplace.

Sales analysis can be either simple or comparative. *Simple sales analysis* is the process of simply listing the sales figures without comparing them against any standards. On the other hand, *comparative* or *performance analysis* requires a comparison between the facts and some performance standards. For example, in the first column in Table 9.2, the actual sales figures are the facts. If the analysis is

Table 9.2 *Actual sales, quota sales and performance index for the first quarter in four territories*

	Actual sales (£)	Quota sales (£)	Performance index
Territory A	1,857,000	2,214,000	83.9
Territory B	2,234,000	2,208,000	101.2
Territory C	1,160,000	925,000	125.4
Territory D	3,498,000	3,501,000	99.9

restricted only to this information, a simple sales analysis has been undertaken. In a comparative analysis, sales figures are compared against some standards. Usually such standards are the sales quotas for each sales area (a similar analysis can be undertaken for each salesperson). When making such comparisons, it is useful to calculate a performance index:

$$\text{Performance index} = \frac{\text{Actual sales}}{\text{Quota sales}} \times 100$$

As already mentioned, actual sales performance can be compared to various other standards. The most common standards used for comparisons include:

- sales quotas;
- previous year(s) sales;
- company level sales forecasts; and
- territory, area, region and country sales forecasts.

On their own, these indicators reveal the direction and magnitude of deviations from the firm's specified objective. However, further insights can be obtained by comparing the performance ratios with other indicators. For example, a comparison between a region's performance index for the current year with those of previous years can be made in an effort to identify trends in sales. Similarly, the difference between the sales ratios of two regions can be traced over a number of years. Such analyses provide a greater understanding of the current sales situation and a more objective picture of the

firm's relative performance. Of course, at the individual level, performance indexes can also be calculated and comparisons between salespeople can be made.

One of the most productive source of information is the sales invoice. However, it is important that the extent and type of sales information collected be guided by the types of comparison the firm wishes to make.

Cost analysis

While sales analysis provides managers with useful data concerning the operation of the salesforce, it does not reveal the costs which are incurred for producing the sales. Therefore, the role of a cost analysis is to:

- determine the difference between estimated and actual costs for achieving a level of sales; and
- reveal the relationship between sales and cost, by expressing the various sales costs as a percentage of achieved sales.

In a similar fashion to sales quotas, which are the benchmarks for evaluating sales performance, selling budgets are the benchmarks for evaluating sales costs. Therefore, in cost analysis, the costs incurred for generating sales are compared to selling budgets to identify whether there are any discrepancies.

In Table 9.3 a cost analysis is illustrated. For reasons of simplicity the cost in this example is limited to training and compensation only. First, the difference between budgeted and actual training and compensation costs, is determined. Next, the actual training

Table 9.3 *Cost analysis for the first quarter in four territories*

	Training and compensation costs				
	Actual cost	Budgeted cost	Difference	Cost as % of actual sales	Cost as % of quota sales
Territory A	108,560	132,840	−24,280	5.8	6
Territory B	133,200	132,480	+720	6.0	6
Territory C	62,380	55,500	+6,800	5.4	6
Territory D	224,720	210,060	+14,660	6.4	6

and compensation costs are expressed as a percentage of achieved sales. If the sales–cost relationship is maintained, then large deviations from the selling budget should not be an issue for concern. That is, increases in costs which are followed by proportional increases in sales should not be considered to be a problem. Contrariwise, when actual costs far exceed budgeted costs and such cost increases are not followed by proportional increases in sales, then this is an alarming situation which needs to be addressed.

In addition to the purpose of identifying the variance between budgets and actual costs and revealing the sales–cost relationship, cost analysis can be used to determine the profitability of the sales function and highlight sources of inefficiency. This is the focus of the next section which concentrates on profitability and productivity analyses.

Profitability analysis

Profitability analysis provides additional information over and above that provided by the sales and cost analyses. There are various types of profitability analyses, two of the most used being:

- income statement analysis; and
- return on assets managed analysis.

In the following sections these two types of profitability analysis are discussed.

Income statement analysis

Income statement analysis looks in detail at a company's various costs in producing sales. The primary purpose of income statement analysis is to evaluate the profitability of the sales organization. However, managers should be fully aware of the difficulties which are associated with the allocation of the indirect costs that cannot be related directly to a specific sales activity. As a result, the income statement analysis can be based on two approaches:

- the full cost approach, and
- the margin contribution approach.

According to the full cost approach, all indirect (or shared) costs are allocated to individual units (i.e. territory, region, etc.) based on a cost allocation procedure. The full cost approach produces a net profit figure for each unit.

The contribution margin approach determines profitability based on the principle that only those costs which are directly related to the unit under consideration are deducted from its net sales. The contribution margin approach therefore produces the profit contribution of the unit under investigation. The general principles guiding the full cost and contribution margin approach are summarized in Table 9.4.

The first step when conducting an income statement analysis is to determine the purpose for which it is conducted. For example,

Table 9.4 *Differences between full cost and contribution margin approaches*

Full cost approach	Contribution margin approach
Sales	Sales
Minus: Cost of goods sold	*Minus: Cost of goods sold*
Equals: **Gross margin**	Equals: **Gross margin**
Minus: Direct selling expenses	*Minus: Direct selling expenses*
Minus: Indirect selling expenses	Equals: **Profit contribution**
Equals: **Net profit**	

is the analysis designed to assess the profitability of salespeople, customers, geographical areas, or products? When the purpose is determined, all costs must be classified as direct or indirect and appropriately allocated to various activities and/or segments of the business. Table 9.5 presents an example which employs a full-cost approach for evaluating the profitability of a district, and uses a contribution margin approach for assessing the areas within the district. Thus, the profit contribution is estimated for the district and its three areas. In addition, after adjusting for indirect costs, a net profit figure for the district is produced. Notice that different cost allocation methods lead to different results.

Return on assets managed

The income statement analysis measures the results achieved in terms of profitability but it does not take into consideration the investment in assets required to produce the sales results. However, just as an organization is evaluated on the basis of return on assets, sales territories can also be evaluated on the basis of the working capital commitment. Working capital commitment refers to assets such as accounts receivable, company cars, etc., which are needed to produce the sales results. Note that only assets which are under the direct control of the sales organization should be included in the return on assets managed (ROAM) analysis. For example, company cars used for non-sales related purposes should not be considered as working capital of the sales organization and must be excluded from the analysis.

The ROAM analysis extends the income statement analysis by including asset investment considerations. Thus, the additional information needed for ROAM analysis is the

Table 9.5 *Income statement analysis*

	Full cost approach	Contribution margin approach		
	District sales	Area 1	Area 2	Area 3
Sales	500,000	250,000	100,000	150,000
Cost of goods sold	400,000	225,000	50,000	125,000
Gross margin	100,000	25,000	50,000	25,000
Direct selling expenses	25,000	12,500	5,000	7,500
Profit contribution	75,000	12,500	45,000	17,500
Indirect (shared) costs	55,000			
Net profit	20,000			

asset investment in a sales territory. Profitability can be either expressed as a net profit or as a profit contribution. By using profit contribution as opposed to net profit approach, sales managers can avoid the rather arbitrary allocation of expenses encountered in the full-cost analysis.

Once the profit contribution and the assets committed to produce the sales results are determined for each sales area, then the ROAM analysis can be performed by using the following formula:

Return on assets managed =
  Profit contribution as % of sales ×
  Asset turnover rate

where:

Profit contribution as % of sales =
  $\dfrac{\text{Profit contribution}}{\text{Sales}} \times 100$

Asset turnover rate = $\dfrac{\text{Sales}}{\text{Assets managed}}$

The example in Table 9.6 illustrates the results of a ROAM analysis. The inventory costs for finished goods in this example is higher for Area 4 than for Areas 1, 2 and 3, and the receivables are different for each area.

The ROAM analysis provides information for an evaluation of the profitability of a sales organization. Therefore, since ROAM is determined by both profit contribution and asset turnover rate, then the return to a business segment can be improved by:

● increasing both the profit contribution and the asset turnover rate;
● increasing the profit contribution while maintaining the asset turnover rate; and
● increasing the asset turnover rate while maintaining the same levels of profit contribution.

Productivity analysis

Profitability analysis incorporates elements of productivity analysis. Productivity analysis is defined as the relationship between outputs and inputs and is usually expressed as the ratio of output measures to appropriate input measures.

Sales productivity = $\dfrac{\text{Output}}{\text{Input}}$

When physical measures, such as number of units sold, number of new accounts opened, cost per sales call etc., are used in

Table 9.6 *Return on assets managed*

	Area 1	Area 2	Area 3	Area 4
Sales	1,000,000	1,000,000	1,000,000	1,000,000
Cost of goods sold	600,000	600,000	700,000	700,000
Gross margin	400,000	400,000	300,000	300,000
Direct selling expenses	200,000	250,000	250,000	100,000
Profit contribution	200,000	150,000	50,000	200,000
Accounts receivable	300,000	350,000	130,000	700,000
Inventory	200,000	250,000	200,000	400,000
Total investment	500,000	600,000	330,000	1,100,000
Profit on sales	20%	15%	5%	20%
Turnover on investment	2	1.6	3	0.9
Return on assets managed (ROAM)	40	24	15	18

productivity analysis, the calculation of various types of productivity ratios can be straightforward. However, in situations where productivity criteria are expressed in non-comparable units (e.g. sales training versus number of service calls), comparability is attained by assigning a price to the units and then multiplying the units involved by their respective prices. For example, if we wish to compare sales training (measured in number of hours) with number of service calls (measured in number of contacts per month) we need assign a price (e.g. monetary value) to both units (price per hour and price per contact) and multiply each unit by its respective price. Following this transformation, the nature of the relationship between these variables can be investigated.

When productivity ratios are calculated and compared, they provide very useful analytical tools for evaluating the performance of a sales organization. For example, the sales per salesperson ratio for one territory may be compared to those of other territories in order to establish whether the sales generated in that territory are above, below or just about average. Similarly, by calculating the cost per sales call ratio, it is possible to compare differences between the cost per call in different regions. These issues have been touched upon in the previous sections on sales, cost and profitability analysis and, as already stated, many of these techniques generalize to the level of the individual salesperson.

The discussion of various types of analyses for assessing an organization's overall sales performance has been completed. The next section provides a discussion of methods for evaluating the performance of individual salespeople.

Evaluating an individual's sales performance

A salesperson's performance can be considered as a set of appropriate behaviours and work outcomes which contribute to the accomplishment of the organization's goals. The performance process consists of:

Practical tip

When sales performance is below established standards and the economic outlook is not promising, it is common practice to reduce costs across the board. This can be fatal to the sales effort if emphasis is placed on the identification of areas where valid cost cutting can be undertaken without identifying other functions and processes where increases in expenditure are necessary.

- evaluating a salesperson's work behaviours by measuring and comparing them with pre-established standards;
- recording the results of these evaluations; and
- providing feedback to the salesperson.

Performance appraisal, one of the most important tools for managing salesforces, involves both a sales manager and a salesperson, and serves two main purposes. First, it provides managers with information for planning, developing, directing and evaluating the salesforce. Second, it offers salespeople feedback concerning their performance and progress towards accomplishing the organizational goals. Clearly stating the objectives and effectively designing and

---

Practical tip

Sales managers conducting the performance appraisal must be properly trained. The objective of such training is to reduce errors and misjudgements by developing a range of analytical skills. The rule is seek professional advice if you are not appropriately trained in identifying, classifying and using relevant information for performance evaluation.

implementing the performance appraisal pays real dividends in terms of motivating salespeople.

The objectives of a performance appraisal can have a judgemental focus, a developmental focus or a combination of both. The judgemental focus is mainly concerned with the assessment and communication of the performance results to a salesperson (e.g. assessing the potential of an individual salesperson for promotion to a managerial position). The developmental focus emphasizes future performance by using information resulting from evaluations of performance improvements (e.g. evaluating performance improvements and determining additional training needs).

Difficulties in evaluating salesperson performance

The appraisal of salesperson performance is considered to be a complicated task because of the unique nature of the sales job. For example, salespeople assume a variety of roles, perform a wide range of activities and work in different regions where the prevailing environmental conditions differ. Furthermore, salespeople are not only involved in selling; they have other tasks such as servicing the account or following up a sale. Thus, given the diversity of role behaviours performed by salespeople, the evaluation of their performance can be problematic. By the same token, objective (i.e. quantitative) criteria, which are, in some circumstances, more desirable than subjective (i.e. qualitative) criteria, are very difficult to establish for some job behaviours (e.g. attitude toward the customer).

Criteria for evaluating salesperson performance

The performance appraisal of salespeople should be based on multiple evaluation criteria because of the diversity of role behaviours which are required by sales representatives. Using several criteria, sales managers can minimize the likelihood of making an error.

The type and number of criteria to be used in a performance appraisal depend upon the objectives of the evaluation. Performance evaluation criteria can be classified into three major categories, namely effort, results and profitability (see Table 9.7).

Effort (or input) criteria which consist of the activities each salesperson engages in when carrying out their job and cover the entire range of role behaviours (i.e. selling activities, professional development, citizenship, etc.), are mainly quantitative. Some of these criteria, however, cannot be quantitatively measured and, as a result, evaluation will need to be based on qualitative assessments. Effort criteria can be used to compare the performance of each salesperson and, later, to link effort to results and profitability outcomes.

Results criteria have always been used in performance appraisals because they are very informative, easy to calculate and simple to understand. However, a potential drawback with results criteria is that they do not provide any information regarding the generation of the results. For example, exceptionally good sales performance in a given territory can either be attributed to the effort of the salesperson or to an advertising campaign run to support the sales effort in that territory. Similarly, sales potential and competitors strategies often differ across territories making cross-territory comparisons very difficult. Therefore, unless actual sales are compared to sales quotas, the use of sales results as performance indicators can be misleading.

The profitability of the sales effort must also be assessed. For example, two sales representatives with exactly the same levels of actual sales may contribute differently to net profits if one has achieved the level of sales by incurring less expense that the other. Thus, profitability measures provide a more complete picture of the performance of salespeople. Furthermore, salesperson profitability is influenced by various factors such as type of product, the level of price negotiated, level of expenditures, etc. Therefore several criteria should be used for profitability assessment.

Table 9.7 *Criteria for evaluating the performance of salespeople*

Dimension	Criteria
Effort	Total number of calls per period
	Calls by type of customer
	Calls by product line
	Selling time versus non-selling time
	Number of telephone calls to prospects
	Number of formal proposals submitted
	Number of service calls
	Number of displays set up
	Number of complaints received
	Product knowledge
	Customer knowledge
	Company policies knowledge
	Development of planning ability
	Development of selling skills
	Good citizenship
	Punctuality
	Rapport building
	Appearance
Results	Sales volume in £s and units
	Sales volume by customer
	Sales volume by product
	Sales volume per call
	Sales volume per order
	New account sales
	Number of new accounts
	Number of accounts lost
	Expenses by type of customer
	Expenses by type of product
	Average cost per call
Profitability	Net profit
	Profit contribution
	Return on assets managed
	Gross margin
	Selling expenses as a percentage of sales
	Order per call ratio

Typically, a salesforce appraisal will need to include criteria from all of the above performance categories. For example, by linking the criteria from each category, the relationships between effort, results, and profitability can be established. However, the effectiveness of a performance appraisal is determined, not only by the criteria used, but also by the method of evaluation. We now discuss this further.

Performance appraisal methods

Sales managers can use different methods for evaluating the effort, results and profitability of their salesforce. These are:

- the essay technique;
- checklists and rating scales;
- ranking;
- management by objectives; and
- behaviourally anchored rating scales.

The *essay technique* is a written statement or a brief narrative developed by the sales manager describing the performance of the salesperson. It is a very easy method and commonly used, despite some inherent limitations caused by differences in writing styles and differences in emphasis when describing the strengths and weaknesses of individuals.

Checklists and rating scales are also widely used for performance evaluation. Each individual salesperson is rated on a scale based on the extent to which they meet established performance standards (see Table 9.8). In its favour, the method is easy to use and understand. However, a weakness of the rating method concerns inter-rater reliability. That is, different raters may have different interpretations of the measures on the rating scale. For example, the level of performance meriting 'Outstanding' may differ from one rater to another.

Ranking is a method which requires the sales manager to order salespeople in terms of their performance on some specific criteria. Thus, the ranking method forces managers to discriminate the performance of salespeople. This method has obvious strengths when assessing quantitative outcomes (e.g. sales volume), but a major drawback is that the sales manager may attach different importance weightings to some qualitative criteria (i.e. personality traits), therefore making the results of the ranking process very subjective.

Management by objectives (MBO) is a goal setting and evaluation process which requires the participation of both the salesperson and sales manager in developing mutually acceptable performance measures and assessing their achievement. This participative approach to goal setting can act as a powerful motivational tool. Perhaps one of the difficulties with MBO is to truly establish mutually agreed objectives. In addition, some of the performance criteria may be difficult to quantify and benchmark.

A *behaviourally anchored rating scale* (BARS) is a set of scaled statements which measure the level of performance behaviours which are associated with achieving desired results. It is a five step process for evaluating salespeople.

1. Salespeople and managers identify and describe a large number of specific critical incidents or occurrences that impact on performance (e.g. unwillingness to contact potential customers, consistently reaching product sales goals).
2. These critical incidents are reviewed and reduced into a smaller number of performance dimensions (e.g. obtaining new customers, reaching individual product sales goals).
3. A group of salespeople is then asked to assign the incidents obtained in (1) to the performance dimensions obtained in (2). Incidents are kept in only if 60% or more of the salespeople assign it to the same dimension.
4. For each performance dimension, its associated incidents are rated by a different group in terms of how effectively or inef-

Table 9.8 *Checklist and rating method*

Criteria	Marginal	Satisfactory	Above average	Outstanding
Expands effort to prospect new accounts	X			
Motivated to perform well				X
Establishes realistic goals		X		

fectively they represent performance on that dimension. Incidents which generate good agreement in ratings are considered for the final scale.

5. The final scale usually includes six to eight levels of performance for each performance dimension.

The sophistication of this method offers clear advantages in that all critical behaviours contributing to effective sales performance are identified mainly by salespeople themselves. However, the criticism extended on the rating scales can be expanded to BARS since no amount of instrument sophistication can remove the limitations involved in a subjective rating system.

None of the above appraisal techniques provides a perfect evaluation. However, by using a combination of methods it is possible to capitalize on the strengths and minimize the limitations which are present in each.

Managing the results of the appraisal

The sales manager must examine very carefully the results of the performance appraisal and identify any difference between achieved and desired levels of performance.

Under the scenario that objectives have been achieved, there is no cause for immediate concern. However, it is important that potential changes in the firm's environment (i.e. competitive, technological, economic, regulatory, etc.) are considered together with their effect on the company's future sales performance.

A second scenario is when the achieved sales exceed performance standards. Here,

salesforce performance should be encouraged and/or rewarded in order to maintain, if not increase, motivation and effort. Reassessment of objectives, as above, should also be undertaken, with an emphasis on determining whether sales forecasts are set too low.

Finally, achieved sales performance may fall short of the standards set. In this case, managers need to identify the causes of the discrepancy. If the low performance is attributed to lack of effort in some area, then managerial actions may include, for example, reassessing motivational programmes, altering remuneration packages, or changing the sales force structure. Poor salesmanship may need to be addressed with changes to the training and staff development programmes. Alternatively, a performance shortfall attributed to external factors may lead to a re-evaluation of sales forecasts.

Practical tip

Sales representatives' response style to performance feedback varies widely. Some salespeople accept critical evaluation, and negative and positive feedback may result in improved performance. Others, however, take criticism very seriously and negative feedback may act as a demotivating factor. Therefore, sales managers need to have a clear understanding of each salesperson's response to different forms of feedback. A tailored approach can then be provided on an individual basis.

Summary

Evaluating the performance of the sales organization is a vital task. Through evaluation, sales managers acquire information concerning the accomplishment of the sales objectives.

To determine performance achievement, sales managers develop various types of forecasts which can be used as indicators for developing sales quotas and establishing appropriate selling budgets.

Sales analysis is the first step in any performance evaluation, providing a preliminary picture of the organization's overall sales status. Due to the fact that sales analysis does not provide any information concerning the expenses associated with the sales function, cost analysis is a further necessary tool to generate insights into performance effectiveness. Profitability and productivity analyses, the other two types of performance evaluation, combine sales and cost data, and examine the relationships between inputs and outputs to provide additional information needed for a comprehensive performance evaluation.

Evaluating the performance of the sales organization is as important as the evaluation of each individual salesperson. A comprehensive evaluation of salesperson performance requires the use of many criteria, from the effort, results and profitability categories. In addition to these criteria, managers must decide which particular performance evaluation method(s) to use. Five methods were presented in this chapter and a combination of approaches should be used in order to compensate for the inherent weaknesses associated with each. These evaluation methods have additional properties in terms of salesperson motivation, overall planning and wider organizational issues (e.g. salesperson empowerment).

The eventual purpose of any performance evaluation is to assess the current situation with a view to enhancing future sales performance. Unless it does this, the performance evaluation is failing in its purpose. Assessing the effectiveness of the evaluation process itself must also be an objective in its own right.

Acknowledgement

I would like to thank John Cadogan for his useful comments and editorial help.

References

Chonko, L.B., Enis, B.M. and Tanner, J.F. Jr (1992) *Managing Salespeople*. Allyn and Bacon.

Churchill, G.A. Jr, Ford, N.M. and Walker, O.C. Jr (1993) *Sales Force Management*. 4th edition, Irwin.

Cocanougher, A.B. and Ivanchevich, J.M. (1978) BARS Performance Rating for Salesforce Personnel, *Journal of Marketing*, July, 87–95.

Ingram T.N. and LaForge, R.W. (1992) *Sales Management, Analysis and Decision Making*, 2nd edition. The Dryden Press.

Johnson, E.M., Kurtz, D.L. and Scheuing, E.E. (1994) *Sales Management: Concepts, Practices and Cases*, 2nd edition. McGraw-Hill Book Company.

Wortuba, T.R. and Simpson, E.K. (1992) *Sales Management: Text and Cases*, 2nd edition. PWS-KENT Publishing Company.

10

Strategic sales planning

Kevin Wilson, Southampton Institute of Technology

 This chapter is concerned with discussing approaches to strategic sales planning. We shall begin by reviewing the reasons why effective and focused planning is important and the reasons why it should be integrated with wider corporate and marketing objectives. Two broad approaches to sales planning will be considered:

- The first will focus upon the development of macro-sales strategies which may be applied across broad customer segments. This approach represents marketing planning as being concerned with the management of the product portfolio in order to achieve market share.
- The second approach focuses upon the development of micro-sales strategies which recognize the importance of key accounts and the need to evolve selling and account development strategies which are tailored to the specific needs of individual customers.

The aim of this chapter is to provide sales managers with a practical guide to the development and implementation of effective sales force strategies which are integrated with the wider marketing and corporate strategies of the organization and which are supported by other functional areas within the firm.

What is strategy?

There is no universally accepted definition of strategy. In a military sense it may be referred to as *the art of the general,* 'the skill of employ-ing forces to overcome opposition'. This link with military thinking has been transferred to the context of management strategy and has perhaps led to an overemphasis upon the importance of competition. Developing strategies which engender competitive advantage is important, but so are those which recognize the value of co-operation – with customers, suppliers, intermediaries and sometimes even with competitors.

Henry Mintzberg proposed five different definitions of strategy – plan, ploy, pattern, position, and perspective. These are outlined in Table 10.1.

Table 10.1 *Definitions of strategy*

Strategy as plan: Strategy consists of formally developed plans which act as a guide to future action aimed at achieving organizational goals.

Strategy as ploy: A company may develop a strategy in order to mislead opponents. By leading competitors to think they will do one thing a company may induce its competitors to make mistakes.

Strategy as pattern: In this definition strategies evolve from a consistent patter of behaviour, not necessarily as the result of a preconceived plan. Strategies may therefore be more or less deliberate or emerge as reactions to environmental stimuli.

Strategy as a position: This definition differentiates between strategy and tactics. Whether a course of action may be considered a strategy or a tactic depends upon where in the organization it was formulated. What may be a strategy to the sales department may be viewed as a tactic by the marketing department or senior management.

Strategy as perspective: Strategy in this sense reflects an organization's *personality*, the way in which the individual people within the organization share a vision of the world. This perspective may be reflected in the organization's approach to the exercise of power in the marketplace, the level of aggressive or co-operative behaviour it exhibits towards customers, suppliers and the competition, or its perceptions about the value of technological leadership or market dynamism.

For the purpose of this chapter we shall be exploring strategy as plan while at the same time recognizing that the nature of the strategic planning process within any organization is effected by the stream of actions which precede it, by the position within the organization where it takes place, and by the culture which has evolved within that organization.

Strategic planning is important in that it provides a framework within which the actions of members of an organization may be guided in order to achieve organizational objectives. Strategic planning is concerned with providing solutions in three problem areas:

1. **Strategic diagnosis:**
   Where are we now?
   Why are we here?
2. **Formulation of strategic choices:**
   Where do we want to go?
   How will we get there?
3. **Implementation of strategic choices/decisions:**
   What actions (tactics) to adopt?
   Are we achieving our objectives?

The ultimate aim of the strategic planning process should be to facilitate actions which further strategic objectives. All too often, however, organizations seem to become entangled in the *process* of developing strategic plans rather than with concentrating upon achieving their desired *outcomes*. The result is often that plans which have taken months to prepare are quietly consigned to the nearest filing cabinet whilst managers give a sigh of relief and say 'now that's over with we can get on with doing the business!' There are a number of reasons why this happens.

1. Theoretical frameworks are taken as prescriptive and used as substitutes for creative thinking. Theory is best used as a point of reference which facilitates the development of judgement, it does not tell you how you should act in a particular situation.
2. Strategy development is often described as a top-down hierarchical process driven by senior management. The problem here

is that there are different views of the organization at different operational levels. The strategic view of a business taken by senior managers may bear little relationship to the day-to-day problems faced by front line managers. If corporate plans appear to have little relevance or flexibility at an operational level then it is not surprising that there is little enthusiasm for their implementation.

3. Much marketing planning takes as its focus the management of portfolios of products whereas sales management maybe more concerned with the management of portfolios of customers. In this case day-to-day decisions taken at operational levels about which customers to deal with, what product adaptations to make to meet particular customer needs and the allocation of resources have significant strategic importance which may conflict with decisions taken at a corporate level.

Practical tip: Strategic planning

Don't get trapped in the 'process' of strategic planning – focus upon real business outcomes rather than the production of glossy strategic planning documents:

- Keep it simple.
- Develop a vision of the future that everyone can share and **get enthusiastic about it!**
- Involve everyone in the process, not just senior managers, and don't surround the process in mystery.
- Make sure you **listen** to customers, to suppliers and to staff!
- Be flexible. Continually review the plan and be prepared to change direction.

Whilst it may be useful in conceptual terms to consider strategy development as occurring separately at different levels within the organization, there is general agreement by writers on strategy that it is essential that integration occurs not only vertically, between different levels within the organization, but also horizontally between different functional specialisms (see Example One). A further requirement is that the strategy formulation process, whilst being driven by management, should be iterative and interactive allowing feedback from operational levels to influence the development of those strategies.

The relationship between sales planning and marketing planning

Most marketing text books identify the role of personal selling as a sub-set of the promotional element of the marketing mix (product, price, place and promotion). They describe personal selling as *personal persuasive communication by sales people employed by the company*. This, in many instances, is too narrow a definition of the role of personal selling because it suggests that it has tactical rather than strategic importance. This definition also focuses upon the role of sales people in creating discrete sales rather than creating long term customers. Traditional perceptions of the salesperson's role also tend to stress the adversarial nature of personal selling rather than its potential for joint value creation and co-operation.

The role and importance of personal selling within the overall marketing strategy of the firm must be viewed against the backdrop of the markets in which the firm operates and the nature of the products and services being marketed. Table 10.2 illustrates the conditions under which the personal selling function may be viewed as performing a largely tactical role within the marketing mix and where the role tends to be of major strategic importance.

Example One

In a small industrial packaging company in Sheffield the lack of co-ordination between sales and operations strategies led to the loss of a major customer.

The salesforce strategy was to focus upon key accounts and to seek competitive advantage by offering product modifications, priority in manufacturing and bespoke delivery to those customers which they believed were of major strategic importance. The culture in production, however, focused upon moving large orders through the manufacturing process irrespective of who they were for.

A major order was won from a key account which stipulated that it would be delivered over the year in twelve equal instalments during the first three working days of each month.

On investigation it was found that even though the works order had been raised in good time the production planning department had ignored the fact that it was for a major customer and labelled it a 'small order'. As such it was put to one side until larger, and in their terms more important, orders had been manufactured.

Where the sales role is perceived as tactical then sales strategies are developed as a response to marketing strategies which focus upon the management of product portfolios. In general, markets in which macro-marketing strategies (those aimed roughly at market segments) evolve and where personal selling is a tactical component, tend to contain large numbers of customers with relatively similar needs. Products for these markets are often simple and low cost, few people are involved in the purchasing decision and the sales cycle is of short duration.

Examples of this are easily identified

Table 10.2 *Selling strategies as tactical and strategic elements of the marketing plan*

Tactical where ...	Strategic where ...
Small sales	Major sales
Short sales cycle	Long sales cycle
Large customer segments	Often segments of one
Simple products	Complex products and systems
Small buying group	Large buying group
Customer needs are similar	Bespoke customer needs
Discrete sales are the focus of selling activity	Long term buyer–seller relationships are the focus of selling activity
Industry culture is adversarial	Industry culture is co-operative

within consumer markets in the cases of the marketing of household consumer services and products such as double glazing, cavity wall insulation, furniture, electrical goods and some insurance, personal investment products and financial services.

In industrial and organizational markets there is a tendency for personal selling to be of far greater strategic importance. This is because customer needs tend to be more diverse, and products are often of high value and complex, in technological terms and in terms of the impact they have upon the customer's own manufacturing process. Even where products are simple and low cost customers still have very specific needs in relation to issues such as delivery requirements and payment terms. Individual customers in business-to-business markets often represent a disproportionately large percentage of total turnover and/or profit, the sales cycle tends to be much longer than in consumer markets and the decision making unit larger and more complex. In these circumstances the salesperson's role is more important because of the need to gather and use information, to understand the purchasing decision making process and to forge and sustain long term multi-functional contacts within the customer organization.

In some organizations sales strategies will reflect marketing strategies which focus upon market share growth and the management of the product life cycle. In others sales strategies will reflect marketing strategies which recognize the overriding need to manage portfolios of customers whilst taking the product as a 'given' (see Example Two).

In many companies selling to other organizations rather than direct to consumers, there is a recognition that a few 'key accounts' demand the development of specialized micro-marketing strategies (aimed at individual customers) and that other, less strategically important customers can be adequately served through the development of generic macro-marketing and sales strategies (aimed at broad categories of customers).

When developing strategic sales plans it is therefore necessary to take account of strategic marketing approaches to both product portfolio management and to customer portfolio and key account management.

Example Two

'In our industry it is becoming increasingly difficult to win competitive advantage from the product alone. Our products are good, they have to be because all the competitors have good products too, but no-one can gain a long term technological lead. The way we have grown our business is to focus upon the way we do business. We target certain key accounts and go out to really understand their business and how we can add value to what they are trying to do. Each relationship is different and we change the way we do things – product formulations, who calls on them, the way they are serviced, anything and everything – to suit the individual customer. Our aim is to grow the relationship so that we are tied in to them, not only supplying the product but managing the process as well.' (Sales director, chemicals manufacturer)

Developing sales strategies ▬▬▬

A major barrier to the effective integration of sales and marketing strategies is poor communications between the two functions within the firm, particularly when they are separated. For this reason many writers advocate that management should not only co-ordinate the marketing and sales functions but actually integrate them under a single manager. In this way there is a much better chance that sales strategies will actually support marketing strategies.

The strategic management process involves three elements: strategic diagnosis; strategy formulation; and the development of tactics for implementation.

Strategic diagnosis ▬▬▬▬

The aim of strategic diagnosis is to answer the questions 'Where are we now?' and 'How did we get here?' For the sales manager this requires a detailed understanding of what corporate and marketing strategies have been adopted by the firm.

Corporate strategies are constrained by a number of factors which are listed in Table 10.3. Not all factors are of equal importance; some of them will be irrelevant in some marketing environments whilst others might be crucial.

From an analysis of the factors listed in Table 10.3 the firm can identify its major strengths and weaknesses in the light of market opportunities and threats. The task facing the corporate strategist is to determine the overall mission of the organization.

Mission statements should define the major arenas within which the firm will operate: the range of industries; the customers to be served; the degree of vertical integration; the technology to be employed; and the geographical scope of the operation. The overall aim of the corporate planning process is to identify opportunities within the marketplace which are compatible with the internal competencies of the firm.

At all levels within the organization, corporate (senior management), functional (e.g. marketing and manufacturing) and operational (e.g. salesforce and production planning and management), objectives need to be formulated which support the overall mission of the company.

At the highest level the major objective has traditionally been expressed as being to maximize profits. It is generally accepted now, however, that managers in fact pursue objectives which are far broader and more diverse. In addition to profitability, companies may set objectives in relation to their standing in the market, the emphasis they place upon technology and innovation, levels of productivity, the use of financial and physical resources and their approach to ethical and public responsibility issues. Objectives set in these areas may have far reaching implications for long term profitability.

Whilst strategic business planning will prescribe the broad objectives of the firm it should not occur in isolation from the planning process at lower levels in the organization. There should be constant modification of corporate strategic objectives in the light of information received from functional departments such as marketing, operations, finance, etc. The process should strive to be dynamic, flexible, entrepreneurial and iterative.

The role of the marketing department is to develop strategic objectives and strategies for their attainment which support the overall corporate objectives of the firm. There should also be continuous feedback to corporate planners about the suitability and viability of their objectives in the light of the firm's marketing position.

The marketing department will have carried out an analysis of the firm, noting the opportunities and threats which exist in the marketplace and the strengths and weaknesses of the organization in relation to internal characteristics and to its position in the network of relationships it enjoys with customers, competitors, suppliers and other stakeholders and interest groups in the industry. Table 10.3 may be used to focus analytical thinking in order to assess the firm's marketing position. In addition sales man-

Table 10.3 *Factors which constrain the development of corporate strategies*

Macro-environmental factors	Political–legal factors Economic factors Socio-cultural factors Technological factors
Industry factors	Market size Growth rate Vulnerability to new entrants Stability/volatility R&D requirements Power/dependency
Customers	Major segments Key accounts Size Needs relative to supplier capability Relationship focus
Competitors	Technological capability Process capabilities Market position
Supplier base	Capabilities Power/dependency Relationship focus
The firm's strengths and weaknesses	Financial capabilities Managerial capabilities Functional capabilities Organizational capabilities Technological capabilities Shareholder interests Internal stakeholders Corporate history

agement need to identify the strengths and weaknesses of the salesforce. The answers to a number of questions outlined in Table 10.4 will help in analysing the strengths and weaknesses of the salesforce.

Marketing decisions are essentially concerned with two major elements: products and markets. A major task facing the marketer which impacts strongly upon both marketing and salesforce strategies is the detailed analysis of both product and customer portfolios.

Product portfolio analysis

One method for carrying out product portfolio analysis was pioneered by General Electric (GE) of America. This involves evaluating the attractiveness of a particular market and then determining the competitive position of a

Table 10.4 *Salesforce strengths and weaknesses*

What is the nature of the selling task?
Order taking, missionary, technical, institutional systems, team, key account, consumer, business-to-business?

What do customers want from salespeople?
Product knowledge, process knowledge, special treatment, commercial skills?

What skills exist to meet those needs?
Is there a match between skills and skills requirements, is additional training needed?

What training is required?
Sales techniques, presentation skills, product knowledge, commercial and managerial skills, team skills?

Does the way in which the salesforce is organized match the needs of the market?
Should the salesforce be organized geographically, by product or by customer type?

Are reward systems designed to support sales objectives?

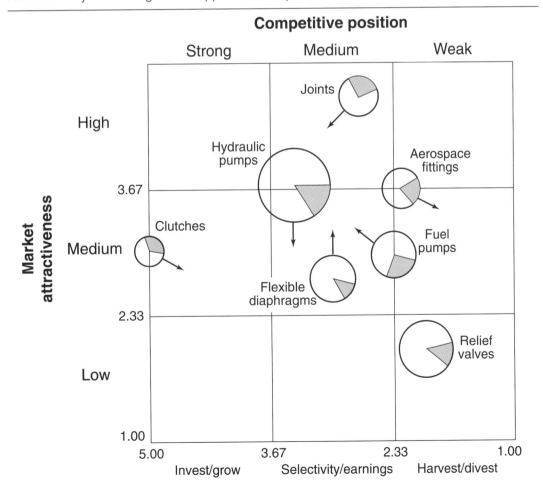

Figure 10.1 *Example of the GE matrix*

Table 10.5 *Market attractiveness and competitive position*

Market attractiveness is judged on the following criteria:
- Market size
- Annual market growth rate
- Historical profit margin
- Competitive intensity
- Technological requirements
- Inflationary vulnerability
- Energy requirements
- Environmental impact
- Social/political/legal

The firm's competitive position is determined by the following factors:
- Market share
- Share growth rate
- Product quality
- Brand reputation
- Distribution network
- Promotional effectiveness
- Product capacity
- Productive efficiency
- Unit costs
- Material supplies
- R&D performance
- Managerial personnel

---

product within that market. Table 10.5 lists the criteria against which markets and products are judged.

Each factor is weighted as to its importance and rated for performance on a scale of 1–5. The rating and the score are multiplied to give a value. The values are totalled and the position of the product is plotted on a matrix. Figure 10.1 is an example of product portfolio analysis using the GE matrix.

- **High market attractiveness** – *strong competitive position products*: These products represent the company's major strength in their product portfolio. It is the earnings from these products which will fund shareholder profits, future growth and product development.

- **Medium market attractiveness – medium competitive position products**: These products are generally at the mature stage of their product life cycles and as such are a valuable source of revenue. They may have varying degrees of competitive advantage and may require some investment in order to maintain or enhance their market position.

- **Low market attractiveness – weak competitive position products**: These products are at the end of their life cycle and serious consideration should be given to their being deleted from the portfolio. An exception to this might be where these products are filling a market niche which would otherwise be available to competitors, or when they are necessary components of a full product line which is required by customers.

The position of a specific product on the matrix suggests the marketing strategy which might be adopted to protect, enhance or change its performance. These will be discussed more fully in the next section on strategy formulation.

Customer portfolio analysis

In many industries it is not so much the product portfolio which is important but the portfolio of customers enjoyed by the firm and its position in relation the each customer.

One method of analysing customers has been developed by Campbell and Cunningham (1983). They suggest a three-step approach to analysing customer relationships.

Step 1: Life cycle classification of customer relationships.
Step 2: Customer/competitor analysis by market segment.
Step 3: Portfolio analysis of key customers.

Step one

The first step enables companies to identify four broad customer classifications: key accounts or today's special customers (those which are of major strategic importance), today's regular customers; tomorrow's customers; and yesterday's customers. Customers are classified on a number of criteria:

- sales volume;
- the demands they make on strategic resources;
- the age of the relationship;
- the supplier's share of the customer's total purchases; and
- the profitability of the customer to the supplier.

By classifying customers in this way sellers are able to identify those on which resources

should be spent and those where investment in their development should be severely limited.

Where the supplier has a portfolio of products then customers should be analysed only in relation to one product category at a time. The reason being that a today's special customer for product category A may be a yesterday's customer for product category B. In some industries, however, where products are manufactured to customer specification or jointly developed, in systems selling, or where the product is only a small part of the total market offering, then this might not be necessary or appropriate.

- **Tomorrow's customers**: These customers have high *potential* strategic importance. They may be small growing companies with a large share of a newly emerging market, they may be former important customers that have been lost and which the seller wishes to regain, or they may be a vital *reference point* within an industry. For example, many textiles companies are keen to deal with Marks and Spencer, and engineering companies with Rolls-Royce and British Aerospace because of their high reputation for quality. If your company supplies these demanding clients then the inference to other potential customers is that you perform to a very high standard also.
- **Today's special customers**: These are the key accounts of a business. Although they may represent a very small proportion of the total customer base they are likely to represent a very high proportion of total turnover and profit. They also tend to demand a great deal of the supplier's time and resources. The relationships that a firm enjoys with these key accounts are likely to be long term, close and require special handling. Today's special customers and tomorrow's special customers require the development of micro-sales strategies tailored to their individual and specific needs.
- **Today's regular customers**: These represent the bulk of a firm's customer base. They

may well be important customers buying relatively large quantities, or they may just be regular buyers. Whichever is the case relationships will tend not to be as close, and total sales and profit from this group of customers will be smaller than that achieved from key accounts.

Generic or macro-sales strategies will be developed for these customers by identifying larger segments of customers with similar needs who can be served cheaply with a basic market offering with limited service content.

- **Yesterday's customers**: Many companies often have a large number of these customers 'on their books'. One East Midlands commercial printer had over 500 customers listed in their records. Of these only 150 had placed orders in the past year, and of those only 20 customers accounted for the bulk of their turnover. Companies must be very sure that yesterday's customers are actually worth doing business with at all, although some of them can provide useful additional income for little effort and serving them may in fact exclude competition from some market segments.

Companies should construct tables which identify how many customers fall into each category, what proportion of sales each category accounts for and what percentage of expenditure they absorb. This provides the company with a general overview of their customer portfolio.

Step two

The second step explores the company's competitive position within their portfolio of customers. Three questions are answered during this process:

1. What is the growth rate of the customer's demand for our products?
2. What is the size of our share of the customer's orders compared to competitors?
3. What is the customer's share of the market they serve?

Practical tip: Customer analysis

When classifying customers involve those people who are closest to them like sales and service personnel *and* those who have the greatest impact upon the level of service which is delivered such as production and dispatch.

Everyone needs to know into which category each customer fits otherwise what happened in Example One will happen to your company.

Once customers have been categorized levels of service must be determined for each category and again it is important that people from all departments which impact upon levels of customer service should be involved. There are two reasons for this. Firstly, where people are involved in decision making they are more committed to the decisions that are made, and secondly they are able to identify any potential problems there may be in implementing those decisions.

The salesperson has an important role to perform at this stage in gathering information. Some of the information will be considered commercially sensitive and it is therefore necessary for the salesperson to seek answers from as broad a range of contacts within the customer organization and industry as possible.

The value of this information is that it allows an assessment of opportunities to further penetrate customers and the threats represented by competing suppliers.

It is also useful at this stage to analyse the nature of the relationship that is enjoyed with each of these customers, whether the relationship is close or distant, whether power is with the supplier or the purchaser, and how critical the relationship is to the long term objectives of the supplier.

Steps one and two are concerned with gathering and analysing information about the whole customer portfolio. They allow the identification of segments of customers for whom macro-sales strategies may be evolved and those individual customers which demand special treatment. Step three is concerned with gathering and analysing information about those customers which require special treatment through the development of micro-sales strategies.

Step three

The final step is concerned with analysing key accounts. Key accounts are not necessarily the largest customers or those which place the largest orders. They are the accounts which management perceive to be of the greatest strategic importance to the long term achievement of corporate and marketing objectives.

Initially all key accounts should be analysed together to give an overall picture, and then individually in order to better understand the nature of individual relationships and the specific needs of customers. The following questions should be asked:

- What is the growth rate of the customer's market?
- What proportion of the customer's demand for our product/service categories do we supply relative to the competition?
- What is the size of the customer's purchases or contribution to profit relative to other customers?

Figure 10.2 represents this information pictorially for a packaging company. It shows the position of the largest customers but also indicates tomorrow's future customers, those of growing strategic importance represented by dots in sectors 1, 8 and 9. It also indicates that the company appears to be investing resources in customers operating in markets with relatively poor growth. This kind of analysis allows companies to identify key and potentially key customers and to begin developing strategies for their development. Which relationships should be developed? Which need to be maintained? Which relationships should

be ended? Marketing, sales management and individual sales people should be involved in this analysis and decision making process.

The identification of key accounts should be based upon criteria established with reference to both the wider corporate objectives of the firm and to the marketing objectives which have been established to support them. The detailed analysis of individual customers should also be carried out jointly by marketing and sales.

The competitive positions shown along the horizontal axis are plotted on a log scale in order to accommodate the wide variation. Thus in square 4 the larger circle represents a major customer where the supplier's share of the customer's business for that product is four times the share held by its largest competitor. In contrast, the share of business enjoyed from those customers represented by dots in square 9 is only one-tenth of that enjoyed by the supplier's largest competitor.

Analysis of key accounts should take place according to the stage of key account development that the seller–buyer relationship has reached (see Table 10.6), on the degree of customer attractiveness and the ability of the seller to serve customer need.

Attractiveness is generally defined in terms of volume, growth potential, market or technical leadership, and the level and nature of the competition for that customer's business.

Other factors which need to be taken into consideration are:

- The complexity of the product or service;
- The buyer's own technical and process capability;
- The nature of the buying team and the purchasing processes they adopt;
- The specific nature of the customer's need.

Customer needs can be thought of in terms of product need, process need and facilitation need.

- **Product need** relates to the customer's requirement for the basic product or service. Product need is likely to be the main focus of the relationship in the pre-

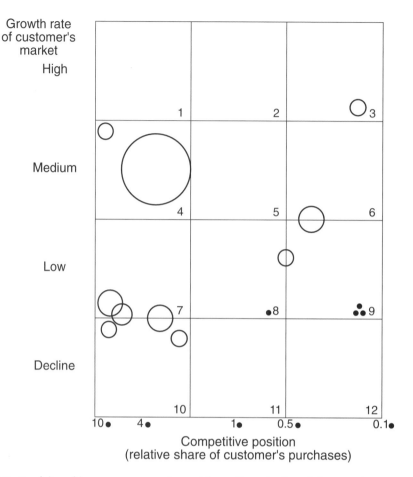

Figure 10.2 *Portfolio of key customers adapted from Campbell and Cunningham (1983). Note: size of circles represents sales volume to each customer*

or early-KAM development stages identified in Figure 10.3. Products may be simple or complex and product need is concerned with assuring minimum standards of quality, performance and conformance to specification.

● **Process need** has to do with how the product or service impacts upon the customer's manufacturing and value creation processes. Customers may require conformance to delivery requirements in terms of quantity and timing (e.g. just in time), products may also be required to be compatible with the customer's technology and the seller may be required to have detailed knowledge of the customer's manufacturing processes. A focus upon

process need tends to characterize mid- and advanced-KAM relationship stages.

● **Facilitation need** represents the customer's strategic focus on developing supplier relationships. If they maintain relationships which are essentially transaction focused (i.e. have little loyalty to suppliers, judge each transaction in isolation and focus upon price), adversarial (constantly pressing for discounts and short term commercial advantage), and opportunistic, then they have few facilitation needs and suppliers are best served by providing basic product offerings to specification and price.

Where customers are interested in forging close, long lasting partnerships with their suppliers, then their facilitation

Table 10.6 *Buyer–seller relationship development stages*

Development stage	Characteristics
Pre-KAM	Relationships at this stage are likely to be distant and transaction focused. Not all relationships are potentially 'key'. Both parties will be assessing the other's potential for relational development and there will be guarded information exchange. If potential exists for KAM relationship then there will be a move to the next stage.
Early KAM	This stage is concerned with exploring opportunities for collaboration. Tentative adaptations may be made to the seller's product and process offering. Sellers will aim to build social relationships and trust.
Mid-KAM	During this stage the relationship will grow in trust and the range of problems it addresses. Cross-firm contact patterns increase and the key account manager takes a facilitating rather than a lead role. There will be increasing involvement by senior managers as the potential for profitable collaboration increases.
Partnership KAM	At this stage buyer and seller are closely aligned. Senior managers from both companies are closely involved and joint teams work on cost saving and quality issues.
Synergistic KAM	Buyer and seller see themselves as a single entity creating joint value in the marketplace.
Uncoupling KAM	Just as not all relationships have the potential to become key accounts, so some relationships cease over time to be strategically important. Contingency plans must be developed to allow uncoupling at this stage.

Developed from Millman and Wilson (1995) and McDonald, Millman and Rogers (1996).

needs will tend to be of major importance. Facilitation is essentially about attitude. Sellers who focus upon meeting the facilitation needs of their key accounts are keen to identify opportunities for joint value creation and to remove barriers to doing business. They are prepared to reduce adminstration, and to alter systems and even organizational structures in order to make it easier for the customer to do business with them. They concentrate on developing their knowledge, not only of the customer's product and process needs, the decision making process and the structure of the decision making unit, but they also develop detailed knowledge about the customer's marketplace and use that knowledge to create competitive advantage for their customers.

The analysis of both the firm's products and markets prior to the development of detailed sales and marketing strategies is essential if a clear understanding is to be gained of the competitive position of the firm.

Strategy formulation

The questions addressed during the strategy formulation process are 'Where do we want to go?' and 'How shall we get there?' These questions need to be answered with reference to both the products and services offered by the company and the markets (customers) they wish to serve.

If companies are to thrive, then they must serve customer needs more effectively and more efficiently than their competition.

Products and services, supported by the internal competencies of the firm and their ability to manage relationships with their suppliers and customers, are the vehicles which deliver need answering benefits to customers. Products represent high levels of investment to supplier organizations and the temptation is therefore to focus upon the management of product life cycles rather than managing customers. Where this happens companies are not truly marketing orientated, they are essentially inward looking and sales led because strategies which focus upon the management of the product tend to focus upon the needs of the seller rather than upon the needs of the buyer.

A focus upon product management to drive marketing and sales strategies may be justified where the company serves markets made up of relatively large segments with homogenous needs. Even here, however, the nature of non-product related needs of customer segments must be taken into consideration. Where the customer base is small or where the marketing and sales strategies need to take account of key accounts, then relationship management rather than product management should provide the main focus for strategy development.

Two general approaches to the development of sales strategies which are integrated with marketing strategies are set out below. The first builds on product portfolio analysis and suggests how marketing and sales strategies may be evolved from an understanding of the product's position within the marketplace. The second shows how to develop marketing and sales strategies which are focused upon managing and developing relationships with customers where the product is only one of the factors which provide competitive advantage.

Strategies which focus upon product management

Three American authors, Strahle, Spiro and Acito suggest a number of sales strategies which support marketing strategies based upon product portfolio analysis. They suggest that there are four basic marketing strategies which correspond to product portfolio stages. These are *build, maintain, harvest* and *divest* marketing strategies.

If we refer back to our discussion of the General Electric portfolio analysis system a number of marketing strategies are suggested by the positioning of products in relation to market attractiveness and competitive position. Strategies for products with high market attractiveness and strong competitive positions should aim to *build* sales volume. Strategies for products occupying positions of medium market attractiveness and competitive strength should aim to *hold* or *harvest* the product, maintaining market share or reducing costs in order to enhance profitability. Where products are found to be in unattractive markets and also have poor competitive positioning, strategies may aim to *divest* them from the portfolio.

The four marketing strategies identified from product portfolio analysis – build, hold, harvest or divest – suggest the sales strategies and objectives which should be employed to support them. These are summarized in Table 10.7.

Build marketing strategy

The strategic sales objectives to support a build marketing strategy will seek to build and maintain sales volume by providing high levels of service, particularly at the pre-sale stage. The emphasis of sales activity will be on finding new customers for the product, carrying out product presentations and demonstrations as well as ensuring that existing customers receive the necessary service to ensure their continued loyalty. In order to build on the product's strong position the activities of other departments need to be integrated with those of sales and marketing. Effective product presentations resulting in full order books will have little lasting effect upon the product's long term viability unless supported by manufacturing, delivery and after-sales service which delivers high quality products at the right time and place and ensures their ongoing performance.

Table 10.7 *Objectives and activities corresponding to marketing product strategies*

Marketing strategy	Primary sales objectives	Sales activities
Build	1. Build and maintain sales volume	1. Provide high service levels, particularly pre-sale service 2. Product/market feedback
Hold	1. Maintain existing sales volume	1. Increase support and service levels to current accounts
Harvest	1. Reduce selling costs 2. Selectively maintain sales volume in key accounts	1. Reduce service levels 2. Maintain service levels 3. Eliminate unprofitable accounts
Divest	1. Clear out inventory 2. Reduce selling costs	1. Inventory dumping 2. Eliminate service

Adapted from Strahle, Spiro and Acito (1996) Marketing and Sales: Strategic Alignment and Functional Implementation, *Journal of Personal Selling and Sales Management*, **XVI**, No. 1, 1–20.

Where the product relies upon intermediaries such as wholesalers or retailers for its distribution the aim will be to increase geographical representation in order to exclude potential rivals.

Salespeople require strong prospecting and presentation skills at this stage, and in the absence of existing relationships with target customers, the ability to build trust quickly and create sales. In addition the salesperson must also have sound product knowledge and knowledge of its applications in the customer's business.

Hold marketing strategy

The sales objective here is to aggressively maintain market position. This may be done in a number of ways. Investment should be aimed at excluding the competition and building customer loyalty; thus discounts, special product modifications, joint promotional activity and the protection of key accounts may all play their part. If sales are through intermediaries then emphasis may be placed on joint promotional activity, whilst direct customers may be 'tied in' by additional service or preferential delivery.

Whilst selling skills are still important, account maintenance skills are of increasing value at this stage. Salespeople need to understand their customers' business and provide higher levels of service which keep, rather than just create, customers. Increasing attention will also be paid to the larger and more productive accounts.

Harvest marketing strategy

The primary sales objective to support this marketing strategy is to reduce selling costs. The aim is to generate cash flow and limit the level of investment expended in supporting this product. At the same time it is important to keep service levels high enough to exclude the competition until a new product is available to replace it.

In line with the overall aim of reducing costs, the salesforce spend as little time as possible selling this product and limit their selling and sales support activities to high volume accounts.

Divest marketing strategy

Here the product is reaching the end of its life cycle and whilst additional cost cutting may allow it to be sold at a price that is still attractive to some buyers there is an ongoing danger that the company will be left with stocks of obsolete product. The primary sales objective at this stage is therefore to reduce selling costs and clear out inventory.

Four issues arise from the adoption of product related strategies to guide the formation of sales objectives:

1. Marketing must communicate the specific product strategy that they wish the salesforce to follow. The establishment of volume targets alone gives no indication of the chosen strategy.
2. Salespeople have an important role in feeding back information about the competition, and about customer reaction to product offerings in order to facilitate changes in marketing strategy. Salespeople are often reluctant to supply information of this nature and sales and marketing managers must develop mechanisms by which this information can be captured.
3. Focus upon product related strategies emphasizes the use of *selling* skills, those related to presentations, overcoming objections and closing, rather than upon skills which build long term relationships with customers. As such they are concerned with the creation of sales rather than the creation of customers. The danger for the selling company is that too heavy an emphasis upon product life cycle issues leads to them being focused upon their own needs rather than those of their customers.
4. Nevertheless, the product portfolio related strategies may be useful where companies identify relatively homogenous market segments that can be served adequately through the development of macro-sales and marketing strategies. Certainly the development of all sales strategies must take some account of

product life cycle, market and competitive positioning.

Strategies which focus upon customer management

An alternative approach is to develop sales strategies around portfolios of customers. By classifying customers as yesterday's, today's regular, today's special and tomorrow's special customers, as we did earlier, it is possible to develop different marketing and sales strategies to serve each category. An understanding of the relational development cycle also allows strategies for the development of individual customers to key account status.

Different strategies for different classes of customers

The same broad strategic approaches of *build*, *hold*, *harvest* and *divest* can be adopted when developing strategies for customer portfolio management (see Table 10.8).

Build relationship strategy

This approach should be adopted for *today's special customers* or key accounts. It involves getting and staying very close to the customer. This involves investing time and resources in the development of the relationship. Over time a great many people will develop cross-functional relationships between buyer and seller organizations and the salesperson or key account manager will perform an important co-ordinating role between these customers and the supplier.

The key account development process will be discussed in detail in the next section of this chapter. For the moment it is worth noting that *build* relationship sales strategies do not only involve planning the activities of the salesforce. They must involve senior managers, and often production, design, service and even finance and purchasing people networking with their counterparts in the customer organization. They also involve a willingness to adapt – product, processes,

Table 10.8 *Sales objectives and activities corresponding to marketing relationship strategies*

Marketing relationship strategy	Customer category	Primary sales objectives	Sales activities
Build	Today's special key accounts/ tomorrow's customers	1. Build relationship	1. Joint problem resolution/bespoke offer 2. Networking/ co-ordination 3. Resource allocation 4. Internal advocate for customer
Hold	Today's regular customers	1. Maintain relationships and share of customer's business	1. Tailor generic sales offerings to market segments 2. Monitor service levels and maintain or increase 4. Use selling skills to present product benefits 5. Address process need selectively
Harvest	Today's regular customers	1. Reduce costs of serving customers 2. Focus on profitable transactions	1. Maintain or reduce service levels 2. Reactive rather than proactive 3. Eliminate unprofitable accounts
Divest	Yesterday's customers	1. Exit relationship	1. Withdraw service

organizational systems and structures – on the part of the seller, and because of the importance of this group of customers, the decisions which impact upon their management are almost too important to be left to salespeople.

A further category of customers which should be managed with build strategies are *tomorrow's customers*. These are customers who may provide small levels of business at the present time but who offer major potentials for long term growth because they are operating in new but fast growing markets

Salespeople should be encouraged to prospect for this type of customer and to analyse their potential for future growth. Once identified an opportunity exists to build loyal key accounts for tomorrow's business by helping these often small and new customers to grow their businesses.

Hold relationship strategy

Hold strategies are adopted for many of *today's regular customers*, those with whom relationships may be of long standing but are less intimate than with key accounts, and less important from a strategic perspective. They also tend to be less loyal and more price sensitive because the the relationship ties are less strong.

Many of today's regular customers nevertheless represent important levels of business and must be protected from incursion by competitors. Other strategies would be concerned with increasing the level of the customer's requirements against other suppliers.

The strategies adopted to hold this type of customer are the macro-strategies, discussed earlier, which reflect the needs of broad customer segments within the customer portfolio. Standard product and service offerings are developed which limit the level of resources which need to be allocated to serving individual customers with limited profit and relationship development potential. With these customers sales strategies are very closely aligned with the product portfolio strategies outlined in the previous section of this chapter.

Salespeople will be instructed to use their judgement in relation to call frequency and will tend to employ standard selling skills and presentation techniques which stress direct product performance and suitability, price, discounts and value for money against competitor offerings, rather than process or facilitation related issues which demand higher resource allocation on the part of the seller.

Service levels need to be maintained and in some instances increased to focus upon process related issues in order to hold the customer, or increase the share of the customer's business, but careful consideration should be given as to whether any increase in service levels will be matched by resultant benefits, e.g. the exclusion of competition, increased customer loyalty, larger orders, greater profitability, etc.

Harvest relationship strategy

This strategy should be adopted for the less attractive of today's customers and yesterday's customers. They are likely to be large in number, spasmodic in their ordering patterns and unreliable in terms of loyalty. Nevertheless they may offer a valuable source of revenue, particularly where their needs are product which is reaching the end

of its general life cycle.

Sales strategies adopted for these customers should be largely reactive. Sales people should be discouraged from making regular calls on them and to limit the level of service they offer. In many instances it should be considered whether these customers may be more efficiently served by telephone rather than field sales staff.

Each transaction with these customers should also be judged for profitability and the level of resources devoted to servicing the account severely limited. Judgements will also need to be made as to whether it is worthwhile continuing to do business with these accounts

Divest relationship strategy

For a variety of reasons some customers are not worth dealing with. The size of order that they place or their focus upon price rather than value may render them unprofitable. They may also be untrustworthy or constantly change their minds about order size, delivery and service requirements making them costly to deal with. Careful consideration should be given in these instances to withdrawing supplies from them altogether.

From time to time all customers need to be reviewed to determine whether their status has changed and decisions should be taken about the strategies which should be adopted for their future management.

Relationship development strategies for key account management

Chapter 5 identified a number of stages through which key account relationships pass. Table 10.6 summarizes the major points. Having identified those accounts which are the key to the achievement of a seller's strategic marketing objectives, it is necessary to develop sales plans which manage the relationship for maximum profitability. Table 10.9 identifies the strategies that may be adopted at different stages in the relational development cycle.

KAM development is a long term process. It can take up to three years to develop relationships which come anywhere near being *synergistic* but the potential for increasing long term profitability leads many companies to believe that the investment in both time and resources is worth it.

The pre-KAM stage

Not all accounts are key accounts. The task facing the sales and marketing function at the pre-KAM stage is to identify those customers with the potential for developing as key accounts. Salespeople and key account managers should be concerned with prospecting for key accounts at this stage and with determining the potential for increasing profitable business with individual customers.

The early-KAM stage

Strategic objectives for the early-KAM stage are to increase levels of business and penetrate the account in order to build a network of contacts. This will enable the identification of potential product and process related issues which may be addressed to add value to the seller's offer.

At this stage a detailed understanding must be gained of the competitive offerings, the decision making process of the customer and their selection criteria, and key decision makers within the organization must be identified and social links forged with them. Efforts are made to persuade customers of the benefits of enjoying 'preferred' status whilst gauging the potential of achieving strategic and cultural 'fit' with the client organization.

The role of the key account manager is to extend the number of contacts he or she has with the customer, to assess whether the customer represents long term potential for profitable business based on partnership and to lead the allocation of resources into the development of the relationship.

The mid-KAM stage

The aim of the key account manager at the mid-KAM stage is to develop trust and enhance the buyer's perception of the seller's credibility so that they are perceived as preferred suppliers. Working with his/her lead contact, the key account manger will increase the number of cross-functional contacts between the two organizations and ensure that the key account is recognized as such within his/her own organization. Joint social events may be held which build trust and facilitate the exchange of information.

The partnership stage

By this stage the number of interfirm contacts is very high. Senior managers will meet on a regular basis and joint projects teams are operating to resolve common problems or achieve partnership objectives. The sales strategy at this stage is to ensure that communication flows are maintained and that nothing is done to sour the relationship. Monitoring the partnership is important and the key account manager may at this stage be reporting to joint board meetings.

The synergistic stage

Some relationships go beyond partnership. Synergistic KAM refers to buying and selling companies jointly creating value in the marketplace. There will be joint business planning, joint strategies and joint market research and implementation. The role of the key account manager becomes that of manager of a quasi-organization composed of joint focus teams of operational staff meeting on a regular basis setting their own objectives and agendas.

Although the main reference has been to key accounts, the strategies that have been discussed could equally well be applied to national or global accounts although the implementation issues may be of a different order. The main problem is how to integrate the efforts of local area salespeople within

Table 10.9 *Strategies for KAM development*

Development Stage	Objectives	Strategy	Key account manager's activity	Characteristics
Pre-KAM	1. Identify as key account 2. Establish product need 3. Establish potential of the account	1. Identify key contact 2. Focus resources 3. Work to establish social contacts and bring organizations closer 4. Show willingness to make token product adaptations	1. Prospect for key account potential 2. Forge social contacts 3. Identify decision making process and criteria 4. Advocate key account status internally 5. Secure trial order	Both parties will be assessing the other's potential. Guarded information exchange
Early KAM	1. Account penetration 2. Increase volume of business	1. If attractive invest in building social relationship 2. If unattractive serve through low cost channels, e.g. telephone or distributors	1. Explore networking potential 2. identify process related problems and show willingness to provide solutions which add value 3. Lead relationship between companies with main contract 4. Involve technical support team 5. Build trust through performance and open communications	This stage is concerned with exploring opportunities for collaboration. Tentative adaptations may be made to the seller's product and process offering
Mid-KAM	1. Establish credibility	1. Identify potential process improvements to gain cost savings 2. Establish key account status 3. Establish preferred supplier status 4. If unattractive develop standardized offer	1. Increase contact patterns – introduce operational staff to opposite numbers 2. Manage implementation of process improvements with key contact 3. Increase information flows	Relationship growing in trust and the range of problems it addresses. Cross-firm contact patterns increase and key account manager takes facilitating rather than lead role
Partnership KAM	1. Develop the spirit of partnership 2. Lock in customer by providing external resource base	1. Integrate processes 2. Establish joint problem solving teams focused on process/cost improvements 3. Multi-level and functional contacts 4. Reduce paperwork and increase information flows	1. Manage the interface 2. Monitor partnership performance for both companies	At this stage buyer and seller are closely aligned. Senior managers from both companies are closely involved and joint teams work on cost saving and quality issues
Synergistic KAM	1. Continuous improvement 2. Shared rewards	1. Focus on joint creation value for the end user 2. Establish joint semi-autonomous project teams 3. Aim for quasi-integration	1. Co-ordinate activities of projects teams 2. Co-ordinate senior management involvement 3. Identify ongoing projects and opportunities	Buyer and seller see themselves as a single entity creating joint value in the marketplace

This table is based upon the work of Millman and Wilson (1995) and McDonald, Millman and Rogers (1996).

the key account management process and this will be addressed briefly in the next section.

Implementation

A number of issues must be addressed at the implementation stage which answer the questions 'What actions should be taken?' and 'Are we achieving our objectives?' These issues relate to how the salesforce is to be recruited, organized and rewarded.

Recruitment

Not all selling jobs are the same. Where the sales cycle is short, the product of low value or importance and the decision making unit small, then presentation and closing skills and the ability to overcome objections may be very important. Contrast this situation with the key account selling process where it would be inappropriate to use traditional selling skills with customers with whom you are trying to develop a close long term relationship.

It is obvious that care must be taken to recruit people with the skills and aptitudes which match the role they are being asked to perform. In the same way it is essential that training programmes are designed to meet the needs of the salesperson, both as an individual and in his/her efforts to achieve strategic sales objectives.

Salesforce organization

The way in which the salesforce is organized should reflect the strategic sales objectives of the company. There are four broad options available: geographical organization; product organization; organization by customers or markets; and organization by selling function.

Geographical organization

Geographical organization assigns individual salespeople to cover separate geographical territories. It has the advantage of being

simple and is the lowest cost option. Another advantage is that since only one salesperson calls on each customer there is no confusion about who is responsible for ensuring that customer needs are met.

> **Practical tip: Recruitment and training tips**
>
> 1. Define the selling task.
> 2. Determine the qualities and skills required.
> 3. Establish a profile of the person you want and recruit to it.
> 4. Establish an induction programme which incorporates an introduction to the company, its products, services and markets, strategic mission and objectives, culture and the role of the salesperson.
> 5. Review training needs regularly and tailor training to individual needs.

There are disadvantages associated with this form of organization. As salespeople sell all the company's products they may not be truly 'expert' in any of them, nor will they be able to develop expertise in all their customers' industries and the problems associated with them. Also salespeople are given a great deal of freedom with this type of organization and the decisions they make regarding which customers to focus upon, which products to sell and which selling functions to perform may not always be consistent with management objectives.

Geographical organization is best adopted where the aim is to keep costs down, where macro-strategies are being implemented, where the customer base is relatively homogenous or where the product range is relatively limited.

Product organization

Product organization is best used where the company has a diverse product portfolio. For example, a company manufacturing electrical switch gear, specialist plugs and sockets and lighting equipment might have three different salesforces to sell the three ranges of product. The major advantage of this form of organization is the level of technical expertise that the salesforce can develop in terms of product knowledge and applications.

A disadvantage is that there may often be duplication of effort where more than one salesperson from the same company is calling on the same customer.

Customer organization

Organizing by customers or markets is a reflection of firms adopting a true customer orientation. Salespeople are able to gain a better understanding of their customers' business, their needs and requirements and can be trained to use different selling approaches for different categories of customer and to implement different sales strategies with each of them.

This method of organization must obviously be adopted where a key account management programme has been adopted but it does require close and careful management, particularly where customers have several sites nationally, or where they are global operations.

Organizing by selling function

This type of organization is a recognition that selling tasks differ and require different skills. One group of salespeople may be used to prospect for and develop new accounts whilst another may be used to maintain existing accounts. Another example might be the use of a sales team organized geographically to sell to today's regular customers and key account managers, unconstrained by territorial divisions, to sell to today's special customers. A specialist salesforce may also be used to assist in the development and early sales of new products. Only once they are

established are they transferred to the wider salesforce.

The choice of organizational form will depend upon a number of factors. The nature of the market, the product and customer portfolios enjoyed by the company, cost, and the strategic objectives the firm has developed. Some companies mix organizational types. For example a materials handling equipment manufacturer operating in several quite different markets uses three methods. The general salesforce is organized geographically and calls on customers in each market segment within their territories. In addition key accounts are managed nationally by a key account manager and both he or she and the salesforce are supported by market and product specialists who provided an internal consultancy service to advise on specific industry applications.

Practical tip: Compensation and incentive programmes

1. Review sales objectives, account management policies and present salesforce performance.
2. Decide what you want to reward – turnover, profit, customer care, account development, sales of specific products, new account generation, etc.
3. Match objectives to compensation and incentive mix: salary, bonus, commission, prizes.
4. Match compensation and incentive programmes to individual salespeople.
5. Take account of non-financial incentives such as promotion, career development, recognition programmes.
6. Do all this openly and communicate the programme to the salesforce.

Rewarding the sales effort _____

The saying that 'you get what you pay for' is never more true than when applied to the salesforce. If you reward salespeople for volume rather than profit, then you will get volume but you may not get profitable volume, particularly if you allow them freedom to negotiate volume discounts.

Another problem with rewarding salespeople on the basis of volume is that they will tend to sell those products which are easy to sell rather than those which the company wishes to be sold. Also there will be a tendency to focus upon closing sales rather than upon building strong customer relationships which will provide sales for the future.

When establishing salary and commission policies it is important to ensure that they reflect and support marketing and sales objectives. The following suggestions outline the process which should be followed in developing compensation programmes.

Summary

Strategic planning is important in that it provides a framework to guide actions in order to achieve organizational objectives.

The strategic sales planning process is concerned with:

1. diagnosing the present position of the firm regarding product and customer portfolios, salesforce performance, skills and capabilities;
2. developing strategies which support the overall company mission and which integrate with marketing and other departmental strategies; and
3. with implementing those strategies and measuring their performance.

Strategic diagnosis addresses the questions 'Where are we now?' and 'How did we get here?' In terms of developing sales strategies, the sales manager answers these questions by carrying out an audit which identifies the opportunities and threats which exist in the firm's market environment and the strengths and weaknesses of the salesforce.

Two broad approaches to developing sales strategies were discussed. The first focused upon the management of portfolios of products, the second upon the management of customer portfolios.

It is important that a thorough understanding is achieved of the life cycle stage reached by each of the company's products and that policies are developed which determine whether they are to be built, held, harvested or divested. If the selling firm is essentially product focused then sales strategies need to be developed in order to support these objectives.

An alternative approach was introduced which focuses upon the management of customers and a method of customer portfolio analysis was suggested which allows them to be categorized as yesterday's, today's regular, today's special and tomorrow's customers. Different sales strategies can be developed for the specific management of each of these categories.

Having identified the broad marketing strategies and management policies which are to be adopted in relation to both products and customers, it was suggested that two types of strategic plans were prepared. The first was called a macro-sales strategy and involved developing generic strategies for selling to broad customer segments. The second was termed a micro-sales strategy and involved developing individual strategies for today's special or key accounts.

In terms of implementation, a number of selling strategies were discussed which related to both the management of the product life cycle and to key account development.

Finally issues relating to recruitment, salesforce organization and reward were discussed.

Further reading

Campbell, N.C.G. and Cunningham M.T. (1983) Customer Analysis for Strategy Development in Industrial Markets, *Strategic Management Journal*, **4**, 360–80.

Millman, A.F. and Wilson K.J. (1995) From Key Account Selling to Key Account Management, *Journal of Marketing Practice: Applied Marketing Science*, **1**, No. 1, 9–21.

McDonald, M. Millman, A. F. and Rogers, J. (1996) *Key Account Management: Learning from Supplier and Customer Perspectives*, Cranfield School of Management in Association with CIM.

Strahle, W.M., Spiro, R.L. and Acito, F. (1996) Marketing and Sales: Strategic Alignment and Functional Implementation, *Journal of Personal Selling and Sales Management*, **XVI**, No. 1, 1–20.

Turnbull, P.W. and Valla J.-P. (1987) Strategic Planning in Industrial Marketing: An Interactive Approach, European *Journal of Marketing*, **121**, No. 5, 5–20. Reprinted in Ford, D. (1990) *Understanding Business Markets*, London: Academic Press.

11

Sales organization effectiveness ——————

Professor Nigel F. Piercy, Cardiff Business School
Professor David W. Cravens, Texas Christian University, USA

 The goal of this chapter is to uncover some critical sales management practices which have been found to relate directly to sales organization effectiveness in major business-to-business companies throughout the world. The issues on which we aim to focus managers' attention are:

- the need to examine salesforce performance as it relates to overall sales organization effectiveness;
- the importance of focusing attention not just on sales results, but also on the activities salespeople perform to achieve results;
- the importance of identifying and concentrating on the characteristics of successful salespeople as the foundation for high performance;
- the significance of the field sales manager as coach and communicator not just commander in the way he or she manages the salesforce;
- recognizing the importance of 'right-sizing' at the level of the field salesforce and sales unit in times of corporate downsizing and adjustment; and
- accepting the overwhelming case that effective sales organizations achieve at superior levels against their competitors as well as their own objectives through their focus on customer relationships.

Each of these issues is considered in turn, and each has a checklist of critical issues for the manager to evaluate in his/her own sales organization. None of these issues provides a panacea, and they are not equally applicable in all companies, but they form a management agenda which focuses on what we can learn about how the most effective business-to-business sales organizations outperform the rest.

Our way of looking at the sources of sales organization effectiveness, on which we will argue that managers should focus their atten-tion, is summarized in Figure 11.1. Our feedback from sales managers points to the performance of the salesforce and the characteristics of the salespeople employed that underpin that performance as drivers of sales organization effectiveness, but also that these drivers of effectiveness are influenced in important ways by sales management activities, the design of the sales organization, and the strength of customer relationship building which is achieved. Each of these areas is evaluated below, drawing on the findings of our studies of effective sales organizations and providing a checklist of issues for sales management attention.

The more effective sales organizations have a number of things in common:

- Their salespeople share several similar success characteristics.
- The salespeople perform exceptionally well on a number of critical dimensions – the drivers of salesforce performance.
- Their field sales managers play a critical role as coaches rather than as commanders.
- They are 'right-sized' and soundly organized at the sales unit level.
- They focus throughout on building long term customer relationships.

There are no magic answers to how to achieve higher levels of sales organization effectiveness, but the more effective sales organizations consistently apply the factors above and achieve dramatically superior performance in the marketplace. The important lessons which can be learned from this form the content of this chapter.

It follows that what we are mainly interested in is business-to-business selling situations where buyers and sellers are both interested in building long term collaborative relationships, and selling situations where management wants to have control over what the salesperson does, and how selling effort is allocated over products, customers, and prospects. These are situations where selling strategies typically rely on more call planning, fewer calls, more sales support activities and customized selling approaches.

Sales organization effectiveness ▄

The modern marketplace is imposing enormous pressures on competitiveness through

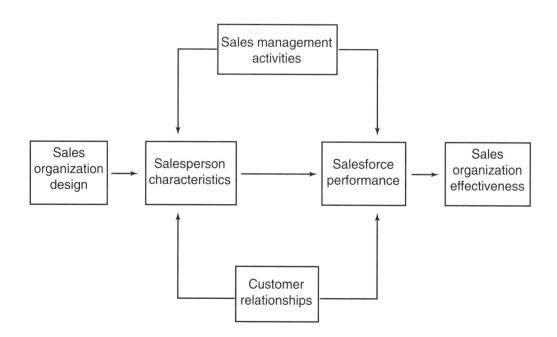

Figure 11.1 *Sources of organization effectiveness*

> ### Practical tip
>
> If we want to encourage long term relationship building with customers to enhance sales organization effectiveness, our sales management processes and methods need to be compatible with our objectives, and everyone should know those objectives. This means placing more emphasis with salespeople on long term results, motivating salespeople more with salary instead of just basing pay primarily on incentive compensation, and working with salespeople to help them achieve high performance.

such factors as global sourcing by major customers and reductions in supplier bases, low economic growth in many countries, and new sources of overseas competition emerging in many product markets. Other pressures come from the goal in many companies to be 'leaner' and to look for savings in the large costs represented by the salesforce.

The result of such pressures has been aggressive efforts by major organizations such as Ingersoll-Rand, Hewlett Packard and General Electric to counteract escalating sales costs and declining salesforce productivity through such mechanisms as: account management, lead generation systems, computer-assisted sales programmes, telemarketing and systems contracts. At the same time, multi-national organizations like Colgate-Palmolive, Compaq Computers, IBM, Proctor and Gamble, Xerox and Kraft are among those undertaking major restructuring of sales organizations to improve effectiveness and competitiveness.

For example, one US study of sales managers in major companies suggests that many of the pressures for change in sales organizations, which are shared by many of our companies, come from the following factors:

1. a growing emphasis on customer-oriented selling which requires more varied types of salespeople of greater sophistication;
2. the need for greater flexibility and faster decision making, which requires structural change to get away from slow bureaucratic organizations;
3. wider corporate restructuring which removes many of the traditional barriers between manufacturing, sales logistics, and customers;
4. budget restrictions causing greater scrutiny of the sales process for effectiveness and profit contribution; and
5. the need to organize salesforces to serve different market segments which demand different selling approaches, managerial structures and compensation systems.

Underpinning these pressures for change in the sales organization is the search for greater effectiveness, which raises the important question of what we mean by effectiveness in this context. There are many well-known technical problems with defining and measuring effectiveness in business operations. However, for our present purposes we can take a simple view. The effective sales organization is the one which is meeting and beating the objectives set for it by management, and which is meeting and beating the competition in sales, profitability, market share and customer satisfaction.

When we are not satisfied with the effectiveness of our sales organization, there are several danger signals to evaluate. These

> ### Practical tip
>
> Do not assume that customer satisfaction and loyalty can only be bought through reduced sales and profit results. It is true that anyone can achieve short term 'popularity' through price cuts, product concessions, free service extras, and so on. What we found is that in the truly effective sales organizations, customer satisfaction, sales and profitability all beat the competitors. This is because customer satisfaction drives sales and profits, not vice versa.

include customers lost to competitors, high salesperson turnover, negative feedback from customers, delays in deliveries and large differences in salesperson productivity.

In fact, we have found that this simple view distinguishes well between the more and less effective sales organizations, and it offers a simple and accessible way for managers to evaluate their own sales organizations and to choose their priorities in where to direct attention for improvements. Checklist 11.1 provides a framework for undertaking this evaluation, as the starting point in searching for superior sales organization effectiveness.

Successful salesperson characteristics

The first of the key drivers of sales organization effectiveness which we consider is the characteristics of successful salespeople. What we have found is that in the more effective sales organizations, salespeople excel in a number of important areas:

1. motivation,
2. customer orientation,
3. team orientation, and
4. sales support orientation.

Checklist 11.1
Evaluating our sales organization effectiveness

Questions to consider   *Score**

Compared to our major competitor, how well has this sales unit performed in the following areas in the last year?

    Sales volume achieved   ....

    Market share achieved   ....

    Profitability   ....

    Customer satisfaction   ....

Compared to the objectives set for this sales unit, how well has this sales unit performed in the following areas in the last year?

    Sales volume achieved   ....

    Market share achieved   ....

    Profitability   ....

    Customer satisfaction   ....

(*Give marks out of 10, where 1 = much worse and 10 = much better)

Implications:

Practical tip

Checklists like the ones shown in this chapter work best if they are used to collect information and opinions from as wide a range of sources as possible, and if they are used to look for trends over time and differences between different parts of the operation – for example using information from salespeople and sales managers to build a picture of how we are doing over a period of time and across different sales units – not just as a way of judging and trying to control more tightly.

Although the term 'motivation' is often used in a very general sense, in this context, *motivation* refers to very specific factors like the extent to which salespeople obtain a sense of accomplishment in their work, and feel a sense of personal growth and development. Their feeling of stimulation from their work and sense of challenging involvement are associated with winning respect from superiors and other salespeople, strong commitment to the company and innovativeness in their work. While these are 'soft', people issues, they are more often found in the more effective sales organizations, and should not be neglected when we are recruiting, and investing in training and developing salespeople.

We have also found that in the more effective sales organizations, salespeople are rated higher in their *customer orientation*. A lot of lip-service is paid to being customer oriented in different departments and roles – few of us would say that we are not. However, we can test this out by being a lot more specific.

Customer orientation in this sense considers such questions as how good are our salespeople in terms of issues like: focusing on satisfying customer needs, employing customized selling approaches to individual accounts, studying customer needs to guide selling strategy, as well as having expert selling skills and extensive product/service

knowledge? This too has clear implications for how we should think about selecting and developing salespeople.

We have also found that salespeople in the more effective sales organizations tend to be rated higher in their *team orientation*. Although many have traditionally perceived the effective salesperson as the individualistic 'lone wolf' or the 'road warrior', salespeople in the more effective sales organizations are rated higher in such things as: co-operating as part of a sales team, and willingly accepting direction and review from the field sales manager and accepting the sales manager's authority. It seems in many situations that traditional qualities associated with effective selling may have to be compared with the potential gains to effectiveness from having salespeople who are 'team players'. This too has major implications for recruitment and development in the salesforce.

Practical tip

Building team-orientation is often difficult, particularly where the traditional success has been associated with the 'lone wolf' salesperson. Some major organizations are countering this by offering salespeople rewards for 'assists', as well as the sales they sign up individually, and this may be a useful approach.

Lastly, we have observed that in the more effective sales organizations, salespeople display a significantly higher level of *sales support orientation* in their selling work. By this we mean that salespeople in the effective sales organizations appear to be superior in the extent to which they spend substantial amounts of time planning sales calls and are effective in undertaking non-selling activities and sales support activities. Our view of sales organization effectiveness suggests that it is achieved particularly by salespeople who invest in preparation and follow-up, even where this is not linked directly to an immediate short term sales success. This has major implications for the orientation towards work that we want from our salespeople, and the management control and incentives that we provide.

The first stage in evaluating the sales organization effectiveness issue is in considering the characteristics of the salespeople, and what this tells us about priorities in recruitment and selection, and in subsequent training and development. Traditional selling skills may be critical, but it seems enhanced effectiveness is also associated with motivation, customer orientation, team orientation, and sales support orientation. This may require us to re-think much of the conventional wisdom about what makes a 'good' salesperson.

An initial stage in addressing this question can be through the use of the questions in Checklist 11.2, which asks us to assess the issues discussed above at the level of the field sales unit.

Practical tip

You may find it useful to compare your scores in Checklist 11.2 across different sales units in your organization. If, for example, one unit is relatively low compared to the others on its motivation or team orientation, then these characteristics may need management attention. We would expect some variation across sales units, so the objective is to look for major differences.

Salesforce performance

To say that higher sales organization effectiveness comes from superior salesforce performance is hardly surprising. However, there are three critical things to bear in mind here.

First, salesforce performance is concerned with how well salespeople undertake the tasks that we believe to be important. Second, sales organization effectiveness is the overall result of that performance, in the light of all the other surrounding issues. In other words, effectiveness depends not just on the performance of the salesforce, it is also dependent on the selling environment and organizational characteristics.

The selling environment is concerned with factors like market potential, economic conditions, competitive activity, and so on – which are outside the control of salespeople. Organizational characteristics of importance may concern the quality of management, the soundness of organizational designs, the production and delivery processes built by the company – and these too are largely outside the control of the salesperson or the sales manager. If we follow the logic that we cannot hold salespeople responsible for things they cannot control, then we need to focus our management attention on the important things they can control.

Third, there are strong arguments that when we examine salesforce performance we should assess both outcome performance in the areas that matter, as well as behavioural performance in a number of critical areas. This has extremely significant implications for how we manage selling, as suggested in the next section of this chapter. For the moment, let us focus on what we should look at in salesforce performance.

As might be expected, one of the things we have identified clearly in the more effective sales organizations is superior outcome performance by the salesforce. By this we mean that salespeople do better in such areas as producing a high market share, making sales of the products with the highest profit margin, generating a good level of sales revenue, quickly generating sales of new products and services, identifying and selling to major accounts, producing sales and contracts with long term profitability and exceeding sales targets and objectives during the year.

It is important that we evaluate the outcome performance of the salesforce, because

**Checklist 11.2
Evaluating salesperson characteristics**

Questions to consider   *Score**

To what extent do the salespeople in this sales unit:

Motivation

  1. Obtain a sense of accomplishment from their work   ....
  2. Feel a sense of personal growth and development in their work   ....
  3. Get a feeling of stimulation and a sense of challenging involvement in   ....
     their work
  4. Have a high level of respect from their supervisors   ....
  5. Have respect from fellow workers   ....
  6. Have a sense of being creative and imaginative in their work   ....
  7. Get a sense of loyal association with the company   ....
  8. Feel a sense of being innovative in their work   ....

Customer orientation

  9. Focus on satisfying customer needs   ....
10. Customize their selling approaches to individual clients   ....
11. Possess expert selling skills   ....
12. Possess extensive product/service knowledge   ....
13. Study customer needs to guide selling strategy   ....

Team orientation

14. Are willing to accept direction from line manager   ....
15. Co-operate as part of a sales team   ....
16. Accept the line manager's authority   ....
17. Welcome performance reviews   ....

Sales support orientation

18. Spend substantial time planning sales calls   ....
19. Perform non-selling activities effectively   ....
20. Perform sales support activities effectively   ....

(*Give marks out of 10, where 1 = not at all and 10 = to a great extent)

Implications:

it is clearly associated with effectiveness. However, what we have also found is that high outcome performance and high sales organization effectiveness are also strongly associated with high behavioural performance by the salesforce. This is more controversial because traditionally managing salesforce behavioural performance has been seen as mainly associated with 'soft' results like salespeoples' capabilities, attitudes, motivation and serving customer needs, while getting sales results was created by focusing on sales and profit targets and financial incentives.

What we have found is a very strong association between salesforce behavioural performance and both outcome performance and overall sales organization effectiveness. We will examine the implications of this for field sales management – behaviour-based control activities – in the next section, but first consider what is meant by behavioural performance in the salesforce.

We have observed superior behavioural performance in the salesforce in the more effective sales organizations in six areas.

First, behavioural performance is concerned with traditional concerns for selling skills and product knowledge. Specifically, we found that salesforces in more effective sales organizations achieved superior performance in *sales presentation* and *technical knowledge*. Sales presentation can be evaluated in performance on such activities as listening attentively to identify and understand customers' real concerns, convincing customers that they understand their real problems, using established contacts to develop new customers, communicating their sales presentations clearly and concisely and working out solutions to customers' questions and objections. Technical knowledge refers to how well salespeople know the design and specification of company products and services and the application of the company's products and services, as well as keeping abreast of the company's production and technological developments.

Performance in these areas is important. However, what we have found is that the more effective sales organizations are not distinguished by superior performance in sales presentation and technical knowledge of their salespeople as much as they are by adaptiveness, teamwork, planning and support. These seem to be the critical aspects of behavioural performance in selling that are associated with effectiveness.

Practical tip

One approach to consider is using the points made here, and summarized in the checklists, as a basis for discussions with customers about their preferences and priorities. This can provide invaluable insight into the different requirements of different types of buyer and customer organization.

Adaptiveness is concerned with such issues as how well salespeople perform in experimenting with different sales approaches, flexibility in the selling approaches used, adapting selling approaches from one customer to another, and varying sales style from one situation to another. It seems that success in modern markets is associated with flexibility and adaptability in selling.

Teamwork can be assessed is terms of how well salespeople perform is such areas as generating sales volume from team sales (in the sense of sales made by two or more salespeople), building strong working relationships with other people in the company, working closely with non-sales employees to close sales, co-ordinating with other company employees to handle after-sales problems and service needs and discussing selling strategies with people from other departments. Successful salespeople in modern business-to-business markets co-ordinate and integrate to get results.

Planning performance is concerned with how well salespeople do in planning each sales call, planning sales strategies for each customer, planning coverage of the sales terri-

---

Practical tip

When issues like sales support, customer orientation and adaptiveness in selling are discussed with salespeople, look for patterns in people's responses, which may be a clue to what can really be achieved and how. For example, one company selling to the construction industry found that, unexpectedly, older salespeople were far more receptive to the ideas of behavioural performance improvements than were younger salespeople. The explanation was that salespeople under 30 had only ever sold in times of recession, while older salespeople knew what it was like in better days. They addressed the problem by having older salespeople act as mentors to the younger.

---

ence to identify new product and service ideas. Superior performance in covering these areas is also characteristic of the more effective sales organization.

We suggest that the underlying drivers of sales organization effectiveness are only partly associated with traditional selling skills in sales presentation and technical knowledge, important though these are. The major gains in sales organization effectiveness seem to be reflected in superior performance by the salesforce in adaptiveness in selling, teamworking, sales planning and the thorough performance of sales support activities.

Practical tip

If the focus of our sales strategy is enhanced effectiveness through stronger customer relationships, this involves more than salespeople. Consider the power of customer visits by key personnel from other departments and senior management made with salespeople. This may show the route to 'seamless service' and a customer relationship focus that improves sales organization effectiveness.

---

tory or customer group, and simply planning daily activities. Many traditional views of planning would see this type of activity as 'downtime'. We found it to be highly associated with the more effective sales organizations.

Support relates to how well salespeople perform in such areas as providing after-sales service, checking on product delivery, handling customer complaints, following up on product use, troubleshooting on application problems, and analysing product use experi-

Evaluation of salesforce performance that encompasses both outcome performance and behavioural performance can be started with the questions in Checklist 11.3.

Practical tip

Every company says they have systems for handling customer complaints, use/delivery problems, and the like. One way of involving salespeople directly in this and encouraging co-operation with other company employees is to consider having salespeople nominate other employees who 'go the extra mile' to get things right for the customer, and reward those who do.

Practical tip

Salespeople need to understand the logic of how (and why) the activities they perform drive sales outcomes. This issue is particularly important when past emphasis in the company has been on sales results only. The sales culture needs to encourage (and openly reward) high performance of the key activities that lead to superior outcome performance.

Checklist 11.3
Evaluating salesforce performance

Questions to consider   *Score**

How well are the salespeople in this sales unit performing in the
following areas?

Outcome performance

1. Producing a high market share   ....
2. Making sales of those products with the highest profit margin   ....
3. Generating a good level of sales revenue   ....
4. Quickly generating sales of new company products and services   ....
5. Identifying and selling to major accounts   ....
6. Producing sales or contracts with long-term profitability   ....
7. Exceeding all sales targets and objectives during the year   ....

Behavioural performance

Sales presentation

8. Listening attentively to identify and understand the real concerns of
   customers   ....
9. Convincing customers that they understand their unique problems and
   concerns   ....
10. Using established contacts to develop new customers   ....
11. Communicating their sales presentations clearly and concisely   ....
12. Working out solutions to a customer's questions and objections   ....

Technical knowledge

13. Knowing the design and specification of company products/services   ....
14. Knowing the applications of company products/services   ....
15. Keeping abreast of the company's production and technological
    developments   ....

Adaptiveness

16. Experimenting with different sales approaches   ....
17. Being flexible in the selling approaches used   ....
18. Adapting selling approaches from one customer to another   ....
19. Varying sales style from situation to situation   ....

Checklist 11.3 *(Continued)*

*Score**

Teamwork

20. Generating considerable sales volume from team sales (sales made jointly by two or more salespeople) ....
21. Building strong working relationships with other people in the company ....
22. Working closely with non-sales employees to close sales ....
23. Co-ordinating with other company employees to handle post-sales problems and service ....
24. Discussing selling strategies with people from various departments ....

Planning

25. Planning each sales call ....
26. Planning sales strategies for each customer ....
27. Planning coverage of assigned territory/customer coverage ....
28. Planning daily activities ....

Support

29. Providing after-sales service ....
30. Checking on product delivery ....
31. Handling customer complaints ....
32. Following-up on product use ....
33. Troubleshooting on application problems ....
34. Analysing product use experience to identify new product/service ideas ....

(* Give marks out of 10, where 1 = needs improvement and 10 = outstanding)

Implications:

Sales management activities ▬▬▬

If the real levers to search out better sales organization effectiveness come from superior behavioural performance from the salesforce, then it follows that a key issue is how well field sales management exercises behaviour-based management and control. This type of sales management process is fundamentally different from one that centres on short term sales outcomes. While the use of incentive payment in the traditional way may be important, what we have observed in the more effective sales organizations is that sales managers spend significantly more of their time on monitoring, directing, evaluating and rewarding activities to get the best performance from the salespeople they manage. What we see clearly here is the role of the sales manager as coach and communicator, rather than as commander.

Monitoring activities are concerned with how much effort the sales manager devotes to activities like spending time in the field with salespeople and making joint calls with them, reviewing call reports, monitoring day-to-day activities and observing the performance of salespeople in the field, as well as paying attention to travelling done, expenses incurred and credit terms given by salespeople.

Directing activities can be assessed as the extent to which sales managers regularly spend time coaching salespeople and helping them to develop their potential, discussing performance evaluations with them and actively participating in training, as well as providing encouragement by rewarding them for their achievements. Evaluating activities in this approach to sales management encompasses issues like evaluating the profit contribution and sales call rate of the salesperson, but also the quality of work and the professional development achieved.

Rewarding activities includes the use of incentive payments to motivate and to reward results, but also addresses the need to reward the quality of sales activities as well as the quantity, and the importance of providing regular performance feedback.

We have found that the extent to which sales managers undertake these forms of behaviour-based management and control is strongly associated with superior salesforce performance and sales organization effectiveness. This is a warning against the temptations of assuming that sales managers are simply senior salespeople who should spend most of their time selling, or that only incentive payment systems get results. A start in addressing the implications of these observations can be made with the questions in Checklist 11.4.

Practical tip

Checklists like those shown here can provide the basis for discussions with salespeople and field sales managers, as well as an assessment device. They can be used to identify the agenda to be addressed in searching out greater sales organization effectiveness.

The link we see between the extent of behaviour-based management control and salesperson performance suggests that sales managers who want to improve salesperson performance should consider increasing the extent of their activities in monitoring, directing, evaluating and rewarding salespeople. The conventional view of salesperson performance is giving way to one which places much emphasis on helping salespeople perform well.

Of course, this also means that sales managers need to be able to perform these supporting activities well. Behaviour-based control calls for a major emphasis on coaching and leading, rather than commanding. Coaching involves working with salespeople to help them develop their selling skills and customer relationship strategies. Sales managers who are good coaches may be very different from the traditional command and control sales manager. This reflects more general trends in management practices: from commanding to collaboration; from criticizing to coaching; from domination to empowerment; from withholding information to sharing; and adapting management processes to individuals. These trends have major implications for sales manager selection and training.

Sales territory design

While salesperson characteristics, salesforce performance and sales management activities are all critical drivers of sales organization effectiveness, it is important to recognize also that the soundness of organizational design impacts on effectiveness. This is because the organization design provides the salesperson with the opportunity to perform at high levels.

For example, if a salesperson is assigned to an area or group of accounts and prospects that do not offer sufficient sales potential, then regardless of the skills and efforts of the salesperson or the sales manager, performance is likely to be low simply because the territory design is faulty. This is likely also to have a detrimental effect on the motivation of salespeople and our ability to retain the best salespeople in the company.

Checklist 11.4
Evaluating sales management activities

Questions to consider   *Score**

To what extent do the sales manager(s)
in this sales unit:

Monitoring activities

1. Spend time with salespeople in the field ....
2. Make joint sales calls with salespeople ....
3. Regularly review call reports from salespeople ....
4. Monitor the day-to-day activities of salespeople ....
5. Observe the performance of salespeople in the field ....
6. Pay attention to the extent which salespeople travel ....
7. Closely watch salespeoples' expenses ....
8. Pay attention to the credit terms that salespeople quote customers ....

Directing activities

9. Encourage salespeople to increase their sales results by rewarding them
   for their achievements ....
10. Actively participate in training salespeople on the job ....
11. Regularly spend time coaching salespeople ....
12. Discuss performance evaluations with salespeople ....
13. Help salespeople develop their potential ....

Evaluating activities

14. Evaluate the number of sales calls made by salespeople ....
15. Evaluate the profit contribution made by each salesperson ....
16. Evaluate the quality of the sales presentations made by salespeople ....
17. Evaluate the professional development of salespeople ....

Rewarding activities

18. Provide performance feedback to salespeople on a regular basis ....
19. Compensate salespeople on the basis of the quality of their sales activities ....
20. Use incentive compensation as a major means for motivating salespeople ....
21. Make incentive payment judgements based on the sales results achieved by
    salespeople ....
22. Reward salespeople based on their results ....
23. Use non-financial incentives to reward salespeople for their results ....
24. Compensate salespeople based on the quantity of their sales activities ....

(*Give marks out of 10, where 1 = not at all and 10 = to a great extent)

<table>
<tr><td>

Practical tip

Although we have found that behaviour-based management is practised more in the more effective British sales organizations, this does not seem to mean that incentive-based pay has been abandoned altogether. In fact, what we found was that the more effective sales organizations typically have a higher incentive element in their salesforce remuneration – mainly with incentive payments in the range of 10–20% of the total remuneration offered. This suggests that the more effective sales organizations have achieved some balance in their approach to providing incentives and control. They have the benefits of behaviour-based control but still retain a sizeable incentive payment as well.

</td><td>

Practical tip

'Right-sizing' at the field sales unit level may be one of the few opportunities we have to cut costs and to improve customer satisfaction at the same time. Where some sales territories are far too large, they may generate more sales than one salesperson can handle, while smaller territories do not justify the salesperson assigned. Consider the potential here for redesigning the territories on the basis of their sales potential, and in this way possibly reducing the selling expense ratio and improving customer relationships by better account coverage.

</td></tr>
</table>

We can assess the soundness of sales organizational design in a number of ways. However, a start may be made by considering the questions in Checklist 11.5. These are concerned with how satisfactory sales territories are in terms of account numbers and particularly large accounts, sales productivity in each territory and the number of sales calls made, the geographic size of territories and the amount of travel required, the market potential of each territory and the equivalence of workload across territories, and the number of sales territories in the unit managed by the field sales manager. This is not an exhaustive list of organizational issues and it can be extended, but it is enough to be indicative of a significant potential source of problems.

One of the things we have observed clearly in comparing the more effective sales organizations with the rest is that they have organizational designs in which managers have more confidence and with which they are more satisfied. To ignore the significance of this issue risks undoing the potential

improvements from building a salesforce with enhanced success characteristics, superior salesforce performance, and behaviour-based management.

We also observed that in the more effective sales organizations, managers see far less scope for improving effectiveness by changing the number of salespeople. Staffing levels are always a sensitive issue in companies, even more so in times of widespread corporate 'downsizing' and restructuring. However, what we have found is that 'right-sizing' in the sales organization is strongly associated with higher levels of sales organization effectiveness. The effective sales organizations seem to avoid overstaffing or stretching too few salespeople too far and missing opportunities.

Conclusions

We have reported here some of the major findings and observations from our international studies of sales organization effectiveness in business-to-business marketing, searching for the hallmarks of superior effectiveness. We have tried to put these findings into practical terms that managers can address in assessing and improving their own sales organization effectiveness.

Checklist 11.5
Evaluating sales territory design

Questions to consider   *Score**

How satisfactory is the design of the territories assigned to salespeople
in this sales unit on the following issues?

1. The number of accounts in each territory   ....
2. The number of large accounts in each territory   ....
3. The sales productivity in each territory   ....
4. The geographic size of each territory   ....
5. The number of sales calls made in each territory   ....
6. The amount of travel required in each territory   ....
7. The market potential in each territory   ....
8. The number of territories in the sales unit   ....
9. The assignment of salespeople to territories   ....
10. The equivalance in workload across territories   ....
11. The overall design of territories   ....

(*Give marks out of 10, where 1 = very dissatisfied and 10 = very satisfied)

Implications:

Looking across many different selling situations and market conditions, we have observed that superiority in sales organization effectiveness is strongly associated with the characteristics of salespeople, the drivers of salesforce performance, the critical sales manager role, and the soundness of sales organization design – and cutting across all these other factors is the supreme importance of customer relationships.

We can summarize our conclusions in the following terms.

The characteristics of successful salespeople

The more effective sales organizations have salespeople who are rated higher in their *motivation*, particularly relating to the sense of personal achievement they get from their work

---

Practical tip

One interesting question to ask of each sales unit is: what would be the effect on sales and profits of allocating one additional salesperson to this territory, and what would be the effects of allocating one less? As long as the answers are backed up with good evidence that the sales managers' answers reflect their real understanding of the market and are not just 'empire-building', this can give a lot of insight into 'right-sizing' at the field sales unit level. ('Empire-building' becomes less likely anyway if people know they have to live with the consequences of more staff or fewer.)

and the enthusiasm they display, but they are also outstanding in their *customer orientation*, their *team orientation*, and their *sales support* orientation. Sales people in effective sales organizations are highly motivated, are driven by customer issues, are team players, and are prepared to invest in support activities, even where these are not directly producing sales results in the short term. These findings have a number of important implications for how we recruit, train and develop effective salespeople, which may cause us to question some of the traditional views about the competencies and capabilities we need in salespeople. The view is that in the more effective sales organizations salespeople are committed team-players, willing to co-operate in implementing company selling strategies rather than operating on an independent basis. Selling skills are important, but being a sales-oriented superstar is not the key to sales effectiveness.

The drivers of salesforce performance

We have also seen that one source of sales organization effectiveness lies in superior outcome performance in the salesforce. This means that the salesforce can be seen to perform at high levels in gaining market share, focusing on selling high margin products and on major accounts for long term business, and exceeding sales targets and objectives. Outcome performance is important and should form part of our evaluation, but we have also seen that it is partly driven by superior behavioural performance in the salesforce.

Traditionally, sales management has focused on developing selling skills. We found that effective sales organizations did, indeed, outperform the rest in selling capabilities reflected in sales presentations and technical knowledge. However, we found these capabilities to be necessary but not sufficient to generate superior results. The major drivers of salesforce performance that characterize the most effective sales organizations come from *adaptiveness* in selling, *teamwork*, *sales planning* and *sales support* activities. The benchmarks here are important to understanding where to focus managerial attention

and development efforts to build a more effective sales organization.

The critical sales manager role

We have observed that in the more effective sales organization the sales manager is more a coach and communicator than a commander and scorekeeper. In the effective sales organization:

- sales manager *monitoring* is really about observing sales performance, reviewing call reports and watching salespeople's day-to-day activities;
- *directing* activities are mainly concerned with helping salespeople to develop their potential, by providing coaching and participating in training;
- the *evaluating* role of the sales manager focuses on appraising salespeople's professional development and the quality of selling, as well as judging sales results; and
- *rewarding* is associated with providing regular feedback and rewards (often non-financial) linked to results (frequently the quality of work, not just the quantity).

These findings suggest that the more effective sales organizations and their increased emphasis on behaviour-based management control, have defined a very different role for the sales manager. This critical position combines the role of coach, communicator and facilitator with the more traditional functions of keeping score and allocating financial rewards. In effective sales organizations the sales manager participates in field sales activities and provides a role model, going far beyond the traditional command and control model of sales management.

These insights are very significant in examining the role of sales managers in our own organizations, and considering the implications for sales manager recruitment, selection and development and appraisal, particularly in balancing the need for 'people' skills and team skills with capabilities in leadership and selling.

'Right-sizing' and organizational design

It is also apparent that sales organization effectiveness is strongly associated with management confidence that effectiveness cannot be increased by adding or subtracting people at the sales unit level, i.e. 'right-sizing', and a high level of management satisfaction with the design of sales territories and units, and the allocation of resources and market potential. Success here impacts on performance and effectiveness, not least because of its implications for retaining salespeople.

This area is problematic. At a time of widespread corporate downsizing and restructuring, staffing levels and allocations may suffer. We suggest that this area should be a high priority in recovering sales effectiveness after large scale organizational changes.

Customer relationships

Cutting across our conclusions in each of these hallmarks of sales organization effectiveness, is our most fundamental finding. *The more effective sales organizations are those which build and sustain long term customer relationships.*

Effective sales organizations outperform the rest in achieving customer satisfaction. Effective sales organizations do not allow salespeople to neglect customer interests by paying wholly or largely by commission and bonus. Effective salespeople are highly customer oriented. Effective salesforces adapt their selling to customer characteristics, work in teams to handle customer problems and provide customer service, plan sales strategy around customers and provide support to customers by checking on performance and responding to complaints.

The pervasive focusing on activities that develop and maintain productive, long term customer relationships characterizes the most effective sales organizations and underpins their dramatically superior results. Indeed, many sales executives who have contributed to our studies throughout the world have made precisely this point: customer relationship building is the most important area in which to focus efforts for improvements in sales organization effectiveness in the future.

While the hallmarks of sales organization provide many new insights and benchmarks, it should be remembered that there are no 'quick-fixes' in the search for sales organization effectiveness, and simply imitating the characteristics of other companies is likely to be unproductive. The challenge to the manager is to appraise his/her sales organization on the criteria we have suggested, and then to develop routes to greater effectiveness that are appropriate to the company concerned and that are capable of effective implementation, and that are appropriate to the markets and products concerned.

The insights which can be generated in this way may challenge many company beliefs about how best to recruit, train and develop salespeople and sales managers, and how best to manage the sales operation. However, realistically, acting on these insights means facing new problems. For example, we have found that the more effective sales organizations focus on developing and maintaining long term customer relationships through teamwork, adaptiveness and customer support in the sales organization. This is highly consistent with the current emphasis on relationship marketing strategy. However, achieving that focus and implementing the relationship marketing strategy may require substantial adjustment to both structural and 'people' issues by sales management. This said, it should not be forgotten that collaborative relationships only make sense when they offer value to both buyer and seller, and both parties favour the relationship.

The goal of those structural decisions is to provide salespeople with high performance situations to exploit – by having a 'right-sized' salesforce, effective territory design, focused sales teams and appropriate spans of control for sales managers. Poor sales management decisions in these areas can establish unnecessary and avoidable performance hurdles. These issues must be addressed alongside the 'people' decisions that aim to develop successful salespeople, capable of winning in the marketplace. These 'people' decisions are critically concerned with having salespeople with the desired success characteristics, and focusing appropriate types of management attention on the underlying drivers of salesforce performance. This is the route to high sales organization effectiveness, based on long term customer relationships.

However, relationship-oriented selling and team-based sales require very different skills and capabilities to those of the stereotypical 'lone wolf, road warrior' salesperson of the past. In the same way, behaviour-based control by sales managers requires a very differ-ent set of skills to the 'command and control' model of sales management.

Sales training will have to emphasize team building, conflict resolution, interpersonal skills and other capabilities relevant to the required success characteristics and management activities. This will require time and money. It may not always succeed – the truly individualistic 'lone wolf' salesperson may not be easily converted into an effective team player; the 'sales commander and senior salesperson' manager may not take well to coaching and communicating as a management style. Nonetheless, our observations suggest that this is the direction in which many companies will have to move in the future to build the truly effective sales organization.

Summary

The goal of this chapter was to look at the sources of sales organization effectiveness, as a basis for managers to focus attention on the most critical issues. We have provided a number of checklists to address this issue in a pragmatic way.

Our view is that sales organization effectiveness, in terms of beating the competition and management goals for sales, profit, market share and customer satisfaction, is associated with a number of critical factors. Those factors are: salesforce performance; salesperson characteristics; sales management activities in control and coaching; the soundness of sales organization design; and success in building effective customer relationships.

Salesforce performance is associated first with outcome performance – hitting the targets for sales profitability, new products and appropriate selling resource allocation. However, effectiveness is driven also by salesforce behaviour: in adaptiveness in selling, teamwork, planning and support, as well as capabilities in technical knowledge and sales presentation. Salesperson characteristics associated with higher effectiveness were: motivation, customer orientation, team orientation and sales support orientation. These points have major implications for the selection and training of salespeople.

Critical too are the activities of field sales managers in coaching and communicating, not just acting as commanders and scorekeepers. The points to focus on here are the extent to which sales managers devote efforts to monitoring, directing, evaluating and rewarding – and the way in which these things are done.

Sales organization design is also important because it is the framework within which motivated and well-managed salespeople can achieve their potential or be denied that opportunity.

Underpinning all these issues, however, is the importance of building long term, collaborative relationships with customers, where this offers advantages to buyer and seller.

Further reading

Piercy, N., Cravens, D. and Morgan, N. (1997) Sources of Effectiveness in the Business-to-Business Sales Organization, *Journal of Marketing Practice: Applied Marketing Science*, in press.

Cravens, D., Ingram, T., LaForge, R. and Young, C. (1992) The Hallmarks of Effective Sales Organizations, *Marketing Management*, Winter, 57–67.

Cravens, D. (1995) 'The Changing Role of the Salesforce', *Marketing Management*, Summer, 49–57.

Hise, R. and Reid, E. (1994) Improving the Performance of the Industrial Salesforce in the 1990s, *Industrial Marketing Management*, **23**, No. 4, 273–9.

12

Using IT in the sales function _____

Lynn Parkinson, Parkinson Training Ltd

 In this chapter we will explore the potential for using information technology in sales management. Despite the increasing availability of computer packages designed to assist in sales management and activities, many businesses are making only basic use of technology's potential. Interestingly, it is not always the most technically sophisticated companies that are making the best use of IT in the sales function. Some IT companies do not use computers to manage and monitor sales activities! In contrast, some small companies have powerful sales management systems to make best use of their limited resources.

Computers are widespread in many business functions, such as accounting. However, unlike accountancy, there is no nationally agreed set of procedures and information requirements for sales management. This means that there is no single framework that is appropriate to all aspects of selling and for all companies. Accordingly, the potential for IT in sales depends on the nature of your sales operation.

In this chapter, we will:

- review some computer technologies and terms and their relevance to sales management;
- outline the range and variety of IT applications in selling and sales management;
- give guidance on the process of introducing new computerized processes in sales management.

Information technology is a major challenge for today's managers. It offers high rewards for those who can exploit it effectively. Even if you don't believe that computers can help you, or you don't know the first thing about them, this chapter will reassure you about their relevance. Experienced users should still find some interesting ideas.

Key IT terms ▬▬▬▬▬▬

You do not need to be a computer expert to be able to apply IT successfully in sales. However, you need to understand some basic terminology and principles. If you are new to (or hiding from!) IT, or have patchy knowledge, then take time to grasp these terms. They will help you understand the information presented later in this chapter. Often the terminology, or its use by another manager (often an IT manager), discourages non-experts from trying to understand it. It's not a problem – if you can understand other chapters in this book, then applying IT in sales is not beyond you. Furthermore, it can even be interesting – finding a new way of winning more business or making more profit always is!

Practical tip

After reading though this section, computer novices should visit a high street computer store or computer 'warehouse' store. Use the descriptions in the text to identify the different products on display. Gather literature on the products, or (better still), if the store is not too busy, discuss the attributes of different types of hardware and software with staff. You will find it easier to understand the rest of this chapter if you can 'visualize' the different types of products.

Hardware

Computer hardware includes all computer equipment, such as computers, printers, or scanners. Players of computer games will be familiar with a Game Boy, which is a form of hardware.

Computers can serve many users or be used as stand-alone computers. The main-frame computer is the traditional form of computer that serves many users. It is commonly associated with large organizations. It is reaching the maturity stage of its life, and is being replaced by computers that have a *server* role. These servers hold the software and data, and distribute it to users, who work at personal computers.

The PC, *personal computer*, is a self-standing desktop computer. It has a screen, a processor (a box) which processes data, reading and recording functions (usually floppy or hard disks, but possibly a CD-ROM or magnetic tape), and input devices (such as keyboards, or a mouse). Increasingly, this PC may be linked to other PCs in a network. A *network* allows people to share data and other hardware, such as printers.

Laptops are portable computers, available in many different specifications. Laptops run from batteries or off the mains power supply. Batteries for laptops have a limited life (currently many batteries run for about 4–8 hours before needing to be recharged). Desktop PCs have more facilities (e.g. more memory or features) or are easier to work with (better keyboards or screens). Laptops can be directly connected to PCs or data can be transferred using floppy disks.

Palmtops or 'hand-held' computers are smaller still. Many people call them 'organizers', as they are the size of a pocket diary. They are very light – about 200–400 grams. They run on penlight batteries (AA batteries) which last for weeks before needing recharging. Many palmtops are ready to use immediately when the 'on' button is pressed, so they are as convenient as a diary, calculator or notebook. Palmtops perform many tasks undertaken by desktop PCs. They share their data with PCs and laptops through cables or infra-red technology. (Many TV remote controls work with infra-red technology.) The screen quality and keyboards on palmtops are poor, so they are mainly used for out-of-office applications. It is the increasing power of the palmtops that is likely to have the greatest long term impact in changing selling practices.

Printers are usually inkjet or laser printers, offering colour or black and white printing. They vary in size, speed and the range of functions, which in turn influence prices. Computer printers are able to print on different types of paper (e.g. glossy and card, or transparency slides). Companies can now print their presentations and stationery, including business cards and leaflets, because the print quality is so high. Paper distributors offer colour-printed papers, which can then be over-printed by a black and white printer. This gives the impression of expensive full-colour printing at cheap prices.

More sophisticated printers perform the same tasks as photocopiers, such as double-sided printing, collating and stapling. Some printers are now being sold as combined faxes, photocopiers and printing tools, offering scanning facilities (the ability to 'read' text or images and convert it into computer data, discussed in more detail below).

Modems link computers and the telephone network, enabling people to send data and information between different locations. For example, a PC with a modem will be able to send a fax message to another location, which prints out exactly as an ordinary fax, or receive a fax from another fax machine. Modems can also send data, such as sales figures, text or graphics, to another computer. They can be internal (i.e. inside the processor box) or external (a separate box or card, like a credit card, which can be plugged into a computer). Modems allow access to the Internet, and the sending of e-mail (electronic mail).

Scanners operate like the outgoing end of a fax, reading the data (whether text or image) line by line. Scanners take data from existing documents for convenient storage and subsequent use. For example, you can scan in a map of your area, and incorporate it in the directions of how to reach your office. Few scanners read handwriting reliably, but they work well with printed text and graphics (including photographs). Office scanners are usually flatbed, which look like small photocopiers, or hand-held, like a roller. Scanners are an essential part of the 'paperless office', as they are required for document processing (or electronic filing).

Software

Programs that run on computers are called software. Game Boys are hardware; Supermario is software. Software is either horizontal or vertical.

Horizontal software

Horizontal software is designed for use by a wide range of customers and in a wide range of market settings. The main types of horizontal software are spreadsheets, word-processors, presentation graphics packages, diaries and databases. All offer benefits in the sales office.

Practical tip

It is difficult for new users to determine exactly what hardware is best for them. It is very easy to believe that the latest technology is the best. To get what you need, and not to pay for more than you need, make a list of essential features for your computer (or other hardware) – like portability, good screen, etc. – then a list of features that sound good – CD-ROM, tape back-up, etc. Ask other users for their experiences of these features. Use their views to revise your original list.

Spreadsheets are computer packages for recording, presenting and calculating numerical data. A spreadsheet can be set up so that the computer automatically totals rows or columns of numbers and/or performs calculations on these figures. The simplest example would be a list of orders received by customer and by sales representative, which could be automatically totalled, and (over time) compared with previous periods.

Many sales office calculations are undertaken routinely. Staff regularly submit expenses claims, detailing travelling expenses, subsistence expenses, parking fees, telephone charges, etc. and charge these against a customer or cost centre. A standard form, called a template or skeleton file, can be prepared on the spreadsheet to total the claim once amounts are entered in each category of expense. Spreadsheet packages can now incorporate 'macros', which are a series of routine commands – for example, they could ask the package to 'look up' information elsewhere in a file (such as the price of an item) or undertake analytical or administrative activities on particular data (such as total the orders placed each week, or the expenses claimed by a sales representative). Alternatively, the spreadsheet could automatically print the names of the top performing salespeople, identified from the list of sales achieved by all sales staff.

Word-processors are software packages for text based activities – writing letters, reports, manuals, etc. These allow letters and documents to be edited and amended without the need for retyping. Word-processors are also used for advanced functions, such as 'mail-merging' – writing customized letters by combining lists of names and addresses with a standard letter. Many word-processors also now offer e-mail facilities. E-mail sends messages directly to another computer, i.e. the letter is sent electronically. The recipient can then look at the message on screen, or print it out.

Many word-processing packages offer limited *desktop publishing* (DTP) capabilities, which takes word-processed text and/or graphics and lays this out to have more impact. DTP is important for documents that need to have impact, such as proposals, newsletters or brochures. Many word-processing packages include 'style sheets', which are document layouts designed by graphic artists. This allows users to get a professional layout with very little effort.

Databases store text, numerical and graphical information that are arranged into 'fields'. Each 'field' is like a file in a filing cabinet. Computerized database packages can sort these files of data in seconds. For example, if you record your customers by name, nature of industry, and location, you will have three 'fields'. In the office before computers, this data would be stored in individual files based (probably) on the customer name. This works when dealing with accounts at an individual level, but managers often need an overview of what is happening by area or industry. For example, they wish to know whether there is a greater percentage of accounts in one business sector than another. In the manual sales office, it could take several days to find the answer. However, if the data are recorded on a database, it takes only seconds.

Presentation graphics software lays out text and graphics for greater impact for presentations. Once again, style sheets designed by graphic artists allow users to choose an appropriate image for their presentation. An informal style can be appropriate for internal sales meetings, with a more formal style for presentations to clients. Style sheets can be customized to include company names and logos. Prepared presentations can be saved on disk and edited, making it quick and easy to customize presentations for clients. Presentation graphics software can print materials, or presentations can be made directly from the computer, and projected onto a screen using a special projector (with an LCD panel, offered by, e.g. 3M or Polaroid). Video and audio materials can be included in presentations made directly from the computer – this also saves having to print out slides for each presentation.

Diary packages allow users to record appointments and reminder dates (such as fixed dates, including birthdays or the tax year end, or on a periodic schedule, such as dental appointments, or meeting schedules), and to summarize main events, prepare 'to do' lists, etc. They also store and recall telephone numbers or addresses, sometimes by accessing data stored in the database package. Diaries can be presented in a range of formats, from daily appointments to a month-at-a-view. They can also track time spent on different activities. For example, travelling time can be given a specific code, and the package can calculate the amount of time spent on this activity. Alternatively, this coding can be allocated by customer or area, to determine the associated costs.

Using computers benefits individuals, but team working and sharing information can be facilitated by computers. Sharing data files gives benefits across the sales office. For example, consider the benefits of several people being able to access electronic diaries:

● Secretaries can set appointments to fit in with the schedule, in the absence of sales representatives.

- If a sales representative is ill, then appointments can be covered by a colleague, or postponed by a secretary.
- Sales managers can monitor their staff's activities.

E-mail messages can be sent 'to keep in touch' or to convey important information. Members of staff can circulate documents for comments and amendments (valuable when finalizing a proposal, for example), and presentations or proposals prepared by one member of staff can be included in another's work.

Practical tip

Horizontal packages are often 'bundled' together into a software suite, such as Lotus SmartSuite, or Microsoft Office. It is easier to transfer data between packages if you have an integrated suite. For example, if you have a customer list in Lotus Approach (a database package), then you can prepare a mailing letter on Lotus WordPro (the word-processing package in the same suite), which uses the customer file. There are similarities in commands and screen display between software packages in one integrated suite.

Vertical software

Vertical software is targeted at one particular type of customer or activity (i.e. at one vertical market). For example, software for telemarketing is vertical software. Vertical software can be independent, or used with horizontal packages. For example, contact manager software allows people to use databases prepared on their office package with letters written on their word-processor, but makes it easier to access and integrate the information.

Sales and marketing systems are examples of

vertical software. There are many relatively small companies offering these packages – the software giants, such as Microsoft, tend to focus on horizontal markets at present.

Practical tip

New users should be wary of promises in advertisements for software, and determine exactly what they need to be able to do, and their budget. Seek the advice of dealers (get more than one opinion, if your dealer hasn't been recommended to you) on how the packages match your requirements. Check computer magazines for reviews of software before buying. If you cannot get a magazine review (it is harder to find for vertical software), ask suppliers for names of other similar users and contact them to ask about their experiences.

Horizontal software packages are cheaper than vertical software packages, because they are targeted at volume markets. An integrated office suite will cost under £500, but vertical software for sales management can cost from this level up to many thousands of pounds. Customized software can cost in excess of £100,000. If you have a limited budget, the general packages will help improve some management operations.

On-line services and the Internet

'Going on-line' uses the computer's modem to access external data. Sending external e-mail is a form of going on-line. Companies can access sources of information (such as software and research data), forums and help groups. Some on-line services are free; others carry charges. You also pay the cost of the telephone call, as being 'on-line' is phoning up another computer network. You will also normally pay a monthly subscription to a company, called a service provider, who will manage your link to on-line services.

On-line information sources are not new. At one time, however, you needed specialist computers to access each type of information source, but now these sources can be accessed from a PC.

On-line management information comes in two main forms – databases and text data. The databases are provided by research or other companies, such as Dunn and Bradstreet, and local, national and international governments. These help in gathering data on new markets or monitoring market trends over time, or getting background information on customers (such as credit history) or identifying new customers in different sectors. On-line text retrieval of business articles and research reports allows users to scan the abstracts or titles of a range of business publications and read or download the full text of those which interest them. Novice computer users will probably find it easier to use a host organization, such as MAID, to gain access to these sources. More accomplished users will 'browse' the Internet, or make direct arrangements with specific research providers.

The Internet is a major IT topic in the 1990s. The Internet is a network of networks. It was originally designed for military and academic users, to allow them access to computers in different locations. Its use has expanded and now private and commercial users also use the Internet. However, despite the hype, only a small percentage of companies and households are actually on-line to the Internet, and few industry experts anticipate that it will become a 'mass' product within the next decade.

Non-users believe that the Internet will provide all the answers to their queries instantly. Users know that the limits of communications technologies make it slow and cumbersome. For example, if you want to gather information on the availability of a specific flight, it could easily take 4–5 minutes to go on-line and make your enquiry. It could be faster to do this on the phone. However, this should become faster and easier in future.

'Forums' – discussion groups on a range of topics – are a feature of the Internet. These can be organized by company, or by people with a special interest. Users ask questions, which other users reply to. For example, computer hardware manufacturers have forums based on each of their main product categories. A user of a computer printer might question how to undertake a specific function with that printer. Other users reply. It sounds strange to non-users – but people both ask questions and reply!

Practical tip

Service providers that enable you to gain access to the Internet offer different levels of support. New users need technical support when going on-line. If you have not got access to technical support in your company, make sure that a technical helpline is included with your monthly on-line service subscription.

There are a few more basic terms that help your understanding of computers. An *operating system* makes the computer work. Microsoft Windows is currently the most successful personal computer operating system, but some computers linked to servers will be on UNIX-based systems. Other operating systems exist (for example, Apple has its own operating system), but more software is designed for Windows and UNIX operating environments.

Computer chips are used to distinguish between computers. The best known chip manufacturer is Intel, and many PCs and laptops carry Intel's logo, the arrow stating 'Intel inside'. Mathematicians and scientists need to have a specific computer chip (because some chips have sophisticated properties), but the choice of chip is not so critical for business users. It is tempting to get the newest chip (often indicated by the computer's price), but often this will only make the computer a second or two faster than an older (and cheaper) chip. An old chip is not a bad chip, nor is a new chip the best chip!

CD-ROMs are compact discs that store large amounts of data to be read by computers. These store far more data than floppy disks, including video and sound data. Computers can read and find information on a CD-ROM quickly. CD-ROMs are cheap to produce, and may replace company manuals and catalogues. Multimedia PCs have CD-ROM drives, and offer audio and video facilities. Currently, PCs cannot record onto CD-ROMs, although the technology will be available in 1997.

The marketing context for sales ▬

We will now move on to apply these technologies in sales management. The company's marketing operations should form the basis for sales activities. Many sales management software packages reflect this link, describing themselves as being 'sales and marketing systems'. Unfortunately, this implies a level of integration between sales and marketing which is rarely achieved. This integration is desirable though, because staff will find a mutual benefit in sharing marketing and sales data. It is expected that these areas will come closer together, partly as a result of computerized systems.

Management decisions depend on information. Data and information are not the same thing. Data are unprocessed information; they are a series of facts with no shape, form or clear purpose. They may be useful, but not in their current form. Information is what results when data are processed or analysed to achieve a specific requirement. In other words, data are like a pile of bricks, while information is like a wall. The pile of bricks has the potential to be something useful, while the wall serves a clear function. Data and information come from a range of sources within the business and externally. This can be gathered routinely and regularly, or undertaken on an ad hoc basis. Ideally, this should be collated into a form of marketing informa-

tion system, including data from other parts of the business. The diversity of data and information means that establishing a marketing information system is complex.

Practical tip

This section is working through issues involved in writing a sales plan. If you have never written a sales plan before, then *Sales and Marketing Success* (available from Dynamic Pathways (UK) Ltd), will help you to write one. It takes you through a series of questions, and integrates the answers to produce a professional looking business plan. It offers a useful checklist for sales managers. The final result is a credible sales plan, which is focused on your business, and prepared quickly.

Customer or contact database _____

The customer database is central to sales effectiveness in the data-based company. A customer or contact database, focusing on distributors or users (either existing or potential), can be maintained on a standard database package or as part of a specialist sales and marketing system. This database can be used for profiling accounts or segmenting the market. Some companies give the responsibility for identifying and monitoring market segments (the macro or broad view) to the marketing staff, while asking sales staff to concentrate on specific account profiles (the micro or focused view).

The database contents depend on the selling environment. Vertical sales and marketing software is available (or can be tailored) for different settings and sales activities.

- Fast moving consumer goods salesforces need detailed data on stores, their stock levels, shelf position, competing brands, etc.
- Industrial sectors, such as engineering or

Practical tip

Standard packages normally include the following fields in their customer database:

- company name
- address
- phone number
- fax number
- e-mail address
- contact name(s)
- position/job titles
- assistant's name
- salutation (Dear ...)

- type of business
- size of business
- status (suspect, prospect, customer, client)
- personal interests
- date of last visit
- proposed next contact date
- purpose of last meeting
- type of products bought

Companies with scanners can add visual images, such as contacts' photographs, the customer's logo, or a map of how to reach the client's premises.

Check how your customer information is stored, and by whom (i.e. sales, accountancy, marketing staff). Identify the categories of information to profile your market or target your sales activities. Use this composite list as a list of fields for your database.

---

pharmaceuticals, need details on the members of the buying centre and their roles during the sales process.

Analysing the customer database helps identify companies currently buying specific products, and companies that match these profiles but are not current users. It also determines whether accounts (or segments) are sufficiently large enough to be viable, and to identify market or account targeting strategies. Over time, it monitors changing trends in the importance of different accounts or segments.

Paper-based systems can be used in similar ways. However, analysis of the database is faster once a computer-based system is established. 'Macro' routines can be put in place to undertake the analysis of this database at periodic intervals.

Example One

Ciba Geigy's Agrochemicals division sells mainly through a network of agricultural distributors. The salesforce also call directly on farmers. They use a specialist sales and marketing software package, Ensure Plus, to record details of the farm and farmer, crops, chemical usage, etc. This enables them to monitor sales by account and by segment (type of farm or farmer, etc.). The sales department can plan calls at an appropriate time for the type of farm.

The role and form of selling

Knowing your customers helps you decide how best to sell to them. Personal or telephone selling can be the principal form of promotional activity, or it may support advertising, direct mail or other activities. The range of promotional options is extensive, and new technology is increasing the options.

The Internet is being viewed as having great potential. It reaches a geographically dispersed audience, cheaper than mass media advertising. It can be used to sell products and services directly (people order them through the Internet) or to generate sales enquiries. The Internet's relevance depends on the market you are targeting. Currently, academics and students are the major Internet users in the UK. Businesses form a smaller share of the market. Only 10% of those on the Internet are home users. However, because users are (or will be) up-market, well-off and well-educated, companies, such as car manufacturers, believe that the Internet will be a valuable part of their promotional strategy in the future.

Sales are a way of delivering a company's positioning – for example, a company can present itself as having a high level of customization, advice or a speedy response. The salesforce role should reflect and support this positioning. Example Three has an IT context, but the principle is not IT specific. This example demonstrates how important it is to 'think through' the company's positioning and the salesforce's role. It also gives rise to a second issue on the role of the salesforce – determining how technology can change the sales role.

Business process re-engineering (BPR) has recently gained considerable attention as a way of reviewing procedures in business. BPR is often aimed at improving customer satisfaction, and improvements to the sales process are part of this process. Frequently, BPR is associated with the application of new technology. For example, Direct Line insurance and First Direct banking could not have been as successful without having substantial computer support. Technology enables companies to change the selling process, at both operational and strategic levels.

● Computers allow 'mass customization'. Routine activities can be standardized, such as standard letters and routines, but each of these can be fully customized by customer name, customer requirements and customer experiences. The improvement in the software capability, coupled with the speed and quality of

Example Two

A company that sells specialist chemical products to breweries has recently gone on-line. At one level, the decision was taken on the technology and competitive stance – they wanted to be the first business of their type to go on-line. A second reason is that many small breweries are developed by people who have a higher than average education, and are highly interested in technical products – often characterized as 'boffins'. They are also more likely to go on-line. The company plans to use the Internet to expand its access to small private breweries.

Example Three

A travel agency has last minute bookings on the Internet. It does not allow customers direct access to prices and schedules, but requests the user's contact telephone number, which its sales team follows through. However, the Internet is a 24 hour service, but the travel agency's sales staff work traditional office hours. If people choose to use it outside traditional office hours, then that is when the sales opportunity exists. Delaying the follow-through on the inquiry until the next working day encourages customers to contact competitors (such as airlines with 24 hour sales teams or companies that sell airline seats directly through the Internet). Customers who choose to use the Internet often do so because they wish to specify how they want to buy, as well as what they want to buy. For example, frequent flyers know the flight times and the fares, and may not want to deal with reservations staff.

modern printers, means that customers feel they are being viewed as individuals.

- Companies selling direct to consumers benefit from QAS (Quick Address) which generates much of the address (such as the street name) from a postcode. This means that account or contact details can be accessed quickly or new contact information entered with the minimum amount of typing time and a high level of accuracy.
- Companies selling products that are bought routinely can introduce electronic meters or counters to identify stock levels and prompt the user to order (by phone, fax, e-mail, etc.) or even order the items electronically. For example, chemical companies have technical gadgets that monitor stock levels and electronically order stock, and retailers use EPOS (electronic point of sale systems, which operate at major supermarkets) in a similar way. The salesforce's role changes when these order procedures are put in place – they no longer need to take orders, but rather focus on developing relationships, on giving advice, etc.

Salesforce objectives

Once the salesforce's role has been determined, sales management needs to turn information into sales objectives and plan how these will be realized. Computers, with relevant sales and marketing management software, focus attention on the accountability of sales activities. Objectives specify what is to be achieved. Sales objectives can be broad, covering the entire sales activities, or detailed, based on breakdowns of sales by products, territories, by sales representative, etc. These are the standard against which performance can be measured.

Sales objectives can be developed in many ways. For example, managers can use market based approaches (based on past or anticipated future sales levels), or develop forecasts based on company requirements of the sales function. Spreadsheet software can be useful in determining quantitative sales objectives, by projecting past sales levels into the future, or by quantitative techniques, such as:

- simple trend extrapolation
- weighted trend extrapolation
- identifying causal variables (these will vary depending on the business sector, but could include prices, interest rates or sales call levels), and then preparing forecasts based on anticipated changes to the variables.

Using the graphics facility in the spreadsheet package, this information can also be presented visually.

Sales objectives can be prepared by breaking down a total sales objective into its component parts. For example, if a company wishes to increase sales by 15% overall, this increase might be unrealistic for all products, all areas, and all sales representatives. The sales manager can develop a spreadsheet to review alternative realistic scenarios and to determine whether various options will achieve the overall target. Each scenario takes only seconds to calculate.

Example Four

A small business needs to set realistic market based objectives for its salesforce. It determines that:

- the market is growing, although the rate of growth has slowed in the past two years;
- no new competitors are expected to enter their market;
- market growth is linked to price – as price reduces, the market increases;
- increasing call frequency can increase sales levels.

The company's spreadsheet offers projections of future sales based on the average annual growth rate (simple trend extrapolation). However, because the company recognizes that the market is slowing, it decides to weight the recent years' growth rates, and use this to produce a weighted average growth rate, from which sales can be forecast.

The company reviews these forecasts, and determines that it needs to stimulate sales volume, without reducing overall profitability. Accordingly, the company analyses the relationship between sales levels and price. The company then uses the spreadsheet to examine 'what if' the price were reduced by 1%, 3%, 5%, etc., and identify sales volumes, revenues and profitability at the different price levels. The company sees that only a marginal price reduction is beneficial in overall profitability terms. Then, the company investigates the relationship between call frequency and sales level, and adds this relationship to its spreadsheet model.

Finally, based on this assessment, the company concludes that the required sales levels could be achieved by increasing call frequency from once a month to once every three weeks.

Example Five

Field sales representatives are often on the road for several days. Inevitably, they need to take some actions – such as information requests and quotations. Instead of waiting to return to the office, or phoning the sales office and asking for information to be sent out, sales representatives update the (computerized) sales records on a laptop. Then, they use their modem and portable phone to send the new information from the sales call to the sales office and get the desired action. Thus, an account could have any requested information delivered the following day, although the sales representative has not returned to the office. As a result:

- the sales call has more impact;
- the customer has increased faith in the company's ability to deliver;
- the records are more accurate, as they are complete at the sales call, or immediately following it;
- the sales records are complete.

Salesforce productivity

Sales and profit figures are common sales objectives, but often other issues, such as salesforce productivity, are also important objectives. Productivity is associated with efficiency (doing things well). There are many ways that computerized sales systems can improve efficiency. In the sales office, sales automation can reduce time spent on administrative chores, such as filing, report writing, updating colleagues on performance, and copying files. This enables the sales force to spend more time with their customers. Field applications also improve efficiency. Many customized sales management packages have remote updating facilities within their software design, which select and send only updated information to a central data collection point.

Example Five demonstrates that automating the salesforce is equally concerned with effectiveness (doing the right things) as a way to improve productivity. The customer database is particularly useful at adding value to the selling process. It can give more information for the sales team to use to make the client feel valued – 'We valued your custom last year, but we haven't visited you since ....', 'It's good to hear from you again. ... I hope you won't wait as long before getting back in touch with us' or 'Thank you for phoning your second order this week. Can I ask one of our sales representatives to call on you to see if we can serve you better?' Making this information available in the sales office means that all staff can be fully informed about clients when they are in contact with them.

Similarly, a shared understanding of the value of customers can ensure that staff treat key customers with the appropriate priority – 'We always despatch your orders immediately, because your business is so important to us....' Details of past purchases can add value to the services you offer – 'Yes, you wish to order some toner. Is this for the Kodak printer which you bought from us? And to the usual delivery address ...'. Furthermore, up-to-date information can be sent from the main office to field sales representatives, enabling them to link in with recent developments at head office – 'I know that you called our office earlier today, ...', 'You may have heard that our company has just announced ...', or 'I've just been advised that your credit status has changed because we haven't received payment for our old account. Is there a problem with this account ...'.

Productivity – both efficiency and effectiveness – can also be improved through call scheduling. If call cycles are set, either on a regular pattern (such as the fortnightly or monthly calls common in van selling in FMCG), or by a sales representative at an earlier call, then computerized diaries can generate 'to do' or call lists. A sales support team can set appointments if required. Some call planning packages have automated dialling facilities. This means that you can complete your records on a previous call, while the next number is being contacted. It seems insignificant, but this can save several minutes of time. Other packages can make your PC 'beep' (like an alarm clock) to remind you to call someone at a specific time – a convenient feature when trying to reach a busy buyer, or someone in a different time-zone.

Call plans can be linked with geographical or route planning software to ensure the best use of salesforce time. Route planning and finding clients are problems when sales staff change territories. Consultants have unique computer systems for route planning, and sell the package or undertake route planning for clients. A cheaper alternative is to buy a general map package (such as Autoroute Express, from Microsoft), which will allow you to enter your destination and give you precise details of your journey. For example, if you want to travel from Bradford to Glasgow, you can enter your journey start time or arrival time, preferred choice of roads (motorways, A roads or B roads), your style of driving (Grand Prix or less hurried!), and any stops on the way. It gives you a route,

with distances and timings, and directions. It prints out itineraries, maps or photographs of your journey.

Hotel guides are available on CD-ROM and some hotels offer on-line booking services, which allow routes to be integrated with accommodation requirements. These arrangements can be made at any time, and do not require guidebooks to be carried round if the software is loaded onto the user's computer or it can be accessed on-line.

These applications may seem minor, but if a sales representative has 250 accounts, improved scheduling and routeing can increase call rates. Information on hotels and easy to use booking services reduce administration for both field and office based staff.

Many specialist sales software packages integrate with horizontal software. So, if your diary tells you that you promised to phone Mr Tidy of Office Cleaning Products today, you can instantly recall all the contact information when you call him. When you agree to meet him, you can quickly print off a standard letter (or fax) confirming the date and time of your agreed appointment, or even a confirmation order should he agree to your offer. If you are required to send a proposal, then you could customize this by adding the logo that is stored in the customer contact record. You could then add your route, and the computer could identify other customers within the same postcode areas.

These activities can also be undertaken with horizontal software packages. A database can be integrated with a diary package to undertake similar tasks. However, the links between packages require specialist knowledge, and the costs of doing this often outweigh the costs of buying a customized customer contact management package.

Finally, simple tasks, like preparing office memos, can be undertaken quickly using e-mail. Instead of printing off quantities of paper and then distributing them, a memo can be prepared and instantly sent to an established distribution list. The ease of this operation encourages people to stay in closer contact. Yet again, this shows that IT can improve efficiency and effectiveness.

Designing the salesforce

Spreadsheets are suited to determining salesforce size and organization. Text books indicate a series of formulae that can be used in identifying the optimum size for a sales team. These work on a few key principles, that:

- The business has a specified number of accounts;
- Each level of sales representative can achieve a set number of sales calls per day;
- There is a feasible number of selling days per year.

This information can be weighted by the priority of account (e.g. ABC accounts, influencing the number of calls that a sales representative would make on each category) or other factors such as distance, or new business selling. These simple formulae can be developed further to consider the cost of each level of sales representative and the costs of sales support, and to design salesforces which meet call levels, within overall salesforce budgets.

Once again, the spreadsheet's 'what if' scenarios can be useful:

- What if the number of accounts increased?
- What if the number of sales calls per day reduced?
- What if the sales representatives' salary increased?
- Etc.

When computerizing the salesforce, it is often possible to remove a level of supervision or reduce the number of staff. Supervisory staff are involved in data collection and analysis, and many routine aspects of this activity can be undertaken swiftly and by less skilled people. Further, shared access to customer records results in a greater team focus in the sales activity. The sales representative is no longer the 'owner' of contacts, but part of a team. These two trends are compatible with overall business trends towards leaner, flatter organizations and a greater emphasis on teamwork.

Once the number of sales staff has been identified, the sales manager can then arrange the sales territories to reflect the market potential. Geographical information packages (packages with maps, discussed earlier) help achieve an appropriate balance between sales territories. Address information in the customer database helps – it calculates the number of customers in each postcode district, and these can be plotted by a map package. Once territories have been allocated, customer lists can be drawn off the database according to postcodes.

Automating the sales office might reduce the need for regional offices. 'Teleworking', i.e. working at a distance, is facilitated by computers with modems. Sales staff normally seek to maximize the amount of time spent with customers, and attending regional offices to clear paperwork takes time. Teleconferencing also increases the amount of field sales time available. It enables geographically dispersed groups of staff to communicate without having to travel. Teleconferencing used to need studios (with associated costs), but multimedia computers allow teleconferencing over ISDN lines. The process of teleconferencing does not have the same interpersonal dynamics as a team event where all the members are in one location, but serves many uses:

● A manager can give a 'pep' talk to staff.
● If a newspaper article puts the company or product in an unfavourable light, then teleconferencing allows the salesteam to be involved in addressing the problems facing their customers, without having to leave territories.
● A sales representative who has gone to a customer may find that the proposed

presentation doesn't cover all the desired aspects. Teleconferencing allows the sales representative and colleagues back at head office to work together to amend its content, in a way that is similar to a face-to-face discussion.
● A sales representative who has gone to an account without having gathered the relevant data can contact the office, and instead of trying to describe it, the files can be viewed to find the appropriate items!

Finally, don't forget that once salesforces are computerized, someone needs to support the use of computers within the sales function, and to check on any problems with computer usage. Managers should remember to include this role within a new sales organization.

Recruitment and selection

Technology is changing recruitment processes:

Example Six

Senior management in NatWest required the international trade and banking services division to reduce operating costs by 40% in 1993. However, it was clear that the 40,000 corporate accounts would not be satisfied by a reduced level of service. NatWest, which uses multi-level selling into their key accounts, looked to computerized sales management to assist in cutting costs. NatWest chose to have two regional centres, rather than many local offices, each with its unique sales records system, with four regional sales managers. Office based (and networked) PCs were installed, and some notebook PCs were also purchased. Despite the cost of hardware, NatWest found savings. The system was geared round what was achieved or undertaken, and so it focused on sales actions. Further, because the sales contact details are held centrally, if a sales representative is out when a customer calls, another team member can take the call and have full information on the client's purchase history and their most recent contact.

- Job advertisements are being placed on the Internet.
- Candidates can 'post' their CVs on the Internet to be viewed by potential employers.
- Software can search or screen potential applicants.
- Applications can be made and jobs filled within hours.

Internet services are designed for both job-seekers and employers. Several Internet listings can be accessed 'free' to applicants, just like newspaper adverts. Employers pay a small amount (under £5.00 per day, currently) to include their vacancies on the Internet. Candidates can register an interest in particular vacancies and companies, and are automatically kept informed of new jobs.

The Internet's wide geographical scope, coupled with the low cost, are attractive to employers. Internet applicants tend to be computer literate, and on-line recruitment services have high numbers of applicants registered (one claims 80,000 on its current database). The process is fast – responses can be made immediately by e-mail.

On-line systems allow candidates to update their CVs or interests easily, and have their CVs made available to a large number of potential employers. They also benefit from the speed of operating on-line, as they can get detailed information on jobs and employers immediately. Applicants can identify industries in which they would not work, so it is targeted. Most services do not charge the applicant for using the service

Computer software can help select sales representatives. Packages used by HRM (human resource management) professionals include psychometric profiling (Myers-Briggs and 16PF) and team role evaluation (such as Belbin). Many are available for Windows based computers, but they should be administered by trained professionals. Some recruiters (such as those on the Internet) also use selection tests, and will produce a personality profile of candidates along with their CV.

Packages are available to assess the suitability of sales personnel. For example, a package called Un-Mask assesses candidates' suitability in three areas – intellect, motivation and sales ability. Intellect assesses verbal, numerical and spatial reasoning abilities. Motivation covers several issues, such as drive, ambition, energy level and need for recognition. Selling skills monitors abilities in lead qualification, handling objections, presentation skills, and time management, according to your requirements.

Finally, computers can track the recruitment and selection process. It is useful to retain details of this for employment legislation purposes. You will also identify problem areas in your recruitment process by monitoring it in this way.

Practical tip

If you are looking for new staff, scan the jobs pages in the Internet. You might find out about expected salary levels, or even competitors' job vacancies.

Consider how you evaluate applicants for your posts. Can psychometric or other assessment techniques be used to improve this process?

Training

Computer based training (CBT) is the term used to describe computer software for training. CBT displays text and graphics on a computer screen, and can deliver knowledge and develop intellectual skills in managing information. Ready-made courses are available from training suppliers, but specific tests can be written to meet corporate requirements. Software packages for this (called 'authoring' packages) are available, but companies wanting customized courses usually pay consultants to write these.

The advantages of CBT are:

- It does not require trainees to come to a central location.
- It can be studied at any time.
- It is good at helping staff learn factual information on new products or the company.
- It can challenge the user to remember key points.
- It can monitor and measure knowledge levels.

The testing and scoring facility identifies gaps in sales representatives' knowledge. Some companies, such as financial service organizations, require salespeople to achieve a minimum score before they are allowed to sell products. Tests can also be designed to identify training needs – a weak score in an area can highlight a need for further training in that area.

Multimedia training packages, which offer audio and video facilities, as well as text and graphics, are generating interest. Currently, these are expensive to produce, and with a limited market (few PCs have CD-ROM drives), most have been designed to teach general skills (like typing skills, languages, telephone skills, customer care, etc.). Some large companies have produced in-house multimedia training packages, but this is very expensive.

A few training organizations use Philips CDi (Compact Disc Interactive) packages. CDi is more like a television format with text and interactivity, but is best suited to group or classroom format. This has not been widely adopted.

Another aspect of IT and the training function relates to training in IT. An automated sales office needs more than a computer. It needs staff who are able and willing to use the system. There are physical, practical and motivational problems in getting people to key in information:

- Many salespeople do not have good keyboard skills.
- Palmtop computers are particularly difficult for those who have limited manual dexterity.

- Some sales representatives try to retain power by keeping information to themselves, believing that their customers belong to them, and not to the company.
- Some sales staff are disorganized, and forget to complete records, or submit 'fictional' reports, believing that they are never used.
- Some sales staff fear that the new systems will be critical of their performance or even threaten their jobs.

Clearly, training is essential when a system is first introduced, but it often takes months before staff master even basic skills, such as keyboard skills. Further, some staff acquire a basic competence, but never master skills in laying text out to a professional standard.

These problems are challenges facing sales managers when adopting new technology. It is important to train staff in the systems, and to monitor sales staff's abilities and performance in sales reporting. Arguably, the most critical job is to sell the idea of the system to staff. It is widely believed that sales management software will only work effectively if both you and your sales staff want it to!

Practical tip

There are many very good CBT and multimedia typing tutors (such as 'Mavis Beacon teaches typing'), which are very inexpensive and fun to use. If your staff (or you!) have weaker typing skills than you would like, invest in one of these packages, and try to practice for about 10 minutes a day. Typing skills will improve rapidly.

Integrated horizontal software package 'suites', such as Microsoft Office or Lotus Smartsuite, are easier for users to learn than separate packages. There are similar commands and layouts in the different packages. Also, look for vertical packages which use common formats and commands, as they will be easier to learn.

Compensation

Salesforce compensation schemes based on quantitative targets (i.e. related to quantitative objectives) lend themselves to spreadsheet models, such as those showing the relative costs of rewarding the salesforce at given sales performance levels. However, salesforce compensation schemes should also consider the number of accounts and the sales potential. This form of analysis should thus be considered alongside salesforce size and territory design. The sales potential can be determined by looking at past sales histories and margins. Motivational effects of other forms of bonuses and incentives can also be monitored and measured against their costs.

Practical tip

If sales increase beyond a certain level, do your production costs fall? If so, use a spreadsheet to calculate the impact of increasing commission levels, based on current profitability and the variable cost levels.

Spreadsheets enable sales managers to undertake a form of job evaluation that deter- mines the broad range of salaries to be paid to different grades of staff, reflecting their skills, responsibilities and efforts. They can review whether quotas can be set beneath which commission is not paid, or beyond which different rates of commission are set.

Finally, the spreadsheet's ease of calculation makes it possible to review the overall sales commission, and then break this down by categories that merit different commission levels, such as product, territory or new business. Thus, more sophisticated forms of commission can be developed.

Salesforce evaluation and control

The applications in this chapter have all referred to IT's role in improving planned sales activities. Many forms of evaluation have already been mentioned. This section will summarize the main forms under three headings:

- sales performance, at company, market or individual sales representative level
- sales productivity
- company performance in the marketplace.

Overall sales performance

The basic purpose of salesforce control is to determine the answer to 'What is happen-

---

Example Seven

A car manufacturer needs to sell 1500 cars at an average cost of £35,000. A simple spreadsheet can examine the cost of the different levels of incentives at different sales levels. This modelling cannot predict the salesforce's ability to achieve these sales levels, but it evaluates the costs of offering incentives, relative to the sales returns.

Example Eight

A chemical company has field sales representatives, key account managers and telesales staff. The key account managers have the greatest responsibility, followed by the field sales representatives, then the telesales staff. All are paid on commission. If a common level of commission is paid to staff, a telesales person could earn more commission than others, by being in the office (thus more available). The sales manager can model alternative commission approaches to ensure that the levels of responsibility are reflected in the salaries, but sufficient incentive is given to all staff.

ing?'. This should be linked with a second question, 'What were our objectives?', and if there is a discrepancy between the two, then a third question 'Why?' needs also to be asked. In this section, the focus is on the first two questions.

All companies record sales data, but few examine these in sufficient detail. Typically, only overall sales figures, or sales figures by one or two favoured breakdowns are used. The problem here is that the iceberg principle – that only a small proportion of a problem is visible, with most of the problem hidden below the surface – is applicable to sales performance review. Overall figures will show minor problems, which could hide substantial threats.

By now, you will recognize that once data have been stored using an appropriate computer package, they can be analysed quickly and easily, and this applies to sales evaluation and control. Investigation of sales problems is possible in the non-computerized sales office. The problem is that it is slow, and the necessary insight is often gained too late. Computerizing sales records enables managers to diagnose problems earlier and more precisely, enabling them to take appropriate and timely remedial action.

The most basic forms of sales control are

examinations of sales by:

- territory
- product
- customer
- time period
- trade channel
- order size.

Practical tip

Identify the most important forms of control – is it related to sales by territory, by product, by customer, etc? Determine which of these are currently available, and from which sources. Determine how long it takes to generate these reports. Could any of these be generated automatically by computerizing an aspect that is not currently computerized?

Sales performance can be evaluated at overall company level, at market (or territory) levels or at individual sales representative level. Clearly, managers could suffer from 'information overload', but the computer can be programmed to identify only those figures that fall outside an acceptable margin. This is called exception reporting. The computer searches for the data, leaving the manager with time to make decisions. More focused analyses can be sought if required to aid this decision making.

Individual sales performance

Ideally, salesforce performance should have both subjective and objective measures. Computers are best suited to measuring objective or quantitative data, for example, reviewing:

- performance against plan
- variations in accounts, products, etc.
- margins, e.g. by sales representative, product, etc.
- call rates

- order levels
- order/call ratios
- etc.

Customized sales packages also identify other forms of evaluation. For example, managers can:

- measure aspects of activity management, such as cost per call or journey planning, for each representative
- monitor sales tracking, to check sales representatives' 'follow through'
- measure aspects of sales representatives' effectiveness in the sales call
- gain qualitative understanding about a sales representative's ability by accessing sales representatives' diaries and/or call reports.

Measuring and monitoring individual sales

Example Nine

Software suppliers are focusing on identifying how computers can assist in performance evaluation. One package – Respond 2 – relates to complaint handling. A better level of understanding of why the problem occurs can be obtained by looking at complaints. Sales staff are well placed to manage these (because they are in contact with customers) and to communicate the complaints to the marketing department. IT can improve the effectiveness of the complaint feedback loop, and improve both efficiency and customer satisfaction levels. Computerized complaints handling systems record information on complaints and complainers, with details of how the problem is being solved. Like sales tracking systems, any member of staff can respond to the customer, because they can view the complainant's history file. It also stores details of the complaint handling process, measuring and monitoring performance in overcoming the complaint.

The marketing department can then examine the customer feedback, the costs of managing complaints, and of the effectiveness of alternative methods of complaint handling, such as personal contact, telephone contact, letters, goodwill offers, etc., as a basis for changing aspects of the product.

representative's performance ensures that individual problems can be identified, and solutions sought. It can also help motivate the sales team.

Sales productivity

Sales productivity was defined earlier in this chapter as the process of doing the right things better – i.e. improving effectiveness and efficiency. This analysis builds on basic sales data, combined with sales cost data. Sales productivity analysis enables the sales manager to examine fixed and variable costs of servicing each customer, and the returns on different forms of sales activities and sales efforts. It can review the proportion of expenses in different regions, or markets, and thus review whether additional investment in these brings an appropriate rate of return.

This information can then be married with costs of servicing individual accounts. Unfortunately, most companies do not measure and allocate costs to accounts because of the time required, even though most sales representatives understand the value of Pareto analysis (the 80:20 rule). However, computerized sales systems offer the potential to record and review the profit by account. It is a straightforward costing process, building on the sales activity logs, sales expenses records and sales records. Once again, the computer's advantage is its simplicity and ease. Specific analysis can determine:

- What is the time spent on this account, including staff time spent in meetings, on proposals, on other admin., on sales support, in travelling time or costs in these areas, etc.?
- What is the revenue from this account?
- What is the profitability of this account?

This enables managers to identify truly profitable accounts, rather than those which appear to be most profitable. Often a customer can order a large volume, but require an excessively high level of support. Alternatively, managers may identify unprof-

itable territories or products. Account productivity tracking enables the profitability to be monitored over time.

This is closely linked with the current attention on customer retention. The rationale for customer retention is that it is cheaper to sell to existing customers than to find new ones. Computer systems can identify and value key customers. Once this information exists, the basic sales performance analysis can be undertaken to identify any fluctuation in the sales pattern of these customers and make early diagnosis of the problem or to review the account's importance.

Sales managers can analyse data on a computerized system. They can use spreadsheet facilities to model alternative levels of investment or activity. Alternatively, companies can use two separate measures to form ratios, such as sales calls/sales, profit/customer, sales/customer, etc. Relevant ratios can become benchmarks for performance. Companies often start using computerized sales and marketing systems to reduce basic administrative tasks. Once these systems are established, they ask for more detailed statistical analysis. Salesforce control is the real benefit of the computerized sales system.

Company performance in the marketplace

Although sales analysis should give insight into performance, a company's performance must also be reviewed relative to competition. An integrated sales and marketing information system allows the sales activities to be related to information on the following, if these are routinely gathered:

- market share
- market size and growth rate
- competitor's price levels
- competitor's marketing activities
- distribution coverage levels
- awareness levels.

Market research packages – especially for survey analysis and computer assisted telephone interviewing (CATI) – can be used for examining the underlying reasons for any changes in market preference, or for recording views on new products or packages. Clearly, the rules of conducting good marketing research need to be followed.

These areas are normally under the marketing department's responsibility. They are mentioned to close the loop between sales and marketing which was referred to earlier in this chapter. There is one further benefit. Corporate marketing managers can access sales management data too, enabling them to react more swiftly to emerging problems within their domain. This makes it easier for the salesforce to sell.

Practical tip

Identify how frequently you access the data you record or analyse – daily, weekly, monthly, quarterly, etc. Identify the breakdowns you need – by region, customer, territory, etc., and ensure that these details are all coded into your records to enable you to make the appropriate analyses. Now identify if there are other data that you should store, and other information that you need to review. Detail these under similar headings. This forms the basis of your sales management system

---

Making it happen

If you have been encouraged by the applications and ideas in this chapter, you may want to implement them immediately. About half the problems with sales management systems come from the users' lack of experience. Gather information, and seek others' views. Start gathering general information, but do not leap instantly into any IT purchase. It takes time to identify the systems requirements (i.e. what do you want to achieve), turn this into a specification, put the systems together (including buying hardware and software, or customizing any packages) and then to get the system up and running (including training the staff on its implementation). On average, it is unlikely to take less than three months to install and implement an integrated package, but for more sophisticated requirements it will take more than a year. Clearly, it is important to get this system right from the start, given this timescale. The practical tips in this chapter guide you through the main issues, and the checklists will also help.

Here is a summary of the main issues.

- **Identify your requirements** – Begin by asking about the system's purpose, and how it fits within the company, its strategy and its people.
- **Developing specifications** – Discuss your requirements with various suppliers to form these into a specification. Use this to guide your purchase, and don't be swayed by non-essential features.
- **Making the purchase** – Evaluate suppliers on service, as well as price. Remember, that if it is a bespoke system, then only that company can give you support.
- **Implementing the system** – Consider staff training requirements, new forms and procedures, reporting cycles, incentives to complete reports, etc. Consider a trial run to ensure that problems are ironed out before it is fully operational.
- **Evaluation** – Establish how you are going to assess the system, and review the sales roles, organization and procedures.

Over time, you will identify necessary improvements. These usually come from the success of the system. Once the initial improvements in sales efficiency and effectiveness have been realized, companies want further improvements – often that the system should be more analytical or broader in scope. Alternatively, as staff develop new IT skills, you could add more sophisticated search or updating tasks.

Later still, 'expert systems' could be developed, in which the computer is given a series of rules to consider, and through these, makes decisions, and suggests actions. In other words, the sales manager identifies the usual questions to be asked of a set of sales figures, programmes these into the 'expert system', and the computer undertakes the assessment of the situation.

Neural networks are a more sophisticated form of 'expert system', where the computer package can be designed to learn from data, by recognizing patterns in the data. This can target sales (by identifying the most promising accounts, given past sales performance) or to set future targets (by extrapolating past sales, and by modifying targets in line with other related targets). These systems are just developing, and they need the expertise of sales managers in the first instance, but just think about the work they would save in the longer term!

Some words of caution

The greater the value of the sales management system to the company, the greater the need for security of this system. You may need to restrict access to parts of the system to ensure that the data cannot be tampered with. Very competitive sales staff could be tempted to enter new data about their perfor-mance, if their bonus depends on it. A greater risk is from damage to the computer system, whether by accident or a virus. Clearly, sales management systems must be kept safe, with security access codes to enter the systems, and routine disk scanning for viruses, and making regular backup disks or tapes.

Practical tip

If you are about to computerize your sales activity, identify one thing that your salesforce complain about in your administration system, such as completing or paying expense claims, or the accuracy of commission payments. Make this a priority, and build this into one of the most central parts of your system. By doing so, you are solving their problems (if they use the system correctly), and you should also be solving your own!

If you are using your computer for busi-ness purposes, and have any personal infor-mation stored on it, you must register under

---

Example Ten

Computers can and will make sales management decisions in future – but based on sales managers' insight. For example, computers check the current overall sales level, and the sales of each product, and compare these figures with the target sales levels, to determine those areas that are falling below the target. This could be undertaken overall, and by territory and/or sales representative. Information could be narrowed down by customer, and compared with past customer order levels, or even with call frequency. The computer could then suggest changes that improve the performance, such as call frequency or territory allocation.

the Data Protection Act. This requires you to undertake to keep all data confidential and accurate.

Finally, watch out that the power of IT doesn't lead to 'over-control'. Many sales people want and need to be independent – so managers must ensure that they do not become so caught up in evaluating computer printouts that they fail to recognize the wants and needs of their salesforce, and of their customers. Misuse can lead to dissatisfaction of both – while satisfaction of both is ultimately the sales manager's responsibility.

Summary

This chapter has examined using IT to improve sales management activity. Clearly, the benefits, like the technology itself, will change in time. Companies that adopt a 'wait and see' strategy will find themselves at a cost disadvantage and less effective than their competitors. Worse still, they will present an image of being dated and even disorganized.

Its benefits are clear:

● Harnessing customer information is essential for maximum sales effectiveness.
● Information technology helps management decision making, by providing data and information which can diagnose problems and identify opportunities.
● Information technology serves as a valuable tool for monitoring and controlling activities.

Information technology can do more than improve operational effectiveness and efficiency. Some companies have gained a strategic advantage through the design of their sales process and in managing their customer relationships. Information technology can change marketing and sales activities, with a resulting impact on the business structures and job responsibilities.

Failing to change in line with this potential will inevitably lead to failure, as others learn to exploit information technology's potential in sales management and sales practice. In the early 1980s, the main business journals carried articles about how computers could be used in sales activities. In the 1990s, it is accessible to most people and companies. In the twenty-first century, it will surely be at the heart of the sales function.

Checklist 12.1
Implementing a new sales and marketing
management system

- **Identify your overall requirements**
  - What do you need this for?
  - What information do you need?
  - How and when will you use this?
  - Who else will use this system?
  - What are their specific requirements?
  - How does this fit with the company's overall marketing and IT strategies?
  - How much data (e.g. customer or transaction details) will you want to store?
  - What is your maximum budget?
- **Identify and screen potential suppliers**
  - Have you approached a range of different suppliers, to determine the potential of different applications for your problem?
  - Do they just sell products, or will they help you implement the technology?
  - Can you ensure that you can get support over time? (If your supplier goes out of business, who can help you?)
  - Have you sought customer references?
- **Detail your specific requirements**
  - Hardware
    1. What hardware is currently available in your business?
    2. What hardware do you need?
  - Software
    1. What software is currently in use in your business?
    2. What software do you need?
    3. Is it available in a standard format, or will it need to be customized?
  - How does this fit with your budget? Prioritize your requirements, and review if necessary.

- **Word-processing**
  - Can your word-processor access your customer or contact database to prepare standard letters?
  - Do you have style sheets for sales letters, appointment, order, or delivery confirmations, proposals, brochures, etc?
  - If you are a small company, or you have a rapid turnover of sales staff, do you have software to enable you to print business cards?
- **Spreadsheet**
  - Do you use 'templates' or skeleton files to prepare standard calculations, such as for quotations, expenses, etc?
  - Have you got 'macros' (formulae) for routine calculations?
  - Can you place any of your forms onto a spreadsheet?
- **Presentation graphics**
  - Do you have a recognized style sheet, including the company name and logo?
  - Do you have a series of basic presentations, on the company, key products, client history, etc., which can form the foundation of future presentations?
  - If you have a product or service where audio or video is important, then have you materials that you could integrate in a multimedia presentation?
- **Database**
  - Have you identified all the major fields for your database?
  - Are there any other fields that could expand the usage of the database (e.g. adding a 'salutation', the name you would call the person in a letter, as well as formal name)?
  - Can you store visuals in your database – e.g. photos, logos, etc. – which could be used for proposals, recognizing clients, etc?
- **Diaries**
  - Are copies of diaries kept centrally, and updated on a regular basis?
  - Do sales staff use diaries in a common way, to enable comparison of activities?
  - Is appointment scheduling prompted by a diary package?
  - Are time planning and usage monitored by a diary package?

Checklist 12.3
Some guidelines for using IT in some sales management activities

- **Salesforce organization**
  - Check the basic data (number of accounts, number of sales staff, number of calls expected per day, etc.) and the territory allocations on a quarterly basis to monitor changes.
  - Check that you have a person designated to give help and support on software for those experiencing problems.
- **Recruitment**
  - Determine what assessment techniques you wish to use, and contact the Institute of Personnel and Development, or read one of their publications, to get information on suppliers.
  - Can on-line services help identify potential candidates? Contact People Bank (or a similar organization) to check whether they could help.
- **Training**
  - Check the extent of computer training in training programmes for new and existing sales staff.
  - Check that staff training is undertaken when you install new software.
  - Contact the Institute of Personnel and Development or a training materials supplier to determine what computer-based training packages could be used by your field salesforce.
- **Compensation**
  - Identify if you can increase sales volume, by paying variable levels of sales commission.
  - Examine the levels of sales commission for different sales staff if you change your sales system because of computerization.
- **Evaluation and control**
  - Determine basic sales figures for evaluation, e.g. sales (volumes/values) this week, month, quarter, year, compared with last week, month, quarter, year; sales (volumes/values) variation by territory; sales (volumes/values) variation by customers – size, industry, etc.; sales (volumes/values) variation by product, each of these compared with plan or quota.
  - Check that you have records of your computer equipment and software, and the current keeper of any field based equipment.
  - Check who needs access to data on the system, and introduce passwords.
  - Develop a corporate policy for checking for viruses.
  - Develop a backup routine for all software and data.

List of suppliers

Dynamic Pathways (UK) Ltd, The Chantry, Hadham Road, Bishop's Stortford, Herts, CM23 2QR. Tel: 01279 465165. Fax: 01279 755039

Intuitive Systems Ltd, Broadlands House, Primett Road, Stevenage, Herts, SG1 3EE. Tel: 01438 317966. Fax: 01438 314368

QuickAddress, QAS Systems Ltd, 7 Old Town, London, SW4 0JT. Tel: 0171 498 7777. Fax: 0171 498 0303

Respond 2, Initiative Software Applications Ltd, Aspen House, Station Road, Kettering, Northants, NN15 7HE. Tel: 01536 310888. Fax: 01536 310898

Symantec Northern Europe, Sygnus Court, Market Street, Maidenhead, Berks, SL6 8AD. Tel: 0118 981 4230. Fax: 0118 981 4222

Tracker Software (UK) Ltd, Winter Hill House, Marlow Reach, Station Approach, Marlow, Bucks, SL7 1NT. Tel: 01628 488866. Fax: 01628 488855

Total Computer Systems (TCS), 117 High Street, Epping, Essex, CM16 4BD. Tel: 01992 575151. Fax: 01992 575147

Tranzline Ltd, St George's House, Knoll Road, Camberley, Surrey, GU15 3SY. Tel: 01276 686968. Fax: 01276 676020

Unitrac Software (Europe) Ltd, Airport House, Purley Way, Croydon, Surrey, CR0 0XZ. Tel: 0181 781 1994. Fax: 0181 781 1999

Un-Mask, Occupational Preference Ltd, Victoria House, 11 Teal Crescent, Worcester, WR4 0LJ. Tel: 01905 458878. Fax: 01905 457274

Consultants

Hewson Consulting Group, Witan Court, 317 Upper Fourth Street, Central Milton Keynes, MK9 1ES. Tel: 01908 677840. Fax: 01908 677850

The Data Consultancy (also offers mapping systems), 7 Southern Court, South Street, Reading, RG1 4QS. Tel: 0118 9588181. Fax: 0118 959 7637. E-mail: sales @data sets.com Internet http://www.datasets.com/datasets/

Major consultancy groups, such as KPMG, also offer salesforce automation consultancy.

Further reading

Hewson Consulting Group Publications, including: Hewson, N., Hewson, W., McDonald, M. and Wilson, H. *The Impact of Computerised Sales and Marketing Systems in the UK*, 4th edition. Hewson Consulting Group.

Sales Arena Magazine. Tel: 01403 752688.

Shaw, R. (1991) *Computer Aided Marketing and Selling*. Oxford: Butterworth-Heinemann.

Part Four

Sales
Approaches

13

International selling

Dr Susan Bridgewater, University of Warwick

 In this chapter we explore some of the issues related to selling in international markets. In particular, the complexity of selling in diverse international markets is considered, paying specific attention to:

- Choice of sales organization;
- Managing international sales;
- The impact of cultural differences on international selling.

A major challenge posed by international expansion is that corporations must decide what type of sales organization is most effective. They must establish and manage salesforces in foreign markets and decide how much centralized control they should exert over these. Decisions must be made as to the use of local or expatriate sales staff. The choice of international sales organization will influence the level of the cultural awareness which sales staff have of the host country.

This chapter reviews the choices which firms make in organizing and managing their international salesforce. It considers the implications of different types of international sales organization, how to manage international sales and the complex task of overcoming cultural barriers to sell successfully.

Choosing the international sales organization

One of the major decisions in international marketing is that of how to organize international operations. Firms must make choices relating to the level of investment they are prepared to stake in entering an international market, and the level of control which they wish to retain over these operations. It is widely accepted that export or use of a sales agent or distributor involve low levels of initial investment (Anderson and Gatignon, 1986). However, the effectiveness of an export salesforce may be inhibited by lack of knowledge of the new market. Whilst sales agents and distributors may have local knowledge, the firm may have little control over the quality of the sales effort. Investment in providing the local partner

Table 13.1 *International sales organizations*

Type of international sales organization	Level of initial investment	Level of control	Distinctive challenges
Export salesforce	Low	High	• Gaining foreign market knowledge and contracts
Sales agent or distributor	Low	Low	• Finding suitable agent • Communicating necessary product knowledge • Controlling quality • May not sell firm's products exclusively
Sales and marketing joint venture	Moderate	Moderate	• Finding suitable joint venture partner • Recruiting staff with appropriate skills • Controlling quality • Managing relationship
Wholly-owned sales and marketing subsidiary	High	High	• Establishing subsidiary • Recruiting staff with appropriate skills • Overcoming cultural barriers

with the necessary product or service knowledge and in the level of service quality which the firm expect may be the price of lower initial investment.

The trade-offs implied by different modes of international sales organization are summarized in Table 13.1. The advantages and disadvantages of these different types of international organization are illustrated by examples of their use in entering Eastern Europe.

Export salesforce

Entry into a new, international market is complicated by the lack of knowledge which the firm may have of macro-environmental differences. A successful formula in the domestic market may not necessarily be transferable. These difficulties can be seen in Example One.

The challenges faced by a firm using an export salesforce include:

• developing or recruiting staff with the necessary linguistic and cultural skills;

• helping export sales staff to identify and build sales leads;

• building a database of sales information;

• creating an incentive structure which takes into account the difficulties of selling in new, or culturally dissimilar markets, compared with more developed or culturally similar markets.

Sales agents or distributors

Use of a sales agent or distributor may overcome the difficulties experienced by expatriate sales representatives. The local agent or distributor adds value by having local knowledge, linguistic and cultural skills. Typically they would be a national of the target country. However, a different but no less problematic set of issues must be faced.

First, the firm must have sufficient market information to identify potential partners. Second, it must evaluate the level of market information and contacts which the agent or distributor has. If the chosen distributor does not have specialist knowledge of the industry,

**Example One
Entering an 'alien' market**

Eastern Europe contains some of the few international markets in which the number of smokers is increasing. Moreover, as communist rule had limited the opportunities available to multinational corporations prior to liberalization in 1989, the early 1990s have seen considerable interest in the region by multinational tobacco firms. The sales manager of one of these firms described Eastern Europe as 'one of the last virgin territories in the world'. In his eyes, these countries are amongst the few left in which the large multinational tobacco firms can jockey for position.

Although unsolicited orders show that western cigarette brands are in demand, the precise extent of the market potential and the decision of how best to serve each country was initially difficult. Some large multinational corporations have decided on early investment in manufacturing operations as a means of gaining acceptance for their brands. However, for other firms the initial investment required for this type of operation is considered too great. One tobacco firm decided to export into the region as a way of gaining a better understanding of the market opportunities. However, the export sales manager encountered a range of difficulties. These included finding suitable business premises. In Ukraine, the manager operated from a hotel bedroom. Also, he did not speak the language and felt that the country was culturally very 'alien'. He was not sure how to begin to find the necessary market information or to build sales contacts.

then an investment in training will be required. In any case, knowledge of the firm's product or service portfolio must be communicated.

More importantly, the firm does not have control over the day-to-day sales activities of the agent. Therefore, it will need to institute a system of monitoring the sales activities of its representative in the country to ensure that an appropriate image of the firm is conveyed. Some agents do not sell the products of one firm exclusively. In such instances, it may be difficult to ascertain whether the agreed priority is given to sales of the firm's products compared to other parts of the agent's portfolio. Promotional expenditure is often required to incentivize the agent. An example of the issues involved in using agents or distributors is given in Example Two.

Joint venture agreements

Joint venture agreements have gained increasing popularity as a means of entering unfamiliar international markets. The level of co-operation involved may span a spectrum from a merger of two organizations to informal co-operation on a particular project. If equity is split between the two organizations, then a joint venture gives greater control over decisions than would be afforded by use of an agent or distributor. This may be attractive to an international firm as it offers better protection of brands and sales quality. However, this control usually requires greater initial investment. Moreover, co-operation must be mutually beneficial in order to be sustainable in the longer term.

Example Two
Distributor selection

One computer manufacturer entering the Ukrainian market decided that the level of market uncertainty was such that it should initially use a distributor. Fortunately, it was able to identify a suitable candidate. Since liberalization in 1991, the distributor, an American, had worked in an international business school where he managed a newly established MBA programme. He had previous international experience of the computer industry. His interest in spending a period working in the country came from his Ukrainian ancestry and ability to speak the language. Therefore, he offered the advantages of local knowledge and cultural awareness combined with a knowledge of western sales practice. Nevertheless, the computer manufacturer had to invest considerable time and effort in communicating knowledge about their products and services. They were able to delegate the recruitment of a local salesforce to the distributor. However, they felt that they had to make frequent visits to the country to monitor quality and ensure that important contracts were successfully won.

Practical tip

The following steps may increase the chances of success for a joint venture:

1. Careful selection of the joint venture partner
Potential joint venture partners should consider what each offers and what each hopes to gain. Are these mutually compatible or mutually exclusive?

2. Openness
Whilst both partners may be cautious in the negotiation stages, joint ventures where there is open discussion of aims and where the partners put effort into developing a trusting relationship stand a greater chance of success.

3. Clear definition of the joint venture's scope
It is worthwhile to spend time early in the relationship deciding exactly which activities will be included in the joint venture and which will remain outside. Remember a joint venture could be any type of agreement from complete merger to informal co-operation on a specific project.

4. Understanding each other's culture
Partners, particularly of different nationality, may have very different ways of working. It is beneficial to try to gain an understanding of areas of similarity and difference between the organizations to avoid possible misunderstandings

5. Regular reviews
Whatever measures have been taken to improve the relationship, the joint venture agreement is likely to diverge from what was originally envisaged at times. Regular meetings to review the satisfaction of the partners with progress should be held to make any adjustments to the scope or operation of the joint venture.

**Example Three
'Walk on the wild side'**

Pioneering Johnson Wax were one of the earliest entrants into the Ukrainian market. Their entry, dating back to 1988, prior to the breakup of the Soviet Union, was triggered by a change in legislation which allowed foreign investors to take a majority stake in joint venture agreements. The partner with whom they were matched by Moscow was located in Kiev, which in late 1991 became the capital of independent Ukraine. Initially, the key challenges faced by the firm were those of achieving an acceptable quality for the products manufactured in the country. Distribution was handled centrally through state-controlled wholesalers to retail outlets whose layout, product range and prices were all determined by government. The plant sold all that it could produce, although some older formulations had to be revived to take into account differences in economic wealth and cultural usage. Since independence, however, the market situation has changed dramatically and in ways which could not have been anticipated. The state distribution system has gradually disintegrated. Johnson Wax have had to find new channels to distribute their products. However, the privately owned kiosks put high margins on products and offer little added value. Moreover, Johnson Wax face the challenge of recruiting and training a direct salesforce in a country which has never had to develop selling skills. Almost all staff have to develop these skills from the beginning. This is a long term and expensive task in which their local partner can offer little assistance.

Kasriel, K. (1994) Walk on the Wild Side, *Business Central Europe*, February.

As with firms using a distributor, the first challenge is to identify a suitable local partner. The process may be fraught with additional concern as a consequence of the higher financial stakes and longer duration involved in equity joint ventures. For these reasons, managing the relationship between the two partners may require considerable time and effort. The advantages and trials of one such joint venture are described in Example Three.

Wholly-owned subsidiaries

If control over the sales of a firm's products or services is paramount, then a wholly-owned subsidiary may be the preferred type of sales organization. This involves 100% ownership of the local subsidiary by the parent company. This category includes sales and market subsidiaries, as well as those which involve manufacture of products in the host country.

Clearly the size of the investment required for this type of operation is higher than for the other modes described. However, this varies significantly between sectors. A sales and marketing subsidiary need not necessarily involve a significant level of investment if it has small premises and a small number of staff. A wholly-owned, or joint venture, manufacturing operation would typically involve substantially greater levels of investment.

The control offered by total ownership may be particularly important to firms whose success is heavily reliant on advanced technologies, knowledge-based assets, such as managerial skills, or high levels of service quality.

An illustration of a situation in which control is seen to justify higher levels of initial investment is given in Example Four.

Managing international sales

Centralization of control

The head office is typically involved in strategic level decisions such as the choice of sales organization, discussed in the previous section. However, they may have little interest in tactical issues such as the setting of sales targets. Gestetner (1974) examines the advantages and disadvantages of centralized management of the sales organization.

Centralized management can be characterized as that in which the head office has a high level of control over the decisions which are made in individual countries. The sales-

---

Practical tip

A wholly-owned sales subsidiary should be considered if:

1. The firm does not wish to share proprietary technology.
2. The firm wishes to protect an established brand name.
3. Providing a high level of or consistent service quality is important to the firm.

Example Four
Protecting an international brand name

The merger activity of the late 1980s gave rise to the 'big six' international accountancy firms: Arthur Anderson; Ernst and Young; Coopers and Lybrand; Deloitte, Ross, Tomatsu; KPMG; and Price Waterhouse. All of these firms now operate in Ukraine, although entry spanned a period of three years. Whilst some of the firms have opted for split control modes of operation, a number have decided that they wish to have 100% control over the Ukrainian subsidiary. Justification of this choice was explained by one country manager as follows: 'We have multinational customers who deal with us in a large number of countries around the world. These customers have expectations of an international accounting firm. We have to provide an understanding of the specifics of accountancy and other business-to-business services in the host country. However, we also have to guarantee a consistent level of service internationally. For this reason it is important that we have control over the operation in a country. If we do not provide the expected level of service quality, an international customer may transfer not only their business in this country, but the whole international account, to a competitor. This risk far outweighs the size of the investment required to control any individual operation.'

force in each country may be modelled upon the salesforce in the home country. Decentralized sales management allows each country to 'do its own thing'.

The advantages and disadvantages of each of these types of sales organization as summarized by Gestetner are shown in Table 13.2.

Advantages of centralized sales management

The ability to access central market information systems may offer benefits to the firm. It may be able to draw on central customer files which contain background information on a firm, previous transactions around the world, the products a customer has bought and the prices it was charged. This both reduces the duplication of market research activity and avoids costly errors.

The growing importance of global customers may make this kind of account management essential. Global customers may have their own records of dealings with a particular supplier and be less than amused if they discover that a component is being sold at different prices by different parts of the organization. Whilst this may be justified by local market dynamics, the customer may expect the lowest price to be provided for all global transactions. In addition to ensuring consistent sales actions, central market research may also allow the sales operation in a particular country to identify products which are selling to one of their customers in another part of the world and to identify new sales opportunities.

For this reason, centralized control of sales activity may be more efficient and less expensive. Furthermore, the company can build its global image by using a standardized style of sales information, although literature will clearly need to be translated and may have to be adapted to meet local preferences.

Table 13.2 *Sales management: centralized or decentralized?*

Centralized sales management	
Advantages	**Disadvantages**
Greater efficiency	Macro-environmental differences
Avoids duplication of market research	Lack of flexibility
Builds global image	Nationalist reactions against parent company
Favours consistency of service levels and sales approach	Reluctance to make local decisions
Country-of-origin effects	Delays
	Problems in communication
	Head office data overload

Decentralized sales management	
Advantages	**Disadvantages**
Freedom of thought and action	Repetition of learning cycles
Local responsiveness	Expensive
Speed of decision-making	Less coherent strategically
Local knowledge	Danger of contradictory actions
	Local factors may be accorded too much importance

Disadvantages of centralized sales management

One of the most significant disadvantages of centralized control is that a local operation may not be able to make decisions which would maximize sales in its own market. This may be particularly frustrating if they are assessed by head office as a separate profit centre. Centralized control may be seen as restrictive, especially if sales targets are high.

In addition to causing resentment amongst sales representatives, centralized management may also result in missed opportunities because of the rigidity of the decision-making process. If potential new business must be sanctioned by head office, then the time involved and limitations on prices charged by the local sales operation may result in lost chances.

Sticking to a centrally defined set of sales targets and sales approaches may be further complicated by local market differences. The products which sell well in each country will almost certainly vary subject to macro-environmental differences such as level of economic wealth, state of technological advancement, and social and cultural differences. Furthermore, the nationality of the parent company will play a major role in determining the perception of its products and services.

The importance of nationality can clearly be seen through recent incidents such as that over the Pergau dam in Malaysia. In a conflict between the governments of Britain and Malaysia over an alleged connection between the construction of the Pergau dam and winning of defence contracts, a number of unrelated British firms were adversely affected by temporary trade embargoes and anti-British sentiments. Subsidiaries less closely associated with the nationality of the parent company may be less affected by this type of inter-governmental conflict.

Conversely, however, the country of origin may have a halo effect which could increase sales of a product. There are strong associations between nationality and the perceived quality of some products. Thus, the local sales organization may benefit from selling Czech beer, Russian vodka or Japanese electronic goods. In this case, close association with the nationality of the parent company may be a plus.

Advantages of decentralized sales management

Gestetner believes that the benefits accruing from a decentralized sales organization may be the absence of too much control and rigidity. The local sales operation has sufficient autonomy to respond quickly and pragmatically to sales opportunities. It can make use of the local knowledge of its salesforce to sell those products or services most likely to succeed in its own market. Hence it is more likely to reach its sales targets.

This local knowledge may allow for the local sales operation to identify new product opportunities which might not have been anticipated by the head office. Johnson Wax have reintroduced liquid starches into Eastern Europe, although these had been discontinued from their product portfolio in most markets. In the Russian market, there is a resurgence of demand for basic cars such as the Lada. Whilst western cars have high status value, spares are difficult to obtain and the vehicles are not designed for extreme weather conditions or poor roads. The robustness and relative lack of technological sophistication of the Lada make it suitable for the local conditions and easy to maintain. The opportunity to penetrate the market with more basic cars might not be considered by a global automotive firm.

Conversely, head office may not understand the impact of market differences on the success of some of its products. Large bottles of soft drinks are less suitable in markets where they must be refrigerated. Drawing upon the knowledge of local sales representatives can avoid this type of blunder.

Disadvantages of decentralized sales management

Allowing each market discretion to determine which products to sell, at what price and how, may involve costly duplication of effort. There is a risk that the firm will lose coherence in strategic approaches and damage international reputation and brands and the possibility that global customers may make unfavourable comparison between sales activity in different markets.

As there are advantages and disadvantages to both centralized and decentralized sales organization, international marketing research stresses the importance of achieving balance in approaches to a number of key issues:

1. **Standardization** of key strategic elements. This may include product features or range, brands, prices or service levels. However, determining which elements are of key strategic importance is clearly firm specific.
2. The lines of **communication** should be as short as possible and clearly defined. Agreement should be reached as to information which could be profitably fed back from the local sales organization to head office and what information and support should be provided to the local operation.
3. The extent and areas of local **autonomy.** Which decisions does head office need to be consulted on and which can best be handled locally? Some agreement should also be reached on priority areas and what speed of response can be expected on different types of decision.
4. **Accountability** for different tasks should also be established.

Multi-market sales management ▬

Example Five illustrates some of the issues which a firm may face in deciding its international sales management. Hill, Still and Boya (1991) identify five factors which influence the choice between separate and multi-market salesforces:

1. geographic and physical dimensions of individual countries
2. level of market development

3. country-level political and legal systems
4. human relations aspects of sales practices
5. local market conditions.

Geographic and physical dimensions __

Factors included under this heading include the size of the market. Hill et al. suggest that large markets warrant their own salesforces and are more likely to have a sales organization independent of the head office. In smaller markets it may be uneconomic to have specialists in different parts of the sales task. Typical consequences in small markets are that a sales representative may double as a sales engineer, or else that representatives may sell a broad range of the company's products.

Degree of market development _____

Hill et al. suggest that differing levels of educational, economic and social infrastructures may have implications for the recruitment and training of sales personnel. A particular problem is identified in recruiting appropriate sales staff in less developed countries. There may be strong local variation in the sources of staff. Examples cited include the use of US business school graduates in target countries by US multinationals, or reliance on military candidates in Central and Southern Africa.

Differing political and legal structures __

Different political and legal conditions complicate the standardization of salesforce working conditions and remuneration. For example, taxation differences may mean that multinational corporations alter the proportion of the total package which is represented by sales incentives as opposed to other benefits, such as higher levels of medical and maternity conditions.

Human relations aspects of personal selling and sales management _____

Social and cultural differences may also determine appropriate management of

The question of whether Europe can effectively be treated as a single market has risen to prominence with the creation of the single European market in 1992. The tension between moves towards deregulation and harmonization and national differences has prompted a debate as to the value of standardized marketing approaches for the 'new Europe'. However, a number of authors believe that the existence of the pan-European market is more myth than reality.

One of the factors which plays a role in determining whether the single European market can be effectively served by a multi-market sales structure is that of differences in the distribution channels most commonly found in the member states. In their studies of marketing in the new Europe, Halliburton and Hünerberg (1993) show the percentage of retail trade through 'independents' rather than 'multiples' to vary between 12% in the United Kingdom and 17% in Norway to 70% in Spain and 83% in Portugal.

These differences in retail structure have implications for salesforce organization. Firstly, the type of sales skills required by a sales representative serving an independent rather than a multiple differs significantly. The sales representative may be required to negotiate the sale and manage the relationship with an independent. However, the product range stocked by the multiple may be pre-determined by the multiple's buyer and the national account manager of the selling firm. The sales role may be closer to merchandizing in this situation. Second, the number of potential outlets for new sales may vary significantly. The extent to which sales representatives can achieve sales targets by their own efforts will vary. This means that different commission structures may be required for each European market. Finally, despite moves towards harmonization of legislation, taxation and labour structures vary significantly between member states. This may complicate regional sales force organization.

human resource issues. In Japan, length of service is the traditional determinant of the level of salary rises, rather than performance in achieving sales objectives. If commission is offered, this would also be dependent upon the combined efforts of the entire sales team rather than the achievements of the individual.

Local market circumstances

Other environmental differences may have an impact upon the features of a product or service which are likely to appeal to the market. In the home fashion industry, variation within the French market for wallpaper relates to climatic differences and a propensity for customers in the warmer south to spend more on outdoor areas of the home. The more expensive part of the portfolio and warmer colours were more easily sold in the cooler northern départements.

A summary of studies of international sales management and of broader international marketing literature produces the list shown in Table 13.3 of influences favouring and

Table 13.3 *Choosing between country-specific and multi-market sales organizations*

Factors favouring multi-market sales organization	Factors favouring country-specific sales organization
Small market size	Large market size
Language commonalities	Geographical and physical differences
Geographic proximity	Level of market development
Free trade agreements	Differing political and legal structures
Harmonization of standards	Infrastructure differences
Convergence of consumer tastes	Cultural and social differences

inhibiting the use of a single salesforce organization to serve more than one country.

The impact of cultural differences on international selling ▬▬▬

Perhaps the most significant difficulty faced in international selling is that of differences in culture. Whilst economic, technological or legal differences may be complex, once identified such variations can be incorporated into decisions on the product offering and preferred sales strategy. However, the cultural differences merit special attention because of their intangibility and the consequent difficulty in isolating their effect on successful international selling.

Culture has been defined as the 'attitudes, beliefs and values of a society'. However, given the differences which may exist in these within a society, management studies often define culture at a national level. Critics suggest that this is a crude over-simplification. Moreover, some argue that national cultures change over time, so that historic data can no longer give any insights. There are, indeed, some obvious instances where external changes have invalidated a previous finding. The most obvious example is that older studies refer to the Yugoslavian national culture. Clearly, subsequent political changes lend weight to the argument that national cultures may not represent cohesive groups. Other obvious examples would be in regions such as Eastern Europe where liberalization

has had a significant impact on individual aspirations, or in Hong Kong, where Chinese influence from 1997 may bring in a different set of values.

The impact of culture on international negotiation ─────────

Despite the difficulty of defining culture, some valuable insights can be gained into the impact of culture on international selling. In Hall's paper (1964) on international business negotiations, culture is classified into high- and low-context. In low-context cultures, the spoken word has great importance. Written and verbal agreements will be carefully worded, as the words are used to define the agreement. Examples of low-context cultures include Scandinavia, Switzerland, Germany, North America and Great Britain. High-context cultures, such as China, Korea, Japan and Latin America, are those where non-verbal signals are of great significance.

Hall focuses upon the misunderstandings which can arise in dealings between individuals from different ends of the spectrum. Thus, a North American sales representative may expect a transaction to be speedily resolved once the features of the product are explained and the contractual details confirmed. However, a Latin American or Asia-Pacific customer may wish to spend time building trust in the relationship before engaging in business dealings. The 'how' of international selling is therefore as important as the 'what'.

Reardon (1984) highlights the fact that, though the world is shrinking, many of the cultural rules of a nationality still persist. She points to the cultural significance of giving a token gift at the beginning of a business acquaintance. This may have a significant effect on the success or failure of the business relationship (see Example Six).

Example Six
'It's the thought that counts'

1. Walter Goferit chooses a typically American gift, a case of his favourite Kentucky bourbon, as a gift for his potential Saudi Arabian client. He also chooses a gold Tiffany bracelet for his client's wife. Having presented the bourbon in person, he tells his secretary that Abdul was literally speechless. Several days later, Walter still has not met his client's wife, so he asks how she is and gives Abdul the bracelet for her. To break the awkward silence which ensues, he compliments Abdul's favourite camel. Abdul looks at him for a long time and then hands him the camel and walks away.
2. Sam Shortfall prepares for his visit to Japan by taking with him a number of gifts which he thinks will make a lasting impression. He wraps the presents in colourful paper and puts large bows on them. He comments: 'Every time I gave someone something the person was really taken aback. I mean, they loved it. No one complained. In fact, they kind of giggled. I even received a number of gifts myself. And to show what kind of impression I made, they always spent more on me than I did on them.'
3. T.J. Ecclente comments that he presented his Latin American business associates with a purple 1984 sedan, as purple is his favourite colour. Nor did he stop there. He also presented kitchen knives and embroidered handkerchiefs to the women.

The consequences

1. Walter is now the owner of a camel named Hank! He still has not heard from Abdul.
2. Sam keeps exchanging bigger and better presents with the Japanese. However his boss has just received a telephone call from the Japanese saying that they feel 'over-obligated.' They still have not sold anything.
3. T. J. kept being offered money for the knives and never did any business in Latin America.

Practical tips

1. Do not give gifts to an Arab man's wife. It is not acceptable to ask about her at all. However, giving gifts to the children is acceptable.
2. Do not admire an object openly in Arab countries, or the owner may feel compelled to give it to you.
3. Do not take alcohol into an Arab home. Drinking of alcohol is often forbidden by religion.

Example Six *(Continued)*

4. Do not try to outgive the Japanese. This causes embarrassment and they feel obliged to reciprocate even if they can't afford it.
5. Take care in selecting colours and deciding on the number of items. Purple in Latin America is associated with Lent. Seven is lucky in some countries but unlucky in others.
6. Take care in selecting the gift. Perfume or jewellery may be considered too personal a gift.
7. Beware superstitions. In Latin America, knives suggest cutting off the relationship and handkerchiefs are reputed to bring the recipient hardship. To offset the bad luck the recipient must give you money.

Source: Reardon (1984)

The composition of culture

Perhaps the most comprehensive classification of factors which may play a role in international selling is that provided for international managers by Hutton (1988). This is summarized in Table 13.4.

These factors may not all be relevant for the sales of a particular product or service. However, they may serve as a checklist of cultural influences which a firm may need to take into account.

Table 13.4 *Components of culture. Adapted from Hutton (1988)*

Component of culture	Composition
Language	Spoken, written, official, foreign languages, mass media, pluralism
Religion	Sacred objects, beliefs, norms, prayers, holidays, rituals, taboos
Values and attitudes	Time, achievement, work, wealth, risk-taking
Law	Common law, codes, foreign laws, international law
Education	Formal, vocational, primary, secondary, higher, literary
Politics	Nationalism, sovereignty, imperialism, power, national interests, ethnic groups
Technology	Transportation, energy systems, tools, communication, urbanization, inventions
Social organization	Kinship, social institutions, authority, interest groups, social mobility, social stratification, status systems

Summary

In this chapter, three questions are posed. First, what type of sales organization should the firm choose? Second, how should it manage its international sales? Third, what are the impacts of culture on international selling and which factors should a firm take into account?

The choice of sales organization involves a trade-off between the level of investment which the firm is able or willing to make and the level of control which it wishes to have. The level of control is highest if it uses its own export salesforce or establishes a sales subsidiary. However, the nature of this control differs. Use of an export salesforce relies strongly on the amount of knowledge within the firm. A potential problem is that, on entering new markets, the firm will have to build contacts and gain an understanding of the complex issues which determine successful selling in that country. The extent of linguistic and cultural understanding of the country are key. Use of an agent or distributor, or else entering a joint venture agreement with a local partner, gives the firm access to the local knowledge of its partner. In return however, the firm will need to invest time in ensuring that the partner has knowledge of the firm's products or services and of the international image that it wishes to convey. Otherwise, this type of operation may damage its international reputation. Setting up a wholly-owned subsidiary protects against this type of risk. Again, the firm gains a high level of control over its operations. However, it must resolve staffing issues such as recruitment of appropriate staff and the balance of expatriate to local staff.

In managing international sales, the firm must decide the level of centralized control which it wishes to have over its sales operation. This will influence not only the type of sales organization which is most appropriate, but also the nature and extent of its involvement in sales decisions. In determining the centralization or decentralization of sales management, the firm must standardize key strategic elements, but allow local autonomy if market conditions dictate it. Areas of autonomy and accountability must be clearly defined. Effective communication between head office and the local sales operation should be established to ensure quick and efficient exchange of key information without overload. If head office makes demands which the local sales organization finds difficult to meet then appropriate support in terms of resources or training should be provided.

Finally, although there is evidence of global convergence in consumer tastes and harmonization of political and legal structures within free trade zones, national differences still persist. The most significant challenge for international selling is that posed by cultural differences. Cultural differences may be difficult to identify without local staff or high levels of local understanding. A comprehensive checklist of factors which might be taken into account is provided.

References

Anderson, E. and Gatignon, H. (1986) Modes of Foreign Entry: A Transaction Cost Analysis and Propositions, *Journal of International Business Studies*, Fall, 1–26.

Gestetner, D. (1974) Strategy in Managing International Sales, *Harvard Business Review*, Sept–Oct, 103–8.

Hall, E.T. (1964) The Silent Language of Overseas Business, *Harvard Business Review*, May–June, 87–96.

Halliburton, C. and Hünerberg, R. (1993) *European Marketing: Readings and Cases.* Addison-Wesley.

Hill, J.S., Still, R.R. and Boya, U.O. (1991) Managing the Multinational Sales Force, *International Marketing Review*, **8**, 19–31.

Hutton, J. (1988) The World of the International Manager. Philip Allan.

Reardon, K.K. (1984) It's the Thought that Counts. *Harvard Business Review*, Sept–Oct, 136–41.

Further reading

Douglas, S.P. and Wind, Y. (1987) The Myth of Globalisation, *Columbia Journal of World Business*, Winter, 19–29.

Halliburton, C. and Hünerberg, R. (1993) Pan-European Marketing: Myth or Reality, *Journal of International Marketing*, **3**, 77– 92.

Hill, J.S. and Still, R.R. (1990) Organizing the Overseas Sales Force: How Multinationals Do It, *Journal of Personal Selling and Sales Management*, **10**, Spring–Summer, 57–66

Hill, J.S. and Birdseye, M. (1989) Salesperson Selection in Multinational Corporations: An Empirical Study, *Journal of Personal Selling and Sales Management*, **9**, Summer, 39–47.

Hofstede, G. (1980) *Culture's Consequences: International Differences in Work-Related Values.* Sage.

14

Selling a service ————————————————

Professor Malcolm McDonald, Cranfield University

 In this chapter, we start by defining what is meant by the term 'service' and the selling process is put in the context of marketing. The process of selling is then described in detail, including the several roles that have to be performed by the salesperson in the service sector.

The growing importance of the service sector

Since World War II, Western Europe has seen a steady and unrelenting decline in its traditional manufacturing industries. Their place has been taken by numerous service-based enterprises, who were quick to spot the opportunities created by both organizational needs and by the increased personal affluence and the consequent raised lifestyle expectations of the population. So successful has been this transition from an essentially industrial society, that today, more than 60% of western economic activity is now in the service sector, whether measured in terms of income or numbers employed.

This shift in emphasis has been so pronounced that some observers refer to it as the 'second industrial revolution'. As individuals spend greater proportions of their income on travel, entertainment and leisure, postal and communication services, restaurants, personal health and grooming and the like, so

has the service sector responded by creating businesses and jobs. In addition, the growing complexity of banking, insurance, investment, accountancy and legal services has meant that these areas of activity show a similar inclination to expand, in terms of their impact on the economy as a whole.

In the UK, government employment statistics (Table 14.1) provide a telling picture of this silent revolution. Whereas employment in the service sector accounted for roughly 50% of the total workforce in 1968, by 1990 this figure had increased to 70%. This pattern has been repeated in most of the developed countries, as Table 14.2 shows.

Although there is a realization that it is essential for a country to have some kind of industrial base, there is little to suggest that this trend towards the service sector is slowing down. Indeed, the manufacturing industry itself is showing a greater propensity to subcontract out a wide range of activities which at one time were carried out in-house.

For example, outsourcing is increasing in areas such as cleaning, catering, recruitment,

Table 14.1 *Total UK employees in employment (thousands)*

	Service employees	All others	Total
1968	11,242	10,944	22,186
1975	12,545	9,668	22,213
1980	13,384	9,074	22,458
1985	13,769	7,151	20,920
1990	15,609	6,771	22,380
1995	15,418	5,616	21,034

Source: *Monthly Digest of Statistics and Employment Gazette*, February, 1991

deliveries, computer services, advertising, training, market research and product design. These are all areas where it has been found that external specialists can provide a cost-effective alternative to a company's own staff. More and more companies are choosing to contract out for specialist services and concentrate attention on their core activities.

Service industries, marketing effectiveness and the role of selling

Throughout roughly the same period, business schools and consultancy firms have been emphasizing how important it is for companies to develop a marketing orientation. At first sight this message would appear to have

Table 14.2 *Civilian employment by sector: international comparison, 1992 (%)*

	Services	Industry	Agriculture
UK	70.7	27.1	2.3
Australia	70.1	23.8	5.2
Austria	57.4	35.6	7.1
Belgium	69.7	27.7	2.6
Canada	73.1	22.7	4.4
Denmark	67.6	27.4	5.2
Finland	63.5	27.9	8.6
France	65.8	28.8	5.2
FR Germany	58.5	38.3	3.1
Irish Republic	57.3	28.9	13.8
Italy	59.6	32.2	8.2
Japan	59.0	34.6	6.4
Netherlands	71.4	24.6	4.0
Norway	70.9	55.3	11.6
Portugal	55.3	33.2	11.6
Spain	55.7	32.4	10.1
Sweden	70.1	26.5	3.3
Switzerland	60.6	33.9	5.6
United States	72.5	24.6	2.9

Source: *Monthly Digest of Statistics and Employment Gazette*, August 1995

hit home, because today many companies claim to be market-led and customer-focused. However, from our position of working with senior managers and marketing staff from a wide range of companies, we can see that this so-called 'marketing orientation' has, for most of them, not been accomplished. There is more emphasis on rhetoric than transactions. In fact, we estimate that less than one service organization in five has a marketing plan worthy of the name.

One of the major UK banks has recruited hundreds of consumer goods trained marketing personnel, yet still has no observable differential advantage in any of its operations. It is clear that such organizations have confused marketing orientation with selling and promotion. The result is that they have merely succeeded in creating a veneer and a vocabulary of marketing.

Recent research by the author into the marketing effectiveness across a variety of service organizations suggested that many of the companies studied operated well below their potential marketing effectiveness. With organizations paying only lip-service to being marketing orientated, the results suggest a dramatic need for improvement in marketing effectiveness.

What is clear is that many service companies are misdirecting their energies and resources and are thereby failing to create competitive advantage and capitalize on market opportunities.

Practical tip

For marketing to take root, not only must new skills be learned, but often new attitudes have to accompany them. Indeed, many of the barriers that hamper the acceptance of marketing can be attributed to outmoded or inappropriate organizational behaviour.

It is clear that selling services, in the absence of professional marketing, will be largely ineffective. The purpose of this opening section, therefore, is briefly to examine the marketing concept and explore to what extent the marketing of services differs from the marketing of products. We will also look at the diverse range of services in terms of establishing some threads of commonality. In doing this, it makes it possible for the service manager to learn from other companies who may not necessarily be in the same business field.

The marketing concept

The central idea of marketing is to match the organization's capabilities with the needs of customers in order to achieve the objectives of both parties. If this matching process is to be achieved, then the organization has to develop strengths, either from the nature of the services it offers or from the way it exploits these services, in order to provide customer satisfaction.

Figure 14.1 provides a visual summary of the matching process, which is the essence of marketing. As it shows, the environment has an impact not only on the matching process, but also on the 'players'. So, for example, local labour conditions might limit the company in recruiting a workforce with the appropriate skill levels. Equally, changed levels of unemployment can have a drastic impact on customer demand, making it either much greater or much less.

Misunderstandings about marketing

Another area of misunderstanding is the confusion of marketing with sales. Some ill-informed organizations actually believe that marketing is the new word for what was previously called sales. Others perceive marketing to be a mere embellishment of the sales process, a sort of 'selling with knobs on'. That such companies exist is a sad reflection on the standard of management and suggests that marketing education has been less than effec-

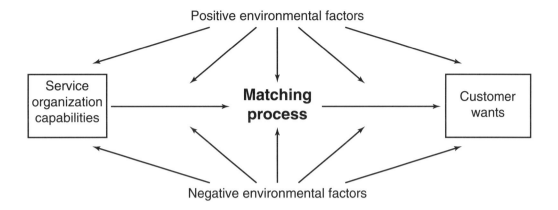

Figure 14.1 *Marketing: a matching process*

tive. By failing to recognize that marketing is designed to provide a longer term strategic, customer-driven orientation rather than a short term tactical triumph, such an organization is certain to under-achieve. Not surprisingly, the chief executive of one such company was overheard to say: 'There is no place for marketing in this company until sales improve!'

A similar misunderstanding occurs which confuses marketing with advertising. Here, gloss is seen as the magic formula to win business. However, without integrating advertising into an overall strategic marketing plan, hard-earned budgets can be completely wasted. Throwing advertising funds at a problem is no way to resolve an underlying issue which might have its roots in the fact that the service on offer has been superseded by another superior offer.

Another misconception is that it is enough to have a high-quality service or product to succeed. Sadly, this has proved not to be the case time and time again. No matter how good the service or product, unless it is appropriately priced and promoted, it will not make any lasting impact.

The final area of confusion is to think that marketing is synonymous with customer service. With misguided enthusiasm, many organizations subscribing to this belief have rushed into organizing 'customer service' pro-

grammes for their staff. Had they bothered to find out what their customers really wanted, perhaps they would have responded differently. For example, train passengers might have travelled in less dirty and cramped conditions, and might have arrived at their destination on time more frequently. Those using banks might have found them open at more convenient times, and with more than one cashier on duty during the busy lunch period (the only time working customers can get there!). Instead, customers have been treated to cosmetic 'smile campaigns', where, regardless of their treatment, they were thanked for doing business with the supplier and encouraged to 'have a nice day'. Most people can recall an incident of this nature.

This is not to say that 'customer care' programmes are not important. What we contend is that, unless the core service and the associated intangibles are right, such programmes will fail. Such programmes ought to be part of the overall integrated set of marketing activities, not a substitute for them. The warning signs are there for those who care to look for them. A recent US study showed that, while 77% of service industry companies had some form of customer service programme in operation, less than 30% of chief executives in these companies believed that it had any significant impact on profit performance.

The nature of services marketing

So far, much of what has been said could be equally applicable to either a product or a service. So, is there anything special about services marketing? Our answer is: 'it all depends'.

A negative answer could be justified because, at one level, the theory of marketing has universal application – the same underlying concerns and principles apply whatever the nature of the business. However, since the nature of some types of services may dictate a need to place more emphasis on certain marketing elements, which in turn could lead to different approaches, a positive answer is also appropriate.

However, it must be borne in mind that the explosive and sometimes erratic growth of the services sector means that there is a diversity of types of businesses, some of which do not readily fit into any neat definition. One of the problems of defining a service is to do with the fact that, whereas a product is seen to be tangible and a service intangible, there are in reality many variations on the degree of tangibility.

Kotler (1996) has identified four categories, varying from a 'pure' product to a 'pure' service. These categories can be placed on a continuum which embraces all possible degrees of intangibility.

Figure 14.2 identifies the continuum of tangible–intangible possibilities. Point (a) on the left-hand side illustrates an offer where there is no service element and so the product is highly tangible. At the other end of the continuum, point (d) illustrates a product which is entirely a service and is therefore highly intangible. Points (b) and (c) show varying mixes of tangibility/intangibility. For example, point (b) illustrates the mix of tangibility and intangibility for a computer company. Computer hardware and programs are highly tangible and can be regarded as commodities; however, the service elements of user training and troubleshooting are largely intangible. Viewed in this way, the difference between a product and a service becomes far less discrete.

Practical tip

The more obvious differences between a product and a service listed below only serve to underline that some differences in marketing approach will often be required:

1. A service cannot be patented and specified with drawings in the same way that a product can.
2. Service quality cannot be guaranteed in the same way as that of a product, which can be controlled accurately at each stage of its manufacture, which in turn is accomplished in controlled conditions.
3. A service cannot be stored on a shelf to be taken down and used at a later time in response to customer demands.
4. An indifferent salesperson does not necessarily obscure the inherent value and quality of a tangible product, whereas with an intangible service the salesperson is often perceived as an integral part of the offer.
5. The value of a product can be assessed at the time of purchase, whereas the true value of a service can only be assessed on its completion. Thus, the purchase of a service is characterized by a much higher component of trust than a product.

It follows that to define services as being confined only to service industries is not strictly true. There is an increasing trend towards differentiating what were once considered to be tangible products by exploiting the intangible service elements of the offer. The service elements can be added to provide unique features matching customer needs. For example, in the highly competitive photocopier business, service has became a major factor in the buying decision. Photocopiers are leased or sold with servic contracts which tie customers to the supplier.

Nevertheless, it will be difficult to proceed without attempting to define a service in some way. Therefore, while recognizing that any definition might prove to be unduly restrictive, and that somewhere a service may exist which does not conform to what we say, our definition is:

A service is an activity which has some element of intangibility associated with it. It involves some interaction with customers or property in their possession, and does not result in a transfer of ownership. A change of condition may occur and provision of the service may or may not be closely associated with a physical product.

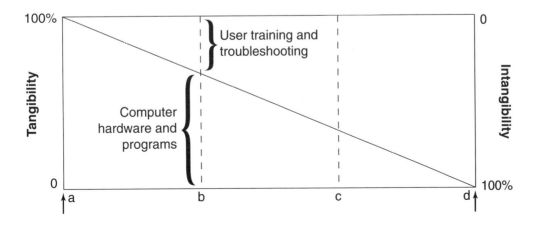

Figure 14.2 *Continuum of tangible–intangible possibilities*

Classification of services

Lovelock (1983) developed a classification framework which yields valuable strategic marketing insights in response to five crucial questions.

Lovelock's five questions (and associated sub-questions) clearly raise a number of interesting and important issues for the service provider. The advantage of this particular method of classification is that it can cut across service industry barriers, thus enabling comparisons to be made with, and lessons to be learned from, service companies in other business fields. They also highlight key issues that need to be addressed in the marketing plans of service organizations.

The strategic value of services in manufacturing

As was shown earlier, the 100% tangible product is a rarity. Apart from a few commodity items or foodstuffs, most products have an element of service attached to them.

Practical tip

You may be able to improve performance by answering the following questions:

1. What is the nature of the 'service' act?
   - What benefits does it provide?
   - Does the customer need to be present as the service is delivered?
   - Is the customer changed as a result of the service?
   - Does the customer have to come to the service deliverer, or can it be provided at home?
2. What style of relationship does the service organization have with its customers (e.g. 'member', informal)?
   - Can anything be done to move 'informal' into 'member' relationship (e.g. random cinema visitors become cinema club members; regular tool hirers get a privilege card; etc.)?
   - Where can there be trade-offs between pricing and usage rates (e.g. season ticket holders for theatre or sports entertainment)?
3. How much room is there for customization and judgement?
   - Is it desirable to limit the degree of customization and thereby benefit from 'standardization' and economies of scale?
   - Should customization be increased in order to reach a wider range of customers?
   - Should services be simplified so that less judgement is required by salespeople?
   - Should the service be updated in order to capitalize on the expertise of staff?
4. What is the nature of supply and demand for the service?
   - How susceptible to peaks and troughs is the service?
   - To what extent can peaks be coped with?
   - Should alternative strategies be adopted to create capacity?
   - Should alternative strategies be adopted for introducing differential pricing?
   - Should a new mix of strategies be adopted, involving both capacity and pricing?
5. How is the service delivered?
   - Should the service be delivered at a single site or through multiple outlets?
   - What is the most convenient type of transaction for customers?
   - Can suitable intermediaries be used to achieve multiple outlets (e.g. franchises)?

Practical tip

Many manufacturers have been quick to realize that, although their basic product might be in the 'me too' category, they can bring about some differentiation from the way they manage the service element of the product. Examine ways you could do likewise.

As manufacturing companies become more sophisticated and as technological advantages become ever more transitory, services begin to represent an area of significant profit potential. This trend has even earned itself a new piece of jargon, 'servitization of business', coined by Vandermerwe and Rada (1988). Not surprisingly, manufacturing is now looking more and more at the service industry in order to learn from its experience. As a result, what was once a clear divide between two quite different types of businesses is becoming increasingly blurred.

This section on the nature of services was prompted by a seemingly simple question about the difference between marketing a product and a service. As we have seen, not only is it difficult to define where a product finishes and a service begins, but even the difference between manufacturing as an industry and the traditional notion of a service industry is becoming ever less clear.

This discussion was important, because it should help the reader to have a much clearer idea about how a business should be defined in terms of the intangibility of its service and the other characteristics that give it a particular identify. Knowing this makes it easier not only to recognize how the marketing process can be best adapted for particular circumstances, but it also provides an essential backcloth for the later section on selling.

The marketing mix

Earlier, marketing was described as being a process which matches the supplier's capabilities with the customer's wants. We also saw that this matching process took place in a business environment which could pose

Checklist 14.1

The types of services that can feature in an expanded 'product package' are:

- Training
- Consultancy
- Service contracts
- Customization
- Fast-moving troubleshooting
- Help with financing
- Special delivery arrangements
- Stockholding or inventory control for the customer
- No-quibble guarantees

threats for the supplier, but which also created opportunities.

The marketing mix is, in effect, the 'flexible coupling' between the supplier and customer which facilities the matching process. Traditionally it was said to consist of four elements, namely:

- **Product**: The product or service being offered.
- **Price**: The price or fees charged and the terms associated with its sale.
- **Promotion**: The communications programme associated with marketing the product or service.
- **Place**: The distribution and logistics involved in making the product/service available.

From this, the short-hand term for the marketing mix became the 4Ps, for reasons which are obvious. However, it must be remembered that within each 'P' is subsumed a number of subelements pertinent to that heading. So, for example, promotion will include not only face-to-face communications provided by contact staff, but also indirect communications such as advertising, sales promotions, publications and direct mail.

Services and the marketing mix ▄

In recent years, those charged with developing the application of marketing in the service sector have questioned whether the 4Ps approach to the marketing mix was sufficiently comprehensive (for example see Booms and Bitner 1981). As a result, there has been a marked shift of opinion which now advocates that the original concept should be expanded, as shown below. This new mix is more appropriate for service businesses and ensures that important elements are not overlooked.

Added to the original 4Ps are:

- **Customer service**: As customers demand higher levels of service, this element

becomes a competitive weapon with which a company can differentiate itself. In the longer term it helps to build closer and more enduring relationships with customers.
- **People**: Since people are an essential element in the production and delivery of services, the quality of the service is largely determined by the quality and behaviour of the company's staff. This is particularly true in respect of those whose jobs involve high levels of customer contact.
- **Processes**: The procedures, routines and policies which influence how a service is created and delivered to customers can clearly be instrumental in determining how 'customer friendly' the company is perceived to be.

This expanded marketing mix will be found to be robust enough to cover most service marketing situations. Of course, with the diversity of services which exist, there could still be a few situations where it might be necessary to vary the constituent elements of this new marketing mix, but they will be relatively rare.

By introducing the marketing mix into Figure 14.1, it becomes possible to arrive at a far more accurate representation of how the marketing process for services really works (Figure 14.3). The output of the supplying company results from the effort it puts into the marketing mix.

Perhaps the service product provided is slightly different, perhaps the financial transaction is varied from segment to segment, perhaps the promotion is different with, say,

---

Practical tip

Just as a master chef will prepare food to a different recipe for customers he or she knows, so will the intelligent marketing organization split its customers into segments and provide a different marketing mix best suited to the needs of each one.

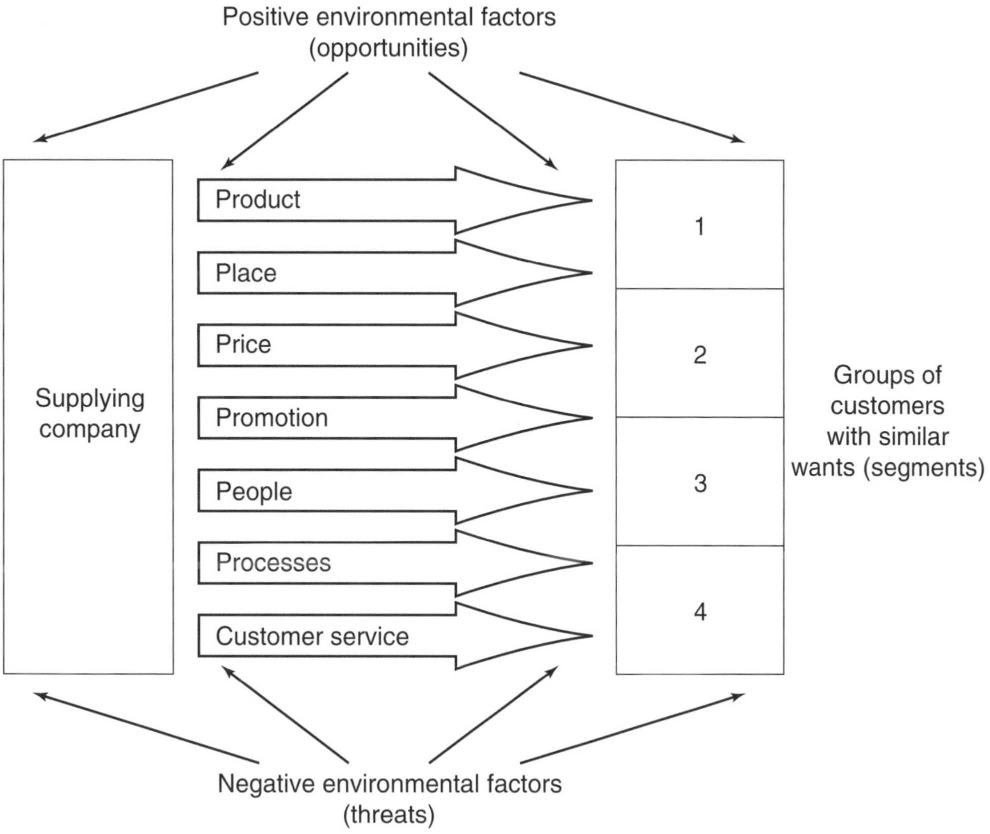

Positive environmental factors
(opportunities)

Negative environmental factors
(threats)

Supplying
company

Product

Place

Price

Promotion

People

Processes

Customer service

1

2

3

4

Groups of
customers
with similar
wants (segments)

Figure 14.3 *The marketing process*

one segment influenced by indirect communications and another by face-to-face methods, perhaps the place element of the mix is
different for each segment, or perhaps it is
customer service which is differentiated.

There is in reality a tremendous range of
options open to the marketer who chooses to
explore all of the marketing mix possibilities,
but of course the whole marketing process
really hinges on how accurately the wants of
customers are known and how astutely they
are grouped into segments which meet the
following criteria:

- Segments are adequate in size to provide
the company with a good return for its effort.
- Members of each segment have a high
degree of similarity, yet are distinct from
the rest of the market.
- Criteria for describing the segments are

relevant to the purchase situation.
- Segments are capable of being reached
through communications.

It goes without saying that a company should
not try to work with too many different segments. There is a danger that some will be too
small but, more importantly, the company
will not be capable of managing its dealings
with too many different segments without
diluting its efforts.

Providing an organization has a customer-
driven philosophy, driven from the board
downwards, and has an infrastructure and
the necessary capability to devise a professional marketing strategy, the personal selling element of the organization will have a
chance of succeeding.

We can now turn our attention to selling a
service.

> **Practical tip**
>
> Like an individual, a company cannot be all things to all people. It must learn to focus on its strengths and on markets where it has the best chance of succeeding.

Salesforce strategy

In this section, we will explore the role of direct selling in the marketing mix, and the sales process itself. For convenience, and to avoid needless repetition, the words 'salesperson' and 'he' have been used. The author recognizes that salespeople are frequently women and no offence is intended.

How important is personal selling?

Most companies have an organized salesforce long before they introduce a formal marketing activity of the kind described throughout this book. In spite of this, salesforce management traditionally has been a neglected area of marketing management.

There are several possible reasons for this. One is that not all marketing and product managers have had experience in a personal selling or sales management role. Consequently, these managers often underestimate the importance of efficient personal selling.

Another reason for the neglect of salesforce management is that sales personnel themselves sometimes encourage an unhelpful distinction between sales and marketing by depicting themselves as 'the sharp end'. After all, isn't there something slightly daring about dealing with real customers as opposed to sitting in an office surrounded by marketing surveys, charts and plans? Such reasoning is dangerous, because, as we have seen, unless a good deal of careful marketing planning has taken place before the salesperson makes his effort to persuade the customer to place an

order, the probability of a successful sale is much reduced. The suggested distinction between marketing 'theory' and sales 'practice' is further invalidated when we consider that profitable sales depend not just on individual customers and individual products, but on groups of customers (that is, market segments) and on the supportive relationship of products to each other (that is, a carefully planned service portfolio). Another factor to be taken into account in this context is the constant need for the organization to think in terms of where future sales will be coming from rather than to concentrate solely on present services, customers and problems.

Investigation of many European salesforces over the last decade has provided evidence that there remains an alarming lack of planning and professionalism in many cases. Frequently, salespeople have little idea of which products and which groups of customers to concentrate on, have too little knowledge about competitive activity, do not plan presentations well, rarely talk to customers in terms of benefits, make too little effort to close the sale and make many calls without any clear objectives. Even worse, marketing management is rarely aware that this important and expensive element of the marketing mix is not being managed effectively. The fact that many organizations have separate departments and directors for the marketing and sales activities increases the likelihood of such failures of communication.

Although its importance varies according to circumstances, in many businesses the salesforce is the most important element of the marketing mix. Personal selling is widely used in many service industries where customers are looking for very specific benefits. Insurance companies, for example, do use media advertising but rely for most of their sales on personal selling. Customers for insurance policies almost invariably need to discuss which policy would best fit their particular needs and circumstances. It is the task of the salesperson to explain the choices available and to suggest the most appropriate policy.

Practical tip

Check out who is likely to be involved in the buying decision by considering these factors:

1. The cost of the service – the higher the cost, the higher in the organization will the purchasing decision be made (see Table 14.3).
2. The 'newness' of the service – the relative novelty of the service will pose an element of commercial risk for an organization. A new and untried proposition will require support at a senior management level, whereas a routine, non-risky service can be handled at a low level.
3. The complexity of the service – the more complex the service offered, the more technical implications have to be understood within the client company. Several specialist managers might be required to give their approval before the transaction can be completed.

Recent surveys show that more money is being spent by companies on their sales forces than on advertising and sales promotion combined. Personal selling, then, is a vital and expensive element in the marketing mix.

The solution to the problem of poor sales-force management can only be found in the recognition that personal selling is indeed a crucial part of the marketing process and that it must be planned and considered as carefully as any other element. Indeed, it is an excellent idea for the manager responsible for marketing to go out into the territory for a few days each year and attempt to persuade customers to place orders. It is a good way of finding out what customers really think of the organization's marketing policies!

Selling to an organization

As we have already indicated, personal selling can most usefully be seen as part of the communications mix. (Other common elements of the communications mix, it will be remembered, are advertising, sales promotion, public relations, direct mail and exhibitions.) In order to determine the precise role of personal selling in its communications mix, the company must identify the major

Table 14.3 *Responsibility for financial expenditure: level at which buying decisions are taken*

Level of expenditure	Board (collective), %	Individual director, %	Departmental manager, %	Lower management clerical, %
Over £50,000	88	11	2	–
Up to £50,000	70	25	4	Less than 0.5
Up to £5,000	29	55	14	2
Up to £2,500	18	54	24	4
Up to £500	4	31	52	14

Source: How British Industry Buys, a survey conducted by Cranfield School of Management for the *Financial Times*, January, 1984

influences in each purchase decision and find out what information they are likely to need at different stages of the buying process. Most institutional buying decisions can involve a large number of people and take a considerable amount of time. Selling to an organization can sometimes prove to be a complex process because it is possible for a number of different people to become involved at the customer end. Although theoretically only one of these is the buyer, in practice he might not be allowed to make any decision to purchase until others with technical expertise or hierarchical responsibility have given their approval.

All those involved in the buying decision are known as the decision-making unit (DMU), and it is important for the salesperson to identify the DMU in all current and prospective customer companies.

A way of anticipating who would be involved in the decision-making processes in a company is to consider the sales transaction from the buyer's point of view. It has been recognized that the process can be split up into a number of distinct steps known as 'buy phases'.

By way of summarizing this section on selling to industry, it can be demonstrated that the successful salesperson needs to be aware of all these things when he approaches a buyer acting on behalf of an organization.

Checklist 14.2
Buy phases*

1. *Problem identification* – a problem is identified or anticipated and a general solution worked out. For example, the marketing planning department find that they have inadequate information about sales records and costs. They need better information made available on the computer.
2. *Problem definition* – the problem is examined in more detail in order to grasp the dimensions and hence the nature of the ultimate choice of solution. Taking our example further, investigation shows that the original software system was not devised with the current marketing planning requirements in mind. A new system is required which can also provide the option for the inclusion of other new data.
3. *Solution specification* – the various technical requirements are listed and a sum of money is allocated to cover the cost of investing in new software.
4. *Search* – a search is made for potential suppliers. In this case, those with the capability of devising a 'tailor made' system to meet the above requirements.
5. *Assessment* – proposals from interested suppliers are assessed and evaluated.
6. *Selection* – a supplier is selected and probably final details are negotiated prior to the next step.
7. *Agreement* – a contract/agreement is signed.
8. *Monitoring* – the service is monitored in terms of meeting installation deadlines and performance claims.

* This section of the text owes much to the original research conducted by the Marketing Service Institute in the USA under the guidance of Patrick J. Robinson.

He needs to know and understand:

1. The relative influence of the buyer in the context of the particular service being offered.
2. What constitutes the DMU in the buying company.
3. How the buying process works.
4. The pressures on the buying decision-maker.

With this information in his possession he is in a better position to plan his work and conduct himself appropriately when face to face with the buying decision-maker(s). Exactly how this information is used will be covered later.

Selling a service to individuals

So far we have only looked at selling to organizations. Is selling to individuals any different? Well, to a large extent, no!

The individual will go through the same set of buy phases as the large organization, the only difference being that it all takes place in his head rather than being institutionalized as a system.

At first sight, the individual is the DMU, but be warned. If the service you offer is going to be relatively costly, as could be the case for specially designed house extensions, or demand a long term level of commitment from the buyer, as in the case of insurance or private health schemes, then undoubtedly other people will be involved in the buying decision. A spouse, a partner or a friend will inevitably be the confidant that the buyer turns to when faced with such a big decision.

Except when the service is either inexpensive or routine, the concept of the individual buyer is something of a myth. It is easy to see why, for the individual buyer is subjected to almost as many pressures as his counterpart in an organization and he welcomes the opportunity to share the burden.

The only possible difference in selling to an individual rather than to an organization is likely to be in the area of what is perceived as the probable solution to the client problem. In an organization, because of the number of people involved in the decision-making processes, the preferred solution will tend to be dictated by more logical and practical criteria. It is not difficult to understand why this should be so. Most managers will wish to demonstrate to their colleagues how rational they are and therefore will tend to present factual, reasoned arguments for proceeding with a proposed purchase.

The individual, without the psychological constraints of satisfying others, will respond to a problem in a more natural way. His choice of solution is just as likely to be made on the basis of feelings as logic. His ultimate choice is likely to be determined by a unique and personal combination of experience and personality type.

Buy classes

Whether or not the salesperson is selling to an individual or an organization, he can divide the decision-making process of his prospects into what are termed buy classes. There are three types of buy class:

1. **New buy** – In effect all the foregoing discussion has focused on the new buy category. It is here that those people who make up the DMU are fully exercised as the buy phases unfold. It is in the new buy class that the needs of all decision-makers need to be met and influenced by the salesperson. Not surprisingly, this takes time and so it is not unusual for a lengthy period to elapse between the initial discussion and landing the contract.
2. **Straight re-buy** – Once the salesperson has had the opportunity to demonstrate how the service can help the customer, further purchases of the service do not generally require such a rigorous examination at all of the buy phases. In fact, should the customer merely want a repeat purchase of the same service, then his only concerns are likely to be around issues such as: Has the price been held to the same level as before? Will the standard of the service be unchanged? Can it be provided at a spe-

cific time? Such issues can generally be resolved by negotiation with the buyer.

3. **Modified re-buy** – Sometimes a modification in the service might be necessary. It might be that the supplier wants to up-date the service and provide better performance by using different methods or equipment. Alternatively, it could be the customer who calls for some form of modification from the original purchase. Whatever the origin, all or some of the buy phases will have to be re-examined, and again the salesperson will have to meet and influence the relevant members of the DMU.

Practical tip

1. A modified re-buy reactivates and strengthens the relationship with the various members of the customer's DMU. To move from a straight to a modified re-buy, reduce the risk of change for the buyer.

2. The more closely a supplier can match his service to the customer's needs (and remember, this matching only comes about as a result of a mutual learning, as communication and trust develop between the supplier and the customer), the more committed the customer becomes to the service.

The higher the commitment the customer has to the particular service and the supplier, the more difficult it becomes for competitors to break in.

Figure 14.4 is a useful matrix for gathering all this information together.

What does all this mean to the salesperson?

So far in this chapter, all attention has been focused on the customer end of the buying

transaction. We have looked at phases, DMUs, buy classes and the pressure on buyers, be they individuals or representatives of organizations.

How does the salesperson use this information to advantage when selling the service?

Clearly, a good understanding of the following can assist the salesperson in three important areas of his work:

1. Identifying the buyer
2. Preparing a sales strategy
3. Clarifying his role in complex sales situations

Identifying the buyer

Recognizing that there is a DMU is an important first step for the salesperson, but having done this, it is essential to identify who actually has the power to make the purchase.

Failure to do so will result in much wasted time and frustration. No matter how persuasive the arguments for buying a service, if the salesperson is not reaching the key decision-maker then all his efforts might be in vain. Finding this person is too important to be left to chance and yet many salespeople fail to do this. Sometimes they have just not done enough research about the company in order to get an accurate picture of how it operates, its personnel and the key issues that they are concerned with. Checklist 14.3 will provide a number of ideas for remedying this particular failing.

Preparing a sales strategy

By understanding the buying process it becomes possible for the salesperson to:

1. Recognize the buying situation and the stage it is at.
2. Plan his response to this accordingly.
3. Identify those people involved in the buying decision.
4. Calculate what benefits the service provides for each of these people.

CUSTOMER ANALYSIS FORM

Salesperson _____
Products _____

Customer _____
Address _____
Telephone number _____

Date of analysis _____
Date of reviews _____

Buy class: new buy   straight re-buy   modified re-buy

Member of decision making unit (DMU)		Production	Sales & marketing	Research & development	Finance & accounts	Purchasing	Data processing	Other
Buy phase	Name							
1 Recognizes need or problem and works out general solution								
2 Works out characteristics and quantity of what is needed								
3 Prepares detailed specification								
4 Searches for and locates potential sources of supply								
5 Analyses and evaluates tenders, plans, products								
6 Selects supplier								
7 Places order								
8 Checks and tests products								

Factors for consideration
1 price
2 performance
3 availability
4 back-up service
5 reliability of supplier
6 other users' experience
7 guarantees and warranties
8 payment terms, credit or discount
9 other, e.g. past purchases, prestige, image, etc.

Figure 14.4 Customer analysis form. Adapted from Robinson, J., Farris, C.W. and Wind, Y. (1967) Industrial Marketing and Creative Buying. Allyn and Bacon

Checklist 14.3
Basic research

1. The company
   - What sort of company is it and what is its business?
   - How big is it?
   - Is it privately owned or part of a group?
   - Is the company profitable?
   - Is it expanding or contracting?
   - What dealings have you had with this company in the past?
   - Does it have a traditional or modern image?
2. Its products and markets
   - What does the company make?
   - Alternatively, what is the range of services it offers?
   - What is the company's standing in its markets (e.g. is it a leader)?
   - Are its markets expanding or contracting?
   - Are new products/services being developed?
   - Is the current business climate supportive or damaging to either the company or its customers?
   - Who are its strongest competitors?
3. Its personnel
   - Who is responsible for buying your type of service?
   - What sort of people are they?
   - Who else is likely to be involved in the buying decision?
   - What do you know about them?
   - Who has the real power?
4. Its systems
   - How does it purchasing system work?
   - Who are the key administrators of the system?
   - How does its invoicing system work (to facilitate the financial transaction)?
5. Its suppliers
   - Has it used your type of service before?
   - Who are the current suppliers?
   - How have they performed?
   - What is the range and price of the service provided?

Not all of this information will be readily available, but it should be possible to assemble most of it by using the following sources:

- your own company records of previous transactions;
- other salespeople;
- other customers:
- telephone enquiries to the company;

Checklist 14.3 *(Continued)*

- informal discussions with gatekeepers, receptionists, van drivers, etc.;
- national and local newspapers;
- trade press;
- the company's own brochures and promotional material;
- chambers of trade;
- trade directories;
- exhibition catalogues;
- Kompass;
- Kelly;
- Yellow Pages;
- Extel cards;
- trade associations;
- etc.

5. Decide how best to influence these people and thereby influence the buying decision.
6. Attempt to convert straight re-buy situations into modified re-buys in such a way as to provide added benefits for the customer.

Although at first sight this might appear to be a fairly logical and straightforward process, in practice it is not because in meeting and trying to influence the various people involved in the buying decision, the salesperson has to play a number of different roles.

The salesperson's role

In order to achieve his objectives the salesperson has to be ready to switch from one role to another. Fortunately, because most people in the DMU have quite specific and individual requirements, it is often possible for the salesperson to act out one role at a time. Here are some of the most common roles.

Information officer

Research has shown that a very large number of companies rely on salespeople to keep them up-dated about new materials, developments in technology and many other aspects of their industry. While some services might lend themselves to advertising, word-of-mouth still seems to be the most potent way of passing on information.

How the salesperson prepares and equips himself for this role will have a profound bearing on his credibility and power to influence certain parts of the DMU.

Consultant

Often information is not enough. There are times when the salesperson will be called upon to perform as a consultant; for example, to help resolve a problem of the client company, to help the buyer make a decision or to influence upwards in his own organization.

To fulfil the consultant role effectively the salesperson must work at building up a relationship with the client which is based on trust and respect. He will not rush into providing solutions, but instead will ask a lot of questions designed to establish the exact nature of the client's needs.

He will listen carefully to the replies and only after analysing them will he recommend the action to be taken by the client. It follows that the salesperson must have an excellent grasp of all the services that can be provided and a creative imagination to tailor them to fit the client's needs.

Salesperson

An awful lot of salespeople get so enamoured with the previous two roles, they forget that their prime task is to sell a service. Somehow, the more professional or technical the service, the more the salesperson is trapped into thinking that he is revered for the specialist knowledge he has. Unless he is in a seller's market, then he could not be more wrong.

Only a fortunate few companies can offer a unique service that cannot be copied or substituted. All the rest have to face up to competition. It is not surprising then, that the old sales axiom still applies to most situations. 'When all things are equal, the orders usually go to the salesperson with the greatest *selling* skills.'

Territory planning and obtaining the interview

Let us now turn our attention briefly to the sales process itself, starting with territory planning and obtaining the interview.

The salesperson must plan his life to ensure that maximum time is spent selling and minimum time is spent on travelling, administration, planning and other activities. A systematic approach to territory planning is needed to ensure that all customers receive regular visits.

Although some calls will be made 'on spec', the majority will be by appointment. Appointments between buyers and salespeople are usually arranged on the telephone. Thorough preparation is needed before the call, to enable the salesperson to decide who is to be spoken to, what is the objective of the call and what lever should be used to arouse the prospect's interest. It is not always easy to get through to the prospect or, once connected, to persuade them to agree to the interview. There is a range of techniques that salespeople can use to persuade the telephone operator and the prospect's secretary to connect them with the prospect, and for persuading the prospect to agree to an interview.

The salesperson should always try to suggest the times for his appointments. This may enable him to fit four or five appointments a day into a schedule that is economical in terms of travel and efficient in the use of time.

Opening techniques

The salespeople will only succeed if they handle sales interviews effectively. They must establish clear objectives for each call and have a plan of how they intend to achieve these objectives.

A useful sequence to follow in any call is the 'ABC' sequence in order to achieve the required objectives. The salesperson should arrest the prospect's attention (A), sell benefits (B) and move to a close (C). The sales offer has to be pre-planned and the necessary facts, information and supporting sales-kit of literature, data and other aids needed to achieve the interview objectives must be assembled.

It is essential to arrive in plenty of time for an interview. The salesperson must be neat and tidy and he must pre-plan his opening remarks in order to create a good impression from the outset and secure the client's immediate interest. Pleasantries and social chat should be kept to the minimum. The salesperson may open by asking a question, giving new information, quoting a reference, using a sales aid, demonstrating something or linking his visit with some previous business. The aim must be to arrest the prospect's interest from the very outset. Since many services are 'people-orientated' the dress and demeanour of the salesperson may provide important cues to the customer abut the quality of the service that can be expected.

Benefit selling

It is obvious that customers do not buy products or services, but rather they seek to acquire benefits. Every product or service has its features, but the potential customer is only interested in the benefits that will accrue from these features. Since people buy products and services for what they will do for them – that is, the benefits of having those products or services – the salesperson must sell these benefits rather than the features.

For the salesperson, a simple formula to ensure this customer-orientated approach is adopted is always to use the phrase 'which means that' to link a feature to the benefit it brings. The salesperson must undertake a detailed analysis to underline the full menu of benefits he has to offer his customers. He should seek to identify standard benefits A (benefits that arise directly from the features of what he offers), company benefits (benefits offered by the salesperson's product or service over those of his competitors). A 'benefit analysis form' should be used to ensure a methodical analysis is conducted and proof should be given to substantiate every claim.

Dealing with objections

The buyer will almost invariably raise objections during the sales interview. An objection is a statement or question that puts an obstacle in the path leading towards closure of the sale. A buyer may raise a fundamental objection when he cannot see a need for the product or service on offer. He may raise standard objections when he recognizes his need but either wishes to delay a decision or needs further convincing before concluding a deal.

The salesperson should always seek to forestall objections before they are raised.

This can be done by identifying possible objections and 'answering them' in this offer. When faced with a fundamental objection, the salesperson has to sell the need for the service in question rather than the benefits entailed. There is a range of techniques for dealing with standard objections but, if the buyer continues to raise objections without actually concluding the interview, there may be a hidden objection. It is often possible to discover what this is by asking an incomplete question, such as 'and your other reason for not deciding is...?'

The salesperson should not fear a price objection. This can usually be overcome by talking in terms of value rather than cost. Furthermore, the salesperson is sometimes able to negotiate the price in order to secure an order.

Closing techniques

The sale is closed when the buyer makes a firm commitment to place an order. The salesperson should constantly look for opportunities to close the sale.

The buyer will often show interest, make committing statements and ask questions; these are buying signals, which the salesperson should follow up by asking a question in order to confirm that he has correctly interpreted the buying signals.

Trial closes should be used throughout the sales offer to test the buyer's reactions, uncover objections, determine buyer interest and speed the sale. Trial closes also help the salesperson retain the initiative and accumulate small commitments from the buyer. The salesperson should use direct and indirect questions to obtain buyer commitment. It is sometimes possible to offer alternatives that lead the buyer into stating a preference, which, once expressed, can pave the way to an immediate close. Other opportunities to close can be created by the summary technique, giving a quotation or by offering a concession. *The salesperson will only achieve a final close if he asks for an order.*

The successful close is the culmination of a great deal of preparation, planning and hard work. It is the moment that makes it all worthwhile. But the close is not the end of the matter, it is just a step in a continuous process. The salesperson must always remember that his objective is not only to close the sale, but also to open up a lasting relationship with the customer. In the final analysis, this is what makes a successful salesperson. Relationships should not be jeopardized by the inappropriate use of closing techniques such as when the decision as to which service provider to use is taken in committee.

Negotiator

Sometimes even getting the customer to say yes is not enough. In these days of information technology and ever-increasing buyer sophistication, the client company might be more discriminating than ever before. On hearing the words 'Yes, I will buy your service if you will just agree to...' from a buyer, the unwary salesperson is so pleased at getting the sale that he fails to grasp the significance of the end of the sentence. If he is not careful he is giving away extras to the buyer, in the shape of special conditions or terms, which can have the effect of wiping out any margins made on the sale.

Thus negotiation is quite different from selling. Negotiation begins when each party realizes that the other has something they want. The art of manoeuvring to get the best deal has sometimes been likened to getting a see-saw to balance. The relative weight and position of each party has a significant bearing on the tilt of the see-saw.

The salesperson has to be able to exert influence on his side by knowing all about the relative costs and margins, his services, the effect of volume, price and sales mix on costs and also how competitors stand by comparison. Using this information intelligently he will perhaps stand a chance of negotiating successfully.

But it has to be recognized that negotiating skills are not the same as selling skills. There are many differences and one of the most obvious is the fact that the selling process follows a linear sequence, as this section has indicated.

Negotiation follows no such pattern, indeed, there is evidence to show that good negotiators do not follow a linear pattern, but move from one issue to another in no particular pre-conceived sequence.

Whatever the role requirements, the successful salesperson will be capable of recognizing what the situation requires and adopting the appropriate behaviour.

Advantages of personal selling

- It is a two-way form of communication, giving the prospective purchaser the opportunity to ask questions of the salesperson about the product or service.
- The sales message itself can be made more flexible and therefore can be more closely tailored to the needs of individual customers.
- The salesmen and women can use in-depth product knowledge to relate their messages to the perceived needs of the buyers and to deal with objections as they arise.
- Most important of all, the salespeople can ask for an order and perhaps negotiate on price, delivery or special requirements.

Once an order has been obtained from a customer, and there is a high probability of a re-buy occurring, the salesperson's task changes from persuasion to reinforcement. All communications at this stage should contribute to underlining the wisdom of the purchase.

Clearly, in different markets different weighting is given to the various forms of communication available. However, in many service businesses, personal selling remains a key element of commercial success. This chapter has outlined some of the basic principles in ensuring that it is a highly successful and cost effective element of the marketing mix.

References

Booms, B.H. and Bitner, M.J. (1981) Marketing Strategies and Organisational Structure for Service Firms. In *Marketing Services* (J. H. Donnelly and W. R. George, eds). American Marketing Association Proceedings Series, Chicago, p. 48.

Kotler, P. (1996) *Marketing Management: Analysis, Planning and Control*, (9th Edition), Englewood Cliffs, N.J.: Prentice Hall.

Lovelock, C.H. (1983) Classifying Services to Gain Strategic Marketing Insights, *Journal of Marketing*, **47**, Summer, 9–20.

Vandermerwe, S. and Rada, J. (1988) Servitization of Business: Adding Value by Adding Service, *European Management Journal*, **6**, 314–23.

Further reading

Payne, A.F.T. (1993) *The Essence of Services Marketing*. Englewood Cliffs, N.J.: Prentice Hall.

McDonald, M.H.B. (1988) *How to Sell a Service*. Oxford: Butterworth-Heinemann.

15

Business-to-business selling

Julian J. Gibas, Automotive Business Development
Daragh O'Reilly, University of Bradford

 The objective of this chapter is to help the business-to-business salesperson work out a practical and successful selling strategy for the markets in which he/she operates. The chapter starts with a definition of business-to-business markets. It then looks at key developments in organizational purchasing in the past decade, and then reviews a number of these changes in more detail to set the scene. It then discusses the importance of seeing both sides of the business-to-business exchange, and the critical difference between transactions and relationships in a business-to-business context. Following this, a number of new buyer analysis frameworks are introduced to take account of buyer power, buyer–seller interaction and strategic buying considerations. The discussion is based on three principles: the salesperson needs to understand the buyer, the salesperson needs to think strategically and sales-oriented marketing is more important than marketing-oriented sales! Finally, as the retail buying aspects of business-to-business marketing have been covered in Chapter 6 on trade marketing, this chapter will tend to deal more (although not exclusively) with industrial marketing – sales of products and services in manufacturing operations.

What is 'business-to-business'? ▬

Once an organization has decided to outsource a component, product, sub-assembly or service and not to originate or make it itself, it is in the business-to-business market. Business-to-business selling is about servicing organizations' needs for products.

This type of market is characterized by:

- **Geographical concentration**: Prospects and customers are frequently clustered around specific locations, for example close to a source of raw materials, labour supply or centre of research excellence. They may even be concentrated together because the desire to take advanatge of state incentives, such as favourable tax regimes!

- **Relative fewness and largeness of customers**: Business-to-business prospects may number as few as six (e.g. leading food multiples) or as many as three thousand (e.g. trade moulders), but never into the millions of prospects which are to be found in a mass consumer market. Their buying potential reflects their often huge size.

- **Professional buyers**: Salespeople are dealing with highly trained purchasing executives who have a clear understanding of their needs and objectives and, in many cases, a better awareness of competitors' specific offerings.
- **Derived demand**: The ultimate source of demand is often at consumer level and far removed from the business-to-business buyer–seller interaction. For example, the supplier of sand to a TV tube plant is separated from the TV viewer by the transactions between the tube plant and the TV plant and between the TV plant and the retailer. In this type of situation, forecasting of demand and organization of operations schedules can be extremely difficult.
- **Level of buyer investment**: The amount of money to be invested in the goods, products or services supplied can be quite considerable; consequently there is a bigger risk to the buyer, as well as the need to look beyond the immediate transaction to the broader relationship. The buyer may be purchasing, for example, a major system reconfiguration, a new production line or a different logistics service, with all the complexities that these entail.
- **Wide fluctuations in demand**: The loss of a single contract can often mean a substantial drop in the supplier's revenue, which can be difficult to replace; as we shall see, there are many reaons why buyers can and do shift work around, often leaving suppliers with the challenge of redeploying or shedding labour if they cannot replace the lost contracts. Likewise, opening on a new customer account can have major implications for a supplier's resource commitments.
- **Importance of personal selling**: The key method of communication with customers and prospects is personal selling. Because the salesperson is often trying to persuade

targets to award or renew a big-ticket contract, he/she has to think strategically on his/her feet.
- **Types of exchange**: The goods exchanged in business-to-business transactions include raw materials, manufactured products, services, components, sub-assemblies, construction services, capital goods and maintenance, repair and operating (MRO) supplies, also termed consumables. In short, any purchase by a retailer, manufacturer, intermediary, government agency, charity, broadcasting or any other type of organization qualifies as a business-to-business market exchange.

Key developments in purchasing ∎

A good salesperson should know his/her prospects and customers thoroughly. In line with this maxim, this section deals with recent trends in business-to-business buying and illustrates the particular challenges facing business developers today. Over the past decade or so, changes in practice include the following:

- shift in large organizations from making to buying-in
- globalization of markets
- buying is now a strategic board-level issue
- decentralization of procurement power within some organizations
- team buying
- increased buyer professionalism
- increased buyer proactivity
- supply base reduction
- new models of buyer–supplier relations and alliances
- vendor rating and benchmarking
- lean production
- flexible manufacturing practices
- stabilization of production schedules
- widespread use of quality standards, practices, systems and team structures
- supplier location closer to manufacturers
- JIT supply arrangements

- open book costing
- multi-functional communication between buyer and seller
- simultaneous engineering and design processes.

Practical tip

It is often a useful exercise to sit down and list briefly the major changes in your customers' negotiating, evaluating and operational scheduling processes over the past, say, three years. By comparing and contrasting the actions of different customers, you can get an accurate pen-picture of how things are changing in your marketplace.

We will now take a closer look at a number of the above developments: buying as a strategic issue, supply base design, type of relationship and globalization of business-to-business buying.

Buying as a strategic issue

Taking up the first point above, that buying has now become an activity with strategic significance, it is important that salespeople be aware of this strategic dimension. All organizations with a 'good practice' approach to buying will go through a strategic purchasing process which usually involves the stages given in Checklist 5.1.

In other words, before the salesperson does any prospecting or calling, his prospects are increasingly likely to have gone through a complex process which locks their whole buying strategy into the overall strategic direction of the company. In the light of this, it would be unwise to place all one's faith in cold calling or the latest product brochure and much more preferable to do some serious thinking about what business exactly is one in!

Supply base design

A key decision for the purchasing organization as far as the design of the supply base is concerned is whether to single-source or multi-source.

Traditionally, multiple sourcing was regarded as a route to the best sourcing value. Making suppliers compete with each other spread the risks of buying and supply and gave the buyer control of costing. Nowadays, however, when many major corporations have slashed their supply bases by significant amounts, e.g. Rank Xerox from 5000 to 300, single sourcing is considered a safer risk, because closer co-operation can lead to more reliable logistics and better design and engineering quality.

As far as the organization of the supply base is concerned, Japanese corporations in the automotive, electronics and office equipment sectors were shown in the 1980s to have hierarchical arrangements of the supply base, with a relatively small number of first-tier suppliers, often systems makers, being responsible for second- and lower-tier suppliers, such as component makers. This system of supply base organization contained many examples of single sourcing, especially where the supply item required heavy tooling investment.

Type of relationship

With supply base reduction, OEM (original equipment manufacturer) and other buyers have been able to devote more time to the development, deepening and strengthening of supplier relationships. Of course between 'make' and 'buy' lies a range of possible types of relationship, for example:

- sole supplier
- preferred supplier
- dedicated supplier
- partnership supplier
- first-, second- or third-tier supplier
- co-makership;
- graded supplier (A, B, C, etc.)

Checklist 15.1
Strategic purchasing process

Does the salesperson or key account manager understand the sequence and outcome of the client's or prospect's thinking on the following issues?

Stage	Actions
Objectives/scope	Define the business – What business are we in? Set priorities Define relevant technology families/product categories Define scope of technological/category opportunity
Analysis	Analyse industry structure, conduct and performance Track and plan the purchasing spend Identify the framework for total acquisition costs Research product and process technologies Identify the prime drivers of cost and performance
Design supply base	Benchmark existing suppliers Develop supplier screening criteria Filter sourcing opportunities Determine sourcing relationship Evaluate potential suppliers
Recruitment	Select suppliers Agree supply contract terms
Operationalize	Initiate operational interaction Set up operational communications Mould cross-functional teams Develop buyer satisfaction measures Measure performance continually Strive for continuous improvement
Feedback	Regular review of process/progress

There are many determinants of these relationships, in particular the nature of the product or service offering, buyer power, technological basis and trends in the relevant business sector, the channel roles of the supplier and buyer, the buyers' core skills, marketing and competitive strategies, and the nature and size of the demand from the final consumer.

Practical tip

List the top 20 companies with which your organization has done business in the past year and write down how you think they rate you: A, B, C or D (or whatever ranking categories are applicable in your business context).

Globalization of business-to-business buying

As far as purchasing is concerned, it is common in business-to-business markets to find organizations whose buying activities occur in many different markets. For example:

- IKEA, the Swedish furniture and furnishings retailer, has buying offices in more than 25 countries.
- Texas Instruments operates an international procurement office in Hong Kong to handle sourcing from the Pacific rim.
- Singer procures its sewing machine shells from the USA, motors from Brazil, drive shafts from Italy, and then makes the machines in Taiwan (Christopher, 1992).
- Ford's European body and assembly procurement is split between Ford of Germany, Britain and Spain. Under the overall control of a German-based director of supply, a German procurement manager handles electrical assemblies and body components, another German-based procurement manager looks after hard and soft trim and tyres, the British procurement manager deals with chassis, engine, plastic and ornamentation components, and, finally, Ford of Spain's procurement manager sources hardware and moulded rubber.
- John Welch, chief executive of General Electric, has commented that: 'You can't be a world-class competitor with a domestic headset. You've got to think of selling not in 50 states, but in 50 nations. You have to think of sourcing not in one state or one country, but in 50 countries'.

Vendor rating and benchmarking

Most professional buying organizations now operate a vendor appraisal and rating system, which scores existing and prospective suppliers on a number of key factors.

Checklist 15.2

An electronics manufacturer, for example, might assess suppliers with a rating scale across the following criteria (among others):

- **business strategy**: customers, growth plans, investment levels, reward levels
- **management strength**: interest, leadership, training, depth, attitude
- **workforce profile**: industrial relations, worker involvement, turnover, experience, morale
- **responsiveness**: due date delivery record, queries, engineering problems, requests to quote; information access for order status, order processing and product availability, schedule stability/flexibility
- **quality**: zero defects, self-assessment, sub-supplier appraisal, worker involvement, standards achieved, continuous/sustained improvement, ship-to-line capability, product performance/reliability in field
- **pricing**: cost reduction programs, payment terms, open book costing, cost-effective design and material specification, economies of scale, choice of technology, labour rates, simultaneous engineering and design.

Suppliers can then be graded relative to one another in a benchmarking exercise. This enables the purchasing organization to learn which are its best product or service suppliers for specific categories of purchase. Leading suppliers can therefore be targeted for e.g. co-operation on more innovative product development projects, or a programme of constructive support (supplier development) to take them to a higher level of capability, where their enhanced performance makes a more significant contribution to the buying company or organization.

One thing which emerges clearly from this 'live' example is that suppliers must be able to compete across all functions and the entire workforce has to become involved in the sales and marketing effort. In addition, in the post-sale operational phase, when, for example, the buying organization's production manager needs to talk directly to his or her counterpart in the supply organization (e.g. pallet-maker to sawmill), the relationship, is constantly under scrutiny and under pressure. The responsibility for the selling effort has to be carried by all those who have operational contact with the customer, from invoicing and credit control, through logis-

tics and production to maintenance and field support. Figure 15.1 illustrates the need for cross-functional inter-organizational communication.

Business-to-business sales and marketing

Having reviewed recent developments in purchasing, we will now consider ways in which salespeople can strategically framework their selling processes when dealing with organizational buyers. First, it is necessary to consider strategic thinking in the context of marketing and selling.

In business-to-business markets, the principal means of communication between suppliers and buyers is personal selling. Whether this selling is done by a salesperson in a presentation to a key buyer, by an account manager to the client principals, or by the commercial director at board level, the key ingredient is the same: people.

All of these people, to a greater or lesser degree, need to be aware of, and able to think and talk with conviction about, the strategic

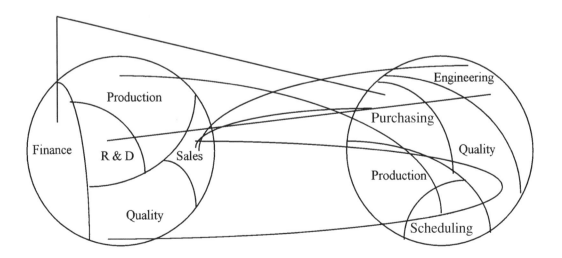

Figure 15.1 *Cross-functional interaction between buyer and seller. Source: Adapted from Turnbull (1979)*

dimensions. A buyer's supply strategy is an inherent aspect of many negotiations about supply contracts and to exclude this from consideration is nonsensical.

However, because the strategic thinking in sales and marketing has been claimed as the remit of the marketer, there is a risk that a false equation might be set up:

Strategic thinking = marketing
Tactical thinking = selling.

Discussion about selling can then, wrongly in our view, often be restricted to the psychological aspects of the sales process. These aspects are critically important, but our point is that the salesperson needs to be able to work in the strategic dimension as well.

To a salesperson, marketing is quite often seen as the 'snob' end of selling, and marketers as intellectuals, poets or poseurs who come apart at the seams when seated in front of a live customer or prospect – if indeed they could even manage to do the prospecting correctly in the first place! This of course is entirely unfair, for marketing has provided many useful insights to counterbalance the salesperson's natural instinctive desire to 'get the order at all costs'. Much of the strategic thinking in marketing, around segmentation, tageting and positioning, for example, has helped to focus salespeople's energies, cut down time and resource wastage or duplication and homogenize the basic pitch, ensuring consistency in the company's communications with prospects and customers.

We feel there has been enough talk about 'marketing-oriented sales', and now there needs to be much more talk about 'sales-oriented marketing'. Selling after all puts the 'bite' into marketing. Without salespeople who are driven to make the top line happen, all talk of contribution and bottom line is academic.

Seeing both sides of the exchange

Good sales thinking means being able to see things from a customer perspective. However, sometimes the very concepts

which are invented to make this easier get in the way!

The need to extend the marketing mix

A good example is the marketing mix ...! Some 30 years ago, Borden (1965) suggested that the following issues or elements should be included in a marketing programme:

- channels of distribution
- physical handling
- personal selling
- advertising
- branding
- promotions
- packaging
- service
- fact-finding and analysis
- pricing
- display.

These came to be known as the 'marketing mix'; essentially, the issues which need to be looked at in business transactions from the seller's point of view. The marketing mix became widely used in a simplified or cut-down version known as the 'four Ps': product, price, place, promotion. This can be restated as: customer need, customer cost, customer convenience, customer communications – a reformulation which turns an inward-looking or one-sided view of the marketing programme into a customer-oriented formulation.

In the early 1980s, it was suggested (Booms and Bitner, 1981) that services marketing needed a seven-point marketing mix to take account of the particularities of services market offerings:

- product;
- price;
- place;
- promotion;
- people;
- physical evidence;
- process.

New thinking about services brought with it an emphasis on process. It was impossible to clearly understand the company–customer interaction without a careful analysis of the process surrounding the business transaction. Later, the emerging importance of quality, with the accompanying need for analysis of process, reinforced the importance of process as a key element in business transactions, whether in consumer or business-to-business contexts. And now, more recently still, the explosive growth in business process re-engineering has accentuated further the vital importance of a process view. Of course, salespeople and marketers have been aware of the process dimension of buying since the 1960s (see Chapter 1, Figure 1.7).

Because of these changes in the salience of process and quality, nowadays it is becoming more widely recognized and accepted that the marketing mix needs to be extended if it is to take account of all the key dimensions of business-to-business exchanges.

The problem with all of this is that it keeps attention focused on what the company is doing rather than on what the customer or buyer needs.

The purchasing mix

What is seldom mentioned is that there is also a purchasing mix, which is the 'flip side' of the marketing mix. The quality and process factors are vitally important to the buyer, as are logistics, price, communication, in short everything which is of importance to the salesperson.

The need for a two-sided exchange framework

Each of these viewpoints – the marketing mix and the purchasing mix – is, in itself, limited and limiting, because it focuses on the business transaction or exchange from only one perspective. Today's successful salespeople and buyers need to be able to see the business deal, transaction or relationship, from each other's point of view.

It would facilitate this switching of viewpoints if there were an exchange framework, or list of transaction issues, which could be used by either party and which represented a neutral and comprehensive checklist of

Table 15.1 *Exchange framework*

Marketing	Exchange	Purchasing
Strategic		
Segmentation	Categorization	Supply base design
Targeting	Focus	Supplier development
Positioning	Positioning	Relationship type
Tactical		
Product/service	Need	Requirement/specification
Price	Cost	Cost/spend
Place	Location	Supply/convenience
Promotion	Communications/ information	Search/sourcing
Process	Process	Process
People	People	People
Quality	Quality	Quality
Budget	Resources	Budget

transaction issues common to both the buyer's and seller's perspectives. Table 15.1 presents such a framework.

Note that the buyer's equivalent of segmentation and targeting, namely supply base design (number and type of sources, single- or multiple-sourcing) and supplier development (focusing on key suppliers to improve their supply and technological quality), affects the salesperson's options even before he picks up the telephone.

To the traditional marketer, the inclusion of quality and budget as part of the marketing mix may seem heretical, but to the business-to-business salesperson/practitioner, the quality and resource aspects are part of everyday working life! The inclusion of resources is important, because it has always been a criterion of an effective marketing approach to customers that it should be consistent with the company's resource base, and because every business-to-business buyer is keenly aware of the cost of buying!

Practical tip

List the key factors (in specific detail) on which your core customers rate their suppliers. Look at these factors from both sides of the exchange, tracking them back to the underlying pressures which make them so critical. This short exercise gives an exchange mix which is adapted to your own context.

Thinking relationship rather than transaction

Taking this idea of a two-sided deal or exchange further, here is a quote from Philip Kotler (1994): 'Exchange is ... a value-creating process [i.e. it] normally leaves both parties better off than before the exchange ... Transactions are the basic unit of exchange. A transaction consists of a trade of values between two parties.'

Everyone knows by now that retaining customers is far less expensive than recruiting them in the first place; repeat business is crucial. This applies all the more in business-to-business relationships, where the loss of a supply contract to a competitor may strip millions of dollars in revenue off the top line at one go.

Successful business-to-business salespeople get beyond the transaction and the deal to the relationship, and try to set up win–win relationships with their customers. It is not so easy to do this if one cannot think from the buyer's perspective.

Clearly there is a close link between exchange and relationship. The quality of the value exchange will depend on the quality of the relationship. The relationship exists because of the need or desire for exchange among the contracting parties. In business-to-business markets, exchange is an ongoing inter-organizational process, not just an event, a one-off transaction. Of course, relationships are built on transactions, and one major transaction can and will affect the entire relationship between two organiza-

---

Table 15.2 *Transaction and relationship marketing*

Transaction marketing	Relationship marketing
Focus on single sale	Focus on customer retention
Orientation on product features	Orientation on product benefits
Short timescale	Long timescale
Little emphasis on customer service	High customer service emphasis
Limited customer commitment	High customer commitment
Moderate customer contact	High customer contact
Quality is primarily a concern of production	Quality is the concern of all

tions (e.g. putting on a new supplier) for an extended period of time; but in the long run it is the relationship which is critical.

It is important to emphasize this distinction between transactions and relationships. Christopher et al. (1994) point out the differences listed in Table 15.2 (see also Figure 1.9, Chapter 1).

Business-to-business salespeople need to work to build relationships rather than win transactions!

Buyer analysis frameworks

Having considered the nature of business-to-business markets, recent developments in purchasing and the importance of a two-sided view of the exchange and of thinking in terms of relationship rather than transaction, in this section of the chapter we will be looking at different ways of analysing buyer's activities.

Buyers' options

Figure 15.2 illustrates eight principal options open to buyers for any business-to-business transaction. The left-hand axis of the matrix shows the supply capability, and the bottom axis the suppliers. Each axis is divided in two, representing new and existing capability and suppliers respectively. The intersection of the axes shows that buyers have essentially four possibilities open to them when working with suppliers.

They can work with existing suppliers and within their existing supply capability. This is a no-change policy, suitable for relatively stable markets, and is therefore called '**supplier maintenance**'.

Buyers can also decide to work with existing suppliers to develop a new supply capability. This process is known as '**supplier development**'. In this situation, the buyers proactively work with the supplier to upgrade the supply capability, for example in the area of just-in-time supply, product inno-

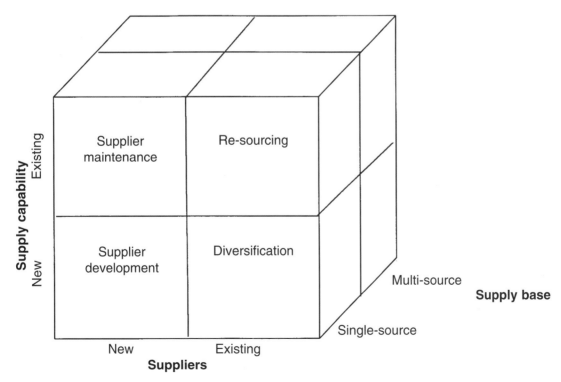

Figure 15.2 Buyers' options

vation, production and quality systems, or order processing.

The third main option open to buyers is to find an existing supply capability, but with a new supplier, which is known as **'re-sourcing'**. This is an all-too-common occurrence for suppliers, who find competitors stealing in to capture an account by providing the same service at lower cost. It is quite common for a number of sourcing contracts for an existing customer to be consolidated and switched to low-cost operations overseas.

Lastly, the buyer can decide that a new supply capability is needed and also new suppliers. This is called **'diversification'**. Clearly a higher risk strategy, an example of this would be where a US company were to set up a manufacturing operation in the Pacific rim area and take the opportunity of this greenfield, state-of-the-art venture to bring in a later generation of technology than it has been accustomed to using back in the States.

A supplier maintenance strategy is clearly welcome news to existing suppliers, but makes it very hard for new contestants to creep in. Supplier development is also an opportunity for those currently servicing the account, although failure to put through the often major consequential changes in financial investment, quality and personnel practice will result in the downgrading and possible exclusion of those which cannot keep up. Resourcing and diversification represent clear threats to existing suppliers' continuity of supply, but opportunities for new competitors to quote for and possibly win the account.

There is a third axis in Figure 15.2, namely that the buyer also has the option to switch from single-sourcing to multi-sourcing or vice versa. For example, an automotive buyer might have three current suppliers of piping, and decide in the interest of supply base reduction to single-source. Alternatively, a buyer who is not happy with a current sole supplier may proactively encourage its competitors to tender for supply – much like warming up the substitutes on the touchline.

Of course, large OEMs, for example, may be

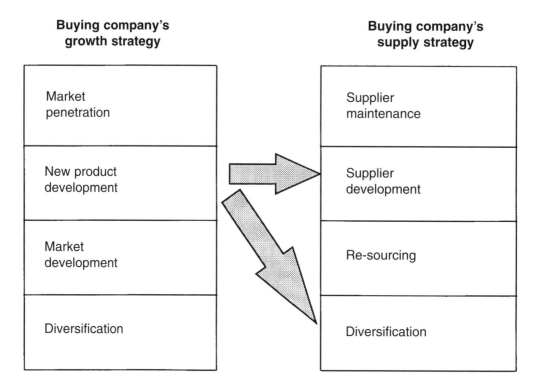

Buying company's growth strategy	Buying company's supply strategy
Market penetration	Supplier maintenance
New product development	Supplier development
Market development	Re-sourcing
Diversification	Diversification

Figure 15.3 *Supply strategy is a function of growth strategy*

applying different strategies to different sections of the supply base at the same time, depending on the capabilities which are being targeted for strategic reasons. This brings us to the buying organization's growth strategies.

Buyers' growth strategy

It is important for the salesperson to see behind the buyer's supply strategy or strategic sourcing to the market reasons which shape and define it. The buying organization clearly has its own customers and prospects to deal with and will be pursuing a board-driven growth strategy in order to attain its marketing objectives. The four main types of growth strategy are: market penetration, new product (or service) development, market development and diversification.

These growth strategies drive the supply strategy. For example, Figure 15.3 shows a buying organization which is pursuing new product development. There are two ways in which it can do this: by enhancing its existing suppliers' capability (supplier development) or finding new suppliers with new capabilities (diversification).

Buying process and buying situation

It can be helpful for the sales strategist to map the target's buying process onto a grid which includes the buying situation, as shown in Table 15.3.

In the new buy situation, when an organization is buying something for the first time, it must go through all of the steps (indicated by the ticks in the table). In a modified re-buy, the company knows it needs to change the product, but can source the new version in the old quantities and characteristics from its existing sources. It can then skip those two stages in the process and just go through the remaining four. In a straight re-buy situation, there is no need for any change in suppliers or specification, the buyer simply makes the order.

Depending on the type of business the salesperson is in, and the circumstances, this table can be used to segment targets and plan the timing of sales calls and other marketing communications, including direct mail and advertising.

Buyer power

It is important for sales strategists to form as clear a picture as possible of the relative power of supplier and buyer organizations. This will give him or her an invaluable negotiating sense of how much leverage the organization actually has. Figure 15.4 offers a simple way of looking at this.

The shaded areas on the lower left and upper right of the matrix represent the areas where the buyer's and supplier's power are greater respectively. In the top right hand box of the matrix, for example, where the

Table 15.3 *Buying process and situation*

Process	Buying process		
	New buy	Modified re-buy	Straight re-buy
Recognize problem or need	✓	✓	
Decide on characteristics and quantity	✓		
Identify and qualify sources	✓		
Acquire and analyse proposals	✓	✓	
Evaluate and select supplier	✓	✓	
Operationalize procurement	✓	✓	✓
Evaluate performance	✓	✓	✓

Practical tip: Prioritizing targets

A simple way of evaluating prospects and customers in order to allocate salesforce time is the following scoring system:

	Low				Score					High
	1	2	3	4	5	6	7	8	9	10
Sales volume										
Sales growth										
Contribution										
Core fit										
● technological										
● size/resources										
● logistics										
Level of competition*										
Level of buyer power*										

*Note that the higher the levels of competition and buyer power, the less attractive the account, other things being equal. These two aspects of account management are often overlooked. Accounts where competition is stiff and the buyer acts like Attila the Hun should of course receive a lowish score! Core fit is about matching the profile of the supplier and the buying organization on all of the critical criteria.

---

supplier's power is high and the buyer's low, the salesperson is effectively in a seller's market (a very pleasant and unusual predicament!). This is the salesperson's dream, with demand for the product high and very few competitors. The buyer has a 'take it or leave it' option. Some buyers will, therefore, try to push the sourcing efforts further afield to try and identify potential suppliers, but in a true seller's market this yields few serious new competitors. Often the suppliers are or become bigger than many of their customers. This means that they can impose terms which improve their efficiency yet possibly hamper the efficiency of the customer, e.g. through setting large minimum order quantities and of course higher prices.

In such an environment, complacency can be the enemy of the salesperson as competitors begin to catch up and alternatives become available. It is a fact of life that a seller's market will not last forever. To keep the seller's market as long as possible the sales representative should give a quality service that negates the need for the buyer to try and look elsewhere. The product quality should be maintained.

In the buyer's market situation, the opposite of the above, demand for the product is significantly lower than the number of companies who want to provide it. Aggressive cost cutting strategies are adopted and often the salesperson is selling on price. In this situation the salesperson needs to be highly incentivized, because as quickly as new business is gained the chances are that other business will be lost. He or she needs to be armed with a unique selling proposition to differentiate the product from the many competitors. In a buyer's market the rep must have something new to tell the buyer. The problem is that differentiating the product usually leads to cost increases rather than cost reductions.

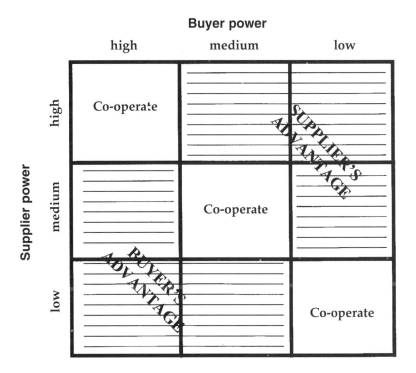

Figure 15.4 *Buyer–supplier power*

Summary

In this chapter, we have considered the many changes in business-to-business purchasing and supply strategy and practice.

In addition, we have considered the need for the sales professional to think in terms of both sides of the business exchange and to focus on the relationship rather than the transaction.

Finally, we examined some frameworks for analysing buyer options for supply strategy, buyer growth strategy, buying process and situation, buyer power and a practical matrix for targeting accounts.

We believe that by taking acount of these changes in the selling environment and by carefully analysing the buyer's options and strategic considerations, the professional sales practitioner can make a difference to his or her organization's success in business-to-business sales.

References

Booms, B.H. and Bitner, M.J. (1981) Marketing Strategies and Organization Structures for Service Firms, in Donnelly, J. and George, W.R. (eds), *Marketing of Services*, American Marketing Association, pp. 47–51.

Borden, N.H. (1965) The Concept of the Marketing Mix, in Schwartz, G. (ed.), *Science in Marketing*, John Wiley, 386–97.

Campbell, N.C.G. (1985) Classification of Buyer–Seller Relationships, in Ford, D. (1993) *Understanding Business Markets: Interaction, Relationships and Networks*, 2nd Edition. Academic Press.

Christopher, M. (1992) *Logistics and Supply Chain Management*. Pitman.

Christopher, M., Payne, A. and Ballantyne, D. (1994), *Relationship Marketing*, CIM/Butterworth-Heinemann.

Kotler, P. (1994) *Marketing Management: Analysis, Planning, Implementation, and Control*, 8th Edition. Prentice Hall.

Turnbull, P.W. (1979) The Interactive Interface in Industrial Markets (Recognition of the Marketing Service Unit), in Ford, D. (1993) *Understanding Business Markets: Interaction, Relationships and Networks*, 2nd Edition. Academic Press.

Index

Account keeper approach, 94
Account management, 122–3
  category management impact, 113
  telephone account management (TAM), 132
  See also Key account management
Account opener approach, 94
Acito, F., 200, 201
Action agreement, 33
Adaptiveness, salesforce performance and, 218, 220
Alternative close, 32
Alternatives, evaluation of, 5–6
Always-a-share customers, 15
Anderson, Arthur, 128
Anderson, E., 261
Appraisal, *See* Salespeople
Audit:
  sales management, 174–5
  trade satisfaction, 115
Availability, 6
Avery Berkel, 148, 149

Bargaining, 48–9
Behaviourally anchored rating scale (BARS), 183–4
Benefit selling, 294–5
Bitner, M.J., 284, 304
Booms, B.H., 284, 304
Borden, N.H., 304
Boya, U.O., 269
Brands:
  equity, 107–8
  loyalty to, 80
  marketing, 123
British Steel, 61, 85
BSE crisis, 135

Bubblegrams, 136–8, 139
Build marketing strategy, 200–1
Build relationship strategy, 202–3
Business process re-engineering (BPR), 238
Business-to-business selling, 298–311
  buyer analysis frameworks, 307–11
  characteristics of, 298–9
  marketing, 303–5
  See also Organizational buying
Buy classes, 289–90
Buyer behaviour:
  buyer power, 309–11
  buyers' growth strategy, 309
  buyers' options, 307–9
  buying orientations, 91–3
  buying signals, 32
  understanding, 20–1
  See also Consumer choice; Organizational buying; Purchase

Call objectives, setting, 20
Campbell, N.C.G., 195, 198
Carelines, 134
Category management, 112
  impact on account handlers, 113
  impact on brand management, 114
  practices, 112–13
  team approach, 114
  trade marketing and, 117, 123
CD-ROMS, 236
Checklist appraisal technique, 183
Choice, *See* Consumer choice
Christopher, Martin, 57, 307
Ciba Geigy, 237
Closing techniques, 31–3, 295–6
Co-operation, sources of, 83
Communication, 116

Compensation schemes, 247
Competition, 110
   competitive position, 193, 194
   key account management benefits, 101
   trade marketing and, 106
Competitor awareness, 72, 74–5
   competitors' products, 19–20
Complaints, 7
Computer based training (CTB), 245–6
Computer chips, 235–6
Computer models, trade marketing and, 117
Computers, 231–2
   See also Information technology
Concession close, 32
Concessions, cost of, 43
Conflict sources, 79–80, 81
Consultant role, of salesperson, 293
Consumer choice, 3–11
   buyers' options, 307–9
   consumer involvement, 7–8
     emotion–driven choice, 9–10
     low emotion choice, 10–11
     low involvement choice, 8–9
   decision guidelines, 141–2
   evaluation of alternatives, 5–6
   implications for selling, 16–17
   information search, 5
   need recognition, 4
   opportunity recognition, 4
   See also Buyer behaviour; Purchase
Consumers, 106
   See also Customers
Core competencies, 64
Corporate strategy, constraints, 191, 192
Cost analysis, 176–7
Cranfield School of Management, 287
   six markets model, 72–9
Crisis management, telemarketing
     applications, 134–5
Cross selling, 138
Culture, 271
   composition of, 273
   cultural distance, 69
   impact on international selling, 271–3
Cunningham, M.T., 195, 198
Curiosity, 4
Customer management strategies, 202–4
Customer markets, 73
Customer organization strategy, 208
Customer orientation, 215

Customer service, 279
   carelines, 134
   core competencies, 64
   telemarketing and, 146–8
   See also Key account management;
     Relationship marketing; Service
     sector
Customers:
   always-a-share, 15
   analysis form, 291
   database, 236–7
   lost-for-good, 15
   needs, 141–2, 197–9
     facilitation need, 198–9
     identification, 21–5
     process need, 198
     product need, 197–8
     recognition, 4
     understanding, 108
   portfolio analysis, 195–9
   relationships with, 227–8
   retention of, 100
     profitability relationship, 57

Daewoo, 129, 130
Databases, 233
   building, telemarketing role, 133–4
   customers, 236–7
Davidow, W.H., 57
Decision making:
   classical model, 3–4
   guidelines, 141–2
   See also Consumer choice
Decision-making unit (DMU), 90–1, 288–90
   identification of, 290
Demonstrations, 25–7
Desktop publishing, 233
Diary software packages, 233
Differentiation, 70–1, 106
Direct Line, 238
Direct Marketing Association, 148, 150
   Broadcast Guidelines, 148
Direct product profitability (DPP), 105, 112
Direct response TV (DRTV), 129
Directing activities, 222
Distance, 69
Distributors, 262–3, 264
Diversification, 308
Divest marketing strategy, 202
Divest relationship strategy, 204

Donaldson, B., 166
Downsizing, 101
Doyle, P., 107

E-mail, 234
Economies of scale, 101
Electronic data interchange (EDI), 112
Electronic point of sales (EPOS) systems, 105, 111, 239
Emotion-driven choice, 9–10
Environment, 57–60
    macro environmental analysis, 59
Essay appraisal technique, 183
Ethics, telemarketing, 148–50
Exchange framework, 305–6
Exporting, *See* International selling

Facilitation need, 198–9
Fallback position, 40
First Direct, 238
Follow-up, 33
Ford, David, 69
Ford Motor Company, 95
Forecasts, 171
Forums, 235
Four Ps, *See* Marketing mix
Framing, 6
Freefone (0800) numbers, 127, 128, 146, 147

Gatignon, H., 261
General Electric (GE) portfolio analysis, 192, 194, 200
Geographical distance, 69
Geographical organization strategy, 207
Gestetner, D., 266–7
Globalization:
    business-to-business buying, 302
    See also International selling
Graphics software, 233
Grönroos, Christian, 66–7
Guarantees, 27

Hardware, 231–2
Hartley, Bob, 147
Harvest marketing strategy, 201
Harvest relationship strategy, 204
Have a nice day approach, 94
Henley Centre, 127–9, 146
Hill, J.S., 269
Hold marketing strategy, 201

Hold relationship strategy, 203–4
Hong Kong Refrigerating Company, 132
Horizontal software, 232–4
Houghton, Chris, 133
Huthwaite Research Group, 22–3, 138–44
Hutton, J., 273

Implication questions, 24
Income statement analysis, 177–8
Industrial Marketing and Purchasing group (IMP), 68–9
Influence markets, 73
Information, 105, 111–12
    consumer decision making and, 5
    salesperson's role, 293
    trade marketing and, 117, 123–5
Information technology, 230–56
    computer based training, 245–6
    recruitment and, 244–5
    sales management and, 236–9
    salesforce compensation schemes and, 247
    salesforce design and, 243–4
    salesforce evaluation and, 247–51
    salesforce objectives and, 239–42
    terminology, 230–6
        hardware, 231–2
        Internet, 234–6
        on-line services, 234–6
        software, 232–4
Internal marketing, 67–8, 78
Internal markets, 73
International selling, 261–74
    impact of cultural differences, 271–3
    management of, 266–9
        centralized control, 266–8
        decentralized control, 268–9
        multi-market sales, 269–71
    sales organization, 261–6
        export salesforce, 262
        joint venture agreements, 263–5
        sales agents or distributors, 262–3
        wholly-owned subsidiaries, 265–6
Internet, 234–6
    recruitment and, 245
    selling and, 238
Involvement:
    in organizational purchase decision, 13–14
    See also Consumer choice

Job description, 160–1, 162

Job specification, 159–60
Johnson Wax, 265
Joint venture agreements, 263–5

Key account management (KAM), 89–91,
    197–9
  conditions for, 91–6
    skills of manager, 94–6
    suitability of supplier's sales approach,
        93–4
    suitability to customer, 91–3
  motives for, 99–101
  process, 96–9
  realizing the benefits of, 101–3
  relationship development strategies, 204–7
Key account manager approach, 94
Kotler, Philip, 280, 306

L&R Group, 134, 143, 145, 146, 147
Laptop computers, 231
Lead generation, telemarketing applications,
    131
Leadership, 164–5
Lo-call (0345) numbers, 127, 128, 146, 147
Lost-for-good customers, 15
Lovelock, C.H., 282
Low emotion choice, 10–11
Low involvement choice, 8–9
Loyalty profiles, 84–6

McDonald, M., 199, 206
Macro environmental analysis, 59
Management by objectives (MBO), 183
Management style, 165
Managing versus doing, 155–6
Market attractiveness, 194
Market forecasts, 171
Market positioning, 108
Market potential, 171
Marketing, 277–8
  brands, 123
  business-to-business, 303–5
  concept of, 278
  internal, 67–8, 78
  misunderstandings about, 278–9
  services, 280–1
  transaction marketing, 15–16, 55–6, 306–7
  See also Relationship marketing;
      Telemarketing; Trade marketing
Marketing mix, 283–4

extension of, 304–5
services and, 284–6
Marketing planning, 188–90
Marketing strategies, See Strategies
Markets, Cranfield six markets model, 72–9
Marks & Spencer, 64
Marsh, Linda, 141
Matching process, 278, 279
Merchandising strategy, 109
Millman, A.F., 199, 206
Millman, T., 73, 75
Mindsets, 35–8
Mintzberg, Henry, 186
Mission statements, 191
Modems, 232
Monitoring activities, 221–2
Motivation:
  basic theory of, 157–9
  motivational mix, 163–7
  See also Salesforce management
Multi-market sales management, 269–71

National call rate numbers, 146, 147
National Power, 85
NatWest, 244
Need pay-off questions, 24–5
Needs, customer, See Customers
Negotiation, 34–5, 296
  outcomes and mindsets, 35–8
  planning, 38–9, 43–50
  preparation, 38–43
Network solutions, 65–6

Objection close, 32–3
Objections, dealing with, 27–31, 295
Objectives:
  call objectives, setting, 39–40
  management by objectives, 183
  salesforce, 239–42
    productivity, 241–2, 250
On-line services, 234–6
Opening techniques, 21, 294
Operating systems, 235
Operational purchasing policy, 63
Opportunity recognition, 4
Order to invoice cycle, 117
Organizational buying, 11–17
  buying centre, 12
    influences within, 14–15
  globalization, 302

implications for selling, 16–17
involvement with purchase decision, 13–14
key developments in, 299–302
management trends, 60–4
operational purchasing policy, 63
process of, 12–13
purchasing mix, 305–7
relationship versus transaction marketing, 15–16, 306–7
strategic purchasing philosophy, 62
vendor rating, 302–3
See also Business-to-business selling; Buyer behaviour
Organizational structures, examples of, 117–21
Outcomes, 35–8
Outsourcing, 101, 276–7
Own label products, 109, 110

Palmtop computers, 231
Partnership, 80–4, 95
key account management, 97–8, 205
See also Relationship marketing
Payne, A., 78
Performance appraisal, *See* Salespeople
Performance index, 176
Performance measures, *See* Sales performance assessment; Salesforce performance; Salespeople
Personal computers (PCs), 231
Personal selling, 188–90
advantages of, 296
importance of, 286–7
selling services to individuals, 289
selling to organizations, 287–9
See also Salespeople
Persuasion, 45
Peters, Tom, 134
Planning:
bargaining, 48–9
behavioural skills, 44–5
marketing planning, 188–90
negotiation, 38–9, 43–50
persuasion, 45
power, 49–50
sales planning, 188–90
sales presentations, 20
salesforce performance evaluation, 218–19, 221

strategic, 187–8
Power:
buyer power, 309–11
planning, 49–50
Preparation, 19–21
negotiation, 38–43
sales strategy, 290–6
Presentation graphics software, 233
Presentations, *See* Sales presentations
Printers, 231–2
Problem questions, 22–4
Process need, 198
Process solutions, 66
Product organization strategy, 207–8
Productivity analysis, 179–80, 250
Products:
knowledge of, 19
competitors' products, 19–20
management strategies, 200–2
own label, 109, 110
portfolio analysis, 192–5
product need, 197–8
product planner, 138
Profitability analysis, 177–9
Promotions, tailored, 116–17
Prompts, 136
Purchase, 6–7
buy classes, 289–90
operational purchasing, 63
outcomes of, 7
strategic purchasing, 62, 300–1
See also Buyer behaviour; Consumer choice; Organizational buying
Purchasing mix, 305–7

Quick Address (QAS), 239
Quotas, 172, 173

Rackham, Neil, 24, 140, 141, 142
Rada, J., 283
Ranking appraisal technique, 183
Rating scale appraisal technique, 183
Re-sourcing, 308
Reardon, K.K., 272
Recruitment:
information technology role, 244–5
markets, 73
strategies, 207
Reference selling, 27
Referral markets, 73

Relationship marketing, 15–16, 56–60, 306–7
  Cranfield six markets model, 72–9
  Industrial Marketing and Purchasing
      group model, 68–9
  network solutions, 65–6
  partnership approach, 80–4
  process solutions, 66
  Scandinavian perspective, 66–8
  segmentation and, 84–6
    loyalty profiles, 84–6
    usage rate, 84
  stakeholders and, 79–80
  supply chain linkages, 69–72
Relationships, types of, 300–1
Remuneration, salesforce, 165–6, 208–9
Representativeness, 6
Respond 2, 249
Return on assets managed (ROAM), 178–9
Rewarding activities, 222
Richards, A., 113
Right-sizing, 227
Risk reduction, 26–7
Rogers, J., 199, 206
Roman, Murray, 127
Roncoroni, Simon, 143
Rules-of-thumb, 5–6

Sales agents, 262–3
Sales analysis, 175–6
Sales forecasts, 171
Sales management:
  audit, 174–5
  information technology role, 236–9, 254–6
  organization effectiveness, 211–14
    customer relationships and, 227–8
    sales management activities, 221–4
    sales territory design, 222–4, 225
    salesforce performance, 216–21, 226
    successful salesperson characteristics,
        214–16, 225–6
  planning, 188–90
  See also International selling
Sales performance assessment, 170–85
  analysis of results, 175–80
    cost analysis, 176–7
    productivity analysis, 179–80, 250
    profitability analysis, 177–9
    sales analysis, 175–6
  sales management audit, 174–5
  sales quota establishment, 172, 173

selling budgets, 172–4
  See also Salesforce performance;
      Salespeople
Sales potential, 171
Sales presentations, 25–7
  category-focused, 114
  planning, 20
  salesforce performance, 218, 220
Sales strategies, See Strategies
Sales support orientation, 215–16
Sales territory planning, 222–4, 225, 294
Salesforce management:
  clarification of sales task, 156–63
  export salesforce, 262
  information technology role, 239–44,
      247–51
  job description, 160–1, 162
  job specification, 159–60
  motivation, 155, 157–69, 214–15
    accuracy and feedback, 166–7
    compensation schemes, 247
    leadership, 164–5
    management systems and controls,
        166
    performance measures, 161–3
    remuneration, 165–6, 208–9
    theory of, 157–9
  objectives, 239–42
    productivity, 241–2, 250
  organization strategies, 207–8
  salesforce design, 243–4
  strategy, 286–90
  telesales, 132
  training, 163–4
  See also Salesforce performance;
      Salespeople
Salesforce performance, 161–3, 167, 216–21
  drivers of, 226
  evaluation of, 220–1, 247–51
  See also Sales performance assessment;
      Salesforce management
Salespeople:
  characteristics of, 214–16, 225–6
    evaluation of, 217
  performance assessment, 180–4, 249–50
    appraisal methods, 182–4
    appraisal results management, 184
    criteria, 181–2
    difficulties, 181
  roles of, 293–6

sales strategy preparation, 290–6
See also Personal selling; Salesforce
    management
Scanners, 232
Scripts, 135–7
Segmentation, relationship management
        and, 84–6
    loyalty profiles, 84–6
    usage rate, 84
Seller behaviours, 138–41
Selling budgets, 172–4
Selling technique, 18–33
    closing, 31–3, 295–6
    demonstration, 25–7
    follow-up, 33
    need and problem identification, 21–5
        implication questions, 24
        need pay-off questions, 24–5
        problem questions, 22–4
        situation questions, 22
    new technology role, 238–9
    objections, dealing with, 27–31, 295
    opening, 21, 294
    preparation, 19–21
    presentation, 25–7
    sales approaches, 93–4
    selling services to individuals, 289
    selling to organizations, 287–9
    See also Telemarketing
Servers, 231
Service sector, 276–8
Services, 280–1
    classification of, 282
    marketing mix and, 284–6
    marketing of, 280–1
    selling, 277–8
        sales strategy preparation, 290–6
        salesforce strategy, 286–90
    strategic value in manufacturing, 282–3
    See also Customer service
Shipley, David, 82
Simon Jersey, 133
Situation questions, 22
SLEPT factors, 58
Social distance, 69
Software, 232–4
    horizontal, 232–4
    vertical, 234
Space management systems, 111–12
SPIN model, 22–3, 138–40, 142

Spiro, R.L., 200, 201
Spreadsheets, 232–3, 247
Stakeholders:
    analysis, 76–8
    multiple relationships and, 79–80
Starkey, Michael, 147
Stevens, Michael, 126, 127
Still, R.R., 269
Strahle, W.M., 200, 201
Strategic diagnosis, 191–9
    customer portfolio analysis, 195–9
    product portfolio analysis, 192–5
Strategic marketing triangle, 58
    network solutions and, 65
Strategic planning, 187–8
Strategic purchasing, 62, 300, 301
Strategies, 186–90
    corporate strategy constraints, 191, 192
    definitions of, 187
    formulation of, 199–207
        customer management strategies, 202–4
        product management strategies, 200–2
        relationship development for key
            account management, 204–7
    implementation of, 207–9
    salesforce, 286–90
STREAK analysis, 49–50
Supplier development, 307–8
Supplier maintenance, 307, 308
Supplier markets, 73
Supply base design, 300
Supply chain management, 69–72, 82–4
Support, salesforce performance, 219, 221
Swiss watch industry, 60
SWOT analysis, 110
Synergistic key account management, 98–9

Takala, T., 79
Targets, 42–3
Team orientation, 215
Teamwork, salesforce performance
        evaluation, 218, 221
Technology, 111–13
    technological distance, 69
    trade marketing and, 123–5
    See also Information technology
Teleconferencing, 244
Telemarketing, 126–50
    applications for, 129–35
        crisis management, 134–5

customer care, 134
database building, 133–4
lead generation, 131
telesales, 131–2
bureaux, 143–6
call success, 143, 144
assessment, 142–3
definition of, 126–7
development of, 127–9
ethics, 148–50
inbound, 126
operation of, 143–6
outbound, 126
selling technique, 135–43
call planning, 135–8
cross selling, 138
seller behaviours, 138–41
understanding customers' decision
guidelines, 141–2
upselling, 138
service quality delivery, 146–8
telephone number selection, 146, 147
Telephone Preference Service, 148
Telesales, 131–2
Time distance, 69
Today's regular customers, 195–6, 203–4
Today's special customers, 195, 202
Tomorrow's customers, 195, 203
Trade marketing, 104
building infrastructure for, 115–25
people and skills, 121–3

roles and organization structure, 115–21
technology and information, 123–5
process of, 106–15
reasons for, 104–6
Trade satisfaction audit, 115
Trade strength, 105–6
Trading limits, 42–3
Training:
computer based (CBT), 245–6
salesforce, 163–4
trade marketing and, 123, 124
Transaction marketing, 15–16, 55–6, 306–7
Trial orders, 27
Trust, 79–80

Upselling, 138
Usage rate, 84
Uusitalo, O., 79

Vandermerwe, S., 283
Vendor rating, 302–3
Vertical software, 234
Vroom's expectancy theory, 157–9

Walters, D., 78
Welch, John, 302
Wholly-owned subsidiaries, 265–6
Wilson, K.J., 199, 206
Word-processors, 233

Yesterday's customers, 196, 204